2000 IDEAS
FOR SPORTSMEN

2000 IDEAS FOR SPORTSMEN

COMPILED BY THE EDITORS OF OUTDOOR LIFE

ANSWERS TO SPORTSMENS' QUESTIONS BY:

Jack O'Connor • William Cary Duncan

Maurice H. Decker • Dr. James R. Kinney

Ray Bergman • J. A. Emmett

OUTDOOR LIFE

353 Fourth Avenue

New York

TABLE OF CONTENTS

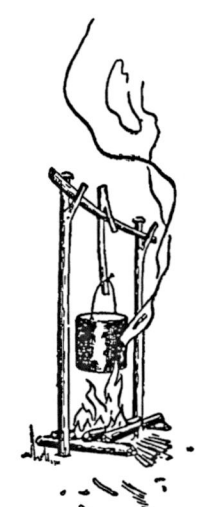

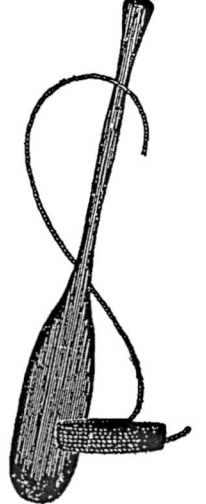

INTRODUCTION

Is a .30/30 Winchester better than a .250/3000 Savage for white-tail deer? Are wet flies better than dry flies for trout? How can a setter be cured of gun-shyness? What is the best method of cleaning and skinning small game? What size outboard is best for trolling?

Questions—Questions—Questions. Sportsmen's questions. Questions from Iowa, Maine, Florida, New York, California—in fact, questions from every nook and cranny of the North American continent wherever there is a man or boy who likes to fish or hunt or camp.

As a service to sportsmen everywhere the Editors of *Outdoor Life* have compiled this book of questions and answers.

The questions are a cross section of the thousands and thousands of inquiries which the Editors receive every year; they represent the true problems of real flesh and blood sportsmen.

The answers to these questions have been written by such outstanding authorities as Jack O'Connor, Ray Bergman and Maurice H. Decker.

All men of the outdoors will find this book to be the true What, Where, How, and When book of Hunting, Fishing and Camping.

THE PUBLISHERS

ALL ABOUT RIFLES

by Jack O'Connor

HOW TO CHOOSE YOUR RIFLE

A GOOD VARMINT RIFLE

Question: I want to get a varmint rifle for use in Maryland and Virginia on chucks, crows, and hawks. I want something in the .22 caliber class that will give me good accuracy up to 250 yd. and which will have enough velocity to shatter upon striking the ground, since ricocheting bullets are dangerous in this part of the country.

The .22 Hornet is a fine little cartridge, but does not have enough soup for me. I've read a lot about the various wildcats, but I want a standard cartridge, if possible. From what I've read and heard, I think the .22/3000 Lovell or the 2-R is about what I want. I prefer a bolt action and plan to mount a 'scope sight on it. Please give me your opinion.—R. F. S., D. C.

Answer: I think that undoubtedly the cartridge you want is the 2-R. I had one of those rifles, and it was a honey. It was on a single-shot action, but how it would shoot! It can give a 50-gr. bullet a velocity of about 3,100 foot seconds with fine accuracy. The 2-R is simply one version of the .22/3000 Lovell. There are others floating around.

My suggestion is that you get a .22 Hornet in the Winchester Model 70, then have a good gunsmith rechamber it for the 2-R and rebuild the magazine to handle the longer cartridge. With about a 6X target-type 'scope you will be nicely fixed up.

THE .30/06 FOR ELK

Question: What do you think of the .30/06 as an elk rifle? I notice several gun cranks lately have been saying that it is not a good rifle for the purpose.

I have been hunting in central Idaho for 20 years, and a .30/06 is the rifle I use. I have killed 58 head of elk and deer with it—all clean, one-shot kills—at ranges from 40 ft. to 400 yd. Of these, 50 were killed with the 180-gr. open-point Western cartridge and the others with the 180-gr. Silvertip. I have seen countless elk killed with .30/06's, and every time one was hit anywhere near a vital spot with a proper bullet he was a dead elk.

So I consider the .30/06 a fine elk rifle. I have tried the .300 Magnum, but I don't consider it so good for the average hunter because of the recoil.—M. H., Idaho.

Answer: You and I vote the same ticket on the .30/06. I consider it and the .270 to be the two best all-round rifles for

American game. If anything like proper bullets are used, the .30/06 will do a good job on elk. It is possible, of course, merely to wound game with any rifle ever made, including the .375 Magnum. The .30/06 and the .270 are excellent compromises between good power and reasonable recoil.

I am inclined to believe that the 180-gr. bullet is entirely adequate for elk or for anything else on this continent, with the possible exception of the big brown bear. I have always felt that the 180 gr. kills better than the 220 gr., because of its higher velocity. It is easier to hit with because of its flatted trajectory.

I have used the 180-gr. Western open point, the 180-gr. Remington Core-Lokt, and the 180-gr. Silvertip. All of them are good, but it is my impression that the open point kills somewhat faster in lung shots.

For deer, antelope, and sheep, however, it strikes me that the various 150-gr. bullets are better killers than the 180's.

HEAVY VS. LIGHT .22

Question: I am thinking of buying a .22 Winchester Model 75 Sporter for target shooting and general plinking. However, I am wondering if the light weight of this rifle (5½ lb.) would make it suitable for target work. I plan eventually to mount a 'scope on it. What do you recommend?—R. M., Ind.

Answer: The Winchester Model 75 Sporter is a fine little rifle, accurate and nicely finished. However, it is much too light for competitive target shooting and even too light for a full-grown man to carry. I am inclined to believe that you would be better off with the Model 75 target rifle. It weighs 8 lb. 10 oz. which is a good weight for target shooting and not excessively heavy for sporting use. If I were you I'd get one with standard Winchester sights—the 84-A peep with

¼-minute clicks and the 99-A front sight.

Later, you could get 'scope blocks put on the barrel and use a target-type telescope sight. As good a compromise as I know of for target and game shooting is the Lyman 6X Junior Targetspot 'scope.

RIFLES FOR WISCONSIN DEER

Question: I want an adequate deer rifle for use in Wisconsin. The hunting country is quite brushy, and in my estimation deer are rarely bagged at more than 200 yd. I am rather stuck on a .300 Savage,

GOOD DEER RIFLES FOR BRUSH COUNTRY

.35 REMINGTON MODEL 141   .348 WINCHESTER MODEL 71   .300 SAVAGE MODEL 99T

Although the .348 has a bit more power than the others, any one of these three rifles is an excellent choice for deer hunting in brush country.

but many people around here seem to think that a .348 Winchester or a .35 Remington would fill the bill more adequately.

I have checked on the ballistics of the three cartridges, and they all seem ideal deer baggers. Of course, I'd like to get all three rifles, but that's financially impossible. So that's where you come in. Which one would you prefer?—B. A., Wis.

Answer: I don't think you can go wrong with any of those three rifles for Wisconsin deer hunting. Any of them will do a very neat and efficient job. Your choice depends on whether you like a pump action such as the .35 Remington Model 141, a hammer lever action such as the .348 Winchester Model 71, or a hammerless lever action such as the .300 Savage Model 99.

For sheer power, the .348 has the edge

over the others, but any of them would give a good account of itself under the conditions you describe.

.270 VS. .300 MAGNUM

Question: I'm planning to buy a long-range rifle equipped with a 'scope sight, the outfit to be used for antelope and possibly mountain sheep, and my choice has narrowed down to the .270 and the .300 Magnum in a Model 70 Winchester. Which caliber do you consider the best for such work?—R. L. H., Ill.

Answer: The .300 Magnum is a big .270 or the .270 is a little .300, depending on how you look at 'em. The ballistic properties of the 130-gr. .270 bullet and those of the 180-gr. .300 Magnum bullet are much the same. The .270, with its muzzle velocity of 3,140 ft. a second, has a slightly flatter trajectory over 300 yd. than the .300 has with 3,060, 5 in. at 150 yd. as against 6 in. for the Magnum. That difference is so small it's unimportant.

However, for sheep and antelope—which I have hunted a good deal—I'd take the .270 any day in the week. It has moderate recoil, better accuracy in a medium-weight barrel, and consequently is my notion of a better bet. Where the .300 would have anything licked is for long-range shooting across canyons at elk in the West, and at grizzly above timber line, where they are most often hunted. However, there are those who use a .270 for such work and swear by it.

.257 BOLT ACTIONS

Question: I hope to buy a .257 Roberts caliber bolt-action rifle. What make do you consider the neatest-looking and most accurate?—Dr. H. A. A., Mich.

Answer: A man trying to choose between a Model 70 Winchester and a Model 30 or 720 Remington would be in a pretty tough spot. To my mind, the first has a better trigger mechanism, the others have the best safety and the best bolt for 'scope mounting. They are all fine rifles, and equally accurate. You might also consider a rifle built up on a Mauser action, if it has a new barrel.

BIG-GAME RIFLE FOR A YOUNGSTER

Question: Within the next two years, if all goes well, my father and I plan a trip to Alaska for Kodiak bear. I'm 18 and weigh 135 lb. I've handled numerous rifles in my young life—principally the .220 Swift, .30/30, and .22 Hi-Power. For Kodiaks, would the .270 have too heavy a recoil for me, or would I get used to it after using it awhile?—W. B. P., Quebec.

Answer: I see no reason why the .270 should be too much for you. Its recoil is somewhat heavier than that of any of the rifles you mention, but it's less than that of the .30/06. For Kodiak bears, however, you'd be wise to get a .30/06 because you'll need a heavier bullet than anything you can use in the .270.

I started shooting a .30/06 when I was 12, and the recoil didn't bother me much. My 12-yr.-old son shoots a .30/06 now and then, and claims that's what he wants when he gets a rifle of his own. You can see, then, that the .30/06 would be easy to get used to.

RIFLE FOR A GIRL

Question: I am a girl, 18, and very much interested in guns and hunting. I have a .22 and wish to purchase a big-game rifle. However, I don't know exactly what I want. I am tall and slender and do not want a rifle with too much recoil. What do you think of Winchester's .257 Roberts? How about a .30/30?—M. L., Calif.

Answer: I am always glad to hear from a girl—I think more of them should hunt. The best bet for you would be the .250/3000 Savage, preferably in the short, light, handy Model 99-T. The rifle is easy to carry and recoil is very moderate.

The 7 mm. or the .257 in Winchester Model 70 would also be nice, but the latter is rather heavy. Don't get a .30/30. I don't think you'd be happy with one or shoot well with it.

LIGHT RIFLE FOR A YOUNG HUNTER

Question: My 14-year-old son has reached the stage where I'll have to take him deer and sheep hunting with me next fall. So I must buy him a suitable rifle.

He has been shooting a .25/20 for some time, hunting coyotes, jack rabbits, and small game. I want to get him a good rifle, but one without too much recoil, since I don't want him to flinch.

Please give the recoil pounds of the following calibers: .250/3000, .257, and .270. I'd appreciate any advice you can give me on this problem.—J. M. L., Nev.

Answer: The free recoil in foot pounds of the .250/3000 is about 6 lb.; that of the .257 is 7 lb.; and that of the .270 is about 14 lb. I do not think recoil would bother a boy so much as owning a gun that was too heavy, although too much recoil isn't a good idea, since it does tend to induce flinching.

You ought to get a lad of that age a relatively light rifle. I would suggest the Savage Model 99-T in .250/3000. It is a good deer cartridge, and the muzzle blast doesn't amount to much. The recoil is light and the accuracy and killing power are good. The 99-T weighs only 7 lb. and is a sweet job to carry.

SAVAGE 99-T FOR THE WOMAN

Question: I am figuring on getting a rifle for my wife. I had been thinking of a .257, but I am beginning to think that a .250/3000 Savage Model 99-T is the business. Am I right, or am I backing too far away from a .257 in such a choice? I plan to mount a Weaver K-2.5 on the rifle when I get it. Please tell me what you think.—M. S., Mich.

Answer: You cannot get a .257 made up any lighter than those Savage 99-T's with 20-in. barrels. Getting one of those babies for your wife would be a very sharp idea. I certainly like the little 99-T. It is a cute little rifle, and unless you are a handloader it has got just as much stuff

.250/3000 SAVAGE, MODEL 99T

LIGHT DEER RIFLE

Good for almost all small and medium game up to and including deer, the .250/3000 Savage is both light and accurate.

with factory ammunition for all practical purposes as a .257. I would get it, by all means.

I think, however, that I would choose a straight-tube 'scope, rather than one with an enlarged ocular lens like the K-2.5, for the simple reason that it is wise to keep the line of sight low. When you get your hands on that 99-T look over the G-88 'scope. I think that would be just what you want.

RIFLE FOR A BEGINNER

Question: I never owned a gun, but I have made up my mind to buy an inexpensive .22 rifle and try shooting. I can afford to spend very little money and have looked only at guns in the low-cost group, among them the Remington Targetmaster, Model 510, and the Mossberg Model 26B. Should I get a peep sight, even if it raises costs a little? Do you think any one of these single-shot rifles is more suited to my purposes than the rest?—D. D., New Jersey.

Answer: I am delighted to know that you have decided to take up shooting. It's a grand sport, and I know you'll enjoy it. Every one of the inexpensive .22 single-shot rifles is a good value. My advice is that you examine the rifles with the idea of finding the one which seems to fit you best; that which comes up most naturally and holds most steadily. See which has the smoothest trigger pull. Find the right combination—that's your gun.

By all means get peep sights. They are better than open sights and easier to learn with. Use the largest aperture, put the front bead on what you want to hit, and then pull the trigger. An adjustable rear sight is a boon. For greater accuracy, have a rifle-shooting friend show you how to sight in the gun, and sight yours in for about 65 yd.; then you can plink from muzzle up to 75 yd.

RIFLE FOR CROWS ONLY

Question: For taking crows from 200 to 300 yd. or more, I plan to build up a rifle on a Model 98 Mauser action. As I see it, it would have a 26 or 28-in. barrel and an 8X Unertl 'scope with medium cross hairs; 90 or 100-gr. bullets would be handloaded.

What caliber would you recommend? I've used a .219 Zipper which, with reloaded ammo, gave me one-minute groups at 100 yd.; but I found it much too wind-sensitive for use on crows at 200 yd. and up. So I'm convinced I need not only accuracy but ability to buck wind.—I. L. O., Wis.

Answer: I am inclined to believe that you would be well fixed with a medium-heavy 26-in. barrel, caliber .270, with six grooves and a twist of 1 in 12 or even 1 in 13, on that Mauser action. The 100-gr. bullet is much less wind-sensitive than any of the .22's. Velocity, as you know, is very high, and trajectory is very flat.

I know quite a few expert varmint hunters who have abandoned all the hot-shot .22's and gone over to the .270, using the 100-gr. bullet at high velocity but having their barrels cut with a slower

twist than the 1-in-10 twist which is factory standard. I have shot such rifles, and someday I'm going to cook one up for myself.

THE .38/55 FOR DEER

Question: Recently I purchased a .38/55 Winchester lever-action rifle. It's in A-1 condition and has a good balance, but I find that at ranges of more than 50 yd. it shoots either high or low. At what distance should I sight it in? Contrary to the opinion of my friends, I think it's a good all-round rifle, and much better for deer than the .30/30.—J. B., Calif.

Answer: For close-range shooting at deer in the woods the .38/55 is still a hard rifle to beat. However, it's by no means a long-range rifle. As a matter of fact, it's adequate up to just about 100 yd.

I suggest that you sight that baby in to hit the point of aim at 100 yd. Then the bullet would strike about 2½ in. high at 50 yd., and about 8 in. low at 150 yd.

RIFLE FOR MICHIGAN HUNTING

Question: I will do quite a bit of deer hunting in northern Michigan, and I am wondering what sort of rifle to buy. How would the military M-1 rifle be for this type of hunting? I realize I couldn't use military ammunition, but do you think it would be advisable to get one of these rifles if the government ever releases them for sale?—H. G. A., N. Y.

Answer: If I were you I wouldn't set my heart on hunting with an M-1 rifle. In the first place, it is on the heavy side for deer hunting. In the second place, an increasing number of states are banning the use of semi-automatic arms.

I am inclined to believe that if my hunting were confined to northern Michigan I would select one of three rifles, depending upon which I happened to fancy most at the moment—a .35 Remington Model 141 pump action, a .348

Winchester Model 71 lever action, or a .300 Savage Model 99 lever action. And I would want a peep sight to go with it.

THE .250/3000 FOR VARMINTS

Question: I am planning to buy a Winchester Model 70 in either .257 Roberts or .250/3000 for use in shooting crows, coyotes, and occasional deer. I believe I'd prefer the .257, but I have heard that generally the .250/3000 performs better with the lighter bullets which I will use almost exclusively. I have also heard that the .257 is better with the 100 and 110-gr. bullets. Is the .257 as accurate with the 87-gr. bullet as the .250/3000? Which do you think would be better?—A. O. W., Wash.

Answer: Since you are planning to use the light bullets almost exclusively, I think the smart thing for you to do is to get the .250/3000. The .250 has a twist of 1 in 14 and handles bullets as light as 60 gr. with accuracy. With the 1-in-10 twist, the .257 is not seen at its best with bullets lighter than 100 gr. Don't worry about the .250 with the 100-gr. bullet not being a crackajack deer cartridge, either.

THE .30/30 FOR DEER

Question: I just bought a .30/30 Winchester carbine, Model 64, which is only a few years old. Is this rifle good for deer? Any advice you can give me about it will be appreciated.—S. J. S., Pa.

Answer: For short and medium-range deer shooting in wooded territory there are certainly no flies on the .30/30. It's the most popular deer rifle in this country, so it can't be so bad. I wouldn't use a .30/30 for open-country shooting in the mountains of the Southwest, but for Pennsylvania it's the business.

I suggest you sight that rifle in for 150 yd. The bullet will strike 2 in. high at 100 yd., and 4 in. low at 200. I'd also equip it with a tang peep sight.

.351 WINCHESTER FOR DEER

Question: Hunters have told me that the .351 Winchester self-loading rifle I bought recently is too light for deer. Please give me your opinion; also tell me the ballistics of the cartridge, and how I should sight the rifle in.—G. D., Wis.

Answer: The .351 Winchester self-loader is a good deer rifle for relatively short ranges, somewhat less powerful than the .30/30. The .351 uses a 180-gr. bullet at a muzzle velocity of 1,850 foot seconds and a muzzle energy of 1,370 foot pounds.

If I were you I would adjust your sights to strike the point of aim at 100 yd. In that case your bullet will hit 1½ in. high at 50 yd. However, you need not sight that rifle very exactly because a deer is a fairly large target and you will be shooting at relatively close range.

ADVICE ON AUTOMATIC RIFLE

Question: For the last two years I have been trying to become better acquainted with my .30 caliber Winchester Model 94 lever-action rifle, but with little success. Previously I had a .32 Winchester automatic which I cherished—until on two successive occasions I had to watch my deer wave bye-bye after direct hits. I was unable to find either animal, and to wound a deer and have to leave it to die is something I want to avoid. So I went sour on the .32 automatic.

Later, seeking a gun with more wallop, I got my Model 94. It has the stuff, but I just can't get used to the lever action.

A hunting pal has suggested that I get a .401 Winchester automatic. What is your opinion? Or what rifle would you suggest for cat and deer hunting—for a guy that is automatic-conscious?—G. J. H., Mass.

Answer: The .401 Winchester automatic may indeed be the answer to your prayer for short and medium-range shooting on white-tail deer. It uses a 200-gr. bullet at a muzzle velocity of 2,140 foot seconds. In other words, its ballistics are practically identical with those of the .35 Remington auto.

Because of its big stubby bullet, the .401 is not a long-range rifle—but you don't need long range for your kind of shooting. It will drop white-tails in their tracks with any solid hit. The cartridge is a good killer because of the large diameter and weight of the bullet, and also because of its fair velocity.

If I were you I would sight it in for 100 yd., then your bullet will hit about 1 in. high at 50 yd.

LONG SHOTS ON DEER

Question: For hunting deer on open, rocky ground, where we often get long shots, I've tentatively picked on the .270 W.C.F. Would that be a good choice for

.270 WINCHESTER, MODEL 70

LONG RANGE DEER OUTFIT

One of the most versatile calibers made, the .270 can be successfully used at both short and long range on practically all types of game. It is made only in bolt action.

such hunting, with maybe foxes, jack rabbits, and woodchucks on the side? What type of action would you suggest, and what about sights?—F. R. McM., Ont.

Answer: I think the .270 is just what you need for those long shots. It's also a good fox, woodchuck, and jack-rabbit rifle, but shooting it at such small game is rather expensive. If I were you I'd most certainly put a 'scope on that .270, to bring out its fine long-range possibilities.

The .270 is made only in the bolt action because no existing lever or pump

action is strong enough to hold it. For many years it was made in a commercial arm by Winchester, Models 54 and 70. More recently it was one of the calibers offered by Remington in its new Model 720. In addition, the Sedgley Co. of Philadelphia, Pa., has built many .270's with Springfield actions, and various private gunmakers have also made .270's up on Springfield and Mauser actions.

GUN FOR LEFT-HANDED HUNTER

Question: After experimenting around (because I shoot left-handed) with two or three bolt-action rifles and a pump, I got a .300 Savage, Model 99-G takedown. That doesn't seem to be the answer either, for when I put it together in the woods, after sighting it in and then take it apart to put away, I get a different point of impact.

Now I'm looking for a rifle with a solid frame which will give consistent results. I need a rifle heavy enough for grizzly but one which won't spoil too much meat. How about the .348 Winchester instead? Also, do the .270 and the .257 come in lever actions?—A. L. S., Pa.

Answer: Takedowns nearly always result in performances like yours. If you had got a Model 99-R or 99-S Savage, I doubt if you'd have had any trouble. Possibly what you want is the Model 71 in the .348 Winchester, which has somewhat more power than the .300. It's a mighty nice rifle, but for most purposes I don't consider it any more accurate or any better-handling than the good Model 99's. It weighs slightly more, but you wouldn't notice the difference.

The .300 uses a 150-gr. bullet (muzzle velocity 2,660 foot seconds), a 180-gr. bullet (2,380), and a 200-gr. bullet (2,200). Comparative figures for the .348 are: 150 gr. (2,850), 200 gr. (2,550), 250 gr. (2,250).

The .257 and .270 are not made in lever actions.

.220 SWIFT FOR WOODCHUCKS

Question: What do you think of the .220 Swift for woodchucks? I am thinking of buying a Winchester Model 70 in this caliber. I have a Lyman Alaskan 2½X 'scope with Griffin & Howe mounts on my Model 54 Winchester .30/06. Can I transfer the 'scope and mounts to the Model 70 or would a powerful 'scope be better?—K. A. L., W. Va.

Answer: The .220 Swift is a very satisfactory and powerful long-range varmint cartridge, and the Model 70 Winchester, of course, is tops. On the other hand, I do not think you would find that 2½X 'scope practical for varmint shooting at the longer ranges. It simply does not enable one to see well enough to hit chucks at more than 150 or 200 yd. at the most.

I think the best 'scope for your purpose would be a target-type 'scope of about 6X —the Lyman Jr. Targetspot or the similar Litschert, Unertl, or Fecker 'scopes. There's no point in handicapping a varmint rifle with a big-game 'scope. I certainly wouldn't use less than a 4X and would prefer a 6X. Many even use 8X 'scopes for the purpose.

32/20 NOT FOR ELK

Question: What do you think of a .32/20 Winchester as a big-game gun for deer, elk, and bears? How does it compare with the .30/30 and other big-game pieces.—A. S., N. J.

Answer: It would be criminal to use a .32/20 rifle on elk and bears. That isn't even an adequate deer rifle. Let us compare that caliber with the .30/30, which isn't any too powerful. The .30/30 used a 170-gr. bullet at a muzzle velocity of 2,200 foot seconds and a muzzle energy of 1,830 foot pounds. The most powerful .32/20 uses a 115-gr. bullet at a muzzle velocity of 1,600 foot seconds and a muzzle energy of only 655 foot pounds. As you can see, the .32/20 is not exactly a power house. I'll kill you an elk with a .22 pistol myself if you let me get within 1 ft. of him, but killing an elk in the woods is another story entirely.

WHAT THE .25/35 CAN DO

Question: What is the biggest game I should use my rifle on? It's a .25/35 Savage, Model 1899. I have shot one white-tail deer at about 35 yd. with it, but suspect it can't be depended on to kill such animals effectively. Also, for crows and the like, at what range should it be sighted in—200 yd.?—A. G. D., Calif.

Answer: With well-placed shots (that is, shots in the chest cavity) the .25/35 cartridge is entirely ample for white-tail deer. Shots in the guts, however, do pretty poorly.

The .25/35 makes an excellent pest and varmint rifle, but I do not think its trajectory is quite flat enough for you to sight in for 200 yd. I'd sight in for 150 yd. instead, in which case the bullet will land 2 in. high at 50 yd., 2 in. high at 100, on the nose at 150, and 5 in. low at 200. If you sight in for 200 yd. your bullet will strike 4 in. high at 100 yd., and that would make you miss small game on the close and medium shots.

FOR ALASKAN BIG GAME

Question: What kind of rifle should I take with me to Alaska that would be adequate on big game, and doesn't cost big money? I am 5 ft. 11 in. tall, left-handed, and weigh 160 lb.—F. J. S., Pa.

Answer: Since you are a southpaw I'd recommend a lever-action rifle, the .348 Winchester in the Model 71. If I were you I'd get it with a Winchester peep sight and a gunsling. Sight it in for 200 yd. with the 250-gr. Silvertip bullet. That cartridge is a power house, and it ought to lay Alaskan moose and brown bears low. They both take a lot of killing!

.30/30 CARBINE FOR WOODS DEER

Question: I've bought a lever-action .30/30 Winchester carbine, Model 94, W.C.F. How can I get the best results from it on deer?—A. E. S., Ont.

Answer: Yours is a good little deer rifle for short and medium ranges and it is certainly ample for white-tails in the woods. The best bullet loaded for the

.30/30 WINCHESTER, MODEL 94

MOST POPULAR DEER RIFLE FOR BRUSH COUNTRY

The .30/30 Winchester is one of the best known and most widely used guns on the North American continent.

.30/30 is the 165 or 170-gr.—preferably the old soft point with considerable lead exposed.

If I were you I would sight that rifle in to put the bullet 2 in. high at 100 yd., and 4 in. low at 200 yd. That means sighting in to hit on the nose at 150 yd.; which gives the best working trajectory for the .30/30.

If you ever decide to get another rear sight I believe your best bet is a tang peep sight like the Lyman 1-A. Marble also makes a similar sight. Being close to the eye, and fast, both are ideal for woods deer.

FOR BIG GAME UP TO 150 YARDS

Question: I have a .303 Savage, sighted at 150 yd., that shoots right on the mark, and am keen to try it out on deer, elk, and bear at moderate ranges. How does that sound to you?—C. S., Idaho.

Answer: The .303 Savage cartridge has always borne an excellent reputation as a killer on even heavy game, at moderate ranges up to about 150 yds. Its muzzle

energy is about like that of the .30/30 or the .32 Special, but because it uses a heavier bullet, with a better sectional density, it seems to penetrate more deeply into the vitals of big game. The standard .30/30 load is a 170-gr. bullet with a velocity of 2,200 foot seconds, whereas the standard load for the .303 is a 190-gr. bullet with a velocity of 1,960.

.32 SPECIAL FOR WOODS DEER?

Question: I have a .32 Winchester Special, Model 64, with 24-in. barrel. Using the 165-gr. bullet, I've had fair luck with it on deer in the New York Adirondacks. Some of my friends tell me this load is too slow, has too curved a trajectory to shoot well at any great distance (150 to 200 yd.), and lacks sufficient penetration and shocking power. I like it very much; what is your opinion?—S. P., N. Y.

Answer: For ordinary hunting in the Eastern woods your .32 Special is a very good cartridge and your Model 64 is an excellent rifle. The .32 Special 165-gr. bullet, with a muzzle velocity of 2,260 foot seconds, is entirely adequate for 200-yd. shooting on white-tails. Sight the rifle in to hit the point of aim at 150 yd., about 2 in. high at 100, and about 4 in. low at 200. That way you will not need to hold high up to 200 yd.

KILLING COYOTES FOR THEIR FUR

Question: First chance I get, I want to buy a better rifle than the one I've been using on coyotes. I kill them for their furs, and need a rifle that will give me good accuracy at 200 yd. and up, when standing, sitting, or prone. I plan on a 4 power Weaver 'scope, and probably a .270 or a .257 rifle. Rifle weight is also a big consideration.—S. B., N. D.

Answer: Probably your best bet is a .270 with the 130-gr. Silvertip or the 130-gr. Core-Lokt. Both bullets have very flat trajectory and do not open up and ruin a lot of fur. Factory .257's and .270's weigh just the same. An accurate .257 can be built quite light; but I think a coyote rifle ought to weigh from 9½ to 10 lb. ('scope included), for it's much easier to hold still.

WILD-TURKEY OUTFIT

Question: What kind of rifle and 'scope would you suggest for turkey shooting? What kind of ammunition should I use for this purpose?—J. D., N. C.

Answer: Some day I'm going to get myself a wild-turkey outfit, and it'll be a

.32/20 SAVAGE, MODEL 23 D

OUTFIT OF EXPERT
TURKEY HUNTERS

If you know where to hold, you can pick off turkeys up to 150 yd. with this .32/20 and a 4X 'scope.

.32/20 (preferably a Savage Model 23) with a 4X 'scope like the Weaver. I'll stick to the 115-gr. bullet at a muzzle velocity of 1,280 foot seconds.

With that rifle sighted in for 100 yd. a man can do a pretty good job, if he knows where to hold, at picking off a turkey up to 150 yd. This is the favorite outfit of some expert turkey hunters.

LIKES LEVER ACTION

Question: I'm planning to buy a big-game rifle, and prefer the lever action to the bolt. What do you suggest for bear, deer, and perhaps moose? What ammunition?—C. W., Va.

Answer: Since you like the lever action I'm going to suggest two rifles—because bear and moose are rather tough cookies and hard to kill. The first rifle is the .300 Savage in the Model 99. With that I would use the 150-gr. bullet for deer

and black bears and the 200-gr. Peters Belted Bullet for moose. The second rifle is the .348 Winchester Model 71, for which the best all-around bullet is the 200-gr., and the best moose bullet the 250-gr. Winchester Silvertip. Either of these cartridges is an excellent modern job of relatively high velocity and maximum effectiveness—superior to cartridges, such as the .30/30 or the .32 Special.

FOR ALASKA'S BIG GAME

Question: I intend to go hunting in Alaska for moose, large grizzlies, and maybe Kodiak and polar bear. Would I have sufficient power with 200-gr. Western Silvertip boattail bullets in a .300 caliber lever-action Savage, Model 99-EG? Or is there a heavier bullet for this rifle—the 220-gr. soft-point H. & H. Magnum, for instance?—W. F., N. Y.

Answer: I'd want a rifle with a little more soup than even that 200-gr. Silvertip. You couldn't use the .300 Magnum—it's much too long and large. The rifle I'd choose would be a .30/06 with the 220-gr. Silvertip, 220-gr. Core-Lokt, or the 225-gr. Peters belted bullet. You might even consider the .375 Magnum for those big bear; everyone who has hunted them tells me that the largest gun is none too large.

.300 GOOD IN BRUSH

Question: Have a chance to acquire either a .300 or a .250/3000 Savage. I'll use the rifle in brushy country on deer. Which rifle is best?—H. K., Wis.

Answer: Since you intend to hunt in brushy country and confine your shooting to deer, I'd pick the .300. With the 150-gr. bullet it's a very fine deer killer at average ranges. The .250/3000 is slightly more accurate, and it's more pleasant to shoot. On the other hand, the brush calls for a heavier bullet than the 100-gr. slug in the .250/3000.

NOT TOO HEAVY

Question: I recently purchased a .401 automatic clip-loader rifle. Is this rifle a little too heavy for deer? Can you give me cartridge ballistics?—P. D., Mass.

Answer: You needn't worry about your rifle being too heavy for deer; the chronic sin of deer hunters is using rifles that are too light. Yours propels a 200-gr. bullet at a velocity of 2,140 ft. a second, has a midrange trajectory of 5.5 in. over a 200-yd. range; that means it's about a 150-yd. rifle. Sight it in so that the bullet strikes about 3 in. high at 100 yd., and you won't have to worry about holding high up to about 160 yd. That rifle is designed as a hard-hitting weapon for deer and large game in forested country, and for that purpose it's a honey.

.375 H. & H. MAGNUM

Question: I have in my possession a .375 Holland & Holland Magnum. How does it compare in accuracy with the .30/06, and could I use this rifle on deer in the New York Adirondacks, also on big game in Canada?—A. F., N. Y.

Answer: The .375 is needlessly powerful for deer, and I'd hate to use a rifle with that much recoil for such hunting; but if you don't mind, go ahead—it will almost always kill a deer with one shot.

In Canada the rifle should be most useful, for it's very powerful and has a flat trajectory. Probably the best all-around bullet for it is that big 270-gr. soft point with its muzzle velocity of around 2,700 foot seconds. In my experience the .375 is just as accurate as the .30/06, and trajectory of the 270-gr. bullet is similar to that of the 180-gr. .30/06.

REMINGTON .35 IS DEADLY

Question: I have been toying with the idea of getting a second-hand .35 Remington pump-action rifle for Pennsylvania deer. Is the cartridge O.K.?—E. S., Pa.

Answer: You bet I do. The .35 Remington cartridge has a well-earned reputation as being one of the deadliest of all medium-range cartridges on deer—or even on elk, for that matter. It's big, fat 200-gr. soft-point slug has a muzzle velocity of 2,200 ft. a second, and hits like a ton of lead. I know of no better choice for the deer hunter who is not an expert rifleman, but who is trained in using a pump-action shotgun.

DOWNING BOBCATS

Question: It has been said that the .22 is impractical for shooting large vermin. What about the .22 Long Rifle hollow point for bobcats?—J. P., Ill.

Answer: Sad to say, the .22 Long Rifle is a long way from being powerful enough to make it a reliable bobcat cartridge. Even the .22 Hornet isn't so hot on them, and I have lost a lot of bobcats and coyotes with the still more powerful 2-R Lovell. An adequate bobcat load would be a .250/3000, a .25 Remington, or a .25/35.

.22 HORNET FOR HAWKS AND CROWS

Question: I should like some information about the .22 Hornet. I know it is inexpensive, has only a mild report, and is accurate. But how is it in killing power? Will it kill a hawk or a crow at 150 to 200 yd.? I am thinking of getting a Savage Model 23-D, equipped with a good 'scope. —C. G., N. J.

Answer: I think a Hornet is exactly what you want. As you say, the cartridge is inexpensive, relatively quiet, and accurate. Either the Savage 23-D or the Winchester Model 70 should do very nicely. The Model 70 is slightly more accurate, but you will get plenty of hawks and crows with the Savage 23-D. You ought to have a 'scope of at least 4X, and a 6X would be even better for your purpose.

HOW TO IMPROVE YOUR SHOOTING

UPHILL AND DOWNHILL SHOOTING

Question: While deer hunting last fall with a party of hunters, the question of the effects of shooting uphill and downhill came up. The old-timers maintained that if you aimed where you usually do, and shot downhill, the bullet would go over the deer. They based the statement on their own experiences, and since I was the greenhorn of the party I couldn't argue.

But I am a student of physics in college, and I can't help thinking that, all other things being equal, it doesn't matter whether you are shooting uphill or downhill or on the level. Wouldn't the acceleration of gravity be the same in all cases?—C. W. D., Minn.

Answer: If you shoot either uphill or downhill at a steep angle, the bullet will strike very slightly higher than if you shot on the level.

Actually, however, when one shoots at an animal on a hill above him, he aims at the lower part of the animal's body. Hits tend to be low for this reason, and in the case of misses, they are usually low. If you shoot at an animal from above, you tend to aim at the upper portion of his body. Hits will necessarily be high, and misses tend to be high.

SHOOTING FROM MOVING PLATFORM

Question: Will you please let me know if there is any difference between the velocity of a bullet fired from a moving platform and that of a bullet fired from a stationary position.—K. D., Pa.

Answer: Whether fired from a stationary or a moving platform, the actual muzzle velocity of the bullet is the same. However, the velocity as compared with the ground varies with the motion of the platform.

If a rifle bullet with a velocity of 3,000 foot seconds is fired from a train traveling at 60 miles an hour—fired in the direction the train is moving—the velocity in relation to the ground is 3,000 plus the speed of the train in foot seconds. If the bullet is fired from the observation platform, in a direction opposite to that in which the train is moving, the velocity in relation to the ground will be 3,000 *minus* the speed of the train.

WHERE TO SHOOT A GRIZZLY

Question: Here is a question that has been bothering a bunch of us guys: Will a good shoulder shot stop a charging

HIGH
SHOULDER
SHOT BEST
FOR GRIZZLY

The first shot at a grizzly should be aimed high on the shoulders, making it impossible for the beast to charge.

grizzly? We think you could set us straight, and I for one would like to know before I meet up with one of those babies.—D. W., Alberta.

Answer: I have killed only four grizzlies so I wouldn't consider myself an authority on them. However, old grizzly hunters say that the best shot is high in the shoulders, so as to break them, making it impossible for the beast to charge. That's what I did on my last grizzly.

HOW TO LEAD RUNNING DEER

Question: What is the proper method of shooting a running deer? How much lead should you give it with a .30/30 if it is running directly across at 75 yd.? I have shot several deer standing or walking, but am confused as to the best method of leading them when they're running. —T. R., N. Y.

Answer: If I were shooting at a deer running directly across my line of sight at 75 yd. I would start behind the deer, swing the rifle rapidly, and touch off the trigger when the bead was on the deer's brisket. This method will almost always make, the bullet land in the chest cavity.

I have killed hundreds of running jack rabbits in this way, and at 75 yd. with a .30/30, the correct lead on a running rabbit seems to be about 1½ to 2 ft. Mind you, the rifle is apparently traveling faster than the running game. Shooting running jack rabbits is wonderful practice for all running game. A man who can make a fairly good average on them will find a running deer so easy there's nothing to it because, after all, a deer is a big target by comparsion.

BUCK FEVER—OR WHAT?

Question: When deer hunting last fall I climbed about 30 ft. into a small oak tree and waited for the drive to come through. From that point of vantage I could cover about 50 yd. The drive came along—five does and a nice buck. They neither winded nor saw me, but stopped in some brush about 100 yd. downhill from where I was. The reddish brush made them rather indistinct, but I drew as fine as I could on the buck and eased one off. I use a 30/30 carbine.

The buck pranced a little, then stopped, facing me. There was a limb near me and, using it for a rest, I fired again. The buck ran toward me about 20 ft., then stopped broadside. Again I took plenty of time, aiming for the front shoulder, and let one go. No luck. And this kept up until I'd fired all seven shots in the magazine. The deer were becoming restless and I levered in one more

shell. But then they spotted me and the final flash shot I took was another clean miss.

When I examined the sign in the snow I found a bit of hair and blood, but it must have come from a superficial flesh wound, for I trailed the deer slowly for several minutes and saw that he hadn't rested once.

Now what in the world could have been the matter? Was it me or my rifle or shooting downhill? I'm a fair shot at target, took plenty of time, and wasn't any more excited than the average deer hunter. I've killed quite a number of them in the past.—R. G. T., Pa.

Answer: There are two possible explanations for your missing your deer that day. The most probable one, from what you say, is that your rifle is not sighted in properly. If you checked it on a target you would probably find that it was shooting 'way off.

Another possible explanation is that you had a bad case of buck fever. I have seen many game animals missed at very close range by experienced, but excited hunters. I have missed a few myself, because of excitement—or buck fever.

I don't think that shooting downhill had anything to do with it. That shouldn't have any effect. My advice is check the sighting of your rifle.

RIGHT BULLET FOR WHITE-TAILS

Question: What is the best bullet to use in a .348 Winchester for hunting whitetail deer in Pennsylvania.—A. H., Pa.

Answer: I think you will find the 150-gr. soft-point traveling at 2,880 to be one of the most sudden-killing of all bullets up to 150 yd.

Although capable of killing the biggest of North American game, there would be fewer wounded deer each hunting season if more hunters used a fairly heavy rifle like the well-stocked .348.

SIGHTS AND SIGHTING IN

DOT RETICULE FOR GENERAL HUNTING

Question: Please advise me on what size dot I should have installed in my Weaver K-4 'scope. I will use it for hunting elk, deer, antelope, and vermin.—L. J., Ore.

Answer: I suggest that you get a dot subtending 3 minutes of angle. A smaller size than that would be useful for varmint shooting, but it would be difficult to see at times when you were hunting big game. I think that the 3-minute dot will be about your best compromise.

'SCOPE FOR BIG GAME

Question: I am going to buy a .270 Winchester Model 70 for use on elk, deer, goats, and sheep, since I think it is better than the .30/06 for that kind of long-range hunting. I am undecided about whether to have a K-2.5 or a K-4 Weaver 'scope put on the new rifle. Which would you advise? Also, what size Lee Dot reticule would be best?—H. M. P., Ore.

Answer: I agree with you that the .270 has a slight edge on the .30/06 for long-range shooting. I would by all means put the K-4 'scope on your new rifle. A dot subtending about 2½ or 3 minutes of angle would be about right for general hunting with the 4X 'scope.

K-4 O.K. FOR RUNNING GAME

Question: I recently bought a new .300 Savage Model 99 which I expect to equip with a Weaver K-4 'scope with medium cross hairs. I am choosing the K-4 because of the condition of my eyes and the fact that I will shoot only standing or slowly moving game. I am aware of the handicap created by high-power 'scopes. So do you think my choice is correct, or should I choose the K-2.5?—E. E., Wis.

Answer: If you are going to take standing shots even in heavy woods, a K-4 is a mighty fine 'scope. In fact, with a well-fitting stock, I would not hesitate to use the K-4 on running game in heavy woods. It has a field of view of around 30 ft. at 100 yd., which is enough for any running game.

SIGHTING IN A .35 REMINGTON

Question: I have just purchased a new Weaver K-2.5 'scope for my .35 Remington Model 141 Gamemaster rifle. Please tell me how to sight it in with the 200- and 150-gr. bullets.—T. K. R., D. C.

Answer: I think you should stick to the 200-gr. bullet in that .35 Remington. The 150 gr. will give you a very different

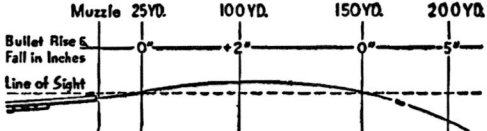

Bullets of different weights have different points of impact. The chart above shows how to sight in the 200 gr. bullet only. The 150 gr. performs quite differently.

point of impact, because of different barrel vibration and because of the higher velocity; and with that cartridge case the bullet cannot be given enough higher velocity to make it any more effective than the 200 gr.

I would do my first shooting at 50 yd. Sight the rifle in to put the bullet 1 in. above the point of aim at that distance. In other words, if you fire three shots the center of the group should average 1 in. above the point of aim.

Now, at 50 yd. each gradation on the elevation and windage turrets of the K-2.5 has a value of 1 in. (At 100 yd. the value is 2 in., and at 200 yd. the value is 4 in.)

Suppose you find that at 50 yd. your

bullets are striking 3 in. high and 1 in. to the right. You will then want to bring them 2 in. down and 1 in. to the left. Turn the elevation screw *clockwise*—in other words, *down*—two gradations. Since you also want to move the point of impact 1 in. to the left, turn the windage screw 1 gradation clockwise.

So sighted, the bullet will first cross the line of sight at about 25 yd. It will be 2 in. high at 100 yd., on the nose at 150, and about 5 in. low at 200.

SIGHTING IN A .300 MAGNUM

Question: I have a .300 H. & H. Magnum —a Winchester Model 70—with a Weaver K-4 'scope. Please give me the dope on sighting it in, and the trajectory of the 180-gr. factory-loaded bullet over 500 yd. —D. S., Calif.

Answer: If I were you I would sight in that .300 Magnum to hit the point of aim at 250 yd. when using the 180-gr. factory

SIGHTING IN THE .300 MAGNUM 180 GR.

Sighted in as illustrated in the diagram, the .300 H. & H. Magnum has a point-blank range of practically 300 yd.

load. In that case, the bullet will first cross the line of sight at around 25 yd. At 100 yd. it will strike about 3½ in. high, at 150 yd. 4 in. high, and at 200 yd. 3 in. high. It will be on the nose at 250 yd. and 5 in. low at 300. That will give you a point-blank range of practically 300 yd.

At 350 yd. the bullet strikes about 11 in. low, at 400 yd. 21 in. low, at 450 yd. 28 in. low, and at 500 yd. about 50 in. low. This bullet is not slow, at the muzzle it travels at 3060 feet per second.

'SCOPE FOR A .348

Question: I have a .348 Winchester Model 71 and would like to equip it with a Weaver K-4 'scope. Would this be a satisfactory combination? If so, what mount do you recommend? If not, what 'scope should I get?—R. S. B., Jr., Ark.

Answer: I do not think I would plan to put a K-4 'scope on a .348 Winchester Model 71. The K-4 is a rather large 'scope, and since it has to be offset to the left because the Model 71 ejects at the top, I do not think you would find it entirely satisfactory. On a bolt action rifle or any rifle that ejects at the side the K-4 is a swell job, however.

If I were you I would get a straight-tube 'scope. A good bet would be to have M. L. Stith, Transit Tower, San Antonio, Tex., put one of his Bear Cub 'scopes on your rifle, using his special offset Streamline mount. This 'scope could be mounted low and offset to the minimum, and the mount is very strong. I know a chap who took a .348 with a similar outfit into the Canadian Rockies and shot everything with great success.

VISIBILITY OF DOT RETICULES

Question: I have about decided to get a Weaver 4X with a 3-minute Lee dot reticule. However, I want the dot to be colored red, so that it would be easier to see in deep timber, where there is very little light. Will this be possible?—C. C. H., Calif.

Answer: It wouldn't do any good to color a dot red, because it is seen against the light and it would look black anyway. At that, I think you will be surprised at how well those dots show up. I used a 'scope with a dot under the overcast skies and poor light of the Yukon last fall, and I never saw anything that the dot didn't look black against—even a black bear in the timber. I am sure you will find the Lee dot very satisfactory.

CHOOSING A 'SCOPE SIGHT

Question: I am planning to buy a 'scope for my .270 and would like advice on the best kind and on the reticule that would be best suited to my type of hunting. This country is mostly wide open, and I do a lot of shooting across canyons at ranges between 300 and 600 yd. I want a reticule that is good for shooting at running game.—C. J., Mont.

Answer: May I suggest that for your .270 you get the new 4X Weaver, running mate of the K-2.5. For long-range shooting such as yours a man needs 4X magnification. Heretofore, the best 'scope in that class has been the 4X Zeiss Zielvier. I understand also that some other 4X 'scopes will soon be coming out. As for a reticule, either a 3-minute Lee dot or a medium cross hair would be O.K.

ADJUSTING 'SCOPE

Question: I own a .22 caliber Winchester pump gun Model 62, with a Weaver 29-S 'scope, and would like to know at what

SIGHTING IN THE .22 LONG RIFLE

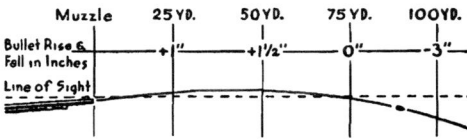

The .22 Long Rifle cartridge is best sighted in to zero at 75 yd. This gives the bullet a point-blank range of 100 yd.

distance I should sight it in. I prefer to shoot long distances.

In view of the drop of the .22 Long Rifle bullet, am I expecting too much to hit an object about 100 yd. away? How would the bullet stand up against coyotes and similar game?—G. M., Colo.

Answer: I would sight in that 'scope-sighted .22 to hit the point of aim at 75 yd. With the ordinary low-speed .22 Long Rifle ammunition, you should do

your first shooting at 25 yd. and adjust your 'scope, temporarily, to put the bullet right at point of aim at that distance.

At 25 yd., each half-minute click with your 29-S 'scope has a value of ⅛ in. For insance, if you shoot from a rest at 25 yd. and find that your bullets strike 1 in. low and 1 in. to the right, give eight clicks up and eight clicks to the left.

Now adjust it to hit 1 in. high at 25 yd., and it will hit about 1½ in. high at 50 yd., at point of aim again at 75 yd., and 3 in. low at 100 yd.

The .22 is not adequate for coyotes, and unless you use hollow-point ammunition it is not even adequate for jack rabbits.

TRAJECTORY OF .22 BULLET

Question: I would like to know, if you please, the drop, in inches, of a .22 caliber Kleanbore Long Rifle bullet at 50, 100, 150, 200, 250, 300, 350, and 400 yd., also the amount of side drift at these ranges.—H. R. B., Miss.

Answer: The drop of a .22 high-speed Long Rifle bullet is 1 in. at 50 yd., 6 in. at 75 yd., 11 in. at 100 yd., 19 in. at 125 yd., 24 in. at 150 yd., and 36 in. at 200 yd. I do not have the dope for longer distances. However, with iron sights adjusted to hit the point of aim at 75 yd., the bullet rises 1 in. at 25 yd., about 1½ in. at 50 yd., falls 3 in. at 100 yd., 8 in. at 125 yd., 16 in. at 150 yd., and 30 in. at 200 yd. The drift would be negligible.

HOW TO USE A PEEP SIGHT

Question: I recently mounted a Lyman tang peep sight on my Model 94 Winchester, but I have trouble sighting with it. As the sight is close to the eye, and the ring around the opening is narrow, the ring becomes just an indistinct blur when I look through it.—J. M., Conn.

Answer: You miss the whole point of a peep sight when you say that the rim becomes a blur. That is what it is supposed to do. To use a peep sight, simply look *through* the peep at the front sight.

SIGHTING WITH A PEEP

When sighting with a peep, you should not be aware of or see the peep at all. Simply put the front sight on what you want to hit.

Don't try to center the front sight in the peep. The eye does it for you naturally. Just put the front sight on what you want to shoot, and pull the trigger. Try that and you will find that you shoot very accurately.

'SCOPE-SIGHT RETICULES

Question: I know some favor the Lee dot as a reticule in a 'scope sight, but what's the matter with a medium cross hair and tapered post? I think it beats the Lee dot all to pieces. The post covers only 2 to 3 in. at 100 yd. Surely that wouldn't blot out too much game.—R. B. S., N. J.

Answer: For many years I used a tapered flat-top post in two or three Noske 'scopes. Those posts subtended 2½ minutes of angle (2½ in. at 100 yd.) on the flat top. I have found the dot a much better reticule for shooting running game because it doesn't blot out any of the game and the shooter can maintain his elevation better with it. However, that's just my own experience. It might not work for you.

CURE FOR SIGHTING IN TROUBLE

Question: Recently I had a 4-minute Lee dot reticule put in my Weaver 330 'scope. It seems to work fine, but I can't see the cross hairs at all in poor light.

In sighting in my solid-frame .300 Savage, I shot at 25 yd., prone, without a sling, and with a rolled-up comforter as a rest. First I tried 150-gr. soft-point bullets and got them hitting where I wanted them to. Then I switched to 180-gr. stuff. These grouped perfectly, but exactly 4 in. *higher* than the 150-gr. bullets. How come? According to all the laws of common sense, they should hit lower. Or should they? Please explain this.—E. M. C., Mich.

Answer: In the first place, you aren't *supposed* to see the cross hairs that are used to suspend a Lee dot reticule. Just look at the dot. That's what you are supposed to see, and you can see it in practically any light.

You cannot sight a rifle in with one weight of bullet and expect it to be on the nose when using a bullet of a different weight. Very often even the same-weight bullets in different brands of ammunition will not hit in the same place. For some reason .30/06 rifles seem to be particularly prone to shoot bullets of different weights away from each other.

In the case of your .300, the 180-gr. bullet strikes higher than the 150-gr. With one of my Springfields, the 150-gr. factory load puts the bullet 9 in. higher at 100 yd. than a factory-loaded 180-gr. With my other Springfield, the 150-gr. bullet hits 2 in. higher at 100 yd. than the 180 gr. A friend of mine, however, has a .30/06 which acts like your .300 and puts the 180-gr. bullet higher at 100 yd. than the 150.

The explanation of all this is barrel vibration. Different weights of bullets cause barrels to vibrate differently. Lever-action rifles like the Savage 99 vibrate slightly more than bolt actions. The thing for you to do is sight in with one weight of bullet and stick to it.

Using the 150-gr. bullet, which I prefer in the .300 Savage, you will find that when sighted in to hit the point of aim at 200 yd., the bullet will first cross the line of sight at 25 yd. At 50 yd., it will be about 1½ in. high; at 100 yd., 3 in. high; at 150 yd., 2½ in. high; at 200 yd., on the nose; and at 250 yd., 5 in. low.

BORE-SIGHTING

Question: Just what is meant by "bore-sighting" and how is it done? I have heard that gunsmiths consider it the best way to sight in a rifle. Will you tell me how to do it?—R. W. K., Utah.

Answer: Bore-sighting is used by gunsmiths in mounting iron and 'scope sights to make sure that the first shot fired will be somewhere on the target. It is no way at all to target in a rifle for hunting purposes, as no two barrels vibrate exactly alike, and one rifle—bore-sighted for 100 yd.—may put its bullet right to the point of aim, and the next may be a foot off.

The procedure is this: Put the rifle in a vise so that by looking through the barrel you can see a conspicuous mark centered through the barrel, the mark being from 50 to 100 yd. away. Then adjust the sights so that they are on the same mark. So adjusted, as I have said, the first shot should be somewhere on the paper, but it is by no means a way to sight in a rifle for game or target work. As an example, a 7 mm. with bore-sighted 'scope that I got from a gunsmith shot only 3 in. low at 100 yd. The same gunsmith mounted a 'scope on a .35 caliber rifle for me, bore-sighted it, and that rifle shot a foot low and a foot to the left!

SIGHTING IN POPULAR RIFLES

Question: Where we hunt in Pennsylvania we have to sight in our rifles at camp, but our grounds aren't large, and we have only a 50-yd. range. Most of us like to sight in for 150, 200, or 250 yd. Can you send us a chart for all popular cartridges, showing how high above the point of aim the bullet must hit, when holding on at 50 yd., in order to be on the nose at long range?—C. F. M., Pa.

Answer: May I suggest that you write to the Western Cartridge Co., East Alton, Ill., for their Western Ammunition Handbook? It contains a very useful chart, showing where all the popular rifle calibers first cross the line of aim, when sighted in for various distances with both iron and 'scope sights. There is a lot of other good dope in the book, and all gun nuts ought to have it.

FAST 'SCOPE SIGHT

Question: I'm looking for a very fast sight for hunting deer in thick timber and wonder if a 1X Weaver 'scope would suit me.—S. W. H., N. H.

Answer: For woods shooting, a 1X 'scope mounted low, and with a conspicuous reticule like the Weaver dot-and-crosshair combination, is the fastest sight I've ever run into. It's a favorite for aerial shooting, and while I've never used one on deer I've tried it on a shotgun and also on a rifle for jack rabibts. I bet you'd like it.

MEANING OF "POINT-BLANK RANGE"

Question: Will you please explain what is meant by "point-blank range"? I have heard it all my life and have not yet been able to determine just what distance it really is. For instance, what's the difference between the point-blank range of a .270 and a .22?—J. E. M., Ill.

Answer: The term "point-blank range" simply means the range at which a rifle can be sighted in so that the game usually shot with it can be hit without allowing for bullet drop.

In the case of a .270, equipped with 'scope, the point-blank range is 350 yd., since the rifle can be sighted in to hit the point of aim at 300 yd., and between the muzzle and 350 yd. the bullet will not depart more than 4 in. from the line of aim. For big game, that is not excessive, so the .270 can be said to have a point-blank range of 350 yd.

With high-speed .22 Long Rifle ammunition, a .22 can be sighted in to hit the point of aim at 75 yd. Between the muzzle and 90 yd. the bullet will not de-

POINT BLANK RANGE

This diagram shows the point-blank range of .270 and the .22.

part more than 2 in. from the line of aim, and small game would not be missed. One can say, then, that the .22 has a point-blank range of about 90 or 100 yd.

FLAT TRAJECTORY

Question: What is meant by "flatter trajectory." How can the trajectory of a given caliber be flattened by changing the load, except that heavier loads give longer range than lighter ones at the same angle of inclination?—W. D. M., N. M.

Answer: All bodies are acted on by gravity at the same rate. However, a bullet traveling at 1 ft. a second would drop almost straight down; one fired at 4,000 foot seconds would travel a long way before it touched the earth, yet both bullets would land at the same time. The faster bullet, then, has the flatter trajectory of the two.

To be more definite: A low-speed .22 Long Rifle cartridge, if sighted to strike the point of aim at 150 yd., would rise about 8½ in. above the line of bore at

75 yd. A 100-grain .270 bullet, at a muzzle velocity of more than 3,500 foot seconds, would rise only 1 in. above the line of bore, if sighted to hit the point of aim at 150 yd. Again, as you can see, the faster bullet has a flatter trajectory.

DOT RETICULE AS A RANGE FINDER

Question: I have heard that it is possible to estimate range by using a Lee dot reticule in a 'scope sight. With a 4-minute dot, how is this done when aiming at an antelope?—M. A. H., Calif.

Answer: A 4-minute Lee dot covers 4 in. for each 100 yd. of range. That is, 4 in. at 100 yd., 8 in. at 200, 12 in. at 300, and 16 in. at 400. An antelope measures approximately 16 in. from back to brisket, or breast. When the dot appears to cover the antelope about halfway from back to brisket, the animal is about 200 yd. away. When it appears to cover the whole distance from back to brisket, the antelope is about 400 yd. away.

When you know the approximate size of your game, it isn't hard to use the dot as a range finder.

SIGHTING IN WITH IRON SIGHTS

Question: When sighting in a sporting rifle is it correct to use a paper target and the 6 o'clock hold? It seems to me that if you use iron sights and hold at 6 o'clock on a 12-in. bull at 200 yd., the point of impact would be 6 in. above the line of sight. If this is true, a hunter with a rifle so sighted would be shooting 6 in. high at 200 yd. Perhaps this is the reason for a lot of overshooting.—H. R., Mich.

Answer: May I suggest that when you sight in you use the 6 o'clock hold, but allow for it. Aim with the top of your front bead, holding it at 6 o'clock on the bull. Then, if you are using a .30/06 with a 180-gr. bullet, adjust the sights so that the bullet will strike 3 in. into the bull at 100 yd. You will then be on the nose at 200 yd. At 200 yd., holding at 6 o'clock, see that the bullets strike at 6 o'clock.

For target shooting, rifles are sighted to put the bullet in the middle of the black with the 6 o'clock hold, but such sighting is useless for big-game hunting. In that case you want the bullet to strike close to the top of the front sight.

'SCOPE MOUNT FOR A SOUTHPAW

Question: I am a left-handed shooter and have a .348 Winchester Model 71. Is it possible to mount a 'scope sight on the side of this rifle, so that I can also use a peep sight?—H. C. D., Mich.

Answer: It is perfectly possible to have a 'scope mounted on the side of a .348. Since you shoot from the left shoulder, I believe that you will find it best to mount the 'scope on the left side. Then you can look across to use it, and your cheek will be firmly on the comb, which would otherwise be too low.

I have not seen any 'scopes mounted this way on lever actions—that is, on the left side—but I have seen pictures of them and have had reports from hunters who found them very satisfactory.

'SCOPE O.K. FOR RUNNING GAME?

Question: Is it possible to shoot running game with a 'scope-sighted rifle?—H. B. T., Wash.

Answer: It most certainly is possible to shoot running game with a 'scope-equipped rifle. I have shot most species of North American big game on the run with 'scope-sighted rifles. And some of that stuff was running mighty fast, too.

Your question shows that you are not at all familiar with a 'scope. In the first place, a good hunting-type 'scope has a wide field of view—about 40 ft. at 100 yd. One simply swings ahead of the game to the proper distance and touches off the shot.

No adjustment of the 'scope is either necessary or desirable before getting off a shot at a running animal. Just how far to lead running game depends on many things—the shooter himself, the velocity of the bullet, the speed at which the animal is running, and the angle at which it is traveling.

When a man first starts using a 'scope on running game, he may be annoyed for a short time because the game appears to be much closer to him than it really is. However, he soon gets used to that and forgets it. I have done a lot better shooting at running game of all kinds when using a 'scope than I ever did with iron sights.

'SCOPE SIGHT FOR .220 SWIFT

Question: I'm about to purchase a Winchester .220 Swift, and want to have this vermin rifle mounted with a 'scope. Frequently I see 8X or 10X recommended, but never 20X. Why is this, and what power is best?—E. G. P., Ill.

Answer: I am inclined to believe that the best bet for you is a 6X or 8X target-type 'scope sight like the Lyman Targetspot, Jr. Targetspot, or the similar Unertl, Fecker, or Litschert 'scope.

As to the choice between 6X and 8X, I suggest that you try both. If the greater magnification of the 8X does not annoy you, I think it will be your meat. Don't go above 8X, however.

The 20X is useful only on a target range, where the 'scope can be focused for the exact distance involved. Used at differing ranges in the field, it would be badly out of focus for all distances except the one for which it is adjusted, and a bad case of eyestrain would result. Furthermore, the field of a 20X 'scope is very narrow.

ONE 'SCOPE FOR TWO RIFLES

Question: I am planning to buy one high-powered rifle and one .22. So I plan to get a .30/06 Winchester Model 70 for deer hunting and a .22 Marlin Model 39-A for general varmint shooting.

Recently I have become interested in 'scope sights and plan to put a 'scope on both these rifles when I get them. I do not, however, want to buy two 'scopes unless it's absolutely necessary. Would it be possible to use a Lyman Alaskan or a Weaver K-2.5 interchangeably on these two rifles? I realize that each rifle would require a different setting, but once this was determined there shouldn't be much of a problem. What's your opinion of these rifles and the possibility of using one 'scope for both.—R. S., Ohio.

Answer: I agree whole-heartedly with your choice of rifles. They ought to make a very nice outfit, and between the two of them you will be able to hunt just about anything. However, I do not think you will find it practical to try to use the same 'scope on both rifles. The only outfit I know of that would do the trick is the Sorensen mount, which has both windage and elevation adjustments on it. With a mount on each rifle, the 'scope could be interchanged. I have never tested one of these outfits, however.

If those two rifles were mine, I would put a 'scope of about 2½X—a Noske 2½X, a Weaver K-2.5, a Maxwell Smith G-88, or a Lyman Alaskan on the .30/06 —using a good permanent mount, and let it stay there. Then I would get a cheaper 'scope for the .22. I understand that some new 3 and 4X 'scopes with ¾-in. tubes will be available very soon, complete with mount, for around $20. These sound like the best thing yet for a .22.

I recommend two 'scopes rather than one, because if you try to use a single one, it will always be on the wrong rifle and you will continually have to be sighting in. I tried it myself once, with a Noske 'scope and bases on two rifles. Many a time I kicked myself for doing

it, and I finally put another 'scope on the extra rifle.

DON'T MOUNT 'SCOPE HIGH

Question: Recently I bought a .30/06 Springfield sporter—one of the last sporters made in 1931—in new condition. It is equipped with a Lyman receiver sight. I'd like to apply a Weaver 'scope, but it seems that would be expensive, what with altering the bolt, changing the safety, and buying the mounts. Would it be practical to use a high mount so the bolt and safety won't require aleration? I like the Weaver T-mount, having used one on my .22.—H. P., Colo.

Answer: If you mount that 'scope high you'll kick yourself so hard you won't be able to sit down. I'd far rather have a good set of iron sights than a high-mounted 'scope. You simply cannot hold the rifle steady enough to shoot well with a 'scope mounted high.

If you want to use a low T-mount, O.K. Then you can get away with just having the bolt altered and mount the 'scope so the eyepiece just clears the safety. The T-mount isn't a bad mount at all. But I strongly advise you to mount that 'scope as low as you can, even if you have to put out $5 extra for bolt-handle alterations.

SIGHTS FOR AUTOLOADER

Question: I've been told that my Remington Model 81 autoloader, caliber .35 rifle cannot be mounted with a 'scope. What sight would be best for me to use on this rifle. B. J. A., Iowa.

Answer: Any of the good side mounts such as Noske, Griffin & Howe, or Neider should do the trick. A 'scope, however, will not be of much value because of the bullet's short range. Why not get a peep or tang sight. They are faster than open sights. You'll shoot much more accurately with a peep sight, too.

SIGHTING IN A .30/06 AND .270

Question: My father and I use a .30/06 and a .270, respectively. Please tell me your method of sighting in these rifles, using 'scope sights.—R. B., Colo.

Answer: I sight my .30/06 rifles with telescopic sights to hit the point of aim at 225 yd. with the 180-gr. bullet. That puts

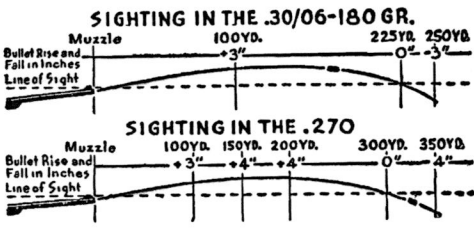

Because of its flatter trajectory the .270 can be sighted in for a slightly longer range than the .30/06.

the point of impact 3 in. high at 100 yd. and 3 in. low at 250. I sight my 'scope-sighted .270's to hit the point of aim at 300 yd. That puts the bullet 3 in. high at 100 yd., 4 in. high at 150 and 200, and 4 in. low at 350.

I believe it is best to sight in a rifle for the longest possible range. For big game, a midrange trajectory height of about 4 in. isn't too bad and will not cause a miss from shooting high at midrange.

PROBLEM IN BALLISTICS

Question: How would you sight in a .30/06, using a 150-gr. bullet at a velocity of 2,960 foot seconds with a low-mounted 'scope, so that the mid-range trajectory height will not be more than 3 in.? Where will the bullet first cross the line of 'scope sight? At what distance will it strike 3 in. low? Please give the same dope on a high-speed .22 Long Rifle 40-gr. bullet at 1,375 foot seconds, also 'scope-sighted.—J. T. W., Mass.

Answer: With a .30/06 using the 150-gr. bullet at 2,960 foot seconds and a low-mounted 'scope you could sight in to hit the point of aim at 225 yd. Then the bullet would first cross the line of sight at 25 yd. At 100 and 150 yd. the bullet would be approximately 3 in. high, and it would strike 3 in. low at approximately 260 yd.

Using the high-speed .22 Long Rifle cartridge, you can sight in to strike the point of aim at 110 yd., and the bullet will not rise more than 3 in. above the line of 'scope sight. It will first cross the line of sight at about 12½ yd. At 25 yd. it will be about 1½ in. high. At 50 and 75 yd. it will be 3 in. high, and at 100 yd., 1 in. high. At 125 yd. the bullet will be 3 in. below the line of aim.

DOPE ON 'SCOPES

Question: I have a .30/06 Model 70 Winchester with a Weaver 'scope and Stith mount. It is very satisfactory except that unless you look directly into the center of the eyepiece it will black out. Would a larger eyepiece, on the order of the Lyman Alaskan, correct this trouble? I do not want a 'scope with more than 2¾ power. I have read of the Eagle 'scope turned out by Litschert. How does it compare with the Alaskan?—A. H., Ga.

Answer: I think that your Weaver 'scope blacks out because, with the Stith Install-It-Yourself mount, it has to be placed too far forward. It is a 'scope of great latitude, but you are using it at the extreme end of that latitude; and besides, the stock probably is a bit long for you.

You could shorten the stock and correct this. You could also solve your problem by returning the rifle to M. L. and M. J. Stith, 500 Transit Tower, San Antonio 5, Texas, and having them install the streamline mount with the 'scope farther to the rear. The Lyman Alaskan is a fine 'scope, but, although it gives a bigger field of view, it doesn't seem to have any more latitude than the Weaver.

PEEP SIGHT FOR .35 AUTO

Question: What kind of peep sight should I put on my .35 Remington autoloading rifle for deer hunting? My hunting is in deep woods.—J. C. W., Wis.

Answer: It doesn't do to get the peep too close to your eye with the .35 Remington auto because the recoil is rather severe. I'd suggest a good, fast receiver sight like the Lyman 41-AT. I'd use it in connection with a large gold or ivory front sight which is big enough to be set quickly in poor light.

'SCOPE ADJUSTMENT FOR 300 MAGNUM

Question: Some months ago I bought a Lyman Alaskan 'scope which is being fitted with a Griffin & Howe mount to a restocked .300 Magnum Winchester, Model 70. I expect to use 180-gr. Silvertip ammunition in the rifle and want to sight it in for 200 yd., but am puzzled about how to set it; and a ballistics table I've consulted only confuses me the more.—A. C. P., Minn.

Answer: The figures in the ballistics table you consulted doubtless had reference to the line of bore, not the line of sight, which in this case is what to base your calculations on.

The Lyman Alaskan clicks for each minute of angle. A minute of angle changes the point of impact 1 in. at 100 yd., 2 in. at 200 yd., 3 in. at 300 yd., and so on. Let's assume that you target your rifle in at 100 yd. and want it to hit on the nose at 200 yd. If you discover, say, that your bullets hit just at the point of aim, as far as elevation goes, but 4 in. to the right, you would then correct by four clicks to the left and two clicks up; for to strike right on the nose at 200 yd. the bullet should strike about 2 in. high at 100 yd. So sighted, your bullets would strike 1 in. above point of aim at 50 yd., 2 in. above at 100, 1¾ in. above at 150, right

on at 200, and about 9 in. low at 300.

You are correct in assuming that each click has a value of ¼ in. at 25 yd., ½ in. at 50 yd., and ¾ in. at 75 yd. You are also correct in assuming that if your rifle is sighted in for 200 yd. and you want your bullet to hit a deer at the point of aim at 300 yd., you would give that 'scope three clicks' elevation. At 300 yd. each click has the value of 3 minutes of angle and that would raise the point of impact 9 in.

To sight in for long-range shooting (which is what I'd do if I were you), have your bullets strike 3 in. high at 100 yd., 4 in. high at 150, 3 in. high at 200, right on the nose at 250, and 5 in. low at 300.

SIGHTING IN A .300 AND A .32

Question: I own a .300 Savage Model 99, equipped with a Weaver 330 'scope sight, and a .32 Remington auto, Model 81,

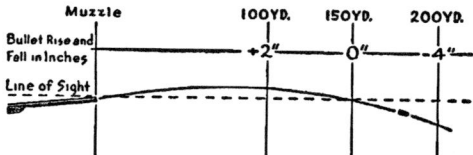

SIGHTING IN THE REMINGTON .32-170 GR.

With the .32 Remington sighted in to hit on the nose at 150 yd., the rifle has a point-blank range of about 200 yd.

with open sights. At what ranges should I sight in these rifles for deer hunting in northern Minnesota? I will use the 180-gr. bullet in the .300 and the 170 gr. in the .32.—H. H., Minn.

Answer: I'd sight in the .32 Remington automatic to hit 2 in. high at 100 yd. with the 170-gr. bullet. That will put you right on the nose at 150 yd. and about 4 in. low at 200.

Using the 180-gr. bullet in the .300 Savage, and a 'scope sight, I'd sight in to hit the point of aim at 175 yd. You will then be 2 in. high at 100 yd. and about 2 in. low at 200.

TRAJECTORY OF .300 SAVAGE

Question: I have installed a No. 70 Redfield sight on my .300 Savage Model 99. I plan to zero my rifle at 150 yd. and use 180-gr. soft-point Core-Lokt ammunition. Where will this rifle shoot at 100, 200, 300, and 400 yd.?—W. F. C., Fla.

Answer: If you sight in to hit the point of aim at 150 yd., your bullet will strike

SIGHTING IN THE .300 SAVAGE MODEL 99

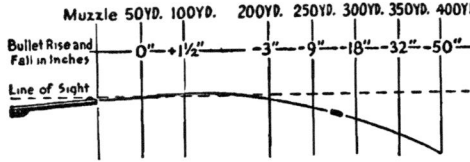

This chart shows how to sight in the .300 Savage 180 gr. bullet to zero at 150 yd. A longer point-blank range is possible with the 150 gr. bullet.

on the nose at 50 yd., 1½ in. high at 100 yd., 3 in. low at 200 yd., 9 in. low at 250 yd., 18 in. low at 300 yd., 32 in. low at 350 yd., and 50 in. low at 400 yd.

As a matter of fact, I think the .300 Savage with the 180-gr. bullet so sighted is only a 250-yd. rifle at best, so I would advise anyone not to try shots beyond that range.

For longer-range shooting I think you ought to target in for the 150-gr. bullet with its higher velocity and flatter trajectory.

RIFLE REAR SIGHT AND SLING

Question: I'm 39 years old and never had the pleasure of hunting when a boy. Now I've got the fever badly. Year before last, I hunted deer alone but never saw a thing to shoot at. Now I've bought a .30/30 Winchester secondhand rifle, Model 1894 and have enough 170-gr. Winchester Silvertip Super Speed ammunition to last the rest of my life—if I don't get more chances to shoot than I did last time.

The rifle has a semi-buckhorn rear sight. For hunting in the southern California mountains, at what range should it be sighted in? Also, I've had a sling put on, for I've seen pictures (not lately, though) of hunters using one to steady their aim when firing. Should I follow suit?—R. C. H., Calif.

Answer: I'd sight that rifle in to hit about 2 in. high at 100 yd. That will put the bullet right on the nose at 150 yd. and about 4 in. low at 200. Suggest replacing that open rear sight of yours with a good tang peep sight, like the Lyman 1-A. And if I were you I wouldn't use the sling except for carrying. When shooting, a tight sling will pull the point of impact down.

SIGHTS FOR THE .30/30

Question: My Model 94 .30/30 has coarse open sights which I don't like, but I don't know what to replace them with— a 'scope, receiver sight, or a tang peep. What would you suggest for woods hunting up to 150 yd.?—H. H., Wash.

Answer: Because of its top ejection, the Model 94 is not much of a rifle on which to mount a 'scope, and the .30/30 is not a 'scope cartridge anyway. If I were you I'd put on a Marble or Lyman tang peep made for the 94. You will then have about the fastest sight you can get for woods and running shots up to 150 yd. For a front sight I'd get a medium-size gold bead; ivory is fine in use, but rather fragile. I have never used the red composition beads, but if they stand up I'd prefer them, as they are the most conspicuous made.

WOODCHUCKS WITH A HORNET

Question: What do you consider the maximum range at which a hit on a woodchuck should be attempted with a .22 Hornet? Mine is a Savage, Model 219, equipped with a 29-S Weaver 'scope and sighted in at 100 yd.; the 'scope's center line is 1⅛ in. above the bore.

I hope you can tell me where the bullets should strike at ranges from 50 to 200 yd.—W. C., N. Y.

Answer: Sighted as you have it now, here's the approximate trajectory of your .22 Hornet: The bullet will strike ½ in. high at 50 yd., on the nose at 100, 2 in.

SIGHTING IN THE .22 HORNET

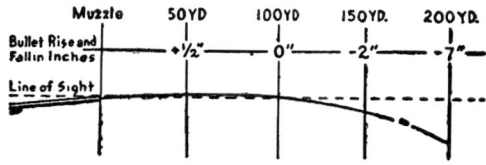

Sighted in to zero at 100 yd, the .22 Hornet has a 7 in. drop at 200 yd If sighted in to zero at 175 yd., the bullet will be 2 in. high at 100 yd. and 2 in. low at 200 yd.

low at 150, and 7 in. low at 200. So as matters stand, the maximum range at which you could hit a chuck without a good deal of holdover would probably be around 150 yd.

If I were you I'd sight that rifle in to put the bullet 2 in. high at 100 yd. Then you would be on the nose at 175, and only 2 in. low at 200.

SIGHTING IN A 99-T SAVAGE

Question: I am having a Weaver 330 'scope installed with B-mounts on my Savage Model 99-T rifle. I would like to sight it in at 200 yd., but to do this job with a minimum of ammunition, here is my theory: If a rifle is being sighted in at 200 yd., at some point between the muzzle and the target the bullet crosses the line of sight; so why not sight the rifle in at that range?

In other words, if the bullet crosses the line of sight at 25 yd., why not sight in at that distance—knowing that you will also be on the nose at the longer range?

If the theory is O.K., just where will

the bullet cross the line of sight when sighted in for 200 yd.?—C. C. S., Calif.

Answer: I think you are exceedingly smart to do your preliminary shooting at the place where the line of sight and the bullet first cross. In your case that point is at 25 yd., so sight in to put the bullet right where you aim at that distance. Then the bullet ought to be about 1 in. high at 50 yd., 2½ in. high at 100 yd., 2 in. high at 150 yd., on the nose at 200 yd., and 4½ in. low at 250 yd.

SIGHTING IN A .30 REM.

Question: Recently I bought a second-hand .30 Remington equipped with an adjustable peep sight. The sight is completely out of adjustment, however, and I don't want to use any more ammunition than I have to, to sight it in again. I'll be hunting in an area where most of my shots at deer will probably be within 100 or 150 yd. For my rifle, three weights are available: 160, 170, and 180 gr. Which weight, and what type of bullet, would you suggest for ordinary deer shooting in brush?—T. W. N., Tex.

Answer: Iron sights differ in their height above the bore, of course; but I would

SIGHTING IN THE .30 REMINGTON

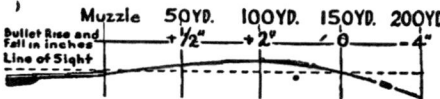

The .30 Remington with the 170-gr. bullet is best sighted in to zero at 150 yd. This gives the rifle a point-blank range of about 200 yd.

guess that if your rifle were sighted in at 100 yd. the line of trajectory would cross at about 25 yd. I'd sight that rifle in to hit right on the nose at 150 yd. In that case the bullet would strike ½ in. high at 50 yd., 2 in. high at 100, on the nose at 150, and only 4 in. low at 200. Then you'd have a good working trajectory.

For your purposes I'd choose a soft-point bullet in the 170-gr. weight.

'SCOPE FOR SQUIRRELS

Question: I have just bought a Savage Model 23 .22 rifle, for use on squirrels, and want to put a 6X or 8X 'scope on it if you think the rifle is accurate enough for one. What 'scope would you recommend? The outfit should cost me no more than $20.—E. B. G., Ga.

Answer: You don't need any advice on .22 rifles, but you do need it on 'scopes. For the love of Mike, don't put a 6X or 8X 'scope on a rifle for squirrel hunting in dark woods. That is too much power. Your field of view would be cut down, you wouldn't get so much light, and since you'd have to do quite a bit of off-hand shooting, the wobble—magnified six or eight times—would be terrible.

The 'scope you need is one of about 3X, and since the outfit cannot cost more than $20, you'll have to shop around.

SIGHTS FOR A .35 REMINGTON

Question: I have been shooting a .35 Remington autoloader with a 200-grain bullet and, using open sights, have been overshooting deer. Recently I purchased a second-hand Weaver 330-S 'scope. I have been told that the T-mount I had installed is not stable, and will vary on account of the recoil. If this is true, what type would you recommend?

After installing the 'scope, I lined the sights on a fixed base, then lined the 'scope at the same spot. With the gun sighted at 100 yd., will the fact that the 'scope is above and to the left of the barrel throw off the bullet at short range—say from 15 to 50 yd.? My shooting is in wooded sections, and I have missed more than one deer at 30 yd.—E. H., Mich.

Answer: I do not think you made a very wise choice in the Weaver 330 'scope for your Remington. It has to be set so far to the left as to destroy the rifle's natural pointing capabilities. To me it is always a pain in the neck to have to hold the head off the comb. Furthermore, the receiver of that rifle is very thin, and it is hard to make a 'scope mount stay put.

If I were you I would get the Redfield Series 102 sight, made for the Remington auto-loader by the Redfield Gunsight Corp., 3311 Gilpin Street, Denver, Colo. It would be much better for your deer shooting than that offset 'scope. You won't have the tendency to overshoot caused by the open sights, which cut off so much of the target. Naturally, wanting to see all of it, one is inclined to hold the front bead too high and, as a result, shoots right over the deer's back.

RECEIVER SIGHT FOR REM. PUMP

Question: I have a .35 Remington pump rifle, Model 141, and would like to put a peep sight on it. What type would be best for hunting in Wisconsin where the brush is heavy?—K. H., Wis.

Answer: Since that pump has rather a heavy recoil I think your best bet would be a receiver sight like the Lyman No. 38, 21, or 56A. With heavy recoil present, the conventional tang sight is too close to the eye and might injure it.

SIGHTING IN A .22

Question: Can you tell me how to sight in my rifle so that I'll know how to aim at various ranges? It's a Model 74 Winchester .22 automatic, with Model 334 Weaver 'scope sight.—A. S., Canada.

Answer: Ordinarily it's best to do your preliminary sighting at 25 yd. Your rifle 'scope has half-minute clicks. That means that each click moves the point of impact $\frac{1}{2}$ in. at 100 yd., $\frac{1}{4}$ in. at 50 yd., $\frac{1}{8}$ in. at 25 yd. Put up a large piece of paper with a definite bullseye. Then shoot from a rest, aiming at the bullseye at 25 yd. Measure the distance off the bull and correct eight clicks for each inch the rifle is shooting off. For example, if the center of your group is ½ in. to the right and 1 in. high, move the 'scope four clicks to the left and eight clicks down.

Now put up a target at 75 yd., shoot, and keep correcting the 'scope until you get the rifle shooting at the point of aim at that distance—75 yd.—which is the best practical hunting range.

Your bullets will then strike about 1 in. high at 38 yd., about at the point of aim at 25 yd., about 1 in. low at 80 yd., and 2 in. low at 90 yd. This means you won't have to hold high on a cottontail rabbit up to 90 yd., so you're pretty well set, since 100 yd. is about as far as you can hit small game with a .22.

VISIBILITY OF DOT RETICULE

Question: I have a .270 Winchester Model 70, equipped with a Lyman Alaskan 'scope with a post reticule, but after studying the ads for the new 'scopes with coated lenses I am considering buying a new Alaskan with a 4½-minute Lee dot. Will this dot show up as well under poor light as the post?—P. N. C., Me.

Answer: The Lyman Alaskan 'scope with a 4½-minute Lee dot is a swell outfit. I have one with a 4-minute dot on my own pet .270 and have used it in Arizona, Wyoming, and the Yukon Territory, often under very poor light conditions. I have never had any trouble in seeing the 4-minute dot at all.

I did experiment with a 2½-minute dot at one time and found it too small. A 4-minute dot is about right, I think, for general big-game hunting with a 'scope of 2½X or so. With a 4X 'scope one can use a 2½ or 3-minute dot, which of course looks proportionately larger.

BALLISTICS OF THE .270

Question: I have a .270 Winchester rifle, Model 70, and my wife has a .257 Rob-

erts with a Model 330 Weaver 'scope. The latter seems to be a very satisfactory rifle for a woman. Both rifles are sighted in for 150 yd. Is that correct for fairly open and mountainous country?

Would you also let me know if my .270 could be handloaded to take a 180-gr. bullet? It seems to me a heavier bullet would be more suitable for grizzly, moose and caribou. Please give me the ballistics on the .270 with both the 130 and 150-gr. bullet.—B. E., Miss.

Answer: I suggest that you sight in for a longer range. Probably your best bet in sighting in the .270 would be for 250 yd. with a 'scope. The bullet will then strike 2 in. high at 100 yd., about 2¾ in. high at 150 yd., 2 in. at 200 yd., on the nose at 250 yd., and 3 in. low at 300 yd. That gives you a very long point-blank range.

With the .257 and the 100-gr. bullet, I certainly would sight in for 200 yd. That would put your bullet 2½ in. high at 100 yd., on the nose at 200 yd., and 5 in. low at 250 yd. With a 'scope, if your .270 is sighted to hit the point of aim at 150 yd., the bullet will strike 4½ in. low at 250 yd., and 9 in. low at 300 yd. You're robbing a fine rifle of its flat trajectory with your present sighting.

The heaviest bullet that you can use successfully in the .270 is the 160-gr. made by Barnes. You can load with 54 gr. of No. 4350 du Pont powder and you'll have a fine elk, grizzly, and moose load with a muzzle velocity of about 2,850 foot seconds. It will be just as effective as the 220-grain .30/06.

BALLISTICS OF .30/06 AND .220 SWIFT

Question: My .30/06 is sighted in for 100 yd., using a 180-gr. bullet. My .220 Swift is sighted in for the same distance, using a .48-gr. bullet. Please tell me the drop of each of these bullets at 200, 300, 400, and 500 yd.—T. B., Wash.

Answer: Better sight that .30/06 in at 200 yd. As it stands now you will do a lot of missing at the longer ranges. Sighted in for 100 yd., the bullet will drop 5 in. at 200 yd., 11 in. at 250, 20 in. at 300, and 47 in. at 400. I'd prefer to sight it in for 200 yd. In that case, the bullet will strike about 2½ in. high at 100, about 11 in. low at 300, and 35 ins. low at 400.

As for the Swift, I think you should sight it in to hit the point of aim at 250 yd. Then the bullet will strike 3 in. high

SIGHTING IN THE .220 SWIFT

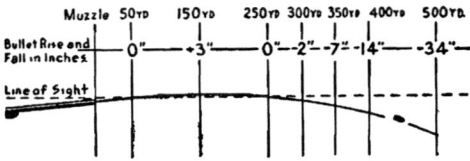

One of the fastest commercial cartridges made, the .220 Swift can be sighted in to zero at 250 yd.

at 150 yd., 2 in. low at 300 yd., 7 in. low at 350 yd., 14 in. low at 400 yd., and 34 in. low at 500 yd.

I think the best stunt by far is always to sight in a rifle for the longest possible range. For a big-game rifle, one can have a midrange trajectory height of about 4 in. without missing anything. For a varmint rifle, the midrange trajectory should not be more than 3 in.

WHAT TO EXPECT FROM A .22

Question: Lying prone, should a fair to good shot with a .22 rifle be able to put five shots in a 1-in. bull at 100 yd.? With iron sights, I think that's a little stiff.—J. F., N. Dak.

Answer: The best prone shots, using heavy-barrel .22's with target 'scopes of from 10X to 15X will keep all their shots in the 2-in. ten-ring of the 100-yd. smallbore target. Most of these shots will be in the 1-in. X ring. In other words, to win a match a man will have to keep more

than three fourths of his shots within a 1-in. circle at 100 yd. With iron sights a man does well to stay in the ten-ring.

SIGHTING IN A .250/3000

Question: If I should sight in my .250/3000 Savage, using iron sights and the 100-gr. bullet, to hit the point of aim at 25 yd., at what greater distance would I be sighted in for?—G. T., Calif.

Answer: If you adjust the sights on an iron-sighted .250/3000 Savage rifle to hit

SIGHTING IN THE .250/3000

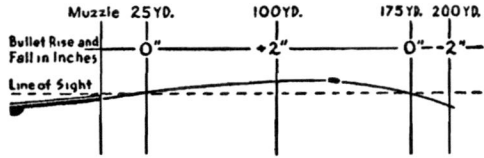

The .250/3000 is a good varmint and deer cartridge. Sighted in to zero at 175 yd. the bullet has a point-blank range of 200 yd.

the point of aim at 25 yd., the bullet will cross the line of aim again at about 175 yd. That will put you about 2 in. high at 100 yd. and about 2 in. low at 200 yd. These figures, of course, are approximate. Do not depend on preliminary, short-range shooting alone. Be sure to shoot at 200 yd., not only to check, but to give yourself confidence that you can really hit at that distance.

'SCOPE TROUBLE

Question: I recently bought a 'scope and mounted it on my .22. Now I can't get it to shoot on the target, no matter how much I try. What did I do wrong?—L. S. D,. Nebr.

Answer: In mounting a 'scope it is necessary to "bore sight" it, which means putting the rifle in a vise and looking down its bore, for the purpose of seeing that line of bore and line of sight coincide at about 50 to 100 yd. If this doesn't work, take it to a professional.

RIFLE CARE, REPAIR AND CONVERSION

NEW BARREL FOR A KRAG

Question: I have an old Springfield Model 1898 (.30/40 Krag) with a 30-in. barrel. It is too long as it is, and too clumsy. I am thinking of getting a new barrel, a shorter one, say 22 to 24 in., but are they available? I'm told that the Krag has not been made since the Springfield was adopted.—J. H., Mont.

Answer: In order to get a new barrel for your Krag you will have to send it to a gunsmith who will either cut off, re-thread, and rechamber an existing .30 caliber barrel for it, or make you a new one from scratch. Winchester and Springfield arsenal barrels were formerly available at a rather low price, but I do not know if they still are.

BEST TO REBARREL MAUSER

Question: I have an 8 mm. Mauser sporting rifle. In the past I've been using a cartridge with a 236-gr. bullet, but I have only a few boxes of these left. I did succeed in getting a box of 8 mm. Mannlicher Schoenauer cartridges with 200-gr. bullets. Would it be safe to use these cartridges in my Mauser?

I have had this rifle for about 10 years. It is just like new and has better lines and stock than any rifle I have ever seen. I have thought of putting a .30/06 barrel on it. Do you think I should do this, or should I sell the Mauser and get a .270 Winchester?—S. C. L., Calif.

Answer: The 8 mm. Mauser cartridge and the 8 mm. Mannlicher Schoenauer cartridge are not interchangeable. The Mauser case is 1 mm. longer and the shoulders are differently placed. The interchange would cause headspace complications.

I would certainly have it rebarreled to some standard cartridge like the .30/06 or .270; then it would live up to its looks.

OLD .22 UNSAFE

Question: After firing a cartridge in my old single-shot .22 caliber Remington rifle, Model 6, I have to use pliers to extract the shell. Can I do anything about this?—W. A. S., Mass.

Answer: Your difficulty probably is due to a badly rusted chamber—the brass of the shell expands into the rust pits. It sounds to me as though that old rifle of yours is about finished. I wouldn't be very enthusiastic about firing it, and I certainly wouldn't use any high-speed cartridges in it.

REBARREL OLD .25/20

Question: The cartridges that I recently bought for my old .25/20 rifle do not fit, being too big around. I have been told that the rifle is an old model, now obsolete, and that shells are no longer made for it. The barrel is marked ".25/20 S.S.," and it was made by Winchester. It is a single-shot lever action. Can you give me any information about this rifle and its ammunition?—D. W., Vt.

Answer: You have a rifle chambered for the .25/20 single-shot cartridge which is obsolete. Your gun could not be rechambered to take the .25/20 repeater case which is shorter and fatter. If I owned that rifle I think I would get it rebarreled to .22 Hornet, 2-R Lovell, or something of that sort.

CONVERTING .22 TO FIELD RIFLE

Question: My present rifle is a Model 52 .22-caliber target rifle, weighing 10 lb., equipped with a Lyman 17-A front sight and a Lyman 48-F receiver. I have ordered a Weaver 'scope and mount so I can use the rifle for shooting woodchucks. I want to leave the barrel at 28 in. but I want the final product to weigh no more than 9 lb. Where should the extra weight be taken from? I would appreciate any other advice you can give me on converting this target rifle into a field rifle.—B. C. B., Wis.

Answer: I think that if you want to make a sporter of lighter weight out of that 52 about the only thing you can do is to cut the barrel off to 24 in. I wouldn't advise you to have the barrel turned down, because it might bend in the process and you would never again obtain very great accuracy. With the barrel cut to 24 in. and a sporting stock installed you would have a sporter of real he-man weight.

On the other hand, I do not think you would ever be satisfied in the long run with a .22 rimfire for woodchucks. It just isn't in the cards for that cartridge to be much of a woodchuck-killer, particularly if you want to knock them over at long range. I think the rifle you should investigate is the Model 70 Winchester .22 Hornet. With this rifle and a 4X 'scope you can take woodchucks quite regularly at ranges up to 200 yd. With the .22 rimfire, 100 yd. is about the limit because of the curved trajectory.

RESTOCKING 8 MM. MAUSER

Question: I recently bought an 8 mm. Mauser which is in good condition, except for the stock, which is a poor homemade affair. Do you think this rifle would be worth restocking? What load should I use in it?—W. E., Wash.

Answer: I think that your 8 mm. Mauser would be well worth restocking. The action is good, and if the barrel is not pitted you ought to get satisfaction out of it. The 8 mm. cartridge is similar to the .30/06 service cartridge, but is not so highly developed in this country. It uses a 170-gr. bullet at a muzzle velocity of about 2,550 foot seconds, and a 236-gr. bullet at about 2,200. Either load is plenty powerful. Plenty of game has fallen from the 8 mm.

DON'T CUT DOWN A SAVAGE .300

Question: I have a Model 99 Savage .300 with a 24-in. barrel. If this barrel were cut down to 20 in., what would be the effect on velocity, energy, and muzzle blast?—W. S. F., Canada.

Answer: Leave that gun alone. In any event, don't cut it down below 22 in. A 20-in. barrel will give you bad muzzle blast and you must subtract 25 foot seconds in velocity for every inch of barrel you cut off.

REPLACING STOCK ON NEWTON

Question: My .256 Newton, which was in perfect condition when I lent it to a friend, was returned with a 6-in. crack in the barrel at the muzzle end. Do you know if I can obtain a stock replacement? If I have to have one made to order, is it possible to switch to a modern caliber?—F. A., N. Y.

Answer: The Newton Company had no successor so I'm afraid that the only way you can get a barrel is to have one tailormade, if indeed you can find anyone to do that. Your action will need no alteration to be used as a .30/06 or a .270 except a new barrel.

CONVERTING "95"

Question: Would it be advisable to convert my Model 95 Winchester over to .270 or .257? I have heard doubts expressed about its ability to handle hot loads.—F. F. D., Calif.

Answer: No. The 95 action is not strong enough to be ideal with the .30/06 cartridge, although it will handle it, but it would not handle the .257 or the .270 since pressures run a little higher. As a matter of fact, .30/06 pressures run 48,000 lb. in most commercial loads and a great many .270 loads run up to 55,000. Many, many hunters have expressed a desire for the .30/06 in a lever-action rifle but to date none have been made.

TIGHT CHAMBER

Question: I have a custom-built Springfield. Two brands of ammunition will fit its chamber, but a third won't chamber at all. How come?—C. D. L., Pa.

Answer: You have a minimum chamber, which one sometimes finds in rifles chambered by private makers and by the Springfield arsenal. Often these tight babies will accept F. A. government ammunition—which is made to minimum dimensions so it will go into dirty chambers during war conditions—and a certain other commercial brand, but will not take a couple of other brands. I had a tight chamber in a tailor-made barrel; it would take F. A. stuff and one other brand. A second "commercial" it wouldn't take at all, and about 50 percent of the hulls of a third brand. Pressures of all commercial stuff were high, with blown primers and primer leaks. I had to cut maximum handloads by 4 gr. of powder. Frankly, that tight chamber was such a nuisance that I had it rechambered for the larger "commercial" chamber. Some gun nuts dote on tight chambers, since they get maximum velocities with less powder, and they swear they get better accuracy. I find tight chambers nothing but pains in the neck.

SHORTENING .30 RIFLE BARREL

Question: I have a .30 caliber Winchester center-fire rifle, Model 1894, with a 26½-in. barrel. As all my hunting is in heavy brush, I find the long barrel too slow, and I'd like to reduce it to 20 or 22 in. I have heard that a barrel must be cut off at a certain place, in order to keep the proper twist as the bullet leaves the muzzle. I am handy with tools and can shorten this barrel myself, if you say the idea is O.K.—L. A. C. L., Manitoba, Canada.

Answer: You can cut the barrel off at any point, down to 20 in., without making the slightest difference in your rifle's accuracy. I, too, have often heard the notion that you must cut off the barrel at a certain magic spot, but there's absolutely nothing to it. Make the cut with a hacksaw, then face the muzzle up with a file. If you can get your front sight on all right, you need have no worries.

CUTTING OFF MOSSBERG

Question: Are all rifle barrels slightly taper-bored? I was told that they are, and that therefore it is bad business to cut off any barrel shorter than the manufacturer made it. However, I know of many guns so changed that seem to shoot all right. I have a Mossberg .22 Model 46AT that I would like to cut down to about 22 in. for convenience. I use a Weaver 'scope, so that barrel length, as I see it, has no advantage for me, and a short barrel would hold steadier offhand, especially in this heavy model.—R. E. K., Ore.

Answer: A few rifles have been made with a taper bore, but conventional rifling is not taper-bored at all, and bore lands and grooves are the same size at the breech and muzzle. You can cut your Mossberg off to 22 in. without impairing its accuracy and without cutting down on velocity.

If you find the shorter barrel steadier to hold offhand your experience is exactly the opposite of mine. I find the longer and heavier barrel better for offhand shooting because it hangs more firmly.

HEAT-TREATING SPRINGFIELD

Question: I'd like to ask you a few questions about the old, low-number Springfield receiver, Model 1903. Can it be strengthened by re-heating so the usual maximum handload can be shot from a rifle in which it is used? A chap who is offering such rifles for sales says they are absolutely safe if properly heat-treated.

I'd like to attach a .270 barrel to this action, if it will stand up.—I. O. S., Mich.

Answer: Those old Springfield actions are made of case-hardened carbon steel; but heat-treating them will fix them up so they are O.K. If the man who does the heat-treating knows his business you will have a good action. The R. F. Sedgley Co., Philadelphia, Pa., has made up thousands of those actions into .270's, .22 Swifts, and other hot calibers.

REMODELING .22 SPRINGFIELD

Question: My Model 1903 Springfield appears to have a standard breech but only a .22 barrel. I've been told that it was a training rifle in the first World War. I have a .30/30 and a .348 but no long-range, high-power rifle. Could the barrel of this .22 Springfield be rebored to a .257, a .270, or a .220 Swift?—A. J. W., Pa.

Answer: Your Springfield is one which was made for use in training troops; it uses the regular .22 rimfire cartridge in an adapter.

It would not be difficult for you to convert that rifle into some other caliber. Not into a Swift, however, because the groove diameter of the Swift is .224, while that of the Long Rifle is .222. On the other hand, you could get that rifle converted to the 2-R Lovell or the .22 Hornet by having the barrel cut off, rethreaded, and rechambered. Or you could have a Model 70 .270 Winchester barrel fitted. I would not recommend a rebore job, as they seldom turn out satisfactorily. Rebored barrels are nearly always crooked barrels, and they change their centers of impact as they heat up.

RING IN RIFLE BARREL

Question: I recently purchased a second-hand .250/3000 Savage and while examining it I found a ring inside the barrel about an inch or so from the muzzle. It is quite deep, but I was told that it was

factory-made. If this is true, what is its purpose?—O. L., New Brunswick.

Answer: The ring in your Savage barrel was not put in there by the factory. Evidently the rifle has been fired with an obstruction in the barrel. You should either have the barrel cut off and a new front sight fitted to eliminate that ring, or you should have a new barrel fitted by the Service Department, Savage Arms Corp., Utica, N. Y.

TO KEEP RIFLE FROM "FREEZING"

Question: I went hunting in the Adirondacks last year with a pump-action high-powered rifle. It was well below zero while I was hunting, and the rifle action froze up as tight as a drum. Why? What does one do about it?—J. B. M., N. Y.

Answer: Those pump-action rifles are fast for woods shooting, but they are as complicated as an airplane engine, and easy to "freeze" up if they are left oiled in cold weather. The next time you brave the wintry blasts with that musket, clean the action thoroughly with gasoline, removing every trace of oil. Then lubricate with dry powdered graphite, which won't congeal.

SHORTS ERODE .22

Question: My single-shot .22 rifle is chambered for the short, long, and Long Rifle, and up to this time I've been using shorts. Now I've bought a large quantity of Long Rifle bullets and find they won't fit into the chamber of the gun properly, and won't eject. Can a gunsmith repair this?—J. K., N. J.

Answer: By using shorts you have eroded the chamber of your rifle and the .22 Long Rifle bullets stick in the portions of the chamber where hot powder gases have roughened it. I believe a good gunsmith could polish the chamber for you if the erosion has not progressed too far. If it has, there isn't anything you can do except stick to shorts.

.250/3000 ON SPRINGFIELD ACTION

Question: Is it possible to have a .250/ 3000 barrel fitted to a Springfield action? Would the cartridge work in the magazine and would the breech pressure be too high?—H. G., N. H.

Answer: It is perfectly possible to have a .250/3000 barrel put on a Springfield action. The Springfield, in good condition, is strong enough for the .250 cartridge. If the job is done by a competent gunsmith, the headspace ought to be correct. I think the cartridges would work through the action a little better if a magazine block is used. However, that is easily installed.

PREVENTING JAMMED CASES

Question: I have a .22 Winchester, model 1902, single-shot rifle. It shoots Remington cartridges well, but when I shoot Western cartridges the empty cases jam in the chamber. Wish you could tell me what to do about this, as I still have a good supply of Westerns.—B. B., Pa.

Answer: You have a very old rifle, and it's my guess that the Western cases jam because the chamber has become a bit rusted. Probably the brass of those Western cases is a little softer than usual and is expanding into the rust pits. Try polishing the chamber a bit with some crocus cloth wrapped around a stick; it may solve your problem.

REBARRELING .25/35

Question: My .25/35 Model 94 Winchester does not shoot accurately. The rifling is so worn down that it does not groove the bullet. I have a .25/20 Marlin barrel in good condition. It is 24 in. long and has the words "special smokeless steel," stamped on it.

Could I have this barrel rechambered to take a .25/35 cartridge and also have it rethreaded so it will fit my Winchester action?—G. R. W., Calif.

Answer: No, you could not rebarrel your .25/35 with a .25/20 barrel, even though both barrels are .25 caliber. The reason is that the .25/20 was designed to use short bullets and has a twist of the rifling of one turn in 14 in. The heaviest bullet it uses is 86 gr.

The .25/35 was designed to use the long 117-gr. bullet at moderate velocity; and to spin that bullet requires the rather sharp twist of one turn in 8 in. Consequently, you would find your bullet keyholing even at 100 yd. if you used that .25/20 barrel.

Better send your rifle to the Service Department, Winchester Repeating Arms Co., New Haven, Conn., and have them install a new .25/35 barrel.

FREE-FLOATING BARREL

Question: My Springfield was recently rebarreled, but I find that the new barrel does not bed perfectly in the stock. Will it shoot accurately in this condition? Could I fit the space with plastic wood, or will I have to have it restocked?— J. W. D., N. C.

Answer: I would hesitate to tell you what you ought to do with that Springfield. Sometimes a free-floating barrel which does not touch the stock will still give excellent accuracy. I would suggest, however that you try the following:

Put a ½-in. wide band of plastic wood about 2½ in. back of the end of the fore-end. Then lay a little strip of wax paper over the plastic wood, put the barrel back in place, and draw the guard screws up tight. Shoot your rifle and see how the accuracy is. If it is all right, fill in between the barrel and the fore-end and at the sides with plastic wood and stain it to match the fore-end.

If the accuracy is poor, however, the thing to do would be to turn the rifle over to a good stocker and have him rebed the barrel or make a new stock. The way the action is bedded in and the way the barrel fits the channel in the fore-end makes a difference in accuracy.

REBARRELING .30/06

Question: I recently bought a model 70 .30/06, but have decided that I'd prefer it in .270. Can a .270 barrel be put on that action without too much trouble? I also plan to get a heavier rifle as I want to hunt Kodiak bear in Alaska. What is your notion of the virtues of the .300 and the .375 Magnums as bear stoppers? Would you consider the .270 and the .375 a good pair of rifles for all American game?—J. P. K., Wyo.

Answer: Any competent gunsmith with head-space gauges can replace a Model .30/06 barrel with a .270 barrel on your rifle. In fact, a Model 70 for the .30/06 (or for that matter, a 98 Mauser, a Model 30 Remington, or a Model 54 Winchester) can be rebarreled to any caliber with the same size case head—for instance, the 7 mm., 8 mm., .35 and .400 Whelen, .250/3000, .257, .270, etc. The .270, and a good many others, began life as .30/06 cases with the necks expanded or necked down for other than .30 caliber bullets. The shoulder slope on the .270 and the .30/06 are the same, and I understand that the .30/06 head-space gauges can be used to adjust the head space on a .270.

I have a .30/06 and a .270, both fine rifles, and have killed a good deal of game with each. My present .30/06 is about my 10th of that caliber. My own notion is that for deer, sheep, and antelope I'd pick the .270, particularly if I could have a good second rifle for the larger stuff, in which case it would be a .375. Thus, the .270 and the .375 would make an excellent pair for all American game.

Judging by the elk I've shot, I'd prefer the .375 to the .30/06, but many excellent elk hunters disagree with me. Now to bear: A man who has done lots of Alaskan hunting, tells me that for Kodiak bear he wants the biggest rifle he can get, and that a .375 is none too big. On the other hand, he says he'd just as soon tackle a grizzly with a .257 if the bullets held together, which the new Silvertips, Core-Lokts, Belted, etc., do. The .300 Magnum simply fires .30/06 cartridges at higher velocities; I wouldn't call it a stopping rifle like the .375.

HORNET CONVERSION

Question: I have a Hornet rifle, and I'm planning to have it changed over to chamber the .22/3,000 Lovell R-2 cartridge. Do you think the increase in efficiency is worth the cost of conversion? —R. B., N. Y.

Answer: Of all the wildcat cartridges, the .22/3,000 Lovell R-2 is probably the best. It's a modification of the original .22/3,000 Lovell, and, I understand, a much more efficient cartridge for obtaining maximum velocity. Both the original Lovell and the R-2 are, you probably know, the .25/20 single shot necked down to take Hornet bullets.

I understand that an R-2 will drive a 51-grain bullet at 3,100, also that the trajectory of the bullet rises but 1 in. above line of sights at 100 yd., shooting at 200-yd. range. That would make it a 250-yd. vermin cartridge. You might also consider the K-Hornet, a modification of the regular case for better burning of powder. That gives about 3,000 ft. a second, instead of the regular 2,650.

It's up to you to decide if the change warrants the cost. If you rechamber for the K-Hornet, you can use regular Hornet ammunition, as the pressure expands the cases to the new shape. Possibly the additional velocity the K-Hornet would give you would be all you'd need. Also, you might consider what a boon it is to walk into a store, lay down your money, and get a box of brand-new bullets to fit your gun.

CONVERTING .25 REMINGTON TO .257

Question: I have had a .25 Remington Model 30 for a great many years. It has always been very satisfactory, but recently I had an opportunity to shoot a .257 Roberts, and it seems to me that it would be a good idea to have the .25 converted to.257. Would it be expensive? —A. A., Calif.

Answer: If that .25 Remington Model 30 has a twist of 1 in 10, you could get it rechambered to .257 by getting the bolt face and extractor altered and having a longer magazine fitted. My information is that that *is* the twist. However, that dope may be wrong, and the twist may be 1 in 8, as it is in the .25/35. If the latter is the case, the twist would be too abrupt for .257, and you would have to have a new barrel fitted.

My advice is to have a good gunsmith look at the rifle, determine the twist, and let you know. If it is 1 in 10, the conversion job will be well worth while. If it isn't, rebarreling and rechambering would be considerably more expensive.

ADVICE ON WINCHESTER MODEL 54

Question: I have a Winchester Model 54 in 9 mm. Mauser, with a 20-in. barrel. This rifle has never been carried. The friend from whom I bought it has fired only five cartridges in it—to sight it in. It is equipped with a Lyman 48 receiver sight. I paid a very reasonable price for the rifle and want to equip it with a Lyman Alaska 'scope on a Griffin & Howe mount. Will that raise the 'scope enough to clear the bolt and safety without altering them? I like the idea of keeping the receiver sight available. Would it be better for me to have it re-

barreled to .30/06 or .270?—T. J. C., N. H.

Answer: For a short time Winchester made the Model 54 for the 9 x 57 mm. Mauser cartridge. It didn't sell well, however, and was quickly discontinued. The 9 mm. Mauser cartridge is now obsolete in this country. It is different from the 9 mm. Mannlicher-Schoenauer.

You could have a good gunsmith rechamber your rifle to the excellent .35 Whelen wildcat cartridge if you wish. The 9 mm. Mauser gave the 280-gr. bullet a velocity of only about 2,150 foot seconds, whereas the .35 Whelen gives the 275-gr. bullet a velocity of 2,450. .

On the other hand, you could return the rifle to the Service Department, Winchester Repeating Arms Co., New Haven, Conn., and have a .270 or .30/06 barrel fitted. The action is just the same as the action for those cartridges.

I strongly advise you against mounting a 'scope high enough to clear the bolt handle and safety. Since you like the double-lever Griffin & Howe mount, get the low mount and have the bolt handle and safety altered for low 'scope mounting. Leave the Lyman 48 receiver sight on. You can remove the slide when you put the 'scope on, and put the slide back when you take the 'scope off.

STEVENS .44 NOT RIGHT FOR HORNET

Question: Can I make a Hornet rifle out of my heavy-barrel Stevens Ideal, Model 44—would the action be strong enough to stand the pressure?—R. C., Mo.

Answer: The Stevens No. 44 action is not considered strong enough for the Hornet. The Stevens action to use is the high-side-wall No. 44½ type, consequently I think you'd better forget about it. You might get away with it and you might not. Furthermore, I think the jacketed Hornet bullets would be pretty tough on your barrel which, I believe, is soft steel. If you want to buy a new gun, both the Savage 23-O and the Winchester Model 70 are chambered for the hornet.

REMOVING OBSTRUCTION FROM BARREL

Question: My little nephew wedged a cleaning cloth and two small nails in my .22 Mossberg repeater. How can I dislodge this obstruction? I've tried poking it out but it won't budge.—W. V., Wis.

Answer: Stand the rifle up on the butt and pour a little of some light penetrating oil down the bore. Let it set for a couple of days, then heat the barrel at the point of the obstruction until it is very hot but *not* red-hot. The oil will lubricate the bore and the heat will reduce the size of the obstruction by charring it. Then you should be able to push it out with a cleaning rod.

CLEANING LEAD FROM BARREL

Question: What's the best way to clean lead out of a rifle barrel? A friend of mine bought a .25/20 which was clogged with lead. He removed most of it, but must have missed some. After firing 15 shots, he retrieved the last bullet and found that it had come out about 3 in. long and no thicker than a pencil lead. Aside from this obstruction in the barrel, the rifle is O.K.—E. B., N. Y.

Answer: I think the best way to get the lead out of that barrel would be to plug the muzzle on the breech and then pour in metallic mercury. The mercury will mix with the lead and clean it out. If there weren't too much lead you might have fair success by using a brass brush with powder solvent.

REFINISHING STOCK

Question: My old rifle has a battered stock that I'd like to refinish. How is it done?—W. E. B., Tex.

Answer: Giving a gunstock a linseed-oil finish is simple. First get a bottle of commercial varnish remover, and rub the contents on the stock until the old finish gums. Scrape that off with a putty knife. You'll have to make two or three applications of the remover, probably, as the varnish may harden up while you're working. When it is pretty well off, sandpaper the stock with medium-fine sandpaper, and finish with a very fine paper. Next wet the stock slightly to raise the "whiskers"—tiny slivers that have been pressed into the wood by the sandpaper. Rub lightly with new fine paper, taking the whiskers off, repeating the wetting-and-rubbing process as long as they show.

Then your stock should be ready for oil. Put on a coat of linseed (the boiled kind dries more quickly) and let it soak in. Repeat until it gums, then rub the gum off after softening it with fresh oil. After that, rub oil in by hand every time you happen to think of it, being sure to remove all excess when you quit, so it won't gum. That's all there is to it, and it's the best way to finish up a gun.

TREATMENT FOR METAL FOULING

Question: Have heard that rifles of .30/06 caliber foul in use. What should I do to prevent this in my new rifle? Should I employ some factory cleaning compound every time I shoot my gun?— W. H. P., Pa.

Answer: I think you're worrying too much about metal fouling. Jackets nowadays don't leave much. In most of my rifles metal fouling is the least of my worries; but I have one, a Springfield with a new, tight, tailor-made barrel that has a tendency to foul. I simply run a Marble's brass brush through it two or three times, then wipe it out with a rag saturated with Hoppe's No. 9, and let it go at that. That treatment keeps the fouling down.

REMOVING RUST FROM BARREL

Question: My Winchester Model 54 .30/06 recently developed serious rust and corrosion in the barrel. It has been excessively damp in my locality lately and the gun was not sufficiently protected against rust. How can I remove this rust and then prepare the barrel against further attacks?—A. A. W., Wis.

Answer: Take out the bolt and put the muzzle of your rifle in a pan of boiling, soapy water. Then put a patch on your cleaning rod and pump the hot water through the barrel until the latter is as hot as fire to the touch. Next dry the barrel with two or three patches and the heat will finish the drying. Now you have all the rust killed—having dissolved the potassium chlorate which it picked up from some old-fashioned primers you probably used. Every time you shoot the rifle hereafter leave the bore coated with a commercial protecting compound which you can obtain at any sporting-goods store. You won't be bothered with rust again.

7 MM. MAUSER

Question: I am about to make up a 7 mm. rifle on a Mauser action, and would like a little advice. I'll use it for deer in the brushy coast-range mountains of this state as well as for a saddle gun. Naturally I want it as light and quick-handling as possible without sacrificing anything. Do you consider a 20-in. barrel too short? The sight will be a Lyman Alaskan with flat-top-post reticule in simple, sturdy, nondetachable mounts.

What does the .270 have the 7 mm. doesn't? Can .30/06 cases be trimmed and resized in a Pacific tool to fit the 7 mm.? I have heard there is a slight difference in the head size and that the necks have to be reamed, as there is a difference in thickness at the neck.—T. L. K., Calif.

Answer: I wouldn't have the 7 mm. barrel shorter than 22 in. Most ballistics figures for the 7 mm. are taken in 30 in. barrels, and that means that even with a 24-in. barrel you are going to lose 150 ft. a second off published ballistics. With a 22-in. barrel you lose about 200.

The 7 mm. is a very efficient cartridge. I had one for some years and had excellent success with it. In fact, I never lost a head of game I hit with it, and if my memory serves me correctly, practically everything I shot with it went down dead in its tracks. The only thing I've got against the 7 mm. is that it is throated for the long loading of the 175-gr. bullet. As a consequence, 7 mm. barrels have a short life if used with the shorter 139-gr. and 150-gr. bullets. When I had a lot of throat erosion in the second barrel of my 7 mm. I swapped it off, although I was very fond of the rifle.

My favorite hunting load was the 140-gr. Barnes bullet or the 139-gr. Western bullet with 45 gr. of No. 4064 powder. Accuracy was very good and killing power excellent. However the 7 mm. is not quite so accurate as the .270 or the .257. Accuracy is about like that of the .30/06, which means you are lucky if you get 1½-in. groups at 100 yd. You're more likely to get 2½-in. groups.

BEDDING KRAG BARREL

Question: How shall I bed my Krag rifle in a Bishop stock? Shall I bed it down solid or leave it floating? Are the two screws on the trigger guard enough to hold the barrel down.—A. K., Calif.

Answer: Bed that barrel in the stock all the way but try to leave slightly more pressure on the fore-end tip than elsewhere. You should be able to feel the stock spring a little when you take the pressure off the front guard screw. Bedded that way, your gun will give groups which will be considerably smaller.

FACTS ABOUT LOADS AND LOADING

CARTRIDGE TERMS EXPLAINED

Question: In all I have read about shooting the writers seem to take it for granted that everyone knows the meaning of the figures they use to describe cartridges. I understand references to caliber but not all of the figures. For example, why are some guns designated as .30 caliber and others .300? What does the 40 mean in .30/40, and what does full patch mean as applied to bullets?—D. P., Ohio.

Answer: The term .30 caliber means that the diameter of the rifle bore is 30/100 of an inch. The .300 caliber means 300/1000 of an inch, which, of course, is exactly the same as the .30. Some rifles are named for their groove diameter (instead of having the diameter measured from the lands, or raised parts of the rifling). For example, the .257 has a bore diameter of .250 (diameter between surfaces of the lands) and a groove diameter of .257.

In .30/40, the 40 means that the case has a capacity of 40 gr. of powder; the .45/70 holds 70 gr. of powder. Full patch means that the bullet point is completely incased in a metal jacket.

.32/20 A GOOD VARMINT BULLET

Question: A friend of mine has offered me some of his specially handloaded .300 Savage cartridges. He has a .300 too, and claims his cartridges are good for groundhogs or for any 100-yd. shot. He uses regular .300 Savage cases and .32/20 soft-nose bullets.

I measured these .32/20 bullets and found they were about .003 in. larger in diameter than the bullets in the factory-loaded .300 cartridges. Since I thought this was dangerous, I haven't used any. Are they safe to use?—A. J. W., Ohio.

Answer: The .32/20 bullet *is* oversize for a standard .30 caliber rifle. However, it swages down as it is forced into the bore and can be used with good accuracy. Actually the lead core of the .32/20 bullet is soft and the jacket is thin. A great many varmint hunters have used it extensively in the .30/06 on woodchucks, and many swear by it.

CURE FOR OVERSIZE CASES

Question: A neighbor who has a Pacific reloading tool, jeweler's scales, and other equipment, reloaded some .30/06 shells for me. The shells had all been fired once and were swollen near the rear. He had not resized them full length. Some of these shells will not go in my Enfield sporter at all, and those that will require a lot of forcing. What should be done to them?—J. E. MacD., Wash.

Answer: You'll have to run those cases through a full-length Pacific die. That will reduce the cases to standard minimum dimensions so they will fit any standard .30/06 chamber. All chambers are not alike. Since the brass expands to fit the chamber of the rifle in which it is shot, it is seldom that any two .30/06 rifles can interchange fired cases, even though they were made by the same chambering tools one after the other.

STORING AMMUNITION

Question: I have a store of .22 rimfire cartridges which I'm trying to take good care of. I store them in an old ammunition box on the bottom shelf of a bookcase in a small storeroom. So that the temperature will stay somewhere between 40 and 60 degrees F., I keep the room door closed, except in damp or rainy weather, when I open it to let in dry air from the rest of the house. The one window in the room faces west, and I don't think the place gets damp. Are there other precautions I should take?—J. P., Conn.

Answer: Ammunition isn't nearly so hard

to store as most people think it is. If you keep yours at ordinary room temperatures, without letting it get too dry (as it would near a radiator) or too damp (as it would in most cellars), it will be perfectly O.K. Strikes me you've been doing some rather needless worrying.

SHORTS IN LONG RIFLE

Question: Is it advisable to shoot .22 short cartridges in a rifle chambered for the Long Rifle, and high and low-velocity cartridges mixed?—A. L., Calif.

Answer: You can shoot .22 shorts in a rifle chambered for Long Rifles, but you won't get the same accuracy you would in

SHORTS IN A LONG RIFLE CHAMBER

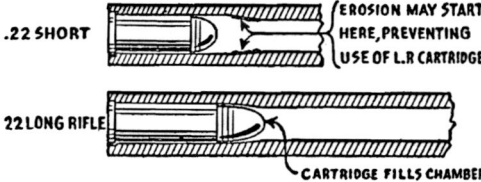

If .22 shorts are used over a long period of time in a chamber which also takes .22 Long Rifle cartridges, the erosion which takes place may make it impossible to use the Long Rifle cartridges in the gun.

a rifle made especially for shorts. And if you continue to use the shorts, you will eventually erode the chamber so that you cannot seat Long Rifle cartridges. As a consequence, I wouldn't recommend that you do that. You may use high and low-velocity cartridges mixed, but they will not have the same center of impact.

LONG RIFLE AND .22 W.R.F.

Question: How does the .22 Long Rifle compare in weight, speed and energy with those of the .22 W.R.F.?—J. M., La.

Answer: Here's the dope on the most powerful forms of the Long Rifle and the W.R.F.: The superspeed .22 Long Rifle hollow-point uses a 37-gr. bullet at 1,400 ft. a second, with midrange trajectory

of 3 in. at 50 yd. over a 100-yd. course. The muzzle energy is 161 ft. lb. The .22 W.R.F. hollow-point high-speed uses a 40-gr. bullet at 1,475 ft. a second, with a midrange 100-yd. trajectory of 2.7 in. The muzzle energy is 193 ft. lb. As you see, the .22 W.R.F. is a little more powerful. However, the rub is this: The .22 Long Rifle is almost as powerful—but it's much more accurate and much more widely distributed.

STEEL-JACKETED BULLETS?

Question: Will you settle an argument? A friend tells me that certain bullets are jacketed with steel. What is the dope on steel jackets?—S. F., Ga.

Answer: A very few jackets of mild steel, mostly coated with cupro-nickel or copper, have been made in the past, mostly in military calibers. However, in Europe, many bullets have steel jackets, both in military and sporting calibers. In the first World War, the Germans even used steel cartridge cases. This country is now making experiments in that direction. But most of the "white" bullets usually termed "steel-jacketed" are really cupro-nickel jackets or gilding metal which has been tinned to give the "steel" color.

GRINDING BULLET TIPS

Question: Recently I picked up some .30/06 M-1. Is it safe to grind or drill the tips without first removing the bullets from the cases? I'm a little leery about doing it and would appreciate any advice you may give me. By the way, how can you tell an M-1 from an M-2 without removing the bullet?—W. B. M., Wash.

Answer: It is perfectly safe to grind or drill the tip of the M-1 bullet without removing it from the case. The M-1 bullets are all copper colored. The M-2 bullet, on the other hand, is white since it is coated with a tin wash. The best way to alter those bullets is to file them down until about ⅛ in. of lead core shows at the tip. Then take a file and thin the jacket for about ¼ in. toward the tip. Then drill a hole about ⅛ in. across and ¼ in. deep into the core. A lot of game has been killed with these bullets.

ONE BULLET—MORE HITS

Question: When I bought a new Model 71 Winchester .348 I got a supply of ammunition with it—150-gr. soft-points, 200-gr. hollow-points, and 250-gr. Silver-tips. I was all set to sight my rifle in at 150 yd.—using the 200-gr. bullets—when lo and behold, I read an article which said that centers of impact will change with different brands as well as with different bullet weights! Now—shall I choose just one weight and one brand? I'll use the gun for moose and bear in Canada and for white-tails in Michigan. Is it too heavy for deer?—A. R., Ind.

Answer: The only way you can be sure where your rifle will put any particular brand of bullet or any particular weight of bullet, is to shoot it and see. It's that mysterious thing called barrel whip. Frankly, though, I think you are fooling around with too many different kinds of ammunition. If you still have an opportunity to trade off your 150-gr. and 250-gr. stuff for 200-gr., do it by all means. The 200-gr. bullet is the best all-round bullet for the .348. It has a good, sufficiently flat trajectory, and great penetration and shocking power. If I were you I'd sight that rifle in for 200 yd., which will mean that bullet will rise about 3 in. above the point of aim at 100 yd. Theoretically, the 150-gr. might appear to be a good bullet; actually, it loses velocity so fast that if sighted in for 200 yd., it will drop about as much, at 300, as will the 200-gr. In addition, it does not penetrate nearly so well.

Don't let anyone tell you that the .348 isn't a good rifle for white-tail deer. It kills them like dynamite without tearing up much meat and the Model 71 rifle is one of the neatest and fastest-handling woods rifles made. Exchange some of that ammunition! That will be better than spending half your time sighting in.

BARREL LENGTH AND VELOCITY

Question: Using the same sporting ammunition in three .30/06 rifles having barrel lengths of 20, 24, and 26 in., what would be the velocities of the bullets? Would there be any difference in their killing power on game?—G. S. S., Ind.

Answer: The velocities of the .30/06 are taken in 24-in. barrels. A longer barrel will give you roughly (and within limits) 25 foot seconds' more velocity for each additional inch. With a shorter barrel, you will lose 25 foot seconds per inch. Using a 180-gr. bullet, the muzzle velocity in a 24-in. barrel is 2,700 foot seconds. You would get about 2,750 with a 26-in. barrel and about 2,600 in a 20 in.

As far as trajectory goes, the difference between a velocity of 2,600 and one of 2,750 would be so slight that you would not notice it in the field. The higher velocity, however, will give a more violent bullet expansion and quicker kills.

My suggestion is not to use a barrel shorter than 22 in. If you do, you will find that the apparent recoil and the muzzle blast are greatly increased.

150-GR. BULLET FOR .300 SAVAGE

Question: None of the deer I have shot with my .300 Savage has been killed in his tracks. All have run several yards before going down. I use the 180-gr. bullet exclusively. If I would use the 150-gr. instead of the 180-gr. stuff, would the killing power be improved?—J. W. S., Me.

Answer: Yes, I believe you will find that the 150-gr. bullet in the .300 Savage kills deer a good deal better than the 180-gr. bullet. In fact, I should say that with the 150-gr. bullet at a muzzle velocity of 2,660 foot seconds the .300 Savage is one of our very best deer calibers. I think what you should do is to try to trade the cartridges you have for some of 150 gr. You couldn't just pull the 180-gr. bullets, seat 150-gr. on the same powder charge, and expect to come out very well.

WHICH BULLET TYPE FOR DEER?

Question: Do you think my .35 Remington autoloader, Model 8, might have lost power? It no longer kills white-tails even when they are hit properly. It used to kill them when I used the regular Express mushroom bullet. Now I don't use that bullet, but am using Core-Lokts. Could this have anything to do with the changed performance?—C. N., N. Y.

Answer: Your rifle hasn't lost any of its power. The answer to your problem lies in the fact you formerly used a bullet which expanded nicely, giving a lot of shocking power. The Core-Lokt bullet you are now shooting is designed to expand a little and penetrate deeply. It is a fine deer killer, but is at its best on larger animals. The white-tail is not a large deer. He needs plenty of expansion and not much penetration. You are shooting through those deer and wasting most of the energy on the far side.

I think the best bullet for those whitetails would be either a hollow-point mushroom, designed to open quickly, or a bullet with a lot of lead exposed.

BULLET WEIGHT VS. VELOCITY

Question: A friend says that a slow, heavy bullet like the .45/70 is deadlier on game than the light, high-speed bullets of the .270 class. He contends that the light bullets stun rather than kill game. Is he right?—R. C., Ohio.

Answer: Only partly. The two deadliest slugs—when they hit—are the big, heavy ones like the .45/70 and the ultra-high-velocity bullets, .270 for one. The .45/70 slug is deadly because of the tissue-destroying and shock-delivering qualities of large diameter and great weight. The .270 knocks them off because of its tissue-destroying high velocity.

I have not seen many kills made with the .45/70, but those I have seen have been just about as sudden and complete as any produced by the .270. Either will kill far more quickly, with hits in the same spot, than the 220-gr. Krag or Springfield or the 170-gr. .30/30, etc.

However, the .270 is much easier to hit with than is the old charcoal-burning .45/70, though for brush shooting the older black-powder cartridges are still deadly on shots at 50–100 yd.

Your friend is wrong when he says the .270 just stuns game. At 300 yd., instantaneous kills with the 100 or 130-gr. bullet are the rule—not the exception.

BULLETS FOR .30/06

Question: What bullets should I use for various game in my .30/06? Does the use of bullets of different weights hurt a rifle?—H. O., Wyo.

Answer: The .30/06 is probably the best all-round caliber in America. By an all-

30/06 BULLETS COMPARED

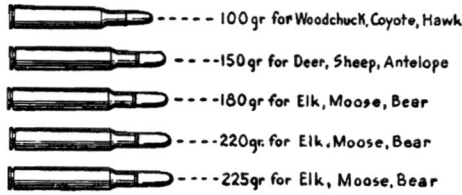

100 gr for Woodchuck, Coyote, Hawk
150 gr for Deer, Sheep, Antelope
180 gr for Elk, Moose, Bear
220 gr. for Elk, Moose, Bear
225 gr for Elk, Moose, Bear

The great variety of bullet weights available for the .30/06 make it one of the most versatile cartridges made.

round rifle I mean one which can be used in a pinch on everything from woodchucks to elk, moose, and brown bear. The .30/06 is a better caliber than the Krag or .30/40, since rifles for it are now made, whereas any rifle for the .30/40 is bound to be old. Actions for the .30/06 are also stronger than those for the Krag and, coupled with greater powder capacity, the .30/06 will drive the same bullets faster.

You can use different weights of bullets in the same rifle without hurting it a bit. However, most rifles will have to be resighted with each different weight, since each sets up different barrel vibrations.

Here is a list of bullet weights for the .30/06, and of the game for which they are best suited:

For vermin (woodchuck, coyote, hawk): 100-gr.; 150-gr. at 3,000 ft.-sec.

For deer, sheep, antelope: 150-gr. bullet at about 3,000; 180-gr. at about 2,700.

For elk, moose, grizzly: 180-gr. at 2,700; 220 and 225-gr. at about 2,400.

For my part I like the various 150-gr. loads for deer hunting, and the 220 and 225-gr. stuff for the big fellows. Many hunters swear by the 180-gr. for elk, but I think it is too light.

.22 AMMUNITION FOR SMALL GAME

Question: I own a .22 Mossberg rifle, Model 46 M, with a Mossberg 4X 'scope. What ammunition would you recommend for rabbits and vermin?—A. P., Manitoba.

Answer: The best ammunition for use on small game is the .22 Long Rifle high-speed hollow point. It has more killing power than the solid bullet and of course more killing power than the low speeds. I prefer greased bullets because they simplify cleaning and protect the bore.

THE .32 SPECIAL

Question: I have bought an almost-new .32 Winchester Special, Model 1894, and two boxes of cartridges loaded with 170-gr. bullets. What are the ballistics of this rifle load? How good is it for deer in Florida, and what is the best hunting cartridge?—W. E. O., Fla.

Answer: That .32 Special is much like the .30/30 cartridge. The best bullet for it seems to be the old-fashioned 170-gr. soft point, having a muzzle velocity of 2,260 foot seconds. The best distance to sight the .32 Special in at is 150 yd. Then the bullet strikes 2 in. high at 50 yd., 2 in. low at 100, on the nose at 150, 4½ in. low at 200, 13 in. low at 250, 28 in. low at 300, and 47 in. low at 350.

As you can see, the .32 Special is no more than a 200-yd. rifle at best, and actually is just about at the end of its rope for practical hunting at 175 yd., especially with open sights.

BULLETS FOR CANADIAN HUNTING

Question: What weight and kind of bullets would you recommend for use in hunting moose in Canada with a .270 and a .30/06?—R. M. C., N. Y.

Answer: I think a 130-gr. bullet of strong construction, such as the Winchester Silvertip or the Remington Core-Lokt, would be best for the .270. A 180-gr. bullet of similar type is best for the .30/06.

2-R AND VARMINTER COMPARED

Question: I would like to know the ballistics of the 2-R Lovell and the .22 Varminter with 46-gr. and 48-gr. bullets. A

2-R LOVELL
50 GR. MUZZLE VELOCITY OF 3,050 FOOT SECONDS

.22 VARMINTER
50 GR. MUZZLE VELOCITY OF 3,600 FOOT SECONDS

This drawings illustrates the differences in velocity between the 2-R Lovell and the .22 Varminter.

friend and I want to compare them with the .220 Swift, with which we are familiar.—W. L. R., N. C.

Answer: The 2-R Lovell is a sort of super-Hornet. It is based on the old .25/20 single-shot case necked down to .22. A standard load gives the 50-gr. bullet a muzzle velocity of about 3,050 foot seconds; the 45-gr., approximately 3,150.

The Varminter is a .250/3000 case necked down to .22. With permissible pressures and good accuracy, it will give 46-gr. and 48-gr. bullets close to 4,000 foot seconds, and even somewhat higher. In other words, ballistically it is very much like the Swift. For the sake of longer barrel life, I have always felt that it was smart to stick to the 50-gr. bullet at about 3,600 foot seconds.

PROBLEM WITH A SPRINGFIELD

Question: I recently bought a Springfield rifle which was supposed to be a .30/06. Then I moved up here into big-bear country. I bought a box of .30 Springfield (Gov't. '06) ammunition and when I tried to load my rifle found the cartridges wouldn't fit.

The rifle is marked "Model 1898 U. S. Springfield Armory." It seems to be in excellent condition, but it's *not* a .30/06!

Please tell me what caliber it is and what bullet weight would be best for grizzlies and black bears, since there are lots of both around here.—C. H. G., British Columbia.

Answer: No wonder you can't use .30/06 cartridges in that rifle of yours. It was made at the Springfield Arsenal, but it is not the 1903 Springfield at all. Instead, it is a .30/40 Krag, and the correct ammunition is the rimmed .30/40 Krag cartridge.

This cartridge, however, is a good one. It uses a 180-gr. bullet at a velocity of 2,500 foot seconds and a 220-gr.-bullet at 2,200. A 150-gr. bullet is also loaded for a velocity of about 2,700, but I think the heavier bullets are the stuff for you, because you live in bear country, and deep penetration might come in handy some day. As you can see, the ballistics of the .30/40 are not too far behind those of the .30/06. It's still a good cartridge.

.25/20 NOT FOR DEER

Question: Have used my .25/20 on everything from woodchuck to deer, and find it a very sweet little rifle. My choice of ammunition is the 60-gr. high-speed. Can you give me some dope on it?—L. B., Pa.

Answer: To be perfectly frank, I think it is criminal to use a .25/20 even on small deer, as that cartridge has neither the bullet weight nor the velocity to make it an effective killer. The smallest cartridge that should be used on deer, and then only with carefully placed shots, is the .25/35. Let us compare the two: The .25/35 uses a 117-gr. bullet at 2,280 ft. a second, and an 87-gr. at 2,650. The .25/20 uses an 86-gr. at 1,450 or a 60-gr. at 2,210. I'll bet you have wounded at least one buck for every one you have killed. The .25/20 should not be regularly used on anything larger than coyote or fox.

STICK TO 170-GR. BULLETS IN .30/30

Question: I have a .30/30 Winchester rifle, Model 94, in which I never have used anything but 170-gr. bullets—soft nose and Silvertips. Would it injure the barrel to use 110 or 150-gr. bullets? Also, would these bullets be suitable for deer and bears?—H. V., Colo.

Answer: I think that you ought to stick to the 170-gr. bullet in your .30/30, since this caliber does its best work with a bullet of that weight. The 110 and 150-gr. bullets would not injure your rifle in the slightest, but you probably would find that they would shoot a lot higher than those of 170 gr. If you didn't adjust your sights to compensate for this difference, you would miss a lot of game. In fact, I think that is one of the most common reasons for missing shots; people change bullet weights without checking and sighting, then they are mystified because they don't shoot accurately.

FASTEST BULLETS

Question: The other day some of us boys were discussing the speed of bullets, wondering whether the .270, .300 H. & H., or .220 Swift was the fastest. Which would you say? Another thing, would the fastest of these bullets be suitable for military use, or is there some other bullet

BULLET SPEEDS COMPARED

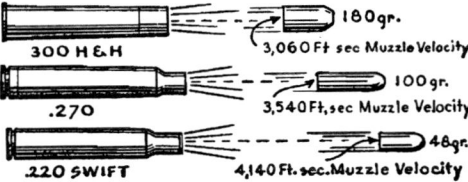

300 H & H 3,060 Ft sec Muzzle Velocity 180 gr.

.270 3,540 Ft, sec Muzzle Velocity 100 gr.

.220 SWIFT 4,140 Ft. sec. Muzzle Velocity 48 gr.

with a muzzle velocity of more than 4,000 foot seconds that has the necessary hitting power and a flat trajectory?—E. S., Wash.

Answer: The fastest commercial cartridge is the .220 Swift which gives a 48-gr. bullet a muzzle velocity of 4,140 foot seconds. The .270, with a 100-gr. bullet, has a muzzle velocity of 3,540 foot seconds. Various wildcat cartridges have been worked out that will drive bullets out of the muzzle as fast as 4,500 and maybe 5,000 foot seconds.

I understand that before the war, government arsenals got muzzle velocities in excess of 8,000 foot seconds, experimentally. The Russians and Germans had antitank rifles with muzzle velocities in that neighborhood now, but they use a taper bore which is smooth, and a vaned bullet which is compressed by the taper.

.270 FOR GRIZZLIES?

Question: Is the .270 cartridge satisfactory for shooting grizzly bears? If so, what weight bullet should be used, and over what distance should it be targeted for hunting in timber?—C. L., Calif.

Answer: I used a .30/06 caliber rifle on the only grizzly I ever shot. However I did see a friend kill one with a .270, and he knocked it very dead indeed. Another friend in British Columbia has bagged about 20 grizzlies with his .270, most of them with one shot.

To my mind, the most satisfactory load for grizzlies at close quarters would be the 160-gr. Barnes bullet with 52 gr. of No. 4350 powder. I sighted both my rifles to hit the point of aim at 300 yd. with the 130-gr. factory load. With the 160-gr. load that puts the bullet exactly at the point of aim at 200 yd. and 2 in. above the line of the scope sight at 100 yd. That makes it very handy, for the rifle, in effect, is sighted in for the correct distance with both loads.

An experienced hunter recently wrote me that he knows a man who has killed more than 100 grizzly bears and brown bears, using the .270 cartridge with a 130-gr. bullet. There's no doubt, then, that the .270 is adequate for big bears.

QUESTIONABLE AMMUNITION

Question: A friend of mine has offered to give me a whole case of .30/06 cartridges, made in 1918. They seem to be in good condition, but I don't want to ruin my Model 70 Winchester by using them if they are dangerous. What do you think?

I also have several hundred rounds of 1943–44 issue .30/06's and some tracers and armor-piercing cartridges. Would it be safe to use this stuff?—H. M. O., Wis.

Answer: If I were you I'd lay off that old 1918 ammunition. It is pretty dangerous stuff. A lot of that powder is decomposed. I have seen old ammunition like that that had a solid plug in the neck behind the bullet. The brass cases have grown brittle with age, too. If your rifle should have a little excess headspace—or even normal headspace on the long side—a cartridge might part and raise Ned with your rifle and your eyes. That ammunition also has corrosive primers which will cause the bore to rust unless you clean it with hot water.

Lay off tracers and armor piercers, too. I understand the armor piercers have very tough jackets which cause a lot of barrel wear. The tracers deposit a very corrosive residue in the bore. On the other hand, with recent stuff like that you could pull the bullets, dump the powder, and reload with regular M-2 bullets. However, M-2's are not safe to use in farm country. Because of their heavy jackets, they richochet badly.

.22 CALIBER HISTORY

Question: What's the dope on high-power .22's. Was the Hornet evolved out of thin air, or is it an older cartridge case necked down? What is the K-Hornet?

What is the .22 Lovell and the 2-R Lovell? What cases were necked down to make them? And how about the .22 Varminter? Can the same bullets be used in reloading all these cases?—T. F. P., Ga.

Answer: The .22 Hornet cartridge is a modernization of the old .22 Winchester center-fire cartridge. The Germans did the same thing with the same cartridge long before we did. The K-Hornet is formed by firing a regular Hornet cartridge in a K chamber. The brass cartridge case expands to give a sharper neck and a greater powder capacity.

The .22/3000 Lovell is the old .25/20 single-shot case necked down to .22. The 2-R is the same case expanded by firing in a 2-R chamber to give a little greater powder capacity and a slightly sharper shoulder. The .22 Varminter is the .250/3000 case necked down to .22.

The groove diameter of the .22 Hornet and the Lovell is .222 in. That of the Swift and the Varminter is .224 in. The bullets can be used interchangeably un-der proper circumstances, but it isn't too good an idea. Swift bullets in a 2-R, for instance, give fairly high pressure.

BEST BULLET FOR .300 SAVAGE

Question: I own a .300 Savage and am very much disappointed with it for long-distance shooting. In the past, I used the 180-gr. bullet. Would 150 gr. be better? What would be the best distance to sight the rifle in at?—H. McC., Pa.

Answer: The 180-gr. bullet in the .300 Savage doesn't have a high enough velocity to be entirely satisfactory for shooting at the longer ranges. A much better bullet is the 150 gr. at a muzzle velocity of nearly 2,700 foot seconds. Using that bullet, sight in so that it strikes 3 in. above the point of aim at 100 yd. That will put you right on the nose at 200 yd. and about 5 in. low at 250. At 300 yd., it will be about 12 in. low.

.30/06 AMMUNITION O.K. IN .30/03

Question: Recently I have missed several shots with my .30/03 Winchester Model 95 which I feel I ought not to have missed. Could it be because I am using .30/06 ammunition? I can't get .30/03 anymore. Furthermore, when I shoot those .30/06's some of them stick in the barrel. What would you advise in regard to a 'scope for this rifle.—F. M. G., Colo.

Answer: It is perfectly safe to use .30/06 cartridges in a .30/03 chamber. But you cannot use .30/03 cartridges in a .30/06 chamber, because the .30/03 cartridge has a slightly longer neck than the .30/06 cartridge.

I believe those cases stick because that rifle of yours is very old. It doesn't have nearly as much extracting power as a bolt action. Also, its chamber is probably rough and pitted.

I wouldn't advise you to put a 'scope on it—it would have to be mounted so high or offset as to be almost worthless.

Frankly, I think you are making a mistake in using full-power ammunition in that rifle. You ought to have some ammunition loaded for it which will give a 150-gr. bullet a muzzle velocity of about 2,600 foot seconds. That would be well within safety limits. As it stands now I think that you are taking a chance.

BULLET FOR MULE DEER

Question: I have been reloading 93-gr. Luger bullets with 50 gr. of Du Pont powder No. 3031. What do you think of this load for Western mule deer?

What is the relative accuracy of the .22 Winchester target rifles Model 52 and Model 75?

And what is the relative accuracy of the .30/06 Winchester Model 54 and the .270 Model 54?—C. H. R. Jr., Nev.

Answer: I would guess that your 50 gr. of No. 3031 drives that 93-gr. Luger bullet with a muzzle velocity of about 3,100 foot seconds—that is, if you are using non-corrosive, non-mercuric primers. I think that load would go to pieces too quickly to be worth a darn on Western mule deer. Broadside shots in the lungs will kill them, but under any other conditions the bullet will not penetrate enough. Try to use the 150-gr. bullets.

Winchester Model 52 is more carefully made and has a much heavier barrel than Model 75, and will give a little better accuracy on the average.

All things being equal, the .270 seems to deliver a little better accuracy than the .30/06 with factory ammunition— and that would hold true with the Model 54. However, the difference is not great. With the best hand loads, a good .30/06 will shoot right along with the .270.

POWDERS FOR HANDLOADING .30/06

Question: I do quite a bit of handloading, and have accumulated a quantity of 172-gr. .30/06 Army bullets, which I am about to alter for use on deer. What load of Hercules Hi-Vel No. 2 should I put behind them?—N. V. G., Wash.

Answer: You've chosen an excellent powder for the .30/06. With the 172-gr. bullet 25 gr. of this powder will give you a muzzle velocity of 1,610 foot seconds; 36.5 gr. will give 2,200; and 49 gr. will give 2,830. Pressures for that last load are rather high—51,000 lb. I'd suggest using 48 gr., which would give a powerful load with pressures around 48,000 lb.

Hi-Vel No. 2 and DuPont No. 4320 are about the best powders for the .30/06.

CARTRIDGE POWDERS

Question: I want to reload some 348 and .30/30 cases so as to duplicate standard factory loads. What and how much powder should I use?—J. N., Pa.

Answer: Cartridges loaded by ammunition companies do not contain standardized lots of powder. Each new lot of powder is tested to discover what charge will give the desired velocity. Consequently, it wouldn't do you any good to know what a company's powder charge is, for it's subject to change without notice.

On the other hand, powder sold to handloaders *is* standardized, and under the same conditions it will give the same velocity. I happen to know that Winchester uses No. 4064 for the .348. With the 200-gr. bullet a charge of 53.5 gr. of powder will give you a muzzle velocity of 2,535 foot seconds. If that sounds a little hot to you, try a charge of 48.5 gr., which will give you 2,315. With the 150-gr. bullet, 58.5 gr. will give a velocity of 2,835.

No. 3031, an entirely different powder, is best for use with the .30/30. A charge of 33.5 gr. will give the 170-gr. bullet a muzzle velocity of 2,300 foot seconds; a charge of 28 gr. will give it 1,945.

The only way to tell exactly what velocity a certain charge will give is to load it up and fire it with a chronograph.

RELOADING THE .30/30

Question: Please advise me as to the correct amount of Hi-Vel No. 2 powder to put behind a 170-gr. metal-cased boattail bullet in reloading for my Savage Model 99.—D. D., Calif.

Answer: The maximum load for that bullet is 30 gr. of Hi-Vel No. 2; seating depth is .489. This gives a muzzle velocity of 2,175 foot seconds and a pressure of 40,000 ft. lb. If I were you, though, I would cut that load to 29 gr., just to be on the safe side.

HANDLOADING VARMINTERS

Question: What loads would you recommend for use in my .22 Varminter rifle? I've had it made up on an Enfield action with a heavy Winchester sniper barrel, 26 in. long with 14-in. twist. At present all I have on hand are some 50-gr. Sisk-Lovell bullets, some 56-gr. high-power Winchester Swift bullets, and some 56-gr. high-power, Hi-Speed Remingtons (mushroom expanding).—V. B. O'G., N. Y.

Answer: Your best bet for that Varminter, I think, is a load of 39 gr. of No. 4350 powder with either of the 56-gr. bullets. With the 50-gr. bullets I suggest trying 38 gr. of No. 4320.

I have never owned a Varminter, but I fooled around a lot with that caliber and it seems to be made to order for No. 4350. As you no doubt know, it's a very progressive-burning powder, and the gentle acceleration seems to deliver the bullets with a minimum of deformation. I have seen some of the damndest groups shot with a 55-gr. 8-S bullet and 39 or 39.5 gr. of No. 4350! The Varminter, I think, is undoubtedly the most accurate cartridge in existence at the present time, and groups of from 5/8 in. to 3/4 in. at 100 yd. are not at all uncommon. Such groups are few and far between.

OVERCOMING MUZZLE BLAST

Question: The recoil and muzzle blast of my .270 Winchester, Model 70, are not terribly unpleasant, but I'd like them toned down just a little. I've been toying with the idea of loading the 100-gr. bullet down to a muzzle energy of 3,000 foot pounds. Am I right in thinking that load would still be extremely accurate and fast enough for varmint shooting (so it breaks up on impact), yet have considerably less recoil? What kind of powder, and how much, should I use?

Also, do you believe a well-bedded barrel shoots more accurately than a floating barrel, especially in the sporting-rifle class?—J. W. C., Calif.

Answer: I see no reason why you cannot load the 100-gr. bullet down to about 3,000 foot seconds of muzzle energy. You would get less recoil and, if your load is well balanced for your chamber, you ought to get excellent accuracy. I believe 48 gr. of No. 4320 with the 100-gr. bullet would be just about right. If that particular load isn't accurate enough try it with a little less or a little more powder until you hit it on the nose.

There's no doubt in my mind that a well-bedded barrel of whatever weight will outshoot a free-floating barrel.

LOAD FOR .35 WHELEN

Question: What can you tell me about the .35 Whelen cartridge? I have a beautiful Griffin & Howe rifle chambered for that cartridge, but I don't know much about its ballistics.—J. H. E., Pa.

Answer: I used to have a .35 Whelen and did a great deal of reloading for it. My maximum loads might be too hot for your particular rifle, so start below and work up. I used 56 gr. of No. 4064 powder with the 275-gr. Barnes or Western Tool & Copper Co. bullet. From the trajectory I figured the muzzle velocity was at least 2,400 foot seconds, maybe more.

Actually, I always felt that 54 gr. was plenty with that bullet.

With the 250-gr. .35 Winchester bullet I used anywhere between 54 and 56 gr. of No. 4064. I used to load 60 gr. of No. 4064 with the 220-gr. W. T. & C. spitzer bullet. You could use 60 gr., of course, with the 200-gr. .35 Winchester bullet and you could use 56 gr. with the Western .35 Newton bullet. My rifle had a fairly heavy barrel and the accuracy of almost any of those loads was surprising. The rifle would shoot as well as the average 9-lb. .30/06. That .35 Whelen is really a power house to use and ought to kill just about as well as the .375 Magnum. From what I have seen, a good .35 Whelen is usually a good deal more accurate than the .300 Magnum with a sporting-weight barrel.

The maximum load with the 220-gr. bullet will give a muzzle velocity of about 2,850 foot seconds. The maximum load with the 250-gr. bullet is supposed to give a maximum muzzle velocity of about 2,750 foot seconds.

NECKED-DOWN .30/06'S IN .270

Question: Will using necked-down .30/06 cases in my .270 Model 70 Winchester for full loads cause more throat erosion due to the slightly shorter neck? I always fire these cases first with a light load before the heavier loads.—B. M., Calif.

Answer: Actually I do not think it hurts the rifle a bit to use .30/06 cases necked down to .270. My own .270 Mauser barrel began to show throat erosion after about 1,000 rounds and to lose accuracy in about 1,500. For a time I thought it was because I had been using necked-down .30/06 cases. I went into the matter with technicians and they felt it did no harm at all, but that using cases with necks that are too long did a lot of harm. As a matter of fact, a .270 case made from a .30/06 is usually stretched enough to be standard .270 length when it has been fired about three times with full-power loads. The history of several .270 barrels with which I am acquainted has been about the same, no matter what has been shot in them. They all begin to show throat erosion after about 1,000 rounds.

CUPRO-NICKEL BULLETS

Question: Recently I bought some bullets by mail, 150-gr. .30/06, and when they arrived I found they were cupro-nickel. Can I use them for reloading in my Enfield rifle? What must I do to keep the barrel clean? I intended to use them on rabbits and chucks. Would you advise using them at all?—H. E. T., Idaho.

Answer: The best thing you can do to keep the barrel of your .30/06 clean when using those 150-gr. cupro-nickel-jacketed bullets is to limit the velocity to around 2,000 ft. a second. If you try to drive those bullets any faster you will have a lot of metal fouling, and you will have to use ammonia dope like Winchester crystal cleaner to remove it. That is an awful lot of trouble. So I'd suggest that you use a load of 32 gr. of Hi-Vel No. 2, which will give you a velocity of 2,000 ft. a second, and you will find it a good killer on both chuck and rabbits.

LOADING .30/40 AND .300

Question: I have a .30/40 Krag and a .300 Savage Model 99. I plan to start reloading my own shells, and have Winchester 120 primers and Du Pont No. 4064 powder. I plan to reload the following bullets: 180-gr. open-point Krag; 165-gr. open-point .30 Remington; 172-gr. government bullets.

Could you advise me how much of this powder I should put behind each bullet of the two different calibers? Also, would full-length, resized cases be less accurate than neck-sized ones? What is the advantage of full-length resizing?—A. M., Pa.

Answer: The maximum loads of No. 4064 powder for the .300 Savage and the .30/40 Krag with the various weights of bullets are as follows: With the 172-gr. government bullet in the .30/40, 42 gr. of the powder will give you 2,565. The same charge would give the 165-gr. bullet about 2,600. With the 180-gr. bullet, your maximum load in the Krag is about 40 gr. for a velocity of 2,425. In the .300 Savage, 40 gr. of the powder will give the 180-gr. bullet a velocity of 2,285. That is the only No. 4064 load I find for the .300. As a matter of fact, No. 4064 is not a good powder for the .300 Savage because of the small case capacity. A much better powder for this purpose is No. 3031. Forty grains of 3031 would give the 180-gr. bullet 2,450.

You can reload your Krag bullets by neck sizing, only because you are using a bolt-action locked at the head. For the Model 99 Savage, however, you will have to full-length resize your .300 cases every time you reload, as they will stretch a bit when fired and will not go back into chamber. This is the only advantage of full-length resizing. It reduces the diameter of the case when stretched. Otherwise it's best to neck-size only.

HANDLOADS FOR A .250/3000

Question: Please give me some information on handloads for my .250/3000. I have thought of the 117-gr. .25/35 bullet and the 125-gr. Barnes bullet for handloading a .257. Would these be practical for the .250/3000? Would they be suitable for deer and bear? What powder charge should be used, and what would be the velocity? A former guide says he uses his .250/3000 for both deer and elk, and states that the only bullet he ever uses is the 87-gr. softnose. In your opinion is this right for elk?—W. E. C., Ga.
Answer: I do not think you would have much success with any of the heavy bul-

lets in the .250/3000 for the simple reason that they would not be accurate. The .250/3000 has a 14-in. twist, whereas those heavy bullets need a 9 or 10-in. twist to spin them out at the longer ranges. I think that the best bet for the .250/3000 is the 100-gr. bullet with 38.5 gr. of No. 4350 for a velocity of 2,900. A man who is a good shot and gets close to his game can kill almost anything with almost any rifle. In the hands of an ordinary hunter the .250/3000 wouldn't be an elk gun since the bullet is too light. A .30/06 is a better elk gun.

FULL POWER LOADS FOR .270

Question: I wonder if you can give me some dope on full-power loads for the .270 Winchester cartridge?—C. K., Calif.
Answer: Good full-power loads are the Barnes 120-gr. bullet with 52 gr. of Du Pont powder No. 4064 or 49 gr. of 4064 with 130-gr. factory bullets. In my .270 their accuracy is good, but being full-powered they should be approached cautiously, starting 4 or 5 gr. below maximum charge. An accurate vermin load is 49 gr. No. 4320 with the 100-gr. factory jacketed bullet; I don't know the velocity, 3,100 to 3,300. With 52 gr. No. 4064 and the 120-gr. bullet, velocity is 3,200; with 49 gr. 4064 and 130-gr. slug, velocity is 3,100.

BULLETS NOT INTERCHANGEABLE

Question: I pulled the bullets from some caliber .30 M-2 government cartridges and replaced them with 110-gr. hollow-point bullets extracted from .30 Winchesters, intending to use them in shooting woodchucks and crows, but the results were terrible. I tried them in my Enfield sporter equipped with a Weaver 440 'scope and from a bench rest the best I could do was 6 or 7-in. groups at 100 yd. I know it is not the fault of the rifle or my holding, since with regular cartridges I can get 1-in. groups at 100 yd.

I would like to know a formula for a good bullet lubricant—one I can make up myself for use with .30/06 gas-check cartridges.—M. J. D., Pa.

Answer: I don't wonder that you don't get good accuracy by simply pulling the M-2 bullets and substituting the 110-gr. hollow-points. The powder used in the M-2 cartridge is designed particularly for the M-2 and I doubt seriously if it is flexible enough to give good accuracy with a lighter bullet. Bullets simply can't be substituted for one another in a haphazard way. A light bullet needs a quick-burning powder, a heavy bullet needs a slow-burning powder.

A good mixture for a bullet lubricant is ¼ lb. Japan wax and 2 tsp. of graphite. Another is equal parts of beeswax and carbuna wax plus enough castor oil to give it flexibility.

RECOMMENDED POWDER CHARGES

Question: Please recommend charges of Du Pont No. 4350 for the following bullets, all of which will be used in modern high-grade rifles: The 220-gr. soft point in .30/06, the 175-gr. in 7 mm., and the 117-gr. in .257 caliber.

The .257 has a 22-in. barrel, the others 24 in. As No. 4350 is a progressive powder, I thought perhaps it might not perform so well in the 22-in. barrel, giving a bad muzzle blast.—W. H. C., Mont.

Answer: My .30/06 has a rather tight chamber, and I find that 52 gr. of No. 4350 is all I can use with the 220-gr. bullet without getting pressures which appear pretty high. But a friend of mine uses 55 gr. for a rifle with a rather large chamber. Start at 52 gr. and work up, quitting when the pressures seem high.

For the 7 mm. I think you will find 47½ gr. of powder about right for the 175-gr. bullet. I have never used that particular load, but I've recommended it to

many 7 mm. users and they report very good results. Muzzle velocity, for a guess, would be at least 2,600 foot seconds.

In the .257 with the 117-gr. bullet you can use at least 45 gr. of No. 4350, for a muzzle velocity of about 2,950. I don't think you'll notice any difference in the muzzle blast, for in the .257 the powder seems to be all consumed in 22 in.

RELOADING EQUIPMENT

Question: I have been thinking of reloading for my .270. What equipment is necessary and what does it cost? Where can I get powder and bullets? What do empty primed cases cost? Are there any inexpensive books which would give me good dope?—R. C., Wyo.

Answer: The .270 is an interesting cartridge to reload, and I do it myself. However, for full-power loads it is comparatively expensive, and a man would have to reload a good many cases in order to effect any economy. However, if you are a vermin shot it would probably be worth it. Here is the equipment you'd need:

1. A reloading tool that will decap, recap, neck-size, and seat bullets. It will cost you from about $7 for a Lyman tong-type tool to $22.50 for a Pacific-straight-line tool. 2. A powder measure (Ideal or Belding & Mull) which will cost about $8. 3. An accurate scale to check the charges thrown by the measure. Cost: somewhere around $10.

Then, of course, you'll need primers, powder, and bullets, with which you can duplicate factory loads in fired cases.

Send 50 cents to the Lyman Gun Sight Co., Middlefield, Conn., for the Ideal handbook, and the same amount to Belding & Mull, Philipsburg, Pa., for the B & M handbook. Send, too, for the catalogue of the Pacific Gun Sight Co., 355 Hayes St., San Francisco, Calif. All three companies furnish powder, bullets, etc.

CAUSES OF GUN RECOIL

Question: For a long time a bunch of my friends and I have been having an argument about what causes a gun's recoil. Since we haven't been able to settle it one way or another, will you please explain it for us? Is there some relationship between the size or weight of the bullet and the kick?—W. L. K., Idaho.

Answer: Recoil is caused primarily by overcoming the inertia of the bullet or the shot charge. The heavier the missile and the more rapidly its inertia is overcome, the more violent the reaction or "kick" will be. A 300-gr. bullet with a muzzle velocity of 3,000 foot seconds would, of course, cause a gun to kick much harder than a 100 gr. bullet at the same velocity.

Secondary recoil is caused by the impact of the powder gases on the air. The larger the diameter of the muzzle, the greater the volume of gas, and the greater the recoil.

RELOADING FULL LOADS

Question: Have been reloading cartridges, reduced charges only, for my Model 70 .30/06, and like the results very much. Would it be safe to reload a full-powder charge for deer, using the 150-gr. open-point bullet and about 47 to 55 gr. of Du Pont No. 4320? Can I use fired factory cases or must I buy new ones? Would the 180-gr. bullet be better with 45–50 gr. of No. 4320?—E. J., Wis.

Answer: There is no reason why you shouldn't reload full-powder cartridges if you have the components and are careful. If you trim the necks of your cases now and then you can use them almost indefinitely with full-powder loads. I have some .270 cases which have been fired 30 times and are still going strong. I think you will find between 50 and 53 gr. of No. 4320 a very fine load in your .30/06 when used with a 150-gr. bullet.

The load which I have settled on for my own .30/06 is 53 gr. of No. 4064, but you can use the same charge of No. 4320 safely unless your rifle has an extremely tight chamber. Fifty grains of No. 4320 will give you 2,800 ft. a second, and 53 gr. about 3,000. For the 180-gr. bullet, 45 gr. will produce a velocity of 2,415, and 50½ gr. 2,790. I wouldn't load more than 49 gr. of No. 4320 with the 180-gr. bullet until I found out how things are.

LIGHT LOAD FOR A .257

Question: I have a .257 on a Model 98 Mauser action. I bought it for use on deer last fall, but would like to use it more than just one week in the year. Can .257 cartridges be handloaded so that they will be light enough for shooting squirrels? If so, please give me the dope on doing it.—G. B. C., Ohio.

Answer: I suggest that you get some cartridges handloaded using a lead, gas-check, lubricated bullet at about 1,600 or 1,700 foot seconds. I think that would be a good all-round practical load with plenty of soup for squirrels—and for midrange target practice too.

If you do your own handloading, 16 gr. of No. 2400 powder would give a 100-gr. bullet a velocity of 1,975 foot seconds, and 10 gr. of Unique would give it 1,470. The latter sounds a little more like what you want.

A full-metal-case .25/20 bullet weighing 86 gr. with 10 gr. of Unique, for a velocity of about 1,600, should also do quite nicely.

EXCESS HEADSPACE

Question: I have reloaded a lot of cartridges for my Model 94 Winchester .30/30 carbine with very good success. Recently a friend of mine who has an older Model 94 in the same caliber brought me a handful of cases to reload for him. On inspecting them, I found that all the primers projected several thousandths of an inch beyond the face of the head. Nothing I have at hand deals with this condition. Can you tell me what might cause it? Is this rifle safe?

I always load my .30/30 cases with the Hensley & Gibbs No. 33 gas-check bullet, hollow-point, and 16 gr. of No. 4759 powder. This seems to be about right for jack rabbits and skunks, which abound around here. I have never recovered more than a small fragment of the base of a bullet.—J. C. McC., Calif.

Answer: The trouble with your pal's old .30/30 is that the breechblock has set back, and the rifle has excess headspace. The pressures are driving the primers back until they meet the face of the breechblock. I am afraid the rifle is about worn out and should be replaced. Your friend will run into trouble when he gets an extra-brittle or extra-soft case.

LIGHT RELOADS CAUSE TROUBLE

Question: A friend of mine recently purchased a Model 70 Winchester in 7 mm. and, in order to get him started, I gave him a few light handloads—6.5 gr. of No. 80 behind an 84-gr. lead bullet. The cases had been fired in my own Winchester Model 54 and then neck-resized and reloaded a few times with these light charges. The cases fitted perfectly in his rifle and seemed interchangeable with mine.

After firing a few of them in his rifle, however, he noticed that the primers were being set back. I examined them and thought they might have been caused by an error in chamber size. Later, however, I found that the same thing was happening in my rifle.

The cases were originally factory loads, were fired first in my own rifle, then reloaded after only neck-resizing. I can see no possibility of the shoulders' being changed in reloading, the primer pockets do not seem to be enlarged, and new primers fit snugly with no evidence of gas leaks.

Of course, there can be no excess pressure with these light loads. Yet the primers protrude $\frac{1}{32}$ in. or more. With full loads, no protrusion is noticed. Can you tell me what's wrong?—H. T. C., Ontario.

Answer: In using those light loads, the powerful primers drive the cases into the chamber and shorten them, thus creating a condition of excess headspace. Such cases can never again be safely used with full-power loads. If you had a cartridge gauge, you would discover that your cases were several thousandths of an inch short in the body and that the neck had been lengthened. That is a little detail which most people forget about light loads.

HANDLOADING FOR SWIFT

Question: Want to do my own handloading for my .220 Swift. What would be a good load with the 55-gr. bullet, say the 8-S—one load up to 200 yd. and another good for 350 or 400 yd. for 'chucks? Do you consider the Varminter a better rifle than the Swift?—L. W. D., Pa.

Answer: The dope I get is that the Varminter is a little more accurate than the Swift, and that Varminter barrels last considerably longer. However, the Swift is an exceedingly accurate cartridge. The maximum load with the 55-gr. 8-S bullet is 42 gr. of No. 4350 for a velocity of 3,600 ft. a second. With the same bullet and No. 4064, the maximum load of 37 gr. gives 3,500 with the Sisk bullet. With the 55-gr. 8-S bullet, 38.5 gr. of No. 4320 give 3,750. These loads were worked out by J. B. Smith, the custom handloader and the man who was instrumental in developing the 8-S bullet. I think I'd use close to maximum loads. I understand that when the Swift is underloaded its accuracy falls off rather badly.

PRIMERS FOR HANDLOADS

Question: I'm planning to make up some light loads for my Springfield .30/06, using smokeless or semismokeless powder and lead bullets. Now, it happens that I have 500 old copper-cup pistol primers on hand which are the same size as 8½ Remington primers. Is it possible to use them in reloading?—P. D., Pa.

Answer: I see no reason why you cannot use those pistol primers for reduced loads in your .30/06. Remember, though, that they are made to stand pressures of only about 15,000 lb., whereas the 8½ Remington primers will stand more than 50,-000 lb. Consequently, you're going to have to use very mild loads in your .30/06—certainly nothing more than 20,-000 lb. at most. That would limit you to some such load as the 169-gr. gas-check bullet with 19 gr. of No. 2400 powder; pressure, about 20,000 lb.

I have shot some .30/06 loads made up with noncorrosive large pistol primers, which are stronger than yours; but even mine weren't loaded up too hot.

DON'T USE CORROSIVE PRIMERS

Question: Please tell me if it's safe to use Frankford Arsenal No. 70 primers when reloading for my Varminter rifle, which I shoot quite a lot.—T. E., Md.

Answer: I would consider it very inadvisable to use Frankford Arsenal No. 70 primers in a .22/250 or Varminter. Even though you cleaned the barrel with boiling water after every use, I believe you would still get rust because of the high concentration of priming salt in the small .22 bore. Better stick to noncorrosive, nonmercuric primers.

HANDGUN PRIMERS FOR RIFLES

Question: I am running short of large rifle primers in the commercial makes such as Remington and Western, but have a lot of Remington primers intended for large handguns. Could they be used in the .300 Savage, .30/30, and similar cartridges?—P. D. F., Wash.

Answer: You can use large handgun primers in a rifle which takes the large-size primer if you keep the pressures low. I believe they will stand pressures to about 25,000 lb., maybe more—but for safety's sake it is wise to keep your pressures below that figure.

As you know, the large handgun and the large rifle primers are the same size, but the handgun primers are made with softer and thinner brass.

In other words, you could use those primers for light mid-range loads, but nothing approaching full power.

THE DOPE ON RECOIL

Question: In an automatic rifle, what causes recoil? Is it the force of the gas pushing the bullet out of the barrel, or does the recoil come after the bullet has left the barrel?—W. K. P., Wis.

Answer: Recoil is principally due to the overcoming of the inertia of the bullet. The heavier the bullet and the faster it is driven, the greater the recoil. Recoil also comes from the impact of the muzzle gas on the air. If a gas is still burning and hits the air violently it will push back. It will push back more with a large-caliber rifle than a small-caliber rifle because of the greater area; but, other things being equal, it will *feel* worse in a light rifle than in a heavy one, because the heavier the rifle, the more inertia there is to overcome and the slower the rifle will move backward. A crooked stock will accentuate recoil, whereas a straight stock will cut it down.

Incidentally, it has been proved that what we think of as recoil is largely psychological and comes from fear of the noise. A man with his ears plugged so he cannot hear the report will swear that his rifle kicks less.

SPECIAL PROBLEMS OF THE RIFLE OWNER

"GAIN" TWIST

Question: Why doesn't the rifling in a rifle barrel start in a slow turn and increase toward the muzzle? Seems to me that the bullet would start its revolution more in proportion to its forward motion and therefore decrease breech pressure and wear, and possibly increase velocity.—O. D. T., W. Va.

Answer: The so-called "gain" twist has been used many times and some experimental barrels are still made with a twist which is sharper at the muzzle than near the breech. It is yet to be proved, however, that this twist has any great advantages, and since it is difficult to manufacture it has never been popular.

.348 FOR LEFT-HANDED SHOOTER

Question: I would like some information on the .348 Winchester Model 71. I shoot left-handed so the lever action would be more suitable for me. How about the recoil?—G. V., Conn.

Answer: I think you are very smart in being interested in the .348 Winchester Model 71. It is a beautifully stocked rifle with a safety that is perfectly O.K. for a southpaw because the safety is the hammer at half cock. Get the model which is equipped with a peep sight.

The recoil of the .348, because of the excellent stock, seems to me to be a good deal less than that of the average .30/06 and a lot less than a 12 gauge shotgun. The .348 is a powerful cartridge and a deer hit with it stays hit. I have seen quite a few deer killed with it.

LITTLE RECOIL IN .220 SWIFT

Question: I had to give up my 12 gauge shotgun because for physical reasons I couldn't stand its recoil. My .410 has a recoil pad, and with that I don't even realize that I have shot the gun. My question, though, is this: I want to go deer hunting in New York State and would like a rifle that's comparable to the .410 insofar as recoil goes. A friend recommends the .220 Swift, and says it has practically no recoil, but since he doesn't notice recoil in his 12 gauge shotgun I'm wondering if he's right.—G. R. D., N. J.

Answer: I think your friend's advice is good. The recoil of the Swift is almost nonexistent, although the rifle has a rather sharp but not heavy report. In addition, the Swift is a good killer if you don't strain it and try to shoot game at too great a distance. The Swift kills almost entirely by shock, and that shock disappears at long range.

I'd use the Swift with a 55-gr. bullet. There is only one rub on using the Swift on deer in New York State, and that is the fact that its high-velocity bullets are greatly deflected by brush and twigs and even leaves. Therefore, it might be wise for you to consider some other caliber which takes a heavier bullet and has but slightly more recoil. Two cartridges you might consider are the .250/3000 and the .257. Neither kicks very much more than the Swift and I don't believe they kick much more than the .410 shotgun. Since these calibers use considerably heavier bullets, they are less deflected by brush, and will probably prove somewhat more satisfactory under practical hunting conditions. It would be ideal if you could try out all three and see which you took a fancy to.

CORRECTING EXCESSIVE HEADSPACE

Question: Every time I fire my .22 single-shot rifle, a big bump forms on the head of the case. Could you tell me what causes this and whether the rifle is dangerous?—E. M. S., Calif.

Answer: Your rifle has excessive headspace, which is always dangerous. If there is a competent gunsmith in your town take it to him to have the trouble corrected.

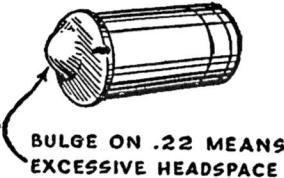

BULGE ON .22 MEANS EXCESSIVE HEADSPACE

If a bulge or bump appears on the head of a cartridge after firing take your rifle to a gunsmith at once.

You might blow out one of those cartridge cases and injure your eyesight with brass fragments or escaping gas.

.348 VS. .32 SPECIAL

Question: How does the Winchester Model 71 rifle, caliber .348 lever action, stack up against the Winchester lever-action carbine, .32 Special? Can a 'scope be mounted on the .348?—A. N., Mass.

Answer: The .348 is far superior in every way, and is a better-stocked rifle with a smoother action. The cartridge itself is much more powerful and slightly more accurate. The .32 Special pushes a 165-gr. bullet at a velocity of 2,260 ft. a second. The .348's 200-gr. bullet goes out at 2,-550. You can see the difference.

A 'scope sight can be mounted on the Model 71, but only Stith—so far as I know—has succeeded in doing it. He offsets his mount to the left and uses a device to deflect the cartridge as it ejects. The reason the Model 71 is hard to mount with a 'scope is that it is a top ejector, like the Model 94.

HORNET AND K-HORNET COMPARED

Question: Just what is a K-Hornet? I know it is a more powerful version of the regular Hornet, but how is it made? I recall reading an article in which the author said that regular Hornet cartridges

were just as accurate when fired in his K-Hornet as were the K cartridges. Is that possible? Can regular Hornets be fired in a K?—D. O., Utah.

Answer: The K-Hornet is simply a regular Hornet which has had the chamber changed in shape to give a more abrupt shoulder and greater powder capacity. Cases are formed by shooting regular Hornet cartridges in the K chamber. That is correct. Regular Hornets will give good accuracy in a K chamber, but a K cartridge could not, of course, be fired in an unaltered Hornet chamber. With the K case the handloader can get considerably higher velocities than with the regular Hornet cartridges.

HOW TO TELL A .30 REMINGTON

Question: Recently I traded my .30/40 Krag for a rifle which looks as if it might be a .30 Remington Special, but I can't tell if it is a Special or not as it has only a 22-in. barrel. I would like to know how long a .30 Remington Special barrel is, and how I can tell a Special from an ordinary .30 Remington.—H. T., Mich.

Answer: You evidently have the Model 30 Remington bolt-action rifle made at one time for the .30 Remington rimless cartridge, which is very similar to the .30/30 except that it has no rim. The Model 30 was also chambered for the .30/06. Rifles of both calibers have been made with 22-in. barrels.

If yours is marked .30 Rem., it is a .30 Remington rimless. If it is marked .30/06, it is .30/06 caliber. The chamber for a .30 Rem. cartridge is much smaller than that for a .30/06, so if you can put a .30/06 cartridge into your rifle chamber you can bet your hat that you do not have a .30 Rem.

There is no cartridge known as the .30 Remington Special. The Remington line of rimless cartridges, originally designed for their pump and autoloading rifles, consisted of the .25 Rem., the .30 Rem., and the .35 Rem. They correspond roughly to Winchester's .25/35, .30/30, and .32 Special.

.30/40 KRAG

Question: Will you please give me some information on a rifle I've just acquired, which is marked "U. S. Springfield Armory, Mod. 1896." Is it safe to use the regular .30/40 220-grain cartridge in it? Would that load be any good for black bear? H. A. Y., N. Y.

Answer: That's the good old Krag, which was used by the U. S. Army from about 1893 until the adoption of the Springfield Model 1903 (.30/06). If the rifle is in good condition it is perfectly safe to use any commercial .30/40 cartridge.

The old 220-grain soft-point load is an excellent one for deer, bear, and even moose and elk. The bullet's sectional density makes it an effective killer, and it is a much more powerful cartridge than the .30/30.

DISCUSSION OF THE .303 SAVAGE

Question: Please give me your opinion of the .303 Savage rifle.—H. L. P., Pa.

Answer: The .303 Savage rifle is a good one, and the .303 cartridge is comparable to the .30/30. It uses a 190-gr. bullet at a muzzle velocity of about 1,900 foot seconds, whereas the .30/30 uses a 170-gr. at 2,200 foot seconds.

Because of the great sectional density of the bullet and the lower velocity, the .303 Savage will usually give deeper penetration than the .30/30 on large game such as elk and bear. On deer, however, I think the difference would be small.

DOPE ON THE .405 WINCHESTER

Question: I would like some information on the .405 Winchester. Does the Winchester Company still make a rifle in this caliber? What are the ballistics of the car-

tridge and what is your opinion of it?—L. E. C., Mo.

Answer: If I remember correctly, the Winchester Model 95 chambered for the .405 W.C.F. cartridge was discontinued about 1936, when the Model 70 was introduced. The .405 was reasonably popular with the lads who hunted the largest game and who believed in large bullet diameter and great weight. Theodore Roosevelt used the .405 in Africa and found it a very good killer. His two sons also used it on their trip to Asia.

However, the introduction of the Winchester Model 70 in .375 Magnum caliber made the .405 pretty much obsolete. The .405 uses a 300-gr. bullet at a muzzle velocity of 2,220 foot seconds and a muzzle energy of 3,285 foot pounds. With a 300-gr. bullet of greater sectional density, the .375 Magnum has a muzzle velocity of 2,540 foot seconds and a muzzle energy of 4,300 foot pounds.

If you want a medium-range rifle which will stop them in their tracks, a new .375 Magnum would be a better bet than a secondhand .405.

LIFE OF A .22 RIFLE

Question: Some time ago I read that in a 10-year period 500,000 rounds of .22 caliber ammunition were fired through one Remington rifle, and that it was still in good working order and fairly accurate. I have had an argument with some friends who think that a .22 is worn out after a few thousand rounds. Please put us straight on this.—M. A. C., Nev.

Answer: Yes, that is the McCoy. A good .22 rifle used with noncorrosive primers and greased bullets—ammunition such as the Remington Kleanbore cartridges of standard velocity—is practically indestructible.

It is a fact that Remington shot 500,-000 cartridges through a .22 and it was still in good shape at the end of the test.

SAVAGE MODEL 20 IS O.K.

Question: Last deer season I purchased a used Model 20 Savage .300. It looks like a new rifle, although I understand it was made many years ago. One of my friends tells me that this rifle in .300 caliber is weak, liable to explode when fired, and was discontinued for this reason. I like the rifle very much, but don't want it around if my friend is right. What is your opinion?—F. C. W., Vt.

Answer: Don't let anybody kid you. Those Model 20 Savages have exceedingly strong actions with locking lugs as large as those of the Springfield or Mauser. Those actions are the only short Mauser-type actions ever built in the U. S. and are in considerable demand. I think the only reason the Model 20 was discontinued is that it was very expensive to manufacture because of special features such as the shotgun-type safety.

IS 1913 RIFLE SAFE?

Question: I recently purchased a 1913 rifle—a .22 Stevens lever-action Crack Shot. Some of my friends say that the rifle is dangerous, that it's so old it might explode. Do you agree?—B. A., Calif.

Answer: Don't use anything but low-speed ammunition in that old Crack Shot. The high-speed stuff would be too much for it. However, if you notice that your cartridges are blowing out at the rim, excessive head space has developed and you'd better lay off shooting the rifle.

RECENT SPRINGFIELD ACTIONS

Question: I have been planning a .22 Varminter using a Springfield action. As pressures occasionally run a little high in these smoke poles, I want to be sure to get a late-number action. What serial number can I use as a guide?

Also, is there a short Mauser action that will stand pressure as well as the Springfield?—R. J. G., Calif.

Answer: The best type of Springfield receiver is the latest type made from nickel steel. It dates from 1927 and begins with No. 1,275,767. The double-heat-treated Springfield Armory receivers are also O.K. They begin with No. 800,000. The original 1903 receivers ought to be avoided for hot loads since they are case-hardened and relatively brittle.

If you get a short Mauser action it will be adequately strong, but be sure you get a Waffenfabrik action. Do not get the old '93 action made by Lowe of Berlin.

.270 BARREL STANDS UP

Question: I am dubious about purchasing a .270 Winchester. I have heard that, in some instances, the barrels of the .270 began to show throat erosion after 1,000 rounds and that they lost accuracy after about 1,500 rounds. Doesn't this make the .270 a very short-lived rifle?

What is the average life of a .270? Also what sight do you recommend in long range (200 to 400 yd.) in the open country of the West?—C. S., N. Y.

Answer: I wore out a .270 barrel in 1,000 rounds, but this happened at a time when I was doing a lot of experimental reloading and shooting many 10-shot groups. That heats the barrel up and makes the life short. Since then I have concluded that I was unduly pessimistic, and that a good .270 barrel, if not used for rapid fire or for a lot of group shooting, has a barrel life not much less than that of the .30/06.

If you don't abuse a barrel and use it only for hunting and a fair amount of target practice, your .270 should give you fine accuracy for many years. I would say it has an accuracy life of 4,000 rounds.

I think the best sight for a .270 for mountain hunting is a good 4X 'scope with the rifle sighted to zero at 300 yd. That will put the bullet 4 in. high at 200 yd. and 4 in. low at 350 yd.

NO LOST ENERGY IN AUTO RIFLES

Question: I'm figuring on buying a new .22 Mossberg automatic rifle, but a friend of mine has told me that an automatic won't shoot so far or so hard as a bolt action, because the recoil action which actuates the reloading mechanism detracts from the velocity of the bullet.

Is this true? I want an automatic, but I also want long range.—J. W., Calif.

Answer: If you want that Mossberg automatic, by all means get it. An automatic will shoot just as hard as any other rifle. There is no difference whatsoever in the trajectory of an automatic and any other type of action, if the same ammunition is used in the same length barrel.

HOW RIFLE CALIBERS ARE NAMED

Question: I see rifles and pistols referred to as .250/3000, .30/06, .30/30, .44/40, and so on. What does the second set of figures signify?—J. R. McC., Tex.

Answer: There are various ways of designating rifle calibers. The old way was to give the bore diameter of the barrel, then the number of grains of black powder the case would hold. Examples: .30/30 and .44/40. In late years many cartridges have been named for the bore diameter in thousandths of an inch. Examples: .270 Winchester, .348 Winchester. Some cartridges are named for the groove diameter. Example: the .22's, whose bore diameter is only about .219. The "06" in .30/06 means that the cartridge was adopted in 1906. The "3000" in .250/3000 means that the original muzzle velocity was 3,000 foot seconds. At one time it was fashionable to add a third figure, which gave the weight of the bullet in grains. Example: .45/70/405.

TROUBLES WITH A LEVER-ACTION RIFLE

Question: I have a Model 99 Savage .300 that I think a lot of. I had our local gunsmith install a Redfield 70 peep sight and a military sling with quick-detachable swivels. I zero-sighted the new peep at 100 yd. and finally got the last nine shots in a 4½-in. group—about 100 percent better than I had ever done with open sights.

About a week before deer season last fall I went out to the range to shoot a few rounds for checkup. After the fourth shot I worked the lever, to eject the empty case; but it just swung down like a pendulum and the breech stayed closed, with the case still in the chamber. I pressed my thumb against the rear of the breech, and then it tipped back and ejected the empty. The case was not expanded or split.

A gunsmith took the rifle apart, but said nothing was broken, bent, or sprung. After he put it together again, I had to resight it, and it seemed to work as well as ever.

I had the new peep adjusted so I was hitting the 6-in. bull with one brand of 180-gr. soft-point bullets at 100 yd. Then I tried another brand of the same-weight bullets and they all hit 4 to 6 in. to the right. How come?—M. F. P., Pa.

Answer: You bring up a couple of interesting questions. In the first place, no lever-action rifle has the camming power of the bolt action. If you get a load which is a little too hot or a brass cartridge case which is too soft, or if the chamber has not been well polished and the reamer marks are left in it, you will encounter ejection trouble with any lever-action rifle.

That is why the armies of the world for the most part use the bolt action. Seating and ejection are both sure.

Some years ago one of the loading companies, working under wartime conditions, turned out quite a few cases of soft brass. I got a lot of squawks about that one particular lot of ammunition from owners of lever-action rifles.

Because of their two-piece stocks, most lever-action rifles are more sensitive to changes in brands of ammunition than are bolt-action rifles. With a lever-action rifle, you will usually find that if you change brands of ammunition the bullets will have a different point of impact, even if they are of the same weight and velocity. The reason is that the rifle is not so rigid, and barrel vibration is not so uniform.

Lever-action rifles have their advantages, but as you can see, any fair appraisal shows that they have their minor disadvantages as well.

CHOOSING BINOCULARS

Question: I am interested in buying a pair of binoculars for use in identifying ducks in the air and on the water. I cannot afford to shell out $75 or $100 for a pair with coated optics. Are there any good cheap glasses available?—W. W., Ga.
Answer: Good binoculars are costly to make. Cheap binoculars have poor definition and often produce severe eyestrain. A man should either get the best or none at all. There is no second best.

BINOCULARS FOR MOUNTAIN HUNTING

Question: I intend buying a new pair of Bausch & Lomb binoculars. Please give me your opinion on the best size to get—8 x 30, 8 x 40, or 7 x 35—for use in mountain hunting.—J. E. G., Mont.
Answer: If I were you I'd get the Bausch & Lomb 8 x 30 binoculars with individual focusing eyepieces. I have used the 8 x 30 with perfect satisfaction from Alaska to Sonora, Mexico. The power is right and the weight is right. The 8 x 40 is a little too bulky to be ideal. It—and the 7 x 35 too—will give you a little brighter field in poor light, but the 8 x 30 will be just about right 95 percent of the time. Definition is actually a little better in the

8 x 30 than in the 7 x 35 because of the slightly greater magnification.

On one trip a friend of mine used a 7 x 50, which weighed three or four times as much as mine. It is a beautiful glass, but too heavy to be ideal, and most of the time it had no edge on my 8 x 30.

EXPLANATION OF BINOCULAR NUMBERS

Question: In advertisements of binoculars, what do the figures mean—7 x 50, 8 x 30, and so on?—R. P. C., Nebr.
Answer: In each case, the first numeral stands for the magnifying power of the glasses. The second numerals indicate the diameter of the objective lenses, expressed in millimeters. Other things being equal, the larger the objective lens in relation to the power, the greater the light-gathering capacity, or "brightness," of the glass.

For general use, 7X and 8X binoculars are about right, but a 10 x 50 glass would be useful in mountain hunting. I prefer, however, to use a 7X or 8X glass for general observation, then pick up small details, such as the size of heads and horns of game, with a spotting 'scope of about 20X.

SPOTTING 'SCOPE OR BINOCULARS?

Question: I intend buying either a spotting 'scope or a good pair of binoculars, and I'm trying to decide which. Please give me the good and bad features of each and let me know which would be best for use in deer hunting in the Colorado Rockies.—W. M. C., Wis.
Answer: May I suggest that you get the 8 x 30 or 7 x 35 Bausch & Lomb binoculars. They have individual focusing eyepieces and are fine, satisfactory glasses. I have used my 8 x 30 B. & L. binoculars all over North America.

A spotting 'scope is O.K. to use for looking over horns and antlers *after* you have located your game.

ALL ABOUT SHOTGUNS

by Jack O'Connor

HOW TO CHOOSE YOUR SHOTGUN

SHOTGUN BATTERY

Question: I'm writing to ask your opinion on the two repeating shotguns I've selected for hunting—both Model 12 Winchesters with 26-in. barrels and a 13¼-in. stock, for I have short arms.

For rabbit and quail: 20 gauge, modified choke. For duck and pheasant: 16 gauge, bored improved modified.

For quail I've used the 20 gauge with No. 8 trap load with good results. How would that combination be for pheasants? Does my 16 gauge have enough choke for duck shooting?—G. P., Mo.

Answer: You've made an exceedingly wise selection, I think. My only suggestion would be to have the barrel of your 20 gauge opened up to improved cylinder, for I think you would kill more quail and rabbits. For killing pheasants with your 20 gauge, try using 1 oz. of No. 6 shot. I too like 26-in. barrels, by the way. I'm a big guy with long arms, but 26-in. barrels point and handle a lot faster for me.

SHOTGUN FOR 13-YEAR-OLD

Question: I am 13 and own a .22. I've used shotguns at skeet events and in the field, and now I'd like to own one. From my past experience, I think a 20 gauge repeater or automatic would be much superior to any other kind.—D. S., Mich.

Answer: I have a 13-year-old boy myself. He hunts a lot with me and he is a good shot, but I should hate to see him have an automatic shotgun. It's the most dangerous and deadly weapon made, and in the hands of a boy as young as you it might lead to promiscuous shooting. Frankly, I think you would be better off with the simple-to-understand and almost foolproof double barrel. Why don't you consider one, instead of letting your mouth water for that automatic?

USING A 12 GAUGE RIOT GUN

Question: Please tell me whether a Model 12 Winchester riot gun in 12 gauge can be used for hunting. It has a 20-in. barrel; would I have to get a longer one? Most of my shooting is for ducks and doves at ranges of about 40 yd.

I have shot the gun as it is, and it gives a pattern of about 45 percent. However, I often shoot high with it, probably because of improper balance.—B. S., Tex.

Answer: The thing for you to do with that riot gun is to have a Weaver-Choke or a Cutts Compensator installed by a competent gunsmith. Either will give you more barrel length and a fine all-round shotgun. With the various tubes which are available for those variable-choke devices you can get any pattern you want.

SEMI-AUTOMATIC SHOTGUNS ARE RELIABLE

Question: Please give me your opinion of automatic shotguns. I have thought of buying a Remington, but since most people here in South Africa use double-barrel guns I can't find anyone who can tell me anything about them. Are automatic shotguns likely to go wrong easily? Do they stand up without the need of new parts every so often? Do they jam easily or damage the shells which are put through the action but not fired?

I am really interested in getting a Remington Model 32 over-and-under gun, but since it might prove too expensive I may settle for an automatic.

Next year I may have a chance to do some big-game hunting out here, so I should also like to know what you think about the Remington .35 self-loading rifle for this purpose.—A. D. C., Cambridge, South Africa.

Answer: I think you will find the Remington 12 gauge semi-automatic shotgun an exceedingly reliable weapon. Possibly it isn't so foolproof as a good double, but it is almost so. Tens of thousands of these guns have been used in every part of the world for many years and have given perfect satisfaction. The same can be said of the other automatics made on Browning patents—the American Savage and the Belgian Browning.

To my way of thinking, an automatic does not handle and balance so well as a good double like the Remington over-and-under, but perhaps that is just my opinion.

Frankly, I do not think that you would find the .35 Remington cartridge satisfactory for South African game. For all-round use, I think you need a more powerful cartridge with a longer and heavier bullet. I would suggest the American .30/06 in some such rifle as the Model 720 Remington or the Model 70 Winchester. From what I understand, you are likely to run into a buffalo or a lion, and the .35 really was intended for animals of the deer class.

SHOTGUN GAUGES AND RANGES

Question: Will smaller gauge shotguns shoot as far and kill game at the same ranges as a 12 gauge?—V. M., Okla.

Answer: The smaller gauges will not kill as far as the larger gauges will. There are two reasons for this. In the first place, the larger gauges carry more shot—and the more shot you carry, the denser will be your patterns at a longer range, and you will kill game more consistently.

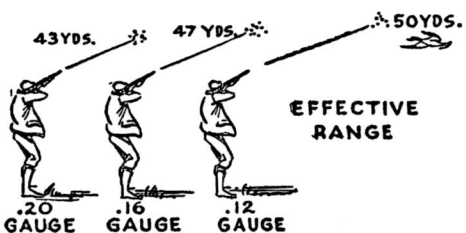

The bigger the gauge the greater the range. This drawing shows the relative effective range of the .20, .16 and .12 gauge guns.

The larger gauges also pattern a little better because the shot columns are shorter, and fewer shot are deformed. That is why, for wildfowl use exclusively, a 12 gauge is better than a 16, and a 10 is better than a 12.

Offhand I would say that by using No. 6 shot in a full-choke 12 gauge, one can kill large ducks consistently at 50 yd.; with a 16 gauge gun, one can kill up to about 47 yd.; and with a 20 gauge, up to about 43 yd. Those figures are more or less relative, but show what I mean.

SLUGS WILL STOP THEM!

Question: A friend and I have shot about all American game with a bow and arrow, and now we've decided to try grizzlies. However, we feel that while one man handles the bow, the other should carry a powerful firearm for "life insurance." We both use pump shotguns, and wonder what you think of the rifled slug for dangerous game. Does it have much of a knockdown blow?—D. M. C., S. D.

Answer: For a stopping rifle at close range you would have to go a long way to find anything better than a rifled slug in a 12 gauge pump gun. Armed with one, I wouldn't be afraid to face an African lion in full charge. Well, not too afraid, anyway.

The British in Africa often use 12 gauge ball loads for a stopping weapon on lions. Much dangerous game has been killed with it, both in Africa and in India. As a matter of fact, the famous 12 bore Paradox gun is much the same, except that the twist on the bullet is given by rifling at the end of a shotgun barrel, instead of by rifling on the ball itself as in the Winchester or Remington slugs. These rifled slugs leave a 12 gauge with a velocity of 1,470 ft. a second, not very much, true, but big, heavy balls of large diameter have knockdown power out of all proportion to their energy, which doesn't mean much. Up to 50 yd. they'll shoot like a rifle too.

20 GAUGE GUN FOR OLDSTERS

Question: I have a 12 gauge automatic that I have killed quail with for 22 seasons. I have always been a fair shot and could generally get one to three birds on a flush, if I was in an open field. For the last two seasons, however, I do not seem to be able to hit them with the 12 gauge. I have in mind getting a 20 gauge double. Do you think this will help my shooting?—C. M. B., Tex.

Answer: I think there probably is something to the theory that as we get older we do not react so quickly with a heavy gun, and that most of us would improve our shooting with a lighter 16 or 20 gauge. I believe your notion of getting a light 20 gauge is a very good one. If I were in your boots, I would get a good 20, weighing between 6 and 6½ lb. and bored about quarter choke and modified. I think you will find it your best bet for quail.

DOUBLE BARREL VS. AUTOMATIC

Question: Will you please tell me what advantages an automatic shotgun has over a double-barrel gun?—H. S., N. J.

Answer: Actually, the only advantage the automatic has over the double-barrel shotgun is more shots. However, there is an increasing tendency to restrict the number of shells in the magazine of the automatic to two, making it a three-shot gun. In some Canadian provinces, only one shell may be carried in the magazine. On the other hand, the double-barrel gun usually handles more easily—it is shorter overall and lighter.

12 VS. 16 GAUGE SHOTGUNS

Question: What do you consider to be the "perfect" barrel length and choke, in a 12 gauge double for rabbits and squirrels? Or is a 16 gauge double more suitable for upland game?

Is it possible that a 12 gauge which is ideal for small game should also be satisfactory for ducks?—R. S. S., Mass.

Answer: Picking out a "perfect" gun is a tough proposition. If I were you, I'd get a 16 gauge gun with 26-in. barrels, single trigger, automatic ejection, and beavertail fore-end. I'd have the right barrel bored 50 percent and the left bored 60 percent. Such a gun handles speedily for fast upland shots and will also take ducks at 40 yards or more from a blind.

I think most people would shoot much better if they carried such a gun. The average man with a 12 gauge having 30-in. barrels, bored modified and full, is greatly over-gunned. He is trying to use a gun made for pass-shooting on ducks for all-round performance.

POWER OF 12'S AND 20'S

Question: The gunners hereabouts are engaged in an argument about the relative killing power of 12 and 20 gauge shotguns. One group, consisting of many old-time duck and fox hunters, maintains that a 12 will reach out 10 to 15 yd. farther than a 20, because of the greater load. The other group maintains that a 20 will go just as far, if not farther, and has deeper penetration, even with less powder and shot.

What is your opinion?—H. J. H., N. H.

Answer: The difference in the killing power of the 12 and 20 gauge is largely expressed in the greater amount of shot carried in a maximum standard 12 gauge load—1¼ oz. of shot. The maximum standard 20 gauge load is 1 oz. of shot. You can see from this that whatever a 20 gauge will do at 40 yd., a 12 gauge will do at 50. As a matter of fact, there is somewhat less deformation of shot in the 12 because of the shorter shot column. As a consequence, the 12 will do a little better than the figures indicate.

Let us say this: A 20 gauge will kill a mallard reliably up to about 45 yd.; a 12 can be counted on to do the same thing up to somewhat more than 55 yd.

LONG VS. SHORT SHOTGUN BARRELS

Question: A friend of mine claims that a long-barrel shotgun will greatly outshoot a short-barrel gun of similar gauge and choke. Will the longer barrel make a closer pattern?—G. L. V., Ind.

Answer: Tell your friend he is not exactly right. A long-barrel gun will not throw denser patterns than a similarly choked gun with shorter barrels.

However, the longer gun has a slightly higher muzzle velocity. Published shotgun velocities are for 30-in. barrels. You will lose 7½ foot seconds in muzzle velocity for every inch cut off. The difference, therefore, between velocities delivered by a 26-in. barrel and a 30-in. barrel is only 30 foot seconds, in favor of the latter. The difference is so slight that one would not notice it in the field.

DAMASCUS STEEL BARRELS

Question: I have a 12 gauge shotgun with Damascus-steel barrels that I used for more than 40 years. A few years ago, however, I got a circular from one of the big shell-manufacturing concerns warning against using modern high-powered loads in such a gun. That scared me, and I started loading my own shells, using semi-smokeless powder.

A lot of my friends have been using guns similar to mine for years with modern ammunition and nothing has happened. In fact, the only guns I have heard about blowing up were two that were supposed to be especially suited to modern loads.

Can you straighten me out on this? It begins to look as if a lot of this talk was just a deal between the ammunition makers and the gun makers to sell more new guns.—T. E. K., Calif.

Answer: Some years ago the Ithaca Gun Co. ran a test with various old Damascus-barrel guns. These guns ran all the way from cheap twist barrels to barrels from the most expensive doubles. The regular Ithaca proof load was used. That load is not excessively hot—just hot enough to take care of the ordinary exigencies in the shooting of a gun. As I remember it, most of those old guns let go at the first shot, and all blew up at the second.

All this means is that a man might

continue to use a gun with Damascus barrels for years, but he is constantly working with an exceedingly narrow margin of safety. A shell left out in the sun might generate enough higher pressures to cause a burst, or some other equally trivial cause might bring the same result. Even a 3¼-dram charge of bulk smokeless powder generates pressures almost as high as the more powerful progressive-burning loads. Their pressure peak, however, comes at a different place.

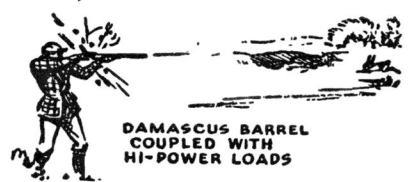

DAMASCUS BARREL
COUPLED WITH
HI-POWER LOADS

Damascus barrels will not stand up under the pressures created by modern shotgun shells.

A few years ago I saw an acquaintance buying shells for an old Damascus gun of good grade. I warned him against it. He told me that he knew gun editors were in cahoots with the ammunition companies to sell a lot of guns. He said he would continue to use it. That very afternoon he blew his right barrel. Luckily he came to no harm, except to get some splinters of wood in his fingers.

Adding it all up, I think you would be wise to get rid of that gun. None of us would think of starting to drive across the country in an 1898 Stanley Steamer. But for some reason no one ever wants to retire a gun as long as it will go bang.

GAUGE AND CALIBER

Question: How did shotguns come to get their gauge designations; rifles, their calibers?—S. J. H., Ont.
Answer: That's a commonly asked question. Gauge was determined by round balls which fitted a shotgun's bore. Twelve of the 12 gauge size weighed 1 lb., and it was called 12 gauge, 16 gauge balls ran 16 to the pound, 20 gauge ran 20, etc. The .410 is named by caliber, and as a matter of fact was originally a rifle caliber.

In black-powder days it was the fashion to name a rifle cartridge from the bore diameter of the barrel and from the amount of powder its case would hold. The bore diameter of the .32/20 is .32, and the case holds 20 gr. of black powder. Other cartridges named like that are the .30/40, .30/30, and the .45/70. In those days sometimes the weight in grains of the bullet was tacked on as a third figure, as in the .45/70/405. As for the .30/06, the 06 stands for the year (1906) when the Army adopted the cartridge. Some rifles are named for their groove diameter instead of their bore diameter: the common .22 really has a bore diameter of about .219 and the .257 is in reality an ordinary .25 caliber.

SHOTGUN WITH SLIGHT RECOIL

Question: Having been ill for quite a while I hesitate to get a 12 gauge shotgun because of its recoil. I hunt mostly rabbits and birds. A single-shot .410 gauge I borrowed from a friend was easy to handle, but I found that it shot rather close. Should I buy a .410, or would a good double-barrel 20 gauge have too much recoil for me?—W. F. T., N. C.
Answer: I think your best bet would be a 20 gauge. The recoil isn't much more than the .410 and it's a much more practical game gun. However, you ought to stick to the ⅞-oz. load, which gives a good deal less recoil than the maximum 1-oz. load. I don't think that shell in a gun of reasonable weight would cause you any inconvenience.

A friend of mine was in bad health

and used a .410 for a couple of years, but he found the 20 gauge much deadlier on game and switched to it.

EVERYTHING IN ONE GUN?

Question: I'm looking for something I can never get—but maybe you can suggest something close to it. I want a duck gun that will throw a 30-in. pattern at 70 yd., will not mutilate teal that flash overhead at 20 yd., is heavy enough to keep superduper loads from kicking me out of the boat, and fast enough for teal. I hunt on a reservoir where most of the ducks stay about 70 yd. up, but teal frequently fly overhead at 20 yd.

A 'scope might help me too. Can a 'scope be mounted successfully on a 10 gauge double-gun? I can afford just one duck gun, and want it as near right as possible.—W. B. S., Miss.

Answer: You are chasing a rainbow if you want a gun that will throw all its shot into a 30-in. circle at 70 yd. The tightest full chokes I ever heard of will keep consistently only 70 or 75 percent of their shot in a 30-in. circle at 40 yd. At 70 yd., the pattern of even a very tightly choked gun will cover the side of a small barn. Furthermore, you couldn't *give* me a gun like you want. The pattern would be so tight at intermediate ranges that you'd have to shoot it like a rifle.

The nearest thing I know of to what you want is the Model 12 Winchester long-range duck gun, which is chambered for 3-in. shells and handles 1⅜ to 1⅝ oz. of shot. That gun will kill single ducks at 70 yd. with some degree of regularity, but baby ducks still will often fly right through the pattern.

A 'scope can be mounted on any gun with some fancy gunsmithing, but it's far easier to mount a Weaver 1X on a gun like the Model 12. I think a 'scope-sighted heavy 12 is your best bet.

DOUBLE-PURPOSE SHOTGUN

Question: I intend to buy an automatic shotgun to use for ducks and other birds; also for use with slugs in deer hunting. What make and gauge is best, and what about choke?—W. T., Mass.

Answer: I don't believe there would be much difference between the various makes. The Remingtons, Savage and Browning guns are all essentially the same, made on the Browning patents which have expired. The Winchester is different, but a good gun.

Since your shooting will include both waterfowl and deer, I think you'd be wise to get a 12 gauge equipped with a Poly-Choke. That is truly an all-round shotgun—you would have lots of range for waterfowl and, with buckshot or rifled slugs, plenty of striking power for deer.

SHOTGUN FOR A BOY

Question: My dad is going to buy me a shotgun. I am 16 years old and weigh 123 lb. I will use the gun on rabbits mostly, but occasionally on squirrels and crows. What barrel length and gauge do you recommend, and should I get a repeater or a single shot?—D. R., Ohio.

Answer: If you can talk your dad into it I think the best gun for you would be a 16 or 20 gauge double-barrel gun with 26-in. barrels, bored improved cylinder in the right, and modified choke in the left. Such a gun is simpler to operate than the pump, and the open boring will make it easier for you to become a good shot.

SHOTGUN FOR A WOMAN

Question: I have never done any shooting, but I want to buy a gun and begin now—my quarry will be rabbits, quail, and pheasants. I am 4 ft. 11 in., and weigh 93 lb. Please tell me what shotgun I should choose.—Mrs. A. L. K., Calif.

Answer: First, let me suggest that you do not either overgun or undergun yourself. A 12 gauge shotgun would toss you all over the lot, whereas a .410 would call for too much skill and close holding.

I think the best prescription for you would be a 20 gauge double-barrel shotgun, bored improved cylinder and modified choke, and weighing no more than 6¼ lb. I would suggest a 1⅝-in. drop at the comb, and 2½-in. drop at the heel. If you cannot get a double-barrel gun, get a light 20 gauge pump with 26-in. barrel, bored improved cylinder.

Be sure that you get an open-bore gun, and that it's not too heavy.

BEST ALL-ROUND SHOTGUN GAUGE

Question: My new shotgun will be either a 16 or a 20 gauge Model 12 Winchester. Which is the better all-round gun? What barrel length and choke should I specify? Our game is rabbits, squirrels, birds, and turkeys.—O. W. F., W. Va.

Answer: I am inclined to believe that the 16 gauge is a better all-round bet for field shooting than the 20, since it has the lightness of the 20 with most of the soup of the 12. It is a very fine compromise and will do anything from quail shooting to duck shooting quite well.

Since you are interested in the Model 12 Winchester, I suggest you get your gun with 26-in. barrels bored modified. This is the best boring for all-round shooting. Still better would be to fit it with one of the variable-choke devices, so you can vary your pattern for the shooting at hand.

LONG-RANGE WILDFOWL GUNS

Question: Where we used to go duck and goose hunting, and where we hope to hunt again, we very rarely have close shots. Most of them are at the extreme killing range of a 12 gauge, full-choke gun. For all-round purposes I swear by

my Browning automatic with Cutts Comp; but would a Magnum be better on those long shots?—W. H., Calif.

Answer: If you want to buy a special gun for long-range duck and goose shooting, and if you are willing to take the trouble to learn to use it, the finest long-range wildfowl gun in the world is the big Ithaca 10 gauge Magnum, which throws 2 oz. of shot. Using No. 3 shot, it will kill single ducks at 80 yd. and ducks out of flocks at 100 yd. It's the darndest cannon you've ever seen.

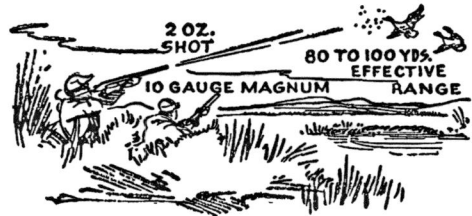

The big 10 gauge Magnum will kill single ducks at 80 yd. and ducks in a flock at 100 yd.

Another good gun is the Winchester long-range Model 12 duck gun, which handles a No. 3 shell and up to 1⅝ oz. of shot. This gun doesn't reach out quite so far as the 10 Magnum—it falls around 10 yd. behind—but it isn't any pea shooter.

.410 NOT PRACTICABLE HERE

Question: I have a single-shot .410 shotgun which I use for squirrels and rabbits. I would like your opinion of it as a dove and quail gun.—D. K., Tex.

Answer: I'm afraid you are in for a great many disappointments if you use a .410 for wing-shooting. It does not throw much shot and the patterns are quite small. An expert can kill a good deal of game with it, but he has to confine his shooting to 30 yd. It is no gun at all for a beginner. It is not a good quail gun because quail are hard to kill and the .410 simply does not carry enough shot.

If I were you I would certainly try to get a 20 or 16 gauge shotgun. Either is much more practical than a .410.

THE 20 GAUGE VS. THE 12

Question: How much more effective, at 30 yd., is a 12 gauge shotgun using a high-base shell with No. 7½ shot than a 20 gauge gun of the same bore using the same kind of shell? I have always used a 12 gauge, and my present one is a Remington auto, but I find it pretty heavy for field hunting.—C. G. F., N. Y.

Answer: At 30 yd. a 12 gauge gun is not one whit more effective than a 20 gauge gun. Actually, it is *less* effective—for the simple reason that the 12 tends to be heavier and slower. Even an improved-cylinder or quarter-choke 20 gauge will kill quail or even ducks just as dead at 30 yd. as a 12. A man who isn't going to shoot at more than 30 yd. is very nicely overgunned with a 12 gauge.

.410 OR 20 GAUGE?

Question: With my 20 gauge shotgun, I used to be very good on pheasant, snipe, and rabbits but only fair on ducks and partridges.

For snipe, pheasants, and rabbits, is a .410 my answer—assuming shots at no more than 25 yd.?—P. S. K., Calif.

Answer: You say you plan to shoot at no more than 25 yd., but I think you will run into conditions where you will want to reach out farther. At 25 yd. a .410 will kill pheasants and even ducks; but even with a full choke it doesn't have a killing range of more than 35 yd., and if you open it up you reduce the killing range materially. Also, the barrel is so thin it's hard to see and aim with.

For your purposes, I think you ought to stick to the 20. It is neat and light and has clean lines; it handles fast; and it has enough weight to be steady.

RIFLED SHOTGUN?

Question: A hunter in our neighborhood claims that some shotguns have rifling in the barrels. I've never heard of such a thing; have you?—J. K., Va.

Answer: Yes, shotguns have been made with rifling at the muzzle. Some have been made deliberately to spread the patterns out so they'll throw a wide pattern at very close range.

In England the British get out various shotgun-rifles. One firm calls its gun the Paradox. A very heavy shotgun, with the last few inches of the barrel rifled, it does fairly well as a cylinder bore, and it throws heavy conical bullets that will stop the largest of big game.

IDENTIFYING DAMASCUS BARRELS

Question: I recently fell heir to an aged 12 gauge single-shot with 30-in. barrel, bearing markings of the Central Arms Co., St. Louis, Mo. The number 812 follows an inscription "King Nitro." How can I tell if it has a Damascus barrel, and hence is unsafe?—W. G. M., Tex.

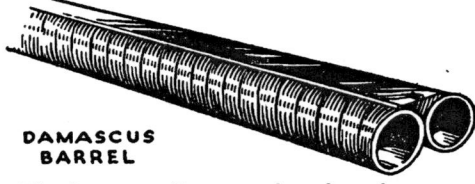

DAMASCUS BARREL

The dangerous Damascus barrel can be recognized by the very definite series of patterns and twists which appear throughout the length of the barrel.

Answer: If that gun has a Damascus barrel, you will be able to discern a fine pattern in the steel in a series of twists and waves. If it has fluid steel barrels they will look like an ordinary piece of steel with no pattern in them. Your King Nitro shotgun was made in Belgium and imported by a St. Louis hardware jobber. It's very old and probably not too good, so don't put anything hot in it.

HOW TO IMPROVE YOUR SHOOTING

'SCOPE FOR SHOTGUN?

Question: Reading about how a 'scope makes for better aim leads me to wonder whether I should get a telescope for my single-shot 16 gauge shotgun, a Model 220 Savage. But since the 'scope would cost twice as much as the gun, would that be a wise investment?—E. H., Pa.

Answer: For shotgun use, I don't think you'd get enough benefit out of that 'scope to pay for it. When I gave a 'scope a thorough tryout some years ago, the best thing I noticed was that with it one doesn't have the tendency to overshoot— a failing most shotgun shooters have because they become excited and don't put their cheeks down on the comb. On a straightway shot with a 'scope you simply put the dot on the bird, touch the trigger, and down comes the bird. But in general, a 'scope functions best on a rifle, where one aims exactly.

TWO SIGHTS FOR SHOTGUN?

Question: For the first time, I have seen a shotgun with two sights, one at the muzzle and the other at the center of the barrel, and it seems to line up faster than one with a single sight. My own gun is a Browning Special with a raised rib. It has a 30-in. barrel, full choke. I use it mostly for duck shooting and am considering having an additional sight installed. Do you think this will help my shooting?—C. A. H., La.

Answer: I doubt that you would get any great benefit from two sights, particularly since your shotgun already has a raised rib. My own Model 21 Winchester has two sights and the only value I can see is that it helps me to check my alignment occasionally. When shooting ducks I never see the rear sight at all, yet I know some people who do. Think the matter over carefully before you install a second sight. Then if you do, keep the two sights at least 18 in. apart.

WHY SHOOTERS MISS BIRDS

Question: I hope you may be able to advise me how to improve my shooting. In hunting ducks and pheasants I have not had much luck. I have missed flying ducks at 50 yd. and less and also have missed a great many pheasants at ranges of from 10 to 50 yd. when I thought I had a perfect bead on them. I have a 20 gauge shotgun with a 26-in. barrel and for the most part I use No. 6 shot—because No. 7½ doesn't seem to me to be heavy enough.—R. K., Mass.

Over shooting and not giving the proper lead cause more misses than any other factors in shooting. Practice makes perfect.

Answer: There are thousands of ways to miss a bird. I wouldn't attempt to tell you just why you are missing them; however, I think the commonest causes are failing to get your cheek down on the comb, seeing too much barrel, and overshooting. That's the tendency of a man when he becomes excited. Another classic reason for missing birds is not leading them enough.

MEASURE OF A GOOD WING-SHOT

Question: I have been in several arguments regarding what constitutes a good wing-shot, and I contend that a man who can kill one duck for every three shells deserves to be classed as good. Don't you agree?—R. C. B., Tex.

Answer: Yes, I think the man who can take on ducks as they come, within 50 yd., and get one duck for three shells is a darned good wing-shot. On the other hand, a man shooting over decoys at 35 yd. wouldn't be much of a shot unless he could get one bird with two shells. In pass-shooting, where all the ducks are between 45 and 55 yd., a man who can get one duck in four shots shouldn't be ashamed to face anybody.

AIM WITH BOTH EYES OR ONE?

Question: Some friends and I have been debating as to the correct way to aim a shotgun. One group maintains that it is best to keep both eyes open, the other favors aiming with one eye. Which is correct?—K. D. R., Me.

Answer: The best way to shoot a shotgun is with both eyes open. This is because the two views thus obtained give the effect of a stereopticon, so to speak, and this aids in judging the range. However, a great many very good shots have learned to shoot with one eye closed, and do very well. If a man has the habit of closing one eye—and can't break himself of it—he shouldn't worry too much. On the other hand anyone who is learning to shoot should form the habit of shooting with both eyes open.

CURE FOR FLINCHING?

Question: Not long ago I went out to do some skeet shooting with a friend of mine. After about 15 rounds I found myself flinching at each shot, using a 12 gauge shotgun.

Now, I enjoy shooting and expect to do a lot of hunting. How can I cure myself of flinching?—J. F. K., Ala.

Answer: Darned if I know what to tell you to do about that flinching of yours, since it comes largely from a state of mind. About the only suggestion I can make is to equip your gun with a Weaver-Choke or a Cutts Compensator, which will reduce the recoil about 30 percent. A rubber recoil pad will also take the sting out of the recoil. Even a 12 gauge, so equipped, shouldn't hurt a flea.

Knowing that you aren't going to be hurt should help you get over that flinching. Habitual flinching is an annoying habit. I think everyone does it now and then, but a man who does it every time is greatly handicapped.

LESSON ON DUCK LEADING

Question: What is the best way to learn how far to lead ducks, and is it necessary to memorize the correct leads at different distances?—W. F. D., Ohio.

Answer: The proper way to learn to lead ducks is to shoot at a lot of them—to miss them and hit them—and to remember how far you led those you hit. I think it is best to look right along the barrel and to swing rapidly, starting behind the duck and ending up ahead of it, then pull the trigger when you think the lead is right. If you swing fast you will hit more ducks than if you try holding the gun stationary.

CURE FOR HIGH AND LEFT!

Question: My Winchester Model 12 shotgun has No. 2 skeet boring. I find that when I shoot it deliberately at paper to pattern it, it puts the charge right in there, but when I shoot hastily, as I would on game, the charge goes high and to the left. I am a good shot and get lots of game, but this patterning business worries me. How come I hit? Do I subconsciously correct? Why do those patterns go that way?—W. B., Calif.

Answer: In shooting game you are not getting your cheek down firmly on the comb. And that, my boy, is one of the prettiest little reasons for missing. That No. 2 skeet boring takes care of some of that sloppy holding, but not all. Practice putting your face right down on that comb every time, and you'll have no more trouble in shooting where you look.

THIS MAN MISSES

THIS MAN HITS

The man who makes consistent hits takes care to see that his cheek is on the comb every time he shoots.

On close shots even a Skeet No. 1 boring won't take care of poor holding. Shooting quail this season with a Skeet No. 1, I found myself missing. I was shooting very fast because I knew I had to bust them right now with that boring. Shots were high and to the left. Reason: My head was up and cheek was not firmly on the comb.

HIGHER COMB SOLVES TROUBLES

Question: Last fall I got a secondhand pump shotgun which feels all right but which I can't shoot for sour apples. When I throw it up and shoot as I would on game the pattern centers about 18 in. low at 40 yd. I think I missed every straightaway pheasant I shot at. What to do?—M. L. H., Mont.

Answer: The comb of that gun is far too low and when you shoot you see nothing but the breech. For bird shooting you ought to see the whole length of the barrel, and it isn't a bad idea to have the gun throw the center of the pattern a little high—about 6 in. high at 40 yd.—since "straightaway" birds are usually rising a bit. The factory can straighten that stock within limits, or you can send it to a good custom stocker. If you don't care about the looks of your stock, you

can dowel a piece of walnut onto it and dress it down until the pattern goes where you want it; in effect, the comb is your rear sight. Another notion would be a Rowley pad, which would raise the comb ½ to ¾ in.

CORRECT LEAD FOR WATERFOWL

Question: With a standard 12 gauge shotgun load of 3¼ dr. of powder and 1⅛ oz. of No. 6 shot—assuming that there is no wind and that the birds are flying at an angle of 90 degrees to the gun—how many feet would you lead different kinds of ducks, such as mallards, teal, pintails, and bluebills? What is the average range at which ducks in flight are killed? What is the average velocity of this shotgun load?—A. L. L., Okla.

Answer: I am sorry, but there is no definite dope I could give you on the correct lead for waterfowl. Even if all ducks flew at the same speed and always passed the hunter exactly at right angles, specific dope would still not be any good because of the different shooting habits of hunters. Some swing their guns faster than others. Some have quicker muscular reactions than others and get off a shot more rapidly after the brain tells the finger to pull the trigger. All in all, wing-shooting is more of an art than a science.

I would say that the average duck is killed at around 30 yd. A 40-yd. shot is actually pretty long for most hunters.

The average velocity over 40 yd. of the 12 gauge low-velocity load you describe is 940 foot seconds. The so-called high-velocity load of 3¾ dr. of powder and 1¼ oz. of shot gives an average velocity of 975 foot seconds.

DOWN PITCH CAUSES LOW SHOTS

Question: For years I used an old Model 12 Winchester pump shotgun, and if I do say so myself I was a red-hot rabbit shot. Now I have a classy, trap-grade over-and-under, and I can't hit a blessed thing. Is it my fault or that of the stocking of the gun?—J. R. F., N. Y.

Answer: I think you're shooting over the rabbits. Your old Winchester 12 had somewhat more drop than the gun you are now using; you tended to shoot low with it and hence got the bunnies. Now, with a longer and straighter stock, you'll do better on birds—and not so good on rabbits. I went quail hunting last season, didn't find many quail but saw a lot of rabbits. I found those bunnies marvelously easy to miss unless I consciously held a good 6 in. under them as they ran off. Then I hit.

You don't mention pitch, and I suspect you need more that you have on your present stock, as down pitch tends to make a gun shoot low. Here is my suggestion, which you can take for what it's worth: Have a gunsmith attach a recoil pad to that stock in such a manner that you will get from 2 to 2½ in. down pitch. You might also have him make the stock come out with a length of pull of 13¾ in. With a gun so stocked, my guess is that you'd hit those rabbits a lot better.

CURE FOR BRUISED KNUCKLES

Question: The stock of my 12 gauge Iver Johnson double-gun is equipped with a rubber recoil pad which was there when I bought the gun. As I grip the stock my middle finger (next to trigger finger) rests tightly against the trigger guard. After six or eight shots in the field the recoil of the gun makes my finger swell, and a few more shots make my whole hand start to swell across the knuckles. Do you think I am gripping the stock wrong, or should I remove the recoil pad?—R. R. R., Mich.

Answer: I think you get bruised fingers because the stock is too short. You probably need about ½ in. more stock or length of pull. If you get an ordinary

lace-on recoil pad and lengthen the stock by that much I believe it will overcome your difficulty.

SLOW SWING CRIPPLES GAME

Question: When I hunt rabbits I usually hit them in the hind legs. What do you think causes this? I use the same 12 gauge Stevens full-choke pump gun I've had for 33 years.—R. W. H., Ohio.

Answer: Those rabbits are probably a little fast for you. It's my guess that they almost get away, but you catch them with the edge of your pattern.

COMB IMPROVES SHOOTING

Question: For 5 years I've had a 16 gauge Winchester, Model 97 repeater with full choke, and am very proud of it. But my shooting of it doesn't altogether satisfy me, for to get hits I have to cover the target with the end of the barrel.

To find out what was happening, I set up a target and, pointing the gun very carefully and trying to hold and cheek the stock as naturally as possible, fired two shots at 90 ft., checking the target after each one. In each case the pattern centered a good 12 in. below the point of aim. Three more shots fired swinging by the target gave similar results. Lastly I replaced the target with a gallon can, swung up from below until it was no longer visible, and let off—and the pattern made shreds of that can.

How can I bring the center of impact up so that it will shoot like that without hiding the target?—W. A. M., Colo.

Answer: Get a higher comb on that shotgun, so that you will see more barrel when you shoot. The comb of the shotgun is, in effect, the rear sight. Raising it will raise the point of impact of the pattern. You can raise the comb cheaply and effectively with a Jostam lace-on recoil pad, or you can fit a piece of walnut to the stock. Either will improve your shooting a great deal.

POOR SWING CAUSES MISSES

Question: I wonder if you can give me some pointers to improve my shooting. I hit ducks in the back of the flock, usually merely wounding, not killing them. I shoot low without knowing why I do it, and my swing is slow.

I use a 12 gauge Remington pump, Model 29, full choke, 28-in. barrel, pitch ¾ in., heel drop 2¾ in., comb drop 1½ in., length of stock 14½ in. (with two boots on because of my long arms). I am 6 ft. 1½ in., arm length 29 in., weight 170 lb., with large hands and long neck. When I shoot I am not conscious of my cheek touching the comb and I never consciously see the barrel. What do you think is wrong?—C. O. F., Mich.

Answer: Sounds to me as though that gun fits you. It has a trifle more heel drop than I like; I use a heel drop of about 2 in. However, your comb seems to be O. K., as does the stock length. There's nothing about the latter which would make you shoot low.

I suspect the trouble is that you stop your swing. You think you lead those birds enough, then, instead of swinging on through after pulling the trigger, you unconsciously stop the gun or slow it down and then pull the trigger. That is what causes most shooting behind birds. Try swinging your gun faster and be sure not to slow down or stop the gun when you touch it off. I don't think there is anything wrong with your shooting that a good fast swing won't cure.

WHEN TO RELEASE THE SAFETY

Question: Many of my friends maintain that it is perfectly safe and proper in the field to carry a shotgun with the safety catch off, in order to be ready for instant firing. I maintain that a gun should *never* be carried with the safety off, that the safety should never be released until the game is actually sighted. It does not seem to me that the speed factor need be considered, since all modern guns are designed so that the safety can be released as the gun is being raised to the shoulder.

If a man will train himself in this simple procedure, his speed in getting off a shot at a fast-flying bird will not be diminished and there will be a lot less chance of his blowing his hunting partner's head off.—W. G. W., Ill.

Answer: You are probably right, but years ago I formed the habit of pushing the safety catch off when I knew I was in the middle of a scattered covey of quail. I still follow the same practice and when I know I am about to jump a bird, I release the safety and leave it off for as long as I think I may have to shoot.

However, I know darned well my gun is ready to fire and so I keep it pointed away from my hunting companions.

Possibly this isn't the best practice, but I know that many expert hunters do the same thing. I'll publish your letter and see what other hunters have to say.

INCORRECT STOCK CAUSES MISSES

Question: Wonder if you can tell me what's wrong with my shooting. I have a fine double-gun which I got two years ago, but ever since I got it I've done poor shooting at quail and pheasants. On crossing birds I do as well as I ever did, but those easy going-away shots have me licked. Last fall I had a friend stand behind me and he told me that all my wads were going right under the birds that were flying away. I am so disgusted that I'm ready to get rid of the gun. What do you advise?—T. O'M., N. M.

Answer: I don't know the measurements of your stock, but I strongly suspect you are shooting with a gun with too much drop. Shooting under is a common mistake when a gun has too much drop. Measure yours and find out. A good field drop is 1½ in. at the comb and 2½ in. at the heel. Quail and pheasants are usually shot rising and driving away from the gun, and the ideal stock for such work is rather straight and throws the charge a bit high, just as a trap gun does. However, trap measurements are, I think, too straight for most field shooting. You can, of course, get a new stock made, or you can get the present stock straightened at most factories for a nominal charge. It might be a good idea for you to try some skeet and see if you can find a gun that suits you before you have yours changed.

SIGHTING TROUBLE

Question: I have been shooting shotguns in the field for about 20 years, but in the last 2 years I have developed a fault in my pointing that has impaired my shooting ability. It seems as if I were looking down the *side* instead of down the top of the barrel when I hold the gun to my shoulder. I point from my right shoulder, with both eyes open.

Most of my shooting is done at doves and quail, using 16 gauge repeaters—one a Winchester, the other an Ithaca with a Poly-Choke. The Winchester has a 28-in. barrel with a solid rib; the Ithaca barrel is 26 in. long. Many birds are just winged, and I don't hit nearly so often as I did in the past. Can you tell me what is the matter?—T. C. S., Tex.

Answer: I think what has happened is that for some reason which I cannot explain, probably from some defect in your vision, your left eye has become the master eye. That sometimes happens with right-handed shooters. When it does, a man finds that he cannot shoot.

I note that you shoot with both eyes open. Ordinarily that is a thing to be encouraged. Now, however, you cannot do that any longer. The only way you can cure yourself, I am sure, is to close your left eye so that your right eye can take over. That would be far easier than learning to shoot from the left side.

SHOTGUN SIGHTS AND 'SCOPES

Question: I am a mediocre shot, and am wondering if installing a Nydar sight on my Remington 12 gauge auto would help me to improve my average on cornfield pheasants.—E. B., Minn.

Answer: I believe either the Nydar shotgun sight or the Weaver 1X shotgun 'scope will help the hunter who has a tendency (and it's a common one) to shoot over his game. Most of us get excited, shoot too fast, see too much barrel —and the charge goes over the bird. With either of the devices mentioned, the fact that the pattern will go over is instantly apparent.

However, all they do is make the picture clearer. The man behind the gun still has to go on from there: swing, lead, and pull the trigger.

EXCITEMENT CAUSES MISSES

Question: In shooting birds I get a very much higher percentage of swinging shots than straightaways. I seem to shoot too quickly on the former and take in too much barrel. What's the remedy— a longer stock?—J. O. M., Mo.

Answer: I do not think there is any particular cure except practice and training for your habit of seeing too much barrel and shooting too quickly on crossing birds. That is a common habit of the excited hunter; he gets his blood pressure up, doesn't get his cheek down on the comb, shoots too fast, and misses.

I suggest that you practice counting *1, 2, 3,* as you shoot—*1* when you mount your gun and get your feet in position, *2* when you get your cheek down on the comb and begin your swing, and *3* as you fire. I think a little more deliberateness will cool you off and start you hitting.

FACTS YOU SHOULD KNOW ABOUT CHOKES

BEST CHOKE FOR BUCKSHOT

Question: I expect to buy a 12 gauge double-barrel shotgun, with 30-in. barrels. This gun will be used only for deer hunting—the law 'in this state does not permit rifles. What choke will give the best pattern when using No. 0 or No. 00 buckshot?—L. E. M., N. J.

Answer: It has been my experience that a gun bored somewhere between quarter and modified choke will give the best patterns with Nos. 0 and 00 buckshot. A full choke seems to give the best accuracy with rifled slugs, but with buckshot I have found that the more open boring is best.

As a matter of fact, improved cylinder often does very well. Some years ago Ithaca built a 10 gauge Magnum to handle large buckshot only and to get patterns as close as possible. When they got through experimenting with barrels, they were getting 100 percent patterns and the amount of constriction in the choke was about that of improved cylinder.

If I were you, I would get a gun that is bored about modified choke. I think you will get very respectable buckshot patterns with it.

REDUCING RECOIL WITH A COMPENSATOR

Question: Although I have never used a Cutts Compensator, I have always understood that it reduces the recoil of a shotgun. A friend of mine in the Ordnance Department says that it has no effect on recoil. Would you mind giving me the facts?

I have a 12 gauge Ithaca Model 37 repeater and would like to get a variable-choke attachment so I can use it for duck hunting. The gun is so light that I hesitate to use heavy duck loads unless the recoil can be cut down.—A. J. S., Va.

Answer: Your pal in the Ordnance Department is a bit off the beam. The recoil of a shotgun *is* reduced about 30 percent by the use of either a Weaver Choke or a Cutts Compensator. However, the diversion of the gases results in a rather sharp muzzle blast. It has never bothered me, but some people profess not to like it.

If you are sensitive to recoil I am afraid that even with the Cutts Compensator or the Weaver Choke, the Ithaca Featherlight might be rather unpleasant to shoot with heavy duck loads. I think, however, that for about 90 percent of all shooting the standard load of $3\frac{1}{4}$ drams of powder and $1\frac{1}{8}$ oz. of shot will be entirely satisfactory.

CHOKE CONTROL

Question: I have a 12 gauge automatic shotgun, bored improved-cylinder. I got it especially for quail, but now that I've taken up duck hunting I find that it hasn't got enough range. Does that mean another barrel or a Poly-Choke? The latter appeals to me.—R. W. P., Va.

Answer: The Poly-Choke, for a better all-round gun. With it you can get any pattern you wish from a true cylinder to about 70 percent. To my notion, the day is coming when all single-barrel shotguns will be equipped with some such gadget.

POLY-CHOKE ON A SKEET GUN

Question: I own a Winchester Model 12 trap-grade shotgun with a ventilated rib, a Poly-Choke, and a 28-in. barrel. The stock is $14\frac{3}{4}$ in., with pistol grip and a drop of $2\frac{3}{4}$ in. In the last few years I have been doing a lot of skeet shooting and find that I keep missing the low-house bird on No. 8. I think it is because the barrel is too long.

If I have the Poly-Choke removed to shorten the barrel, what will I have left? Will there be enough choke remaining to make any sort of pattern?—V. E. H., Ill.

Answer: Why don't you simply send your gun to the Poly-Choke Co. and have them install that Poly to give an overall barrel length of 26 in.? That would be handy for skeet.

All the choke was removed from the barrel when the Poly-Choke was put on, so that it could function properly. If you simply removed it, you would have only a straight-cylinder barrel which would give you patchy and unreliable patterns.

DETERMINING CHOKE

Question: Will you please tell me how I can measure the choke of my shotgun so I can tell what choke it is?—N. B., Wis.

FINDING CHOKE

To determine choke, tack up a 5-ft. square of paper and follow the steps as illustrated.

Answer: The only way to determine choke is to try it out for pattern, since the gun manufacturers bore their chokes to definite formulas. The standard method of determining choke is by the amount of shot it will put into a 30-in. circle at 40 yd. from the muzzle of the gun. Fire three or four patterns at the centers of as many 5-ft. squares of paper, and then inscribe each with a 30-in. circle—taking in as much shot as possible. Count the number of shot within each circle, average them, and then compare the final figure with the amount of pel-

lets in the particular charge you are using. A full-choke gun should shoot patterns of 70 percent or better. A modified choke shoots around 60 percent, an improved-cylinder from 50 to 60. Actually there are only about three real chokes: improved-cylinder, modified, and full. However, various companies list all kinds: skeet, improved-cylinder, quarter choke, half choke, modified, improved-modified, and full.

REPLACING SHOT WITH SLUG

Question: I would appreciate receiving your answers to the following questions:

1. When a variable-choke device such as the Weaver, Cutts, or Poly-Choke is installed on a full-choke barrel, must the choke be cut off?

2. When using slugs in a shotgun, must the barrel be cylinder bore?

3. If a shot load is removed from a shell and replaced with a much heavier slug, does the chamber pressure increase and is this dangerous?—F. S., Ariz.

Answer: Yes—if a Weaver, Cutts, or Poly-Choke is mounted on a shotgun, the barrel has to be cut back to the true cylinder portion, or else all of the choke has to be bored out of it to give a true cylinder.

Slugs can be used in a full-choke barrel because they are hollow at the base and contract when they hit the choke.

I never have tried removing the shot from a shell and replacing it with a slug, but I have heard from many people who have tried it and who got away with it. I am not guaranteeing it, however.

VARIABLE CHOKE IMPROVES SHOOTING

Question: I used to shoot a 12 ga. single-barrel Stevens, and my hitting was close to 100 percent. Not long ago I acquired a Winchester 12 ga. automatic (Model 40) and my shooting now is way below par. The barrels of the two guns are of the same length, as are the stocks. However, the auto is 4 in. longer overall than my old gun. I've figured it out that this extra length, and the fact that the auto has modified choke, cause my poor shooting. Do you agree? And, if you were I, would you have the barrel of the automatic shortened and install a variable-choke device?—E. H., Mich.

Answer: I think you are correct in your assumption that the long barrel and the modified choke are handicaps to you. It may also be that using a heavier gun makes you a little slower in your swing. I believe that shortening the barrel and installing a variable-choke device will cure a lot of your trouble. In case you select a Poly-Choke, have the barrel cut off to 25 in. If it's a Cutts or a Weaver, I'd suggest shortening the barrel to 23 or 24 in. Your gun so altered will swing and handle faster, and by using an open adjustment, will be right there with a good improved-cylinder pattern.

QUARTER CHOKE TOO OPEN FOR PHEASANT

Question: Please tell me if my quarter-choke tube is all right for pheasants if I use No. 6's and low-velocity shells. What tube would be best for doves and ducks? Do high-velocity shells improve upland shooting?—P. W., N. M.

Answer: I believe you would find the quarter-choke tube a bit too open for most pheasant hunting. I'd use about a half choke (because of its denser pattern) and standard shells with 1⅛ oz. of No. 6 shot and 3¼ drams of powder.

For all-round dove shooting I'd use No. 7½ or 8 shot with a half choke. If you expect to take most of your doves close to a water hole the quarter-choke would be better. If your duck shooting is exclusively pass-shooting, the full-choke tube is best.

For upland shooting I don't think there's any advantage in using high-velocity loads.

ADVANTAGES OF IMPROVED CYLINDER

Question: I have a 12 gauge Remington automatic shotgun with an improved-cylinder barrel. Is this a suitable type of choke for general hunting? How does it differ from modified choke and full choke?—J. H. J., Okla.

Answer: The improved cylinder is a very good choke to use in upland gunning for quail, woodcock, and cottontails. It is easier to hit at close range with the improved-cylinder bore, and because of the wide dispersion of shot the game is less torn up than when a tighter choke is used. Up to 30 yd. an improved cylinder will kill just as well as anything else, and as a usual thing it will take even ducks to more than 35 yd.

The improved cylinder will usually pattern between 45 and 50 percent of its shot in a 30-in. circle at 40 yd. The modified choke should pattern at least 60 percent, and the full choke 70 percent or better.

SKEET CHOKE GOOD FOR GAME

Question: I have an opportunity of buying either of two shotguns, for use on rabbits and birds, but both are "skeet choke." What kind of choke is that? Would it be any good for the kind of hunting I want to do?—J. S., Pa.

Answer: The skeet choke is a very good one for either rabbit or bird hunting. In fact, the skeet bore is one of the best game chokes made, as it will throw a wide, even pattern at the closer ranges in which game is generally killed. Actually, the skeet chokes are simply variations on the improved-cylinder. The right barrel usually patterns about 45 percent and the left barrel from 50 to 55 percent, although some left barrels in skeet guns are true modified chokes and pattern about 60. I have done a lot of shooting with a skeet gun and have found the choke about the finest for short-range work that I have ever run into. As a matter of fact, those skeet chokes will kill ducks well up to nearly 40 yd., and most shooting is done at less than 35.

CHOKE OF DOUBLE-BARREL GUN

Question: I have a 16 gauge Fox double-barrel shotgun with 28-in. barrels. Is it true that each barrel has a different pattern? I will appreciate your explaining the difference.

Also, I'd like your opinion of No. 7½ and No. 6 shot. I expect to do a lot of rabbit, grouse, and pheasant hunting in New Jersey. What is the best load for this kind of game?—P. D., N. Y.

Answer: As a usual thing the standard double-barrel shotgun is bored to give modified—about 60 percent—patterns in the right barrel, which is fired by the forward trigger, and full choke, or about 70 percent patterns in the left barrel. Ordinarily one uses the front trigger and fires the more open right barrel for his close shots and the rear trigger for more distant ones.

For New Jersey pheasants any size shot from No. 7½ through No. 6 would be perfectly O. K. If I were you I would use the standard load of 3¼ drams of powder and 1⅛ oz., of shot such as found in the Winchester Ranger or Western Xpert. The maximum loads give rather severe recoil and often make a flincher out of a beginner.

BEST GUN FOR SHORT RANGE

Question: In the fall I intend to buy a 20 gauge double-barrel shotgun to be used only on grouse and woodcock. What choke would you recommend? Most of my hunting is done in the brush, and

the range at which most of my game is taken is from 15 to 25 yd. I snap-shoot a great deal and very seldom shoot at birds that are 30 yd. or more away, as I don't like to take a chance of catching them with the edge of the pattern and wounding them.

Another thing, do you think I should get a pistol grip, and do you recommend automatic ejectors?—E. R., Nova Scotia.

Answer: A good many companies make a gun that would be ideal for you—the double-barrel skeet model as put out by Winchester, by Parker, by Marlin, by L. C. Smith, by Fox, and by Ithaca. These guns are bored exactly right for grouse and woodcock hunting in thick cover—a wide improved cylinder in the right barrel, and about quarter choke or 55 percent in the left. In most of these guns you have an option of pistol grip or straight grip; I prefer the pistol grip. And by all means get automatic ejectors.

OPENING UP A .410

Question: I have a Marlin .410 over-and-under with both barrels full choke, which for my purpose is too close, as I want to have a good boring for skeet and for quail and doves. What boring should I ask for when I send the barrels back to Marlin to be opened up. I average 18 x 25 with the gun at skeet, and once broke 24.—C. C. C., Ky.

Answer: At best you can't open a .410 to improved cylinder or any other skeet cylinder, since you simply don't have the shot to throw around. I don't know just what the boring of the .410 skeet gun is, but from having shot a couple of patterns with one, I imagine it is about 60 percent, whereas a 12 or 16 bore pattern would run 45–45 percent. You simply have to hold those babies closer than the larger bores.

Breaking 24 straight at skeet! My hat is off to you. If I ever do that with a .410

I'll declare a legal holiday.

Send that gun back to Marlin and tell them just what you want—as good and even a pattern as you can get at 20 yd. with one barrel, and a killing pattern at 30 with the other. Your 30-yd. barrel should run about 65 percent, I imagine. If you open it up more you surely aren't going to get many doves with it.

NO TRUE CYLINDER BORE

Question: Will you please explain just what is meant by the old "cylinder bore," the "cylinder bore" of today, and "improved cylinder"? Some authorities claim that there is no true cylinder bore made today, and yet I've seen choke listed in catalogues as cylinder, improved cylinder, etc.—H. N. W., Md.

Answer: As I understand it, no straight-cylinder guns have been manufactured for a long time, except for the riot guns intended for short-range shooting with buckshot.

A true cylinder bore gives about 35 percent pattern and is almost useless for game shooting. What the arms companies call the cylinder is, in reality, a very-wide-open improved-cylinder, with a very slight construction. Most so-called cylinder guns will give a pattern of between 40 and 45 percent. Skeet borings are of that type.

Improved-cylinder patterns run from 40 to 55 percent. Some companies call anything beyond 50 percent and less than 60 "quarter choke." Modified runs from 60 to 65, and full choke from 70 percent up. I'll admit that the whole thing is rather confusing, and that the various companies have not standardized on their names. It would be lots better to say that with a certain shot size and powder charge that a gun would average 40 percent patterns, instead of calling a gun a cylinder bore.

Lou Smith of Ithaca says that there ought to be only three borings—improved-cylinder, modified, and full, and that nobody can guarantee patterns closer than that.

CHOKES NOT STANDARDIZED

Question: One of my pals claims the reason shotguns of the same size and choke shoot patterns of different size is because the gun manufacturers do not have a standard measurement for each of the various chokes. Is this correct?

What is the inside diameter of a full-choke 12 gauge barrel measured at the choke?—J. J. B., Mass.

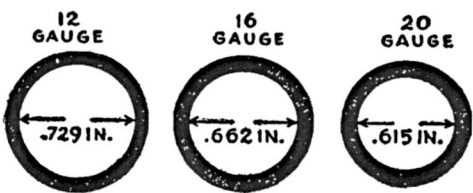

This diagram shows the standard bore measurements of the 12, 16 and 20 gauge shotgun. These gauges are very popular.

Answer: The standard 12 gauge shotgun bore measures .729 in., the standard 16 gauge .662 in., and the standard 20 gauge .615 in. Occasionally manufacturers depart from these standards, particularly for handling large shot for long-range shooting, when they make the bores larger.

The various chokes are given various amounts of constriction. The difference between the bore and the parallel of the choke will run anywhere from .003 to .040 in. An improved-cylinder boring will have from .003 to .005 in. constriction, and a full choke around .040 in. As you can see, the degree of choke is not at all standardized, and often it is found that the gun will throw denser full-choke patterns if the choke is relieved a little. In other words, you simply cannot measure the constriction in a shotgun barrel and tell offhand just what kind of patterns you will get.

The same choke may give 75 percent patterns with No. 4 shot and a certain powder charge, but only a 60 percent or modified pattern with some other size shot and different powder charge.

VARIABLE CHOKE

Question: I'm thinking seriously of having a Poly-Choke installed on my 16 gauge Stevens pump gun, Model 620. It has a 28-in. barrel, bored modified.

I am planning to hunt grouse in New Hampshire, and I believe a more open bore would help me, for I'm only an average shot.

How short would you have the barrel cut for a Poly-Choke? My idea is to make a brush gun out of it, as I have two shotguns with long barrels bored full choke for long-range shooting.—N. C. L., Mass.

Answer: I think it would be well worth your while to convert your Stevens to an upland-grouse gun by the addition of a Poly-Choke. I suggest an overall length of 25 in. You'll probably get a very fine upland pattern with the choke set between cylinder and improved cylinder.

My own 16 gauge Winchester Model 12, equipped with a Poly-Choke, has an overall length of 25 in., and I like it very much.

SKEET NO. 1 AND 2 CHOKES

Question: I have just purchased a new 12 gauge Winchester, Model 21, skeet gun. I have already tried it on clay pigeons thrown from a hand trap and missed very few. I think it will prove fine for rabbits and pheasants, which is about all we have to hunt around here. What do you think?

Could you also tell me something about the No. 1 and 2 Skeet chokes? I'd like to know their approximate killing ranges on the above game.—J. G., Wis.

Answer: You have a very fine shotgun— in my estimation one of the best field guns made, with an excellent beavertail and fine dimensions.

For some shooting, however, that gun is rather open. Skeet No. 1 is a wide-open improved cylinder giving patterns of 35 to 40 percent. Skeet No. 2 is about one quarter choke, giving patterns of 55 percent. Both chokes will kill very dead up to about 35 yd., and on animals the size of small ducks you will kill well at 40 yd.

Let me give you a tip, however. Those two chokes do not pattern worth a hoot with high-velocity ammunition like Nitro Express, Super-X, or Super-W. You will get your most even patterns with the mildly loaded trap and skeet loads. And you will have a very deadly gun on any game, provided you don't try to strain it.

SWAGED OR RECESSED CHOKE?

Question: I have a 12 gauge Remington automatic—Browning patent, cylinder bore, 26-in. barrel—which was once used in the police department here; and I'd like to have the barrel converted to full choke without installing a choke device.

One gunsmith says that for $3 he can constrict the bore to full choke by using a choke roller. Would that be as good as a factory choke?—T. A. P., Calif.

Answer: That gun of yours has a straight cylinder bore with no constriction whatever. I don't know exactly what your gunsmith means by a "choke roller," but I suspect it's his name for swaging.

Two things can be done to give your gun a little choke. It can be swaged—that is, have the muzzle constricted a trifle— or a recessed choke can be bored into it. Neither method is any too hot. Swaged chokes (used on the cheapest of single-barrel guns) are exceedingly unreliable. Recessed chokes are tricky to bore, and it's difficult to get anything but an improved cylinder with one.

Frankly, I think you'd be better off with a Poly-Choke, a Cutts Compensator, or a Weaver-Choke.

WHAT CHOKE FOR UPLAND GAME?

Question: I am having a Poly-Choke installed on my 12 gauge Winchester Model 12 for an overall barrel length of 26 in. Most of my hunting is confined to quail and rabbits at present. I want to pattern my gun and find the proper choke setting. Please suggest some loads to try out. Would you recommend my using Super-X shells?—W. C., Ill.

Answer: About as fine a quail load as I have ever used is the standard trap load, using 3 drams of powder and 1¼ oz. of No. 7½ shot. Another good one for you would be the standard "low-power" hunting load of 3¼ drams of powder and 1⅛ oz. of No. 7½ or 8 shot.

For short-range upland shooting I think you will find that you get very nice improved-cylinder patterns with your Poly-Choke set either at improved cylinder or at the click between improved cylinder and modified.

If I were you, I would certainly not use Super-X or any other maximum load for upland shooting. It is unnecessarily powerful, and the recoil is fairly severe. There is no use in using a long-range duck load on upland game.

VARIABLE CHOKE

Question: I've toyed with this question of choke long enough; so thought it best to ask one who knows. I have a Winchester Model 12, trap grade, with 30-in. barrel and ventilated rib, which I use for all my game-bird shooting, starting with doves. It's a perfectly choked job, but I'm wondering if I'd do better with a variable choke.—C. C. R., Ariz.

Answer: If you set great store on a really full choke, you can get just as good or even better full-choke patterns from a Cutts Compensator and one of the extra-full-choke tubes. I wouldn't hesitate to whack that barrel off and install a choke device. In your case I believe I'd select the Cutts Comp, and since you've been used to a pretty long barrel I'd cut it down to 24 in. and then have the choke added.

I imagine that your present choke is an improved modified, giving patterns of between 67 and 70 percent. The gun companies long since discovered that people who say they want full choke don't really mean it. Consequently, the gun marked full choke is not ordinarily a "very full" full choke.

Just wait till you turn loose on doves with the Cutts all-purpose choke. You'll be surprised how well you can shoot!

SHOTGUN LOADS AND CHOKES

Question: Will you please answer the following questions: 1. What system of weights is used in measuring powder for shotgun loads? 2. What does the expression, drams equivalent mean with reference to high-velocity shells? 3. A barrel that gives a 50 percent pattern is said to be quarter choke; 60 percent is half choke, and 65 to 68 percent is three-quarter choke; how did these terms originate?—H. A. L., Mich.

Answer: The avoirdupois system is used in loading shotgun shells. A dram (or drachm) is equivalent to $27\frac{11}{32}$ gr.

The term, drams equivalent, means simply that the shell is loaded with dense powder to give the velocity equivalent of that amount of black powder or bulk smokeless.

As a usual thing, a barrel between 50 and 55 percent is supposed to be quarter choke; a 60-percent-choke barrel is a half choke; and one of 65 to 68 percent is improved modified. Those terms have been used for many years, but different companies have different notions of what constitutes the various choke.

FACTS ABOUT LOADS AND LOADING

USE OF BUCKSHOT FOR DEER

Question: I have failed to stop the last five bucks I shot at, at 40 yd. or less, using standard 2¾-in. shells with 27 pellets of No. 4 buck, which I prefer for the same reason that some duck hunters prefer No. 7½. For many years I hunted deer in Maine and Pennsylvania with a rifle, killing nine out of the last 10 I shot at. Five of these were running shots, and six required only a single bullet. So you see my marksmanship is all right. What about a 10 or 12 gauge Magnum for shooting deer in my state, where the law calls for a shotgun?—J. D. S., N. J.

Answer: I have never had any great respect for the shotgun as a deer killer, even at short ranges. From the dope I get from old buckshot hunters, however, the best stunt seems to be to use the smaller size of buck, rather than No. 00 buck, because the chances are better that a vital spot like the heart, brain, or backbone will be struck.

As far as I can learn, the 10 gauge shell comes with only one type of buckshot load—16 pellets of No. 0 buck—as against 12 pellets of the same size shot in the 12 gauge. The 10 and 12 gauge Magnums are long-range wild-fowl shells only and are not loaded with buckshot.

As a wild guess, based on the use of BB shot for coyotes and bobcats, I should think that probably the most deadly load one could get for deer would be a 10 gauge Magnum with a 3½-in. shell loaded with 2 oz. of BB shot.

AGE LITTLE FACTOR WITH SHELLS

Question: Do shotgun shells lose their power after a few years? Last winter I was hunting with some shells that were about 4 years old. My gun is a 20 gauge Ithaca and I shot a great horned owl five times before he dropped.—R. R., Ill.

Answer: Modern shotgun powders do not deteriorate with age. If anything, they get drier and give higher pressures—in other words, they are stronger rather than weaker.

RANGE OF SLUGS AND BUCKSHOT

Question: At what approximate range will rifled slugs kill a deer when fired from a 16 gauge shotgun? Also, what is the maximum range of buckshot when used in the same gun?—B. C., N. H.

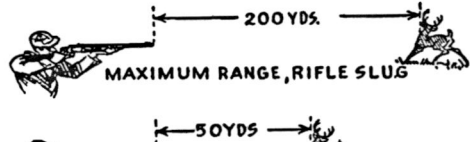

Hitting a deer in the lungs with a 16 gauge rifled slug will score a hit at 200 yd, while the most effective range of the best patterning buckshot is only about 50 yd.

Answer: If you hit a deer in the lungs with a 16 gauge rifled slug I believe you will kill him up to 200 yd. Catch is, however, to hit him in the lungs at that distance. I would say that a man who is a pretty good shot should be able to hit a deer up to about 100 yd. with those rifled slugs; and at that range the heavy, large-diameter slug should kill pretty well with almost any solid body hit.

Buckshot is something else. It's my guess that the effective range of the best-patterning buckshot is only about 50 yd.

ARGUMENT ABOUT SHOT-SHELL VELOCITIES

Question: Please settle an argument about shotgun-shell velocities. One man claims there is no difference in the speed of shot fired from an ordinary heavy-load

12 gauge shell, and that of the 3-in. Magnum shell of the same gauge. The other side maintains that the shot from 3-in. shells fired in his over-and-under shotgun travels faster and has more shocking power at 40 yd. than the regular heavy load. Neither party will accept any evidence the other can produce, so now it's up to you!—W. B. L., Minn.

Answer: Here's the dope to settle your argument: The Winchester 3-in. Super Speed Magnum load, with 1⅝ oz. No. 6 chilled shot, has an average velocity, over 40 yd., of 965 foot seconds; the standard Super Speed load of the same make—but using 1¼ oz. No. 6 chilled shot, has an average velocity over the same distance of 975 foot seconds. In other words, the lighter shot charge travels slightly faster.

However, the 3-in. Magnum shell would have greater killing power for the simple reason that it would hit the bird with more shot.

LOADS FOR DUCK AND DEER

Question: Do you think the 4C load in a 20 ga. is good for large ducks at medium range? How does No. 3 buckshot rate for deer?—C. M., Tex.

Answer: I don't think very much of using No. 4 chilled in the 20 ga. for ducks. I wouldn't use anything larger than No. 6. If you do, your patterns are going to be awfully thin. I think you will do fairly well with No. 3 buckshot for deer. That's O. K. for the 20.

SHORT SHELLS IN STANDARD CHAMBER

Question: I recently purchased a standard 16 gauge pump gun with a 2¾-in. chamber. The only shells I have been able to buy for it are 2⁹⁄₁₆-in. long. Is it all right to use these short shells in the gun?—N. Z., Mass.

Answer: Almost all 16 gauge shells have 2⁹⁄₁₆-in. cases, although the standard 16

gauge chamber is now 2¾ in. You needn't worry. You can get good patterns with the 2⁹⁄₁₆-in. case in the standard chamber.

RIFLED SLUGS WON'T HARM BARREL

Question: Many people claim that the use of rifled slugs in shotguns injures the barrels. If this is so, why don't the firms which make these shells discontinue them or warn prospective users of the danger involved?—C. R. A., Md.

Answer: Do not worry. Rifled slugs have hollow bases which contract when they hit the choke. Their use will not harm a good gun at all.

SHELLS FOR A 12 GAUGE AUTOMATIC

Question: I recently bought a 12 gauge Remington autoloader in new condition. Is it safe to use this gun with long-range factory loads?—G. H., Calif.

Answer: Do not worry; your Remington autoloader is perfectly safe with any standard 2¾-in. 12 gauge shell. That means you can use anything like Super-X or Nitro Express, but of course you cannot use the 3-in. 12 gauge Magnum shells.

BIRDSHOT FOR DEER?

Question: A friend of mine claims a deer's hide is so tough that neither No. 5 nor No. 6 shot in a 12 gauge Super-X shotgun load will penetrate it at 25 yd. I say that it will not only penetrate but mortally wound the animal if it strikes a vital spot. Please set us straight on this matter.—J. H., Ohio.

Answer: I believe you would find that either No. 5 or No. 6 shot would penetrate a deer's hide at 25 yd. Whether the deer would be killed outright, however, is a question, although he undoubtedly would die, sooner or later, of his wounds. At 25 yd. even a full-choke pattern is opening up quite a bit.

I think that No. 2 shot would probably kill a deer with a chest hit at that distance, but I am doubtful about No. 5 or No. 6. I know I have knocked down coyotes at what I estimated to be 25 and 35 yd. with No. 7½ shot, only to have them get up and run away.

PROPER LOADS

Question: Will you please tell what loads of chilled shot should be used on partridge, crows, pheasants, ducks, geese? I use a Savage skeet automatic, 12 gauge, with Cutts Compensator.—E. H., N. Y.
Answer: Partridges: 3 drams powder, 1⅛ oz. of No. 6 or 7½ shot. Crows: 3¼ drams, 1⅛ oz. 6's. Pheasants: 3¼ drams, 1⅛ oz. Lubaloy 6's. Ducks: 3½ drams, 1¼ oz. 5's or 6's (rarely 4's). Geese: 3½ drams, 1¼ oz. of 2's.

KILLING POWER OF LIGHT SHOT

Question: Most of my hunting is done in the tall timber of Arkansas, and it is tricky long-distance shooting. However, I've never had to use a 10 gauge with No. 4 shot to make kills at 60 yd., as is often recommended. I use a Remington Model 26 with a 30-in. barrel, with any one of a number of duck loads, but always with No. 7½ shot. I wouldn't trade those 7½'s for any load, and I'm not troubled by an undue number of crippled birds. I might use No. 6 shot for geese when shooting from an open sand bar, but I prefer 7½'s in oat fields and other feeding spots.

Why do so-called sportsmen clamor for blunderbuses that kill hapless birds more by their report and concussion than by their shot?—E. A. B., Ark.
Answer: I too have often advocated the more general use of smaller shot sizes, but I am afraid that if you actually measured it you would find you were not making very many 60-yd. kills with No. 7½ shot.

That size of shot is O. K. up to about 45 yd. It is so light, however, that its velocity falls off rapidly beyond that, as does its power to penetrate.

Just for the fun of it, get off a full 60 yd., someday, and shoot a load of No. 4's and a load of No. 7½'s into a soft-pine board. Then dig the shot out. When you see how much farther the No. 4's will penetrate because of the greater retained velocity and greater energy, I think you will agree with me. I suspect your 60-yd. shots have been about 45 yd.

OPEN BORE BEST FOR BUCKSHOT

Question: Last fall I shot a deer with buckshot—a Super-X shell loaded with 16 pellets which I had molded myself—at about 50 yd. Upon skinning him out I found three pellets in him, one in the shoulder and two along the backbone. I was astonished at this evidence of fairly close patterning, since my gun is cylinder bore, not full choke.

My uncle tells me that a cylinder bore will always give a denser pattern with buckshot than will a full choke. Is this true?—C. M., Ala.
Answer: I think your uncle is right. Usually a more open bore *will* throw denser buckshot patterns than a full choke. I do not know exactly why this is so, but it works out in practice.

Once the Ithaca Gun Co. built a special 10 gauge Magnum to handle nothing but buckshot, for use on polar bears from a pitching boat. Ithaca succeeded in getting that gun to pattern *all* the buckshot load into a 30-in. circle at 40 yd., and the constriction of the choke was about that of an improved cylinder.

DUCKS GET AWAY

Question: I have a 12 gauge Remington automatic shotgun and do very well with it on squirrels and rabbits. But on ducks, I generally just make them lose a little altitude and a few feathers. My friends tell me that chilled shot will not kill a duck unless it hits him in a vital spot. Is this true?—W. S. G., Tenn.

Answer: The reason those ducks you shot at didn't stop was that you didn't hit them with enough shot. It's just an old wives' tale that soft shot will expand and deliver more shock to a bird. If you feather a bird, and he continues to fly, it shows that you were either shooting out of range or catching the bird on the edge of your pattern.

BB'S FOR SHELLS?

Question: Is it possible to remove the rifled slug from a 16 gauge shell and fill it up with regular BB pellets, as other shot shells are filled, or must I put in only a certain number of these pellets? If this procedure is possible, would the result be a good shell for turkey and wild geese?—M. S., Pa.

Answer: You could remove the slugs and load those shells with 1¼ oz. or BB shot. If I were you, however, I would confine the load of BB's to 1⅛ oz. I wouldn't say that such shells would be first-rate geese loads, as you wouldn't have very many BB's and the pattern would be pretty thin. I think No. 2's or No. 3's would be better for geese.

.410 SLUG NOT FOR DEER

Question: I've seen 20, 16, and 12 gauge slugs used on deer, and noted that they carry terrific shock and kill very cleanly. How would the .410 shotgun slug be as a deer killer?—J. T. R., Ill.

Answer: It would be criminal to use that little slug on deer; it would wound far oftener than it would kill. The .410 slug weighs only 93 gr. and has a muzzle energy of only 460 foot pounds. The 20 gauge slug is an entirely different proposition, weighing 282 gr. and having a muzzle energy of 1,245 foot pounds.

BEWARE OVERSIZE BALL SHOT

Question: I have a 20 gauge single-barreled shotgun which I use for deer. I used a Lyman mold to make the balls I load with. Now, the ones I turn out this way are bigger than factory-made balls. They will sit right on the end of the barrel, whereas the factory-made ones drop right through. Will the homemade balls hurt my gun? When I fired ten of them the gold-and-ivory part of the front sight came off.—H. R. C., Nova Scotia.

Answer: Don't use those balls if they are larger than the choke. Evidently the mold you have is for a 20 gauge *cylinder* bore. When you use those oversize balls you are getting high pressures and are probably damaging the choke of the gun. The factory-made balls are sized so that they will pass through a tight choke. I would bet that you are getting very high and dangerous pressures.

00 TOO THIN FOR GEESE

Question: Is it true that No. 00 or No. 1 buckshot will groove or injure a shotgun in any way? Would buck be of any use on geese?—R. J., Utah.

Answer: No, buckshot will not harm or groove your barrel. However, either No. 00 or 1 has too thin a pattern for geese —or anything else except deer.

RIFLE AMMO IN A SCATTERGUN?

Question: I have a .410 gauge Iver Johnson shotgun chambered for the 3-in. shell and have been thinking about buying a rifle for deer hunting. However, a friend tells me that he uses .44/40 rifle cartridges in his .410 for deer hunting. The cartridges do seem to fit the chamber all right, but I would like to know if this is a safe practice.—G. R., Quebec.

Answer: If you want to live to a ripe old age all in one piece, don't try to use .44/40 ammunition in your .410 gauge shotgun! Those rifle cartridges develop about three times as much pressure as shotgun shells, and I would not dream of shooting them in a scattergun under any circumstances. You might get away with it once or twice—or the gun might blow up at the first shot. It's best to be on the safe side and use in any gun only the ammunition for which it was designed.

VELOCITIES OF 12 GAUGE SHOT

Question: What is the muzzle velocity of maximum loads such as Super-X in a 12 gauge shotgun with a 30-in. barrel? How many foot seconds are lost if the barrel is shortened to 24 in.?—E. C., Tenn.

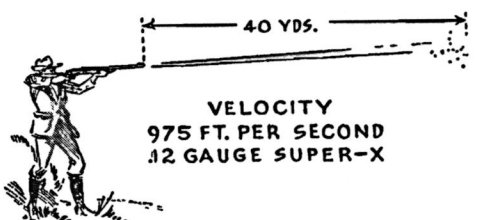

VELOCITY
975 FT. PER SECOND
12 GAUGE SUPER-X

A maximum load in a 12 gauge shotgun with 30 in. barrel gives a velocity of 975 foot seconds over a 40 yd. course.

Answer: The velocity of 12 gauge Super-X ammunition with 3¾ drams equivalent of powder and 1⅛ oz. of shot in a 30-in. barrel is 975 foot seconds, average over a 40-yd. course. For every inch you cut off the barrel, subtract 7½ foot seconds.

LOAD FOR A LIGHTWEIGHT 12 GAUGE

Question: Recently I bought a brand-new Stevens 12 gauge single-barrel shotgun with a 2¾-in. chamber. I'd like to know if it is safe for me to use Super-X shells in it. I have some which measure 2½ in. before firing. Are they the right length for this gun? What game is this gun best suited for?—J. S., N. Y.

Answer: Yes, you could use Super-X shells in that new gun of yours. I wouldn't advise you to do so, however. That is a light gun, and using those

maximum loads will kick you into the middle of next week. Their use might well make a flincher out of you. Stick to the standard load of 3¼ drams of powder and 1⅛ oz. of shot, and you'll be perfectly safe.

The length of the shell should be measured after it has been uncrimped by firing, not before.

In a pinch you could hunt anything from sparrows to wild turkeys with your gun and suitable ammunition.

DON'T USE MAGNUMS!

Question: Can I use 3-in. shells and 3-in Magnum shells in my Stevens 12 gauge, barrel No. 3141?—H. R., Wis.

Answer: It would be positively dangerous for you to use 3-in. Magnum shells in your Stevens 12 gauge. It's chambered for the 2¾-in. shell and I should not think you'd need anything hotter than the high-velocity 12 gauge ammunition, such as Nitro Express and Super-X. Don't use those three-inchers or you may run into some serious trouble.

12 GAUGE AND 12 GAUGE MAGNUM

Question: Can I shoot ordinary 12 gauge shells in a 12 gauge Magnum shotgun, or is this unsafe?—L. M. C., N. Y.

Answer: Ordinary 12 gauge shells can be used in a Winchester Model 12 Magnum. However, your patterns will open up a bit.

EFFICIENCY OF SHOTGUN LOADS

Question: Please tell me if a shotgun load of 3 dr. of powder and 1⅛ oz. of shot is more efficient in a 16 gauge gun than the same load in a 12, both guns being full-choke and all other conditions being equal.—C. G., N. J.

Answer: No, the 1⅛-oz. load in the 16 gauge is a shade *less* efficient than the same load in a 12. The reason is that 16 gauge pressures run a little higher and, because of the longer shot column, there are more deformed shot which fly off. Of course, the difference is more theoretical than practical, but it is true.

POWDER WEIGHT IN SHOTGUN SHELLS

Question: What is the standard weight of powder used in 12 gauge shotgun shells? I have never seen any that were loaded with more than 3¾ drams of powder—regular or highspeed.

Is shotgun-shell loading regulated by federal law?—M. D. C., Pa.

Answer: The maximum load for the standard 2¾-in. 12 gauge shotgun shell is 3¾ drams of power with 1¼ oz. of shot. This holds true for Super-X, Nitro Express, Super Speed, or any other maximum load. Magnum 12's are chambered for 3-in. shells and handle more powder and shot, but they are not true standard 12 gauges.

No federal law controls the amount of powder or shot in shotgun shells. It does, however, forbid the use of any gauge larger than 10 for taking waterfowl, and many states outlaw even the 10 gauge for any hunting. The federal government can regulate only the hunting of migratory birds. Upland game, such as quail and pheasant, is in the hands of the individual states.

HOW TO STORE SHOTGUN SHELLS

Question: I'd like some information on the proper way of storing shotgun shells. I've been told that they belong in a cool, dry place and have been keeping mine in the basement in a room away from the furnace. The room is dry and cool. I could transfer them to the furnace room, which is warmer but not hot. Which would be better—the cooler or the warmer room?—W. P. A., Neb.

Answer: I don't think you need to worry. As long as the room is dry and fairly cool you can keep shotgun shells indefinitely. Don't keep them in a very hot place, or

the powder will dry out. Don't keep them in a very damp place, or the shells will swell.

2¾-IN. SHELLS, 2½-IN. CHAMBER

Question: Ever since I was 15 (I'm now 22) I've been shooting a double-gun that used to belong to my father—a 6¼-lb. L. C. Smith, with 30-in. barrels, that kicks like a mule but fits me like a glove. Is it safe for me to use heavy buckshot loads, and Super-X duck loads (No. 5 chilled)?—F. W. S., N. J.

Answer: It depends on the chambers of your L. C. Smith double. If it was manufactured since about 1925 it has 2¾-in. chambers and will be safe with any modern loads you put in it. On the other hand, some of those 20 gauge guns made before that time had 2½-in. chambers; and shooting 2¾-in. shells like Super-X would raise your pressures dangerously high.

Safest thing for you to do is to write to the service department, Hunter Arms Co., Fulton, N. Y., giving them the serial number of your gun. Ask them what kind of chambers it has, and about using Super-X.

MAXIMUM LOADS IN OLD GUN

Question: I have a 12 gauge J. Stevens Arm & Tool Co. shotgun with single barrel of electro-steel, purchased 30 years ago. I have found that many kinds of ammunition work very well in this gun, and lately have been using Remington Kleanbore Shur Shot and Westen Xpert shells in it. These shells are 2¼ in. long and are loaded with 3¼ drams of powder and 1⅛ oz. No. 6 shot. Is it safe to use loads like this in my gun?—E. H. R., Pa.

Answer: I think you'd be smart to lay off maximum loads like Super-X, Nitro Express, and Super Speed. Stick to the standard load of 3 to 3¼ drams of powder and 1⅛ oz. of shot and you'll be all right. Actually, this load is better than the super-duper stuff for about 95 percent of all hunting anyway.

I consider it unwise to use maximum loads in any old shotgun no matter what grade of steel the barrel is. It's something akin to cramming a 1910 automobile full of high-octane gas and seeing how fast she'll go. Chances are the car will stand up to it, but she might not. It's the same way with a gun; age doesn't improve a gun and modern steels are superior to old ones.

.410 LOAD FOR PHEASANT

Question: What is the most effective size of shot to use in a .410 gauge shotgun on pheasant?—F. D. M., Pa.

Answer: In the first place, I'd be leery about using a .410 on pheasants, which come big and tough, because it would be pretty easy to overstrain your gun. If I had to do so, however, I think I would use No. 7½ or even No. 8 and count on hitting the pheasant in the head or some equally vital spot, rather than hitting him hard with larger shot. Used in the .410 gauge, No. 6 shot—which I believe I'd select for pheasant in a 16 or 12 gauge —would give too thin a pattern.

RIGHT LOAD FOR SMALL GAME

Question: I own a Model 12 Winchester repeater. One barrel (No. WS-1) is for skeet; and, using a Winchester crimp trap load of 3 drams of powder and 1⅛ oz. of No. 7½ chilled shot, patterns 37 percent at 40 yd. in a 30-in. circle. The other barrel is improved modified, shooting a 65 percent pattern with the same load. What shot sizes should I use in each barrel, and at what distances could I kill doves, ducks, pheasants, quail, rabbits, and squirrels?—D. S. S., Wis.

Answer: I've done a lot of game shooting and patterning with chokes identical with yours, and with similar shells, so I think I can give you some fairly accurate data on what to expect.

Doves are pretty easy to kill, and I think you can count on getting them at 35 yd. cleanly with your skeet barrel and No. 7½ shot. Anything larger wouldn't be so hot because your pattern would be thinner. Using the improved-modified barrel and No. 7½ shot, you should be able to take doves up to 45 and sometimes 50 yd.

Because ducks are a little larger than doves, you'll find you can kill them a little farther off, say up to 50 yd., quite regularly. For the skeet barrel I'd recommend No. 7½ shot; for the i.-m. barrel, No. 7½ or No. 6.

Pheasant? I think you'll be safe in assuming you can kill them at between 25 and 35 yd. with No. 7½ shot with your open barrel. Some would prefer No. 6, but the greater number of the smaller No. 7 shot permit broken wings, and head shots which kill instantly. With the i.-m. barrel and either No. 7½ or No. 6 shot, you will drop pheasant cold at between 40 and 45 yd.

Quail are small and have a lot of vitality, so I don't think you'll have much luck with your open barrel at more than 25 yd. You'll kill them farther than that, but you'll also merely wound a good many. The same thing applies to squirrels. But with the i.-m. barrel and No. 7½ shot you'll make clean kills up to about 40 yd. on either quail or squirrel.

Rabbits are larger and do not have much vitality. With No. 6 shot I think you could count on killing them up to 35 yd. in the open barrel, and up to 50 yd. in the choke.

DROP SHOT VS. CHILLED

Question: Is a box of No. 6 shells marked "drop shot" all right to use on pheasants and rabbits? I didn't notice that mark until after I'd bought the box. I have another just like it, except that it's just marked "6."—S. H. E., Pa.

Answer: The terms "drop shot" and "chilled shot" are confusing. Drop shot is simple soft unalloyed shot. Chilled shot has been hardened by some alloy— usually antimony. Drop shot usually does not produce as good patterns as chilled shot does, because when it hits the bore it tends to flatten on one side, or otherwise become deformed. These deformed shot fly off to make a wide pattern; which is why many Southerners like drop shot for quail.

LONG BARRELS DECREASE MUZZLE BLAST

Question: My 16 gauge double-gun has 28-in. barrels and weighs 7½ lb.; right barrel modified and left full choke. It is a very satisfactory gun—comfortable and easy to handle—but seems to produce excessive muzzle blast, which often throws me into a slump where I can't hit anything. I hunt mourning doves and turtle doves, shooting Super Speed shells (3 drams of powder and 1⅛ oz. of shot). When I go to standard loads the blast is slightly decreased.—R. C. P., Cuba.

Answer: I have a gun similar to yours except that the barrels are 26 in. long instead of 28. It ought to have more muzzle blast than yours, and as a matter of fact when I use maximum loads I do notice the blast. However, I never use these shells except for pass shooting at ducks. For most of my shooting, I have found that the ordinary skeet and trap loads do excellently. With them the recoil is much less severe and they are just as deadly. I can see no reason why you should use Super Speed for dove shooting, since the trap and skeet loads with 2¾ drams of powder and 1⅛ oz. of No. 8 chilled, or 2½ drams and 1 oz. of No. 9's do very well.

There's no other way you can reduce the muzzle blast in your double-gun except by getting longer barrels.

STEEL PELLETS UNSATISFACTORY

Question: Is it O.K. to use small steel pellets in my 20 gauge shotgun shells? They are cylindrical, about ¼ in. in diameter and ¼ in. long.—C. T., Iowa.

Answer: No, you cannot use those steel pellets in your shotgun. If you do you'll damage the bore very badly. Furthermore, steel is so light that it would not carry well and would lose its velocity very quickly.

28 GAUGE O.K. FOR UPLAND

Question: It seems to me that judging from the size of the shell, the 28 gauge could be loaded to handle ⅞ oz. of shot instead of the ¾ oz. with which it is now loaded. With the heavier charge it would be an upland gun hard to beat, whereas now it has only the shot charge of the heavy .410.—B. F. B., Calif.

Answer: That could be done without too much trouble, probably, but what would be the point? With ¾ oz. of shot, the 28 is a nice little upland gun, better than the .410 since it seems to shoot better patterns, and probably handles its charge at higher velocities. Another load for the 28 would simply complicate further an already complex situation. If a man wants to shoot more shot he ought to get a 20 gauge and let it go at that. As it is we have too many shot sizes, too many loads, possibly too many gauges.

Seems to me that we have worked too hard trying to make 20's out of .410's, 16's out of 20's, and 12's out of 16's. Ammunition would cost us less if we didn't have to pay the overhead on the manufacture of a lot of odd sizes and loads which only a few men buy. The 28 is a grand little gun, and with its ¾ oz. it's an adequate medium-range upland scattergun right now.

PROPER LOAD FOR OLD 10 GAUGE

Question: I own an old 10 gauge Winchester lever-action shotgun—the "wild-goose gun," I believe they call it. It's well preserved, action is good and tight, original blue is still on all metal parts, inside of barrel is clean. Will it safely take modern 10 gauge shells?—W. P. C., Wyo.

Answer: You'll be all right if you confine yourself to the mild 10 gauge loads for which that gun was designed. I recently had some correspondence with the Winchester people about that model, and they recommend sticking to the Ranger shell using 4¼ drams of powder and 1¼ oz. of shot.

That gun is definitely not safe with anything more powerful—like Super-X or Nitro Express, say, with 4¾ drams of powder and 1⅝ oz. of shot, even though (being 2⅞ in. long) they'll chamber in your gun. And by all means avoid those 3½-in. 10 gauge Magnum loads which handle 2 oz. of shot and are made only for extra-heavy doubles.

As you can see, the old 10 gauge load is nothing more than a high-velocity 12 gauge load; so I doubt if it will kill any farther than an ordinary 12 gauge handling the same amount of shot.

2¾-IN. SHELLS, 3-IN. CHAMBER

Question: My 12 gauge heavy duck gun, a Winchester Model 12, is chambered for 3-in. shells. Would 2¾-in. shells jam the mechanism, or affect the pattern in any way?—V. I., Calif.

Answer: Don't worry; 2¾-in. shells will function perfectly in your 3-in. chamber. They will open up your patterns slightly —between 5 and 10 percent. They will reduce your full choke to something approximating modified choke.

TWIST BARRELS ARE DANGEROUS

Question: I own an old 12 gauge double-gun with 30-in. twist barrels—made by Meriden (Conn.) Firearms Co. and bearing the serial number 36599. Do you think it safe to use high-power stuff in this gun. It's in very good condition. Five years ago I shot at least 2 boxes of Western Super-X (with No. 5 shot) and several boxes of Remington Kleanbore medium load (with No. 6 and 7½ shot)— with excellent results on quail, pheasants, and ducks and no harm to me or the gun.—P. E. L., Calif.

Answer: I'll answer you by telling you a story. About 3 years ago a friend of mine had an old shotgun of good trade but with twist barrels. I told him it was unsafe to use it with any modern smokeless-powder loads and advised him to retire the gun. But he had fired hundreds of Super-X shells through it already and felt perfectly safe in continuing to use it. A week later, when he was shooting doves, the barrels blew out, ruined the gun, and scared him out of 10 years' growth. The same with your gun, you might shoot it the rest of your natural life without a bit of trouble—and it *might* blow up tomorrow.

RANGE OF LEAD SLUGS

Question: What kind of accuracy can one get with lead slugs in the 20 gauge shotgun—at ranges of 100 and 200 yd.? Also, what is the trajectory with high-velocity loads?—C. H., Calif.

Answer: A few years ago I did a good deal of shooting with slugs in 12, 16, and 20 gauge guns. I found that most shotguns put the bullets close enough for one to shoot about a 1-ft. group offhand at 50 or 60 yd. If the shotgun were carefully targeted in with the Weaver 1X 'scope one could hit by holding about 1 ft. high at 100 yd. Beyond that distance the trajectory is so curved that hits are a matter of luck and guesswork. I'd say it would be poor practice to shoot big game with those slugs at more than 75 yd.

INFORMATION ABOUT RIFLED SLUGS

Question: I think the subject of rifled slugs gets too little attention. Many deer are killed and plenty are wounded by slugs, but I dare say that most of the slugs shot at them miss their mark. I have some questions to ask about them:

What can you tell me about the trajectory of the rifled slug? What is the maximum range at which it should be used on deer? In what gauge is the slug most accurate? How does the choke affect accuracy?—S. W. H., N. Y.

Answer: Although I hunt in rifleman's country, I have shot rifled slugs experimentally. Using a 12 gauge pump gun, equipped with a Weaver 'scope, I could get 6-in. groups at 100 yd. from a rest, and 1-ft. groups offhand. With the gun sighted in at 50 yd. I found I had to hold about 9 in. high to connect at 100 yd. The range up to 65 yd. is virtually point-blank. I wouldn't advise using a slug at a range much more than 100 yd.

It has been my experience that the best accuracy is obtained with a full-choke barrel. It seems to be generally agreed that rifled slugs will kill with any solid hit. The 12 gauge slug really is a power house. It weighs 415 gr., and has a muzzle velocity of 1,470 foot seconds.

I believe that the reason a lot of people miss shots with slugs is that they do not have the proper sights on shotguns. Many hunters take quick shots, see too much barrel, and shoot too high.

HARD SHOT IS BEST

Question: Can you tell me why I cannot buy 16 gauge shotgun shells of any of the popular makes with No. 6-C (chilled) shot? I carefully patterned my Browning, several years ago, with No. 6 chilled shot, but for several years now all the shells I've been able to buy are marked merely "6." What does this mean?—R. W., Ohio.

Answer: The shells you have been buying are the same as those you used before. The reason you can't buy shells marked "6 chilled" is that the designations "chilled" and "soft" have been discontinued. I recently picked up a box of Remington Express 12 gauge shells, and they were marked plain "6." As a matter of fact, I think the use of soft shot is going to be discontinued entirely. There is no real use for it. Hard or chilled shot always gives a better pattern and kills better.

SHOT FOR DUCKS

Question: Last season I used a duck load of 3 drams of powder and 1⅛ oz. of chilled No. 6's in a pump gun with modified choke. Patterns ran about 60 percent but were patchy. I wonder if the old trap load of 3¼, 1¼, No. 7 chilled, would get me better patterns? About 20 percent of my birds were cripples.—K. E., Mich.

Answer: A man has to shop around a bit and pattern his gun with various sizes of shot and different charges of powder if he is to obtain full efficiency. Some guns will pattern No. 6's like a million dollars but won't pattern 4's, etc., as well. Others will pattern 7's and not 6's, etc.

Some Sunday when you don't have anything to do, why not take that gun of yours, and about five boxes of shells (each a different combination of powder load and shot size), and pattern the piece. Put up big pieces of paper, draw 30-in. circles on them, and shoot at least three patterns with each load. You'll learn which shells feed best results into that gun of yours. For example, maybe that 1⅛ oz. of shot will actually give you a better pattern and a longer killing range than 1¼. You may find, too, that your gun has a decided preference for one size of shot. Anything from 7½ to 6 shot is O.K. for most duck shooting and for pheasants too. At least 95 percent of your kills will be at less than 45 yd.

SHOTGUN CARE, REPAIR AND CONVERSION

BETTER NOT RECHAMBER GUN

Question: My 12 gauge Winchester double-barrel shotgun, Model 24, is chambered for 2¾-in. shells. Could I have this gun rechambered for those powerful new 3-in. shells the company puts out—and if so, would the patterns from 2¾-in. shells still be as good as they are with the present chamber?—W. H. B., Jr., Conn.

Answer: While I am quite sure that your shotgun is strong enough for the rechambering you have in mind, I would advise against your having it done. Your patterns with the shorter shells would not be as good, and the recoil from so heavy a load in a light gun would bounce you around. To handle those 3-in. cannon crackers, a shotgun should be at least a pound heavier than the average 12 gauge gun.

SHOTGUN RECHAMBERED?

Question: I know where I can pick up some 3-in. shells, and I'm wondering whether I ought to have my shotgun rechambered to take them. It's an Ithaca 12 ga. new field grade, with 30-in. barrels, full and modified choke, single trigger, auto ejectors, and has recoil pad and straight stock. I understand these 3-in. shells kick pretty hard. What is your opinion on this?—J. S., Iowa.

Answer: Ithaca wouldn't recommend your having your gun rechambered, and I'm afraid I can't either. Of course it can be done, and in times past Ithaca has put out some guns like yours with 3-in. chambers. But for 3-in. shells you should be using the heavier gun with the longer frame. In a gun of the weight of yours, recoil would be very severe, and when you used the regular 2⅝ and 2¾-in. shells in that long chamber, your patterns would open up a lot through excessive shot deformation. Better leave that gun the way it is. The excessive recoil would be likely to make you a flincher and take away all the fun of shooting.

MAUSER CONVERTED TO SHOTGUN

Question: A friend with whom I do considerable partridge shooting each year is using a Mauser rifle converted to a 16 gauge shotgun. As you probably know, this is a bolt-action job, and it does not appear to me to be any too safe. Will you please give me your opinion on this type of firearm, particularly as to its safety.—G. J. D., Ontario.

Answer: I believe your friend is taking grave chances in using that old converted Mauser. In order to convert a Mauser to a shotgun the locking lugs at the head of the bolt are made inoperative, and the bolt is kept from blowing back only by the auxiliary lug at the root of the bolt handle. Right after the first World War the market was flooded with Mausers converted to shotguns. A good many of those guns have blown up, they're cheap jobs and it's my guess that your friend has one of them. If I were you I'd warn him of the risk he is running.

DON'T SAW OFF THE BARRELS

Question: Please advise me if the 28-in. barrels of my 12 gauge double-barrel shotgun (bored full and modified choke) could be cut to 25 or 26 in. by a good gunsmith; and if doing so would give me a better bird gun? We have some quail hunting here, but it is pretty rough shooting with plenty of cover. I have known several hunters who have had their guns shortened, but the reports of the results are so conflicting that I cannot get a conclusive answer. What would the pattern be if I have the barrels shortened?—W. W. J., N. C.

Answer: I would advise you not to get those shotgun barrels sawed off. Afterward you would have nothing left but straight cylinders which would give patchy and very unreliable patterns. You might kill with a good hold on one shot, and only wound on the next one. The best thing would be for you to send your gun back to the service department of the manufacturer and have the choke opened up somewhat.

RECHAMBERING 12 GAUGE STEVENS

Question: I am wondering whether to have my 12 gauge Stevens rechambered for 3-in. shells. This gun has 30-in. barrels, the right modified, the left full choke.—R. A., Ind.

Answer: I am extremely doubtful of the advisability of rechambering a 12 gauge Stevens double-gun for 3-in. shells. Even if the gun is strong enough, the recoil would be excessive and shooting it would be unpleasant.

I suggest you write the service department, J. Stevens Arms Co., Chicopee Falls, Mass., asking their opinion. Give them the serial number of the gun.

SHOTGUN RECHAMBERED

Question: I have a double-barrel .410 Springfield shotgun. I'd like to have the chamber rebored at a machine shop so that it will handle the 3-in. shells—provided it will continue to take 2½-in. shells as well.—L. E. McC., N. M.

Answer: Yes, I believe that shotgun of yours can easily be rechambered to take 3-in. shells. I'd advise you to send it to a gunsmith, for the average machinist doesn't know much about guns.

ON SHORTENING A SHOTGUN BARREL

Question: I have a Winchester Model 97 shotgun with a 30-in., full-choke barrel. I would like to know if it is possible to cut off part of the barrel and make a modified choke out of it. How much should be cut off?—M. V., N. Y.

Answer: If you cut off much of that barrel you will destroy all of the choke. If you cut off any of it, what choke you would get would be open to question.

My advice would be that if you want a shorter barrel, which is advisable, you should fit a Cutts Compensator or a Weaver-Choke to give an overall length of 26 in. with the spreader or skeet tube in place. Or you could have a Poly-Choke installed to give the same overall length. In either case, you would then have a shorter barrel that would have some choke in it.

SHORTER BARREL ON PUMP

Question: My 12 gauge pump shotgun has a 30-in. barrel, on which I am planning to install a Poly-Choke for all-round hunting; everything from grouse to ducks. After using a friend's pump with 26-in. barrel, I decided it handled much faster than my own; so have been thinking of having my own barrel cut off considerably when the Poly is installed. My only worry is that I might lose considerable pattern and range. What do you advise?—V. A. M., Wis.

Answer: I agree heartily that a pump with a short barrel is much faster and easier to handle than one with a long barrel. The long receiver on the pump gives plenty of sighting radius, even when the barrel is chopped off considerably. Loss of velocity between a 30 and a 26-in. barrel is so slight that one could never tell the difference in the field. Get that long-Tom barrel chopped off by the Poly-Choke people by all means. As for loss of pattern—well, I have a 16 pump with a Poly-Choke and a barrel of 25 in. overall. It gives me from 70 to 74 per cent patterns, set at full choke and using the 1⅛-oz. duck loads with No. 6 shot.

CHANGING GUN'S DOWN PITCH

Question: The down pitch of my 20 gauge Winchester pump gun is 2¼ in. I have shot the gun for three years and it seems to shoot low, especially if I fail to keep my cheek down hard on the stock. Please tell me how I can correct the pitch.—R. C. G., Ky.

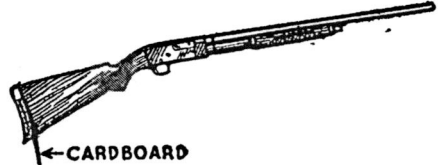

←CARDBOARD

Change the pitch of a shotgun by inserting cardboard underneath the lower end of the stock between the wood and the butt plate.

Answer: Try putting some pieces of cardboard underneath the toe (lower end of the butt) of your stock, between the wood and the butt plate. You can change the pitch that way very easily, experimenting until you get it just right.

CORRECTING SHOTGUN PITCH

Question: For 20 years, or more I shot a 20 gauge Parker, with 28-in. barrels and about 2¾ in. of down pitch. I used it for everything from jacksnipes to geese and it shot very well. A couple of years ago I picked up a little higher-grade Parker which was a mate to my old one except that it was a little heavier and had 30-in. barrels. It did not have a recoil pad on it, so when I had one put on I had all the pitch taken out.

Now while I find this new gun is just as good on ducks as the old one was, it doesn't handle so well in the field. I attribute some of this to the extra 2 in. of barrel length and its feel of being a little muzzle-heavy. I'm planning to put back about 1 in. of down pitch, and am wondering if this can be accomplished by

buffing off the toe of the recoil pad a little?—P. H. O., Wash.

Answer: I think you have correctly diagnosed your trouble. A gun with zero pitch doesn't handle very fast.

To correct it, you won't need to take much off the toe. I'd suggest simply buffing the toe down until the gun feels about right. You'll probably find it fits snugly to the shoulder and handles fast when you reach a down pitch of somewhere between 1½ and 2 in. So as you buff, keep trying it and measuring the pitch. A little off the toe makes considerable difference at the end of the barrel, where it's measured.

TO PLUG SHOTGUN MAGAZINE

Question: What is the best way to plug my pump gun so that it will conform to the migratory waterfowl laws? My gun is a 20 gauge Winchester, Model 12, and I thought perhaps I could do the job.

Another thing, this gun fits me perfectly and I do rather good work with it, but it has one drawback—it will take only the short 20 gauge shells. Would it be possible to have the gun fixed so that I can shoot both the large and the small sizes?—R. A. S., Neb.

Answer: About the best way I can suggest for you to plug that gun is to get a screwdriver, remove the front end of the magazine, insert the plug inside the spring, then put it together again.

Why not send your shotgun to the service department of the Winchester Repeating Arms Co., New Haven, Conn., and have it rechambered and otherwise altered for 2¾-in. shells? You could then use anything in it.

WAYS TO CORRECT LOW SHOTS

Question: I had a variable-choke device installed on my shotgun and now I find that the gun shoots about 6 in. low at 20 yd. I have been told that the gun barrel may be bent up to correct that condition, but I am wondering if it is a safe thing to do. I would like to know if there are any other methods by which I could raise the pattern?—C. E. F., Calif.

Answer: I do not think it would hurt your barrel at all to give it a slight bend. That is very often done with perfect satisfaction. When a choke device is put on a gun it makes it shoot a little low because you sight low with it and as a usual thing the barrel is bent to offset that.

Another method is to raise the comb of your gun by building it up with walnut. Also you could use a Jostam cheek pad. The comb is, in effect, the rear sight of the gun, and raising it will raise your point of impact. What has happened to your gun is that you have, in effect, put on a higher front sight—and a higher front sight lowers the point of impact.

BENT BARREL CENTERS PATTERN

Question: I recently had a Poly-Choke installed on my 16 gauge Winchester Model 12 shotgun. Upon trying the gun, I found that the center of the pattern was about 16 in. below the point of aim at 40 yd., when using a high-velocity load and No. 6 shot.

Since you have the same model and gauge gun, perhaps you have had similar trouble and can tell me how to correct it. I realize that it is caused, at least in part, by the high bead which is an integral part of the Poly-Choke. But how can I get around it?—P. H., Md.

Answer: I suggest that you return your gun to the firm which fitted the Poly-Choke and ask to have the barrel bent slightly to throw the pattern higher. Installing any choke device is like adding a high front sight to a rifle. It makes the weapon shoot low, and as a usual thing the barrel should be bent a bit, to center the pattern. As a matter of fact, that is done in the best gunsmithing circles.

SHORT STOCK CAUSES INJURY

Question: I have been using a 12 gauge Winchester Model 12 with a 13½-in. stock and 30-in. barrels ever since I was 15 years old, and have done very well with it. Now, however, I am having trouble. When I shoot I lay my cheek tightly against the stock, and after a few rounds find that my cheek gets very sore. I do not seem to feel any recoil when I pull the trigger.

I am 6 ft. 2 in. tall, weigh 230 lb., and have high cheekbones, although I have no Indian blood. I have tried putting various-sized blocks on the stock, and have loosened the bolt and given the stock a slight twist to the right. This has resulted in centering my game better, but the gun still bangs my face. Can you suggest any remedy?—E. J. N., Canada.

Answer: I think that the primary cause of your trouble is the short stock of that Winchester Model 12. It is just about 1 in. too short for you. That results in your putting your cheekbone right at the point of the comb, and you get very nicely cracked every time you pull the trigger. No wonder your cheek is sore!

From what you tell me, you must have a rather full face which complicates the problem. What I would do is install a recoil pad to lengthen the stock, giving you a length of pull of 14½ in. and a pitch-down from 30-in. barrels of about 2 in.

That 14½-in. stock length should just about fit you. If you find the comb is still a bit high for you, take a piece of broken glass and scrape it down until it no longer punishes you when you shoot.

DANGEROUS CONVERSION

Question: Not long ago I was struck by what seemed at the time to be a bright thought. Now I'm suspecting that it may not be so bright, but I'd like to get your opinion before I junk the idea. I have a 12 ga. single shotgun with 36-in. barrel and hammer action. I thought I'd like to send this to the Poly-Choke Co., and have the barrel cut down to 12 in. or so and a Poly-Choke installed. Meanwhile I'd go to work on the stock, retaining the pistol grip but removing the rest. After I had replaced the barrel I would have something like a dragoon's pistol. What I'd like to know is whether such a weapon would be dangerous to use. Would the recoil be too heavy? What would be the effective range? And could I use rifled slugs?—L. J. H., Me.

Answer: If I get what you mean, you are going to shoot that 12 ga. gun in one hand. Wow! You're a better man than I am, Gunga Din. Frankly, I think you would be making a sad mistake to cut the butt stock off back of the pistol grip. 1. You wouldn't be able to hold it. 2. The recoil would break your arm. 3. You couldn't hit anything.

On the other hand I think you have an idea when it comes to getting a Poly-Choke with a lot of barrel whacked off. If I were you I would have a foot of barrel removed. Then you'd get good patterns and have a light, handy gun suitable for almost any purpose. Forget that horse-pistol notion. It won't work.

OPEN CHOKE GETS GAME

Question: For the last 20 years I have shot a pump with a barrel between modified and quarter choke, mostly at ducks. It will kill plenty far for me. The measurements are: $1\frac{4}{5}$ x $2\frac{1}{2}$ x $14\frac{1}{4}$, with a $2\frac{3}{4}$-in. pitch. Recently I acquired a 16 gauge Greener, both barrels full choke. I have tried it at clay birds and ducks, and can't hit a thing. The measurements are $1\frac{1}{4}$ x $2\frac{1}{2}$ x $14\frac{1}{2}$. I am thinking of having the Greener opened up. Do you think 55 and 65 percent would be too open? I am also thinking of having the dimensions changed. What do you think is wrong?—F. R. C., Canada.

Answer: Just why you aren't hitting with the Greener I can't say. It might be due to several causes. However, my own guess is that the principal cause is not the dimensions of the stock but the fact that your Greener is bored full choke, whereas you are used to a more open boring. By all means, have some of the choke removed. I would guess that 55 and 65 percent would be about what you want. Even for duck shooting I think you would do better with such boring than with the conventional full choke. Last season the most expert and deadly duck shooting I saw was done by a man using a gun bored improved-cylinder and half choke. He knocked down so many birds at what appeared to be long range, that the hunters in near-by blinds thought he was using a Magnum. Actually, he was killing those birds at between 40 and 50 yd. My favorite double is a 16 with both barrels bored 55 percent.

Why don't you have the double changed to the exact specifications of the pump you like so well? Actually, there is not much difference between them. You do not mention the pitch on the double; possibly there is none, or an inch or less down pitch, in which case your gun would tend to shoot high, since you keep your head erect. The faster a man shoots a scattergun, the more important are the dimensions.

You use, with that pump, more comb drop than I like. I'd prefer a drop of $1\frac{1}{2}$ in. myself; however, I keep my cheek on the comb.

TO CUT DOWN AND OPEN UP

Question: My 12 gauge hammerless field gun shoots too close. Could the barrel be cut to 28 in., and could our local gunsmith do it?—R. A. G., Ill.

Answer: I'd write to the service department of the factory that made your gun, tell them your troubles, and ask if they will open up those barrels—to 55 percent in the right and 60 percent in the left. They might even cut those barrels down to 28 in. and give you a recessed choke. In any case, it's a job for the factory; most local gunsmiths don't have the necessary equipment.

NEW STOCK FOR OLD SHOTGUN

Question: Please tell me where I can get a new stock fitted to my old 16 gauge Parker double-barreled shotgun. I can't seem to locate one.—J. R. H., Ark.

Answer: The thing for you to do is get in touch with the Service Department, Parker Gun Division, Remington Arms Co., Ilion, N. Y., and see if they can furnish and fit a new stock for that 16 gauge of yours. Give them the serial number of the gun, since it might be an obsolete model. It would be far cheaper for you to have the stock fitted by Parker, because they have machine-inletted blanks while custom stockmakers would have to do the inletting work by hand which would naturally be quite expensive.

THE STOCK MUST FIT

Question: In the last 15 years I've developed considerable skill with my 16 gauge Western Field model, often bagging 20 pheasants with 25 shells. I cut about 1½ in. off the stock, making an ideal gun for snapshooting.

Last fall I bought a .410 gauge Winchester pump, Model 42, and am well pleased with it. Only trouble is, it's straight as a broomstick and the stock is big enough for a 7-ft. man. With the butt plate square on the floor and the breech against the wall, the end of the barrel is about ½ in. from the wall. When I set my 16 gauge in this position the muzzle is about 6 in. from the wall. When I throw the .410 to my shoulder I have to pull my neck way in to sight down the barrel; with the 16 I'm looking straight

down the beam.—A. I. P., Wyo.

Answer: Probably the best thing would be to buy a shotgun buttstock from a mail-order house and restock that .410 pump yourself. I had a friend who did it very successfully. It isn't hard for a man handy with tools.

It takes all kinds of people to make a world, and all kinds of shotguns to fit those people. I couldn't hit a flock of barns with your 16 gauge, but it suits you, so go to it and try to make your .410 as near like it as you can. A man is certainly justified in sticking with what works for him.

REMOVING DENT IN BARREL

Question: A short time ago I bought a brand-new 16 gauge Fox double-gun. When the express company delivered it there was a dent about the size of a large nailhead in one of the barrels. Will this cause any harm? It doesn't show up much on the inside of the barrel.—C. T., Iowa.

Answer: You had better get that dent removed. If you shoot with the gun as is, the shot will in time wear off the protruding metal and weaken the barrel there. It's not difficult to have such a dent removed. Any good gunsmith can do it, or you can send it back to the maker.

If the express company is responsible for the damage you should take the matter up with them.

CURE FOR LEADED CHOKE

Question: I have a Lefever single-barrel field and trap gun, 12 ga., full choke, hammerless, Model 2. It throws a good pattern, but leads badly in the choke when I use ordinary drop shot. It doesn't lead so much with chilled shot. Can you suggest any remedy?—C. L. C., Mich.

Answer: You might try gun slick and see if that cuts down the leading. If that doesn't work, I suggest that you saturate a tight patch with Winchester rust remover, a mild abrasive. Then polish the choke where you encounter the leading. I imagine the trouble is that the barrel was not well polished originally. In time the lead would polish it, but that's rather a slow process and you can speed it up by the method I've described.

BRUSH REMOVES LEADING

Question: I have a 12 gauge automatic which I used for the first time last season. Throughout the season I had trouble with leading in the barrel, so when the season was over I sent the gun to the manufacturer. They cleaned the lead out and returned the gun, charging me $3. After shooting a few shells, the gun was leaded again.

I have tried several well-known solvents, but they seem to remove only part of the lead.—J. W., Neb.

Answer: The best way to take lead out of a shotgun barrel before it gets bad is to go after it with a brass shotgun brush every time you use the gun. Do not use a steel brush, since it will scratch the bore. I have found that it helps to have a little light powder solvent in the barrel when you are working on it.

If the leading is allowed to get bad, I have had good results by using some blue mercuric ointment on it. I wipe it in the barrel with a patch on the cleaning rod and let it set for a week or so. When I wipe it out, the mercury has usually amalgamated with the lead, and the lead comes right out. I have seen very badly leaded, guns, however, that needed more than one application.

REMEDY FOR FOULED BARREL

Question: I have a new double-gun which has leaded so badly in the few times I've shot it that the barrels look like the inside of a smokestack. Will it always be that way?—C. H. G., Minn.

Answer: A lot of new shotguns lead up like the very devil for a while. However, continuing to shoot your gun will "lap" out the barrel by polishing it with shot. In the meantime, take out the lead with a brass brush and a light solvent like Hoppe's No. 9, or if that doesn't work try an application of mercuric (blue) ointment, which can be bought at any drug store. Leave the stuff in and let the mercury amalgamate with the lead—then wipe it out.

Don't lose patience with the gun and the situation will right itself.

BADLY PITTED GUN HOPELESS

Question: I have a 16 gauge Winchester shotgun which is badly pitted. Can this damage be repaired?—G. D. H., Pa.

Answer: I am very sorry, but it will not be possible to remove those pits. When a gun is badly pitted the rust has eaten away the metal. There is no way to replace it.

SELF-LOADER FIRES TWICE

Question: I have a Winchester self-loading shotgun, Model 11, which fires twice with one pull of the trigger. What do you suppose causes this, and what would you advise doing?—J. E. R., Va.

Answer: Whatever the trouble is, it's plenty! You should send your shotgun at once to the Service Department, Winchester Repeating Arms Co., New Haven, Conn., for checking and overhauling. It is dangerous to do any shooting with it in its present condition.

INTERCHANGEABLE BARRELS

Question: My Fox Sterlingworth 12 gauge shotgun has 26-in. barrels. Would it be well to have a set of 30-in. barrels too, for use on certain types of game? To what degree would the longer barrels affect balance, and how would one correct such a condition? Would the change affect my shooting?—L. J. M., Pa.

Answer: While it would be possible for you to have an extra set of 30-in. full-choke barrels made—particularly good for shooting waterfowl at long range—probably your gun will seem to handle somewhat sluggishly because you are accustomed to 26-in. barrels. Consequently, I would recommend that you get the extra set not longer than 28 in.

To have this change made, send your gun to the Service Department, Fox Gun Division, Savage Arms Company, Utica, N. Y.

CUT BARREL TO 26 IN.

Question: I have a 12 gauge full-choke Remington repeater, Model 29, with 32-in. barrel. It is fine for ducks but practically useless in rabbit hunting. I would like to open the choke and also would like a shorter barrel. Is it advisable to saw off the barrel? Do you think I could cut it to 28 in. without making it a scattergun?—W. E. W., Ind.

Answer: Since all the choke in a Remington is in the last 2½ in. of barrel, if you cut off more than ½ in. your gun would shoot like a hose spraying, and no ducks would be killed. I'd cut the barrel down to 26 in. and put a Poly-Choke on it. Then your gun would be right in weight and barrel length, and you could always get any degree of choke you wanted by simply turning the Poly-Choke, 10 seconds' work. And the total cost would probably be less than that of a new barrel.

LONGER STOCK IMPROVES SHOOTING

Question: I have a 12 gauge Ithaca pump gun with raised rib, Poly-Choke, 28-in. barrel (overall), and 13¾-in. stock. My trouble is this: When I grasp the gun and let my cheek fall naturally against the stock, my thumb bumps my nose—sometimes painfully—upon recoil. Except for that, the gun seems to fit me O.K.; but to avoid getting bumped I have to place my thumb unnaturally, and that bothers me. Would it weaken the stock too much to have a gunsmith cut a groove in the grip for my thumb to rest in?—M. K. S., Iowa.

Answer: Evidently you are rather tall, or you have long arms or a long neck, or both. Your remedy is to lengthen that stock about ½ in. First try shooting the gun with a lace-on pad which will lengthen your stock about that much. When you find the length of pull which fits you and keeps that thumb away from your nose, you can have a permanent recoil pad fitted to the stock, to increase length of pull as much as need be.

HIGH COMB CAUSES MISSES

Question: I have shot a couple of rounds of skeet and have patterned my gun as I would on the field, and find that even though I bring my cheek firmly to the comb each time, the shot charge goes high and to the left. Is my gun barrel bent?—R. B. J., N. J.

Answer: What is wrong, I think, is that the comb of your shotgun is too high and too thick, and your eye is not in line with the barrel. Take a rasp and work down and thin the comb until you look right down the barrel without effort, and then your patterns will hit where you point.

WHITE SPOTS ON SHOTGUN BARREL

Question: The barrels of my L. C. Smith shotgun have suddenly developed a lot of little white spots near the rib. I have wiped these spots off several times, but they come back the next day. Can you tell me what causes them?—H. G., N. C.

Answer: What has happened with your shotgun is that the bluing solution which was used (evidently the Houghton process) has stayed between the barrels and the rib and is working out. This can be cured by boring a couple of little holes under the rib and flushing with water.

DOGS AND THEIR HANDLING

by William Cary Duncan
Dr. James R. Kinney

HOW TO CHOOSE YOUR HUNTING DOG

ALL-AROUND DOG

Question: I want a dog that will be good for pheasant hunting, will also retrieve ducks, and have a good disposition as a home dog.—J. C. W., Ore.

Answer: For retrieving ducks in water not too cold, the German shorthair pointer would be about right, but they're hard to find in most parts of the country. Some of the setters do good retrieving in water of moderate temperatures, and they, as well as the shorthair, point their game. Wirehair pointing griffons and German wirehair pointers are even harder to find than the shorthair. So, I'd say a setter or the shorthair.

BEST DOG FOR WOLF AND LION

Question: Which dog is the best fighter—and how do the bull mastiff, great Dane, and Irish wolfhound stack up in this category? Could a great Dane catch a wolf, and could any of these dogs handle a mountain lion?—C. L., Calif.

Answer: I assume by "best fighter" you mean the dog best suited to cope with the timber wolf and the mountain lion. The Irish wolfhound will be your best bet of

those you mention for the former, especially if your hunting terrain is fairly flat and not too rocky. Neither the great Dane nor the bull mastiff is fast enough to catch a wolf.

Mountain lions offer a different problem. Usually these animals are hunted with hounds and are shot when they tree. An Airedale will handle a cat in case one jumps from the tree.

RETRIEVERS FOR UPLAND GAME

Question: Both my springers have died of old age, and I'm thinking of getting another dog. They were fine hunters, but I'm too old to run miles across country as I had to do to keep up with them when they were after pheasants. What about a golden retriever for pheasants and quail? Do these dogs spring their game like spaniels?—H. M. S., N. J.

Answer: Golden retrievers are very definitely duck specialists, but they sometimes do very well on pheasants when trained to that game. I doubt if you would find the breed satisfactory for quail. They do not point, but work up to their game slowly as spaniels do.

LABRADOR—A DUAL-PURPOSE DOG

Question: What do you think of the Labrador retriever as a combination child's companion and duck dog? Would the Texas climate be too hot for this type of dog?—H. T. H. Jr., Tex.

Answer: I couldn't recommend a better dog for your requirements than the Labrador; a friendly animal and a good companion for children. I don't think the heat of Texas will affect it to any extent. Certainly the Labrador will not feel the heat more than some of the other breeds used for duck shooting.

SPRINGER SPECIFICATIONS

Question: What size does the springer spaniel attain? I'd also like to know if he will work on quail as well as pheasants and rabbits. Would this breed stand up under hard hunting?—R. O. B., Ill.

Answer: The standard for English springers calls for a weight of 42 to 50 lb. and a height at shoulder of 17½ to 19 in. The average individual is an excellent worker on rabbits and pheasants and can be used on quail if properly trained. Springers are strong and can stand the gaff with any of the bird dogs.

They come in liver and white; black and white; liver and tan; tan and white; black, white, and tan; liver; black; roan, and similar combinations—anything except red and white or lemon and white.

PHEASANT DOG FOR COLD CLIMATE

Question: I plan to buy a dog solely for hunting pheasants. Having no basement, I wonder if either a cocker or a springer could stand Minnesota winters in a kennel. As I don't hunt more than four or five times a year I wonder if a cocker wouldn't be dog enough for me. What is your opinion?—D. L. K., Minn.

Answer: Either dog would be O.K. in an outdoor kennel if it is dry, has a good bed, and a heavy piece of carpet or something similar hung over the door for warmth and to prevent drafts.

As to the cocker-springer question, it all depends on the cover you will hunt in. If it is very tough and heavy, I'd choose the springer, but in either case make sure the pup is from good *hunting* stock.

BEST SETTER FOR PHEASANTS AND DUCKS

Question: I am 16 years old and want to buy a setter pup to train by myself for pheasant and duck hunting. I have a lot of patience and think I could do the job. I would like your advice on which would be best for me to get—an Irish or an English setter. What is the difference between the two?—D. A., Neb.

Answer: I am glad you are going to own and train a setter and I am sure you will do a good job and have a lot of fun besides. It will pay you to get a book on training, unless you have had more experience than most boys your age. I know I ruined my first bird dog when I was about 14, not because I lacked patience, but because I overtrained him before he had a chance to find out how much fun he could have hunting.

As to the difference between an Irish and an English setter, it's hard to answer that question because so much depends on the individual dog, his breeding and so on. As a rule, however, English setters are more easily trained and handled than Irish setters. On the other hand, if the English setter is of the Llewellin strain, he would probably be too fast and heady for a boy to handle.

The average English setter is a more natural pointer, and stancher on point, than the average Irishman. As for ducks, neither is a duck dog, but I think you would have fully as much luck with an Irish as with an English setter, perhaps more. So it's a toss-up.

SPRINGER FOR SMALL GAME

Question: I want to get a good dog for small game in New Jersey and Pennsylvania. I'd prefer a small dog since I live in the city. What breed would you recommend?—F. B. D., N. J.

Answer: A well-trained springer spaniel should be just right. Such a dog is good for both fur and feather and is small enough to accommodate himself to relatively confined quarters.

HOW TO CHOOSE BEST OF LITTER

Question: In exchange for breeding my Chesapeake Bay retriever with a neighbor's bitch of the same breed, I have been promised my pick of the litter—the usual stud fee—when they are 10 weeks old. I don't know too much about the Chesapeake breed; so can you tell me some points to look for so that I can make a wise selection?—A. T. G., Calif.

Answer: It's difficult to pick the best pup in a litter that's only 10 weeks old. Generally speaking, however, look for a good strong pup with straight front legs, plenty of bone, well-sprung ribs, a well-curved stifle, good tight feet (not splay-footed), and a clear eye. But even more important than conformation (at this age) is disposition. Your choice should be a smart, active pup that uses his nose and *shows no tendency toward shyness.* By smartness, I mean paying attention quickly when you speak to him, being first to notice the feed dish when you set it down, etc.

AIREDALE SIZES

Question: I have been trying to get a very large, strong Airedale for hunting. The owner of a kennel tells me that the dog I want is an Oorang Airedale. He says this is the largest breed of Airedale, a male weighing about 85 lb. and a bitch 65, the height being about 24 in, at the shoulder. Is this a lot of height and weight for an Airedale?—J. J. N., N. Y.

Answer: The Oorang Airedale terrier, which is simply a strain, not a breed, is usually a good, big dog, as Airedales go, but 85 lb. is a lot of weight, even for an exceptionally large one. For show purposes, Airedales are bred on the small side nowadays, which I personally think is rather unwise. The maximum size for an A-show specimen is 45 lb. for males, slightly less for females. Using this as a gauge, you can see that your 85-lb. dog is the next thing to a giant, or else excessively fat. But if you like a big dog, and the 85-pounder is well put together, I see no reason to pass him up.

BEST DOG FOR BOBCATS

Question: What would be the best dog for bobcats and lynxes in northern Massachusetts and New Hampshire? Will a coon or foxhound do, or must I get a real lion dog from the West? Aren't these three actually all the same breed, but trained for different animals? I already have a springer spaniel that I use on birds and rabbits; would it be dangerous to try him on cats?—G. C., Mass.

Answer: I believe a good, big foxhound, trained to trail and tree bobcats and lynxes would be O.K., though an Airedale-foxhound cross might give you a gamer fighter. In a way it is true that coon, fox, and lion hounds are all the same general breeding in many cases, but coonhounds are being bred very carefully nowadays for work on coon, and are almost a distinct breed.

Don't take any chances with your springer. Bobcats and lynxes are no game for a spaniel. As a rule they will tree when hard pressed by dogs, but all rules have exceptions.

WHEN TO START A SETTER

Question: At what age should an English setter be bought for eventual hunting use? Which sex is best?—B. T., Minn.

Answer: I think it's a good idea to buy a setter pup when 2 to 3 months old, so that you can have his handling and training from the start. But this is by no means necessary. Real training for field work need not be started until the pup is 8 or 9 months old, and many professional trainers do not attempt to do much with a pup younger than that. As for the sex, that's all a matter of how you are situated. Females, as you know, have to be kept in close confinement for about 17 days twice a year, and for that reason are sometimes considerable trouble. Then too, in most states the license fee for females is higher. All things being equal, I'd choose a male.

HOUND FOR WOLF AND COYOTE HUNTING

Question: Would you recommend a Russian wolfhound for hunting wolves and coyotes in northern Wisconsin? Has the breed a good nose?—R. P., Wis.

Answer: The consensus seems to be that the best wolf and coyote dog to *catch and kill* his game is a cross between the Russian wolfhound and a good big greyhound. As to nose, neither the wolfhound nor greyhound is a trailer in the sense that a foxhound is, both being really sight runners.

DACHSHUND FOR RABBITS?

Question: Do you consider the dachshund as good a rabbit dog as the beagle? Does he bay on a trail as other hounds do? Is he slower than the beagle, and would he run after deer or fox trails? Do you favor the black-and-tan or the redbone for fox hunting?—J. K., N. Y.

Answer: At the present time the dachshund—as a breed—is not considered as good for rabbits as the beagle as a breed. All breeds have exceptionally good and bad individuals.

The dachshund usually barks on trail, and both he and the beagle are comparatively slow trailers, with the dachsie perhaps a little the slower. As far as I know, *all* hounds will run deer, as deer scent seems especially attractive to them. This goes for fox, too, to a lesser degree.

I never like to compare two breeds or strains that are supposed to do the same job in the same way, but I'll say that—in my opinion—your chances of getting a good foxhound are a trifle better with a black-and-tan than with a redbone. The latter makes an A-1 coon dog, as a rule.

THE GORDON AS A PHEASANT DOG

Question: We plan to move to the grouse country of northern Michigan and are thinking of getting a Gordon setter. Will this breed also work on pheasants? How does its disposition compare with that of the Irish setter?—Mrs. D. L. R., Minn.

Answer: A Gordon setter from *good hunting stock* usually makes an A-1 grouse dog and is equally useful on pheasants; but I'd hate to risk spoiling a good grouse dog on those sprinters.

As a rule, Gordons are inclined to be one-man dogs, at least more so than the Irish setters—but that trait, like most others, depends on the individual dog.

DOGS FOR BEAR AND DEER

Question: We are planning a bear and deer-hunting trip, and want to know if Irish terriers, fox terriers, and Airedales could be used.—R. P. M., Calif.

Answer: Either hounds or Airedales would prove more satisfactory for bear and deer than any of the small terriers, like fox or Irish terriers. By hounds, I mean good, strong foxhounds that are fairly strong and game.

GOLDEN GOOD FOR BIRDS

Question: I plan to buy a retriever bitch to use on ducks, pheasants, quail, and doves. I want one with a good disposition, that's easy to train, can stand cold water and bad weather, and will make both a good house pet and a good car dog. I am undecided between the golden retriever and the black Labrador. If they're about equal, I'd prefer the lighter of the two. W. McH. Calif.

Answer: A golden will be the better of the two for the work you have in mind. It's the lighter dog—and the Labrador is a stocky, boisterous animal which I'd hesitate to recommend for a house pet.

SPRINGER AS A RUNNING MATE

Question: I am thinking of buying a springer spaniel pup to run with my beagle, and would like to know what you think of the idea. Is a springer a good trailer, and would it work on rabbits with another dog?—Miss H. G., Ohio.

Answer: As a rule, springers make first-class rabbit dogs, but they do not hunt exactly as a beagle does. They usually jump the rabbit when working close to the gun, whereas beagles are likely to go out independently, jump the rabbit, and work out the trail rather slowly so as to drive the rabbit around to the gun.

I can't say how a springer and a beagle would work together, but I'd guess the combination would be rather discouraging to the beagle.

AIREDALE FOR SQUIRRELS?

Question: I'm looking for a squirrel dog, a silent trailer. Would an Airedale be suitable? Are there two types of Airedales, the large and the small or terrier Airedale, and is the small one better for hunting?—E. B. F., Tex.

Answer: Airedales are not actually trailers in the sense that hounds are, and neither are any of the other terriers, but nearly all of them make first-class squirrel dogs. There is no definite breed of small Airedales, however. You may be thinking of the Welsh terrier, which

looks like a very small Airedale, the size of a fox terrier. Incidentally, wirehair fox terriers make excellent dogs for small game, but like Airedales are not real trailers, either open or silent; they usually jump their game and tree it or drive it to earth after a short run.

COON AND BEAR HOUND

Question: What type of hound or other breed could I use on both raccoon and black bear in Michigan?—A. K., Mich.

Answer: I believe you would find foxhounds as satisfactory as any breed for the type of work you mention, but you should pick dogs that are good and sturdy and from practical working stock. Airedales often make good bear dogs, and so do Airedale-hound crosses in many cases. Much, of course, depends on the individual dogs.

LABRADOR VS. CHESAPEAKE

Question: I would like your advice before buying a retriever for use here in Louisiana. We hunt the hard way—wading swamps to a duck blind that's knee-deep in mud and water. This requires a dog to swim a lot, be constantly wet with cold salt water, and heavy with mud. Often he can't even find a place to shake himself. Floating vegetation makes swimming with large ducks difficult and cripples must be retrieved from dense cane, practically impassible to man but duck soup for the ducks.

I am undecided between a Labrador and a Chesapeake. I understand the Lab is the smaller of the two. Can he do hard jobs as well? Also, is his nose as good, and would his black coat frighten ducks? Another factor, which is better around children?—R. B. W., La.

Answer: In the case of two dogs as similar in size, character, and disposition as the Chesapeake and the Labrador—both extremely popular with practical hunters—it is a question of the individual dog, not of the breed.

The average Labrador is little if any smaller than the average Chesapeake, and certainly can stand cold water and hard work just as well. If the black coat of the Labrador were a real handicap he certainly wouldn't be as widely used by duck hunters as he is.

In general both breeds have exceptionally even dispositions and are remarkably intelligent. If I were in your shoes I'd just pick an individual that appealed to me, making sure it is from practical working stock, and has a good disposition.

TERRIERS FOR KILLING CHUCK AND WEASEL

Question: I would like a dog, smaller than the bull terrier-Airedale class, that would be good at killing woodchucks and weasels on my farm. What would you suggest?—W. R. S., Ontario.

Answer: Picking a breed for someone else is pretty risky business at best, but I'll stick my neck out and suggest one of the small terriers—a wire-haired or smooth fox terrier or a Scottie, or better still a Welsh terrier, although you may have difficulty locating one of the latter as they are not very common. A Welsh corgi, another fairly rare breed, would be a good bet too. As always, of course, much will depend on the individual dog.

THE GORDON

Question: Would appreciate any information you can give me about the Gordon setter, as I am interested in getting a dog with its characteristics. I can't find anyone who knows anything about the Gordon.—A. W. B., Mich.

Answer: There is no better gun dog, I believe, than a good Gordon setter, especially on grouse and woodcock. But, of course, all depends on the individual dog. There are aces and two-spots in all breeds of dogs.

The typical Gordon is black with tan "points," by which I mean tan spots over the eyes, a tan muzzle, tan at root of tail and below the vent, tan on inside of hind legs, tan on lower part of front legs, tan feet, and usually a tan dumb-bell on chest. The setters vary in size, the typical bench Gordon being a big dog, larger than the average English setter; but many of the field-type Gordons are only medium size. They are inclined to be one-man dogs, and if you buy one *make sure it is not man-shy.*

HOUND FOR RUNNING COYOTES

Question: Am considering the purchase of hounds for running coyotes. Which hound do you think is suitable for this purpose?—J. M., Ore.

Answer: I believe a cross between a greyhound and a Russian wolfhound (borzoi) has been found the top dog for chasing, catching, and killing coyotes. But I think it is agreed that it takes more than one dog to *catch and kill* a coyote. For running purposes, I think you would find a good, tough greyhound, from racing stock, quite satisfactory, and I'm not saying that two or three of them would not catch and kill.

AMPHIBIAN DOG

Question: What breed would you advise for a combination duck and pheasant dog? How would a Labrador do for this type of hunting?—T. C., Utah.

Answer: As a rule, there is no better duck dog than a Labrador, and they can be trained for hunting pheasant as well. This is also true of any of the retrievers.

I suggest that you give a little thought to a springer spaniel, which is aces on pheasant and, as a rule, a better than fair retriever for duck. Of course, in all cases it's as much the individual dog as it is the breed—so, take your pick.

BEAGLE STANDARDS

Question: I am trying to locate some good beagles of the small type. Please give me a brief description of points to watch for.—H. D. S., Jr., Ga.

Answer: By show and field-trial standards, the height limit for beagles in this country is 15 in. (in England, 16 in.) at the shoulder, and dogs larger than that are not eligible to compete. A popular height for small beagles is 13 in. The head should be of good size and well proportioned, the expression rather soft and very intelligent, the neck long and clean, with sloping shoulders that go neatly into a body that is close-coupled with good spring of rib. It's important that the dog have plenty of bone in the legs and small, well-arched cat feet, and the hocks should be set low to the ground. The tail should be moderately high-set, with a good brush but never a curly one. Any true hound color is permissible.

CHOOSING A BEAR PACK

Question: Can you tell me how to go about assembling a good pack of bear dogs?—W. C. R., Vt.

Answer: I advise obtaining hounds from a reliable kennel which will guarantee that they won't run deer or rabbits, but have been trained only on bears. As a complement to the hounds, Airedale terriers should prove satisfactory.

BRITTANY FOR IDAHO BIRDS

Question: What do you think of a Brittany spaniel to hunt pheasants and quail around Twin Falls, Idaho? I'd like to get a puppy and train him in the spring and summer for work next fall. Our fields are mostly stubble, corn, and sugar beet—with plenty of cockleburs and an occasional brushy ravine. The main requirement, so far as I am concerned, is that the dog point.—H. H. G., Idaho.

Answer: A Brittany spaniel should do the trick. He should point to perfection—and, in view of the training you're willing to give him, should be in fine shape by the fall.

JOB FOR A SPRINGER

Question: What breed would you suggest for flushing and retrieving game in heavy brush country and for retrieving ducks in comparatively cold water?—A. J., Wash.

Answer: A rugged springer spaniel is the best dog for this job.

DOG FOR PHEASANTS AND DUCKS

Question: What dog would be best for hunting pheasants and ducks in South Dakota?—R. S., S. D.

Answer: A Labrador retriever is the answer to your problem.

SETTER BEST FOR UPLAND BIRDS

Question: I want to get a dog as a house pet and for hunting quail, grouse, and pheasants. Would a Chesapeake Bay retriever be as satisfactory as some other breed, such as the English setter for these purposes?—G. C. C., Va.

Answer: Get a setter; a Chesapeake couldn't hope to equal his performance on upland birds.

BASSET HOUND FOR RABBITS

Question: Since I am no longer young—more than 60—I find following a good beagle pretty strenuous, yet I like to hunt rabbits. I have been wondering whether a basset hound wouldn't be better for me, since I feel it would be slower in the field. I don't want to go out when the snow is deep, so the dog's short legs wouldn't be any drawback. What do you think?—R. S. R., N. Y.

Answer: The basset hound is the equal of the beagle in every respect, except that it is a slower dog because of its shorter legs. This seems to be just what you require, so I'd recommend a basset hound.

HOW TO TRAIN YOUR DOG

KEEPING DOGS AWAY FROM TRAPS

Question: I am going to do some trapping this season, and want to take my dog with me. How can I train him to keep away from traps?—C. M., Mass.

Answer: There is no way that I know of to train a dog to stay away from traps. By employing the following device, however, you may be able to keep him from getting caught:

Sapling arched over trap allows small game to spring the trap, but forces dog to jump.

Cut a sapling, lop off the branches, and stick each end firmly in the ground so as to form an arc over the trap. This will allow small game to spring the trap, but force a dog to jump over it.

IT'S EASY TO TRAIN DACHSHUND

Question: I've just bought a 5-month-old dachshund which I want to train to trail rabbits and skunks. At what age can I start his lessons, and how do I go about training it?—M. E. T., Mo.

Answer: Start at once. You won't find your dachshund hard to train; that breed possesses a good hunting instinct and remarkable intelligence. Give him his first lessons on rabbits. When the dog is not in the immediate vicinity, drag a freshly killed rabbit over the ground. Then liberate the dog. By trial and error he'll soon find where you've put the bunny— and at the end of a few such lessons your dog should be an accomplished trailer.

Skunks, however, present another problem. In the first place, I don't know whether a dachshund can handle a skunk —and if the two ever tangle, the dog's eyes and your nose are going to suffer. However, if you want to try it, just take the dog out on a rainy night and he'll soon locate the whereabouts of a skunk. Whether the upshot of this will be to your satisfaction or sorrow, I don't know.

LET DOGS DIG HOLES

Question: For the last eight or nine months my 3-year-old hound has had the habit of digging holes in the ground wherever he may be. Please tell me what is the reason for this, and is there anything I can do to stop it?—P. L. O., Pa.

Answer: Practically all dogs love to dig in the earth and the earth is good for them. To lie in it is like taking a tonic. I have owned setters that dug actual tunnels like fox burrows. Of course, a surface of cement or hard ashes in your dog's yard would tend to overcome this digging habit, but unless there is some good reason for preventing it, I'd let him dig.

CURING GAME BURYING PUP

Question: My 6-month-old pup, a cross between a springer spaniel and a terrier, buries the game he retrieves. How can I correct this?—J. R., Calif.

Answer: This fault, probably caused by his terrier blood, will be difficult to remedy. Fit him with a modified spike training collar and to this tie a long length of tarred salt-water trolling line such as is used for bluefish. Coil the line carefully in the blind. When the dog swims out to retrieve, pay out the line so that it will not restrict him. Then when he returns to shore and starts to bury the bird, call him back and pull sharply on the cord. The spike collar will persuade him to bring in the bird. A few of these lessons, which can be taught with land birds as well as waterfowl, should stop this habit of game burying.

BREAKING HARSH-MOUTHED SETTER

Question: How can I break a young setter from mashing and crushing game when he retrieves?—A. E. H., N. C.

Answer: Thrust short knitting needles through the body of a freshly killed bird and throw it out for the dog to retrieve. The sharp points will discourage him from biting down hard. Repeat several times, and this fault of crushing game will be corrected in no time at all.

HOW TO CURE GUN-SHYNESS

Question: My 2-year-old cocker spaniel is an excellent rabbit and quail dog, but he is afraid of the sight or sound of a gun. How can I cure him of this?—D. W., Mo.

Answer: Gun-shyness is a serious fault and hard to cure, but if you have patience you may be successful.

Take your cocker out hunting, but carry no gun, not even a pistol. If and when he becomes thoroughly fond of the sport take a small pistol along and, when the dog is working busily on scent or flushing a bird, fire the pistol—but be sure you are a good distance away from the dog. If he seems to be afraid of the report wait a week or so before trying it again. But never fire unless the dog is working on hot scent or flushing and even chasing game.

When and if he pays no attention to the report, work nearer to the dog when you fire. Finally you should be able to change from pistol to shotgun.

TEACHING SPANIEL TO RETRIEVE

Question: What is the best method of teaching my 20-month-old female water spaniel how to retrieve?—N. M., Wyo.

Answer: Find a secluded spot, preferably in short grass, where the dog's attention will not be diverted. Throw a glove stuffed with soft material a short distance and urge her to bring it to you, rewarding her with a tidbit for each success. Repeat this performance a dozen times but no more, or the dog may become bored.

In each succeeding lesson throw the glove farther until you have reached the limit of your throwing range and the dog is thoroughly proficient. Then hide the glove and encourage her to find it by using her scenting powers and again reward her for her first few successes.

Gradually increase the weight of the object until it weighs 1 lb. or more, but be sure it is always compact and does not have loose ends protruding. Try a piece of wood packed in duck feathers and then stuffed into a rabbit skin.

Since most spaniels are born with an instinct for retrieving, you'll probably have no difficulty in training yours.

A GOOD WAY TO CURE DEER CHASING

Question: My 3-year-old beagle performs very well on rabbits, pheasants, and an occasional fox. However, his desire to chase everything has extended itself to deer. Since I hunt in New York State, and in a section where deer abound, this habit is dangerous as well as annoying.

Bitter-tasting deerskin bib—a cure for deer chasing dog.

I have heard of putting deer musk in the kennel; of starting the dog on a goat's trail, and letting the goat butt him; and of whipping the dog off a laid trail of deer musk. Do you know of a better method?—J. C. L., N. Y.

Answer: Here is one which, if you are able to arrange it, is about as good as any:

Make a bib of a piece of deerskin—with the hair on—and tie it around your hound's neck, so that he can lie and chew it. After he has chewed it awhile, doctor the bib with a good dose of something very bitter, like aloes or bitter olive; and keep it doctored with the stuff. A deer hoof works about as well as the bib. This is no sure cure, but it *is* worth a try.

TEACHING OBEDIENCE TO WHISTLE

Question: I want to teach my 3-month-old beagle to come to me when I blow a whistle. Can you tell me how to go about it?—G. S., N. J.

Answer: To teach your beagle to obey the whistle, simply hitch a 20-ft. rope to his collar and let him drag it while giving him a lesson. As the dog runs about, keep up with him, carrying any type of whistle that can be heard over a reasonable distance. Use the same whistle.

Every few minutes blow the whistle and, as you do so, step on the rope. If the pup is traveling fairly fast it will pull him up with a jerk or even throw him end over end. Repeat the whistle and haul him in with the rope, patting and praising him when he reaches you. Continue these lessons as long as necessary, which shouldn't be long if you do your part conscientiously.

PROS AND CONS OF ELECTRIC FENCES

Question: My experience in using an electric fence around my springer spaniel's yard does not bear out your contention that such a device will spoil a hunting dog. A few years ago he developed the habit of climbing over his pen and running away, to be gone several days at

a time. I put a smooth wire above the woven-wire fence and charged it with my high-line-operated fence controller. He got one good shock and it cured him of climbing out. It had no effect on his hunting.

Think twice before using an electric fence—it may cause serious harm to your dog.

Since this first experience, I have installed another charged wire around his pen near the ground to prevent him from digging out. One or two shocks were enough to make him leave the fence strictly alone. As a matter of fact, the charger has been turned off for the last three months and he hasn't once tried to dig out.

A homemade device operated from the high line might very well be dangerous, but I think a commercial fence controller is safe.—K. M. C., Mich.

Answer: I *am* on record as not favoring the use of electric fences for hunting dogs. The reason is that I have to be very careful in all cases of this kind. Purebred gun dogs are often high-strung and no two are ever exactly alike in temperament. A device like an electric fence might be completely harmless to one dog and disastrous to another.

TRAINING BEAGLE FOR FOXES AND DEER

Question: Can beagles be trained to hunt foxes and deer?—H. E. H., Ontario.

Answer: Yes. In fact, the main difficulty usually is to stop them from running deer and to concentrate on one sort of game. The strong deer scent apparently offers an inducement which dogs find it hard to ignore, and if your beagles cross a deer track while you're out hunting rabbits you'll probably have a long wait until they return again. To train them to hunt deer, merely put them on a fresh deer track and see what happens.

TRAINING GERMAN SHORTHAIR FOR DUCKS

Question: I have recently acquired a German shorthair pointer, age 18 months, a big, well-built dog. He has had no training, good or bad, and if possible I would like to train him for all-around hunting. Do you think he could be used as a duck dog? Also, our best rabbit hunting is in the winter, after the pheasant season. Do you think that using him on rabbits after birds would spoil him for the bird season next year?—G. W. P., Utah.

Answer: One of the claims made by sponsors of this breed is that it makes A-1 duck dogs, and I know some individuals are just that. As in all breeds, it's usually a case of the individual dog—there are good ones and clucks.

If you plan to use the dog on birds, I would not allow him to run rabbits. Except in the case of some of the spaniels, which do not point, birds and rabbits just don't mix as game for a dog. This in spite of the fact that it is claimed the shorthair can handle successfully pheasants, quail, grouse, snipe, woodchuck, ducks, raccoons, opossums, and deer. That's a pretty big order, and if I were you I'd forget rabbits if you wish to use the dog on birds.

PATIENCE PRODUCES GOOD RETRIEVER

Question: In teaching my English setter force retrieving I found she will return to my hand a gag on which I have tied feathers, but she will not pick up a dead bird in the field unless her ear is pinched.

It was hard training her with the gag, and I had to bribe her a great deal. Now she'll retrieve a dead bird for me, but she still expects something to eat in return. What method would you advise me to use in order to arouse her interest in retrieving?—R. C. J., Tex.

Answer: I wonder if the "dead bird" you speak of was shot over her flush or point or was merely a dead pigeon or something of the kind. If the latter is the case, I think that when the bitch becomes used to having game birds shot over her she will pick up interest, and the birds too. I have an idea she just needs more experience. In any event don't expect success too quickly. It often takes time and patience to produce a good retriever.

If she expects something to eat for her efforts, carry a few little tidbits in your pocket and give them to her when she brings in game. Later on, unless I'm greatly mistaken, it won't be necessary to give her a reward for retrieving.

BREAKING RUNAWAY HABIT

Question: I was recently given a 2-year-old springer spaniel and he continually leaves home for a day or two at a time after staying around close for a week or so. He loves to hunt, but ranges about 200 yd. from the gun. I've tried breaking him, but he pays no attention to me. He hunts constantly, paying no attention to commands. At home, he obeys nicely and is a fine pet.

Do you think I will be able to make anything out of this dog? Do you advise locking him up to keep him from running away?—C. W., Mont.

Answer: I assume that your springer does not visit his old home on his runaway trips, or you would have said so. That being so, it looks as if you have a real runaway to deal with—a rather unusual thing for a spaniel.

As for a cure, I can't promise anything,

but suggest that you cut a piece of old broomhandle to about 18 in. in length, then carve a notch in the center of this piece so that you can tie a cord around it. Fasten this cord to the dog's collar in such a way that the stick will hang as nearly horizontal as possible about half-way down the dog's legs. If this is properly done, your dog will find that running away is very difficult.

You might also try shutting him up in his kennel after one of his trips, but be sure not to whip or strike him at such times. If you do, he'll think he's being punished for coming home.

As for his wide-ranging qualities in the field, I believe he needs a thorough yard-breaking. Any good book on the training of hunting dogs will give you the details.

3 WAYS TO TRAIN CLOSE HUNTER

Question: How can I convert a wide, fast bird dog into one that will hunt close to the gun in heavy cover without impairing his hunting ability?—D. A. C., Pa.

Answer: A combination of three things should do what you want:

First, yard breaking with a long check cord attached to the dog's collar, so that you step on it and check him if he keeps going when you whistle. This throws him, and usually makes him realize that a whistle or call means "Come in." Keep this up until the lesson is thoroughly learned and the dog responds promptly.

Second, hunt the dog with the check cord dragging and in heavy cover if possible, to slow him down. Or you can attach a piece of broom handle to the collar so that it hangs as nearly horizontal as possible and interferes with any fast running he may try to do.

Third, kill as much game as possible over the dog and teach him to retrieve it. This almost invariably makes a dog inclined to "hunt to the gun," and slows him up considerably.

SHOOT BIRDS OVER PUP WHEN TRAINING

Question: I have had my 5½-month old springer spaniel out three times on pheasants. On several occasions he walked right by birds without giving any indication of their presence, although when he hit the trail of one running hen he had no difficulty in flushing the bird. Do you think he lacks a good nose, or am I expecting too much of him at his age? How far away should he be able to get the scent of a bird?—J. B., Wis.

Answer: From what you say I judge your pup will have a good nose. When he's had a few birds shot over him and learns what it's all about, I think you'll see a wonderful change in his behavior. As a general thing, a dog should catch body scent at about 10 yd., although the distance varies greatly with different conditions, such as moist or dry weather, a moving or "stuck" bird, etc. I once saw Comanche Rap, one of the greatest of field-trial winners, run along a stubble row parallel to a quail running in the very next row, and never catch the scent. Five minutes later he gave a great exhibition of long-distance nose.

HOW TO TRAIN COON HOUNDS QUICKLY

Question: I have just bought four 2-month-old hounds of good hunting stock. With 4 months left before the season starts, could I get them trained for coon and possum hunting this fall? Would using a pet coon help?—H. C., Tenn.

Answer: Your pups will be pretty young to do much real work in the coming season unless they're very exceptional. But the more you take them out in the woods the faster they will learn. All hound breeds really train themselves, either by working with an older dog or even by themselves. If convenient, you could use a tame coon, leading it across country to make a trail, then fastening it high in a tree where the pups can't reach it. The same process should work with opossum.

EXPERIENCE BREAKS BEAGLE OF BACK-TRAILING

Question: Last fall I bought a beagle rabbit dog. She is very good in picking up trails, but I have found that when she loses one she back-trails. Please tell me if she can be broken of this and how it may be done.—F. F. N., Del.

Answer: You do not state how old the beagle is nor what experience she has had. All rabbit hounds develop ability rather slowly, and often are practically pups at 3 years old. They learn primarily by running rabbits, rather than by any specific method of training.

Try to keep as close to your hound as possible when she is on trail, and when you find her back-tracking set her right, going along with her a way to keep her on the move. Better yet, run her with an old, thoroughly experienced hound. If you do this, make sure that the old dog is faster than yours. Otherwise your dog may forge ahead and then start back-tracking, even though she may be only trying to get back to the other hound.

Experience and plenty of it is what makes a good rabbit hound. Many are not at their peak as trailers until they are 6 or 7 years old or even older.

TRAINING DOG TO BE OPEN TRAILER

Question: Hope you can give me some advice about my 3-year-old beagle. A year ago he was a good open trailer, but would run off and go hunting by himself whenever he got the chance. Now he barks only when he starts a rabbit, then goes silent. He is still a good hunter, has a fine nose and is a hard worker. Do you think anything can be done to get him to open up?—M. H., Mass.

Answer: I know of but two ways to make an open trailer out of a silent one, and can't guarantee that either will work. The first is to run the hound with a good open trailer that makes plenty of noise. This sometimes does the trick. The other plan is to jump a rabbit yourself, if possible; then call the hound and start along the trail with him, showing plenty of excitement—run and holler and beat your arms. Both methods are certainly worth at least a try.

HOW TO MAKE DOG GIVE UP GAME

Question: I have a 3-year-old English springer spaniel who does her hunting and retrieving excellently, but refuses to give up pheasants or rabbits when she brings them back.—W. H., Ind.

Answer: If you will press your springer's teeth against her lips, or vice versa, sharply enough to hurt the lips, I think the dog will readily drop any game she has in her mouth. You might also yard-break her for the hard mouth by using a 6-in. piece of broom handle with game feathers glued to it and spikes set in the wood which will discourage biting.

SETTERS AREN'T GOOD RABBIT HUNTERS

Question: How would you advise me to start training my young dog to hunt rabbits? Should I train him alone, or with another dog? Do you think a setter could be trained for this work?—C. M., Mich.

Answer: The best way to train a young dog to hunt rabbits is to yard-break him at home, then take him out to learn for himself. Training with another dog is all right for a short time, but if continued, may make your dog dependent instead of independent in his hunting.

I do not think setters are suited for rabbit hunting. They are not true trailers and, when they jump a rabbit, they usually push him so hard he holes up.

HOW TO TRAIN PUP FOR FIELD

Question: I recently acquired a 4-month-old English setter of good breeding. I have had him in the field several times, and on each occasion he has been inclined to stay quite near me. Is this a natural tendency for such a young dog? Also, do you think I should take him out when the bird season opens, and shoot birds over his head?—F. M., Ind.

Answer: You couldn't expect a pup of this age to do more than stay near you when you take him out in the field—he's still a baby. But he'll mature fast, and the more you take him out in hunting country the faster he'll develop. Take him out as often as you wish; if he runs into birds, so much the better. But be careful not to shoot too close to your pup until you're sure he has no tendency toward gun-shyness.

BREAKING HOUND OF RABBIT CHASING

Question: My 3-year-old coon hound was running coon well when I bought him last year. I took him out with another dog, which turned out to be a good rabbit dog instead of a coon dog, and now my hound has taken to running rabbits. I've tried whipping him off the tracks, but it seems useless.—W. P. R., Pa.

Answer: Your problem is not an easy one. Since whipping the dog off the trail does no good, you might try whipping him good and hard with a dead rabbit, making sure that you hit him over the head and face. The messier he gets, the better. It may make him dislike the smell of rabbit, and it may not, but it's worth a try. Another scheme that often works, at least with hounds that run deer, is to have some man, a perfect stranger to your dog, hide in the brush along the trail, catch the dog, and give him a good hiding. The trail may be laid with a dead rabbit for more effective results.

FLASH POINTING AND BLINKING

Question: I have a setter pup 11 months old, that seems to have a good nose. When I take him to good pheasant cover, he will point for about a minute, sometimes as far as thirty feet from the pheasant; then he will rush it. When the pheasant flies up he will chase it a little way, come back, and smell the ground excitedly. Lately he has developed the habit of pointing at the spot where the pheasant has been sitting, then rushing it. When no pheasant flies up he gets more excited than ever. A friend tells me the dog is blinking.—P. G., Mich.

Answer: The pointing you refer to, which lasts only a minute, is simply what is known as a flash point, and nearly all young and inexperienced bird dogs do it. The same goes for chasing. When your dog points at the spot where the pheasant has been sitting he is not blinking—blinking is backing away from a point already established. Chances are that as your pup grows older he will readily distinguish a bird from the bed or spot where a bird has sat.

WHY POINTER LOSES INTEREST

Question: When taken afield my 4-year-old pointer bitch works well for about 20 minutes, then leaves and goes back to the car to hide under it. She isn't gun-shy. What's wrong?—R. L. F., Pa.

Answer: Without knowing the dog's whole hunting history, I can only guess. But unless she's an experienced dog and has had many birds killed over her, I'd suspect that she simply loses interest when she begins to tire. If you kill a reasonable number of birds over her there's no reason why she should quit. However, if you consistently miss birds, and the bitch has been accustomed in the past to a gunner who consistently scores, I should say she simply goes sour, as many good dogs will do under these conditions.

FACTS ABOUT DOG HEALTH

FITS IN THE FIELD

Question: I have a 3½-year-old dropper. He is big and strong—weighs about 75 lb. Last October I was hunting chickens with him in Kansas. After three hours of hard, fast going he had a fit—fell over, whimpered, and stiffened out. I carried him to the car, which luckily was near by, and covered him with my hunting coat. Two hours later he had perked up considerably, and the veterinarian, a very good man, said it was worm fits, and gave him some pills. He was not hunted again until the middle of November, in the Ozarks in southern Missouri. There was no recurrence. However, the next four times I took him out he again had fits; each time about three hours after starting. On the advice of another veterinarian, I changed his diet and put him on milk and raw horse meat. Your opinion on this matter will be greatly appreciated.—M. H. J., Mo.

Answer: Fits are due to various ills. They may be the result of a brain lesion, an intestinal disorder, or possibly, a kidney disorder. Some dogs have a habit of eating grass or chewing on branches and bushes when hunting. This will cause some digestive disorder, and a convulsion may follow. It is advisable not to hunt your dog for too long a period. Give him 1 tbsp. cod-liver oil daily. Also, 1 vitamin capsule (ABCDG) daily. Add 5 gr. potassium iodide to the drinking water once a day. Have the blood examined for filaria, too.

STANDARD DOG DIET

Question: Please give me a good, inexpensive diet for dogs.—R. F., Tex.

Answer: I suggest the following diet:

Lean, chopped beef, raw or slightly cooked, with stale whole-wheat bread or shredded wheat biscuit and some cooked vegetables such as carrots, spinach, onions, celery, asparagus or tomatoes. This mixture may be given every day. If the vegetables do not agree with the dog, you may eliminate them. Also, cooked lamb, mutton, or beef heart may be substituted for the beef occasionally. Milk may be given daily, and a raw or soft-boiled egg three or four times a week. For puppies, add cod-liver oil to the food.

TEMPORARY BLINDNESS

Question: Last fall my 4-year-old setter almost died of distemper, but good care and vaccination by a veterinarian pulled him through. Last season I took him hunting. The first few times out he ran into fences, bushes, and logs. By the fourth day, however, his sight had improved, and on the fifth day it was normal again. What, in your opinion, caused this temporary near-blindness? Will it recur?—J. B. K., Md.

Answer: It is not unusual for dogs to suffer temporary blindness after distemper. It may, in fact, last for several months. Give the dog 1 tbsp. cod-liver oil (with viosterol) and 1 vitamin ABCDG capsule daily. Add 5 gr. potassium iodide to the drinking water each day. Feed him a normal diet of rare beef mixed with stale whole-wheat bread and some cooked vegetables, also milk, and a raw egg daily. Give him 1 tbsp. mineral oil two or three times a week to prevent constipation.

PREVENTING CAR SICKNESS

Question: Please give me a treatment for car sickness in dogs.—H. L. L., Mass.

Answer: When you expect to take the dog on a trip, skip his last feeding before starting time, and don't let him drink water for 2 hours before leaving. One hour before the trip, give him ¼ grain phenobarbital, and repeat this dose just before you start out. Many dogs are subject to car sickness, but they generally overcome it as they grow older.

CHOREA

Question: I have a registered setter puppy, 8 months old, which has recently recovered from a bad case of distemper. He is active and has a good appetite, but the muscles of his right shoulder twitch almost continuously. What should be done for him?—C. R. W., N. C.

Answer: Your dog probably has chorea, resulting from the distemper. Give him 5 gr. calcium lactate with $\frac{1}{20}$ gr. parathyroid three times a day. If the twitching seems to make him uncomfortable, give him $\frac{1}{4}$ gr. phenobarbital twice a day for 10 days.

The twitching will subside so as to cause your dog no discomfort, but it may take weeks or even months before his condition improves noticeably.

BEAGLE HAS COLD

Question: My 17-month-old beagle has coughing spells—almost as if he had something caught in his throat—his eyes are bloodshot, and his appetite is ravenous.—J. G., Mich.

Answer: Your dog probably has a very severe cold, which may lead to other trouble unless treated. Give him 1 tsp. sirup cocillana three times a day, and 2 tsp. cod-liver oil with viosterol daily; also bathe the eyes with a 2 percent boric-acid solution three times a day, and put one drop of 5 percent argyrol in each eye after each bathing. You may also give him $\frac{1}{2}$ tsp. brandy in a dessertspoonful of honey two or three times a day. Keep him in a warm, dry place.

CONSTIPATION

Question: My two dogs are constipated and drag their rear ends on the ground. What should I do?—F. H., Jr., N. C.

Answer: Give them each 1 tbsp. mineral oil or milk of magnesia twice a week. Have the stool analyzed to determine if worms are present. If segments of tapeworm are found, give the animal $\frac{1}{20}$ gr. arecoline hydrobromide on an empty stomach, followed an hour later by a saline enema of 1 tsp. salt in 1 pt. warm water. Repeat this treatment in 3 weeks if necessary. The dogs may have rectal irritations, so cleanse the areas with a solution of 1 tsp. bicarbonate of soda in a glass of water.

TREATING DIARRHEA

Question: My beagle has been suffering from diarrhea for the last 2 months. His stool is like jelly, and sometimes red, other times brown and red. What should I do?—G. G. E., N. Y.

Answer: Give the dog 5 gr. bismuth subnitrate every 3 hours until the stool is normal. If he drinks too much water, substitute weak tea or barley water occasionally. Feed him beef mixed with stale whole-wheat bread twice a day, and when his stool is normal add cooked vegetables, cereal, and milk to his diet. Have the stool analyzed for worms.

DISTEMPER

Question: I recently acquired a cocker spaniel about 6 months old. He sneezes and coughs quite a bit. Is this distemper, and, if so, what should I do for it? In other respects he seems healthy and happy.—R. B., Kan.

Answer: It is likely that your dog has distemper. Cleanse his eyes with a 2 percent boric-acid solution three times a day. Also, give him 1 tsp. sirup cocillana three times a day, and half of a 5-gr. aspirin tablet twice a day.

The diet should consist of rare beef mixed with stale whole-wheat bread and some cooked vegetables. Also some milk, and a raw egg three or four times a week.

Add cod-liver oil to the diet once a day. If the stools are loose, eliminate the vegetables and milk till they become normal.

EXCESSIVE DROOLING

Question: My 7-month-old springer spaniel is subject to considerable drooling of saliva from the backs of his jaws. Is this any particular ailment?—C. C. C., Wis.

Answer: This drooling may be due to nervousness when hunting. It is also possible that the dog may chew on various things, such as weeds, wood or grass, that would induce drooling. I believe the condition will disappear as he grows older, but try giving him a thiamin chloride tablet (1 mg.) two or three times a day.

DEEP EAR INFECTION

Question: My 5-year-old springer spaniel has been bothered with an itching in both ears, accompanied by a dark, smelly discharge which comes from deep down in the ear canals. I have been told that it is an infection due to a minute organism similar to that which causes athlete's foot.—N. L., Wis.

Answer: Try cleaning the ears with cotton dipped in hydrogen peroxide, then wiping with dry cotton and applying a 2 percent yellow mercuric-oxide ointment. Massage gently and remove surplus ointment. Every fourth day, dust sulfanilamide powder into the ears instead of using the ointment. After this ear disturbance seems to have been corrected, examine the ears occasionally, as they may require repeat treatments.

IRRITATED EYE

Question: One of the eyes of my year-old English pointer has suddenly become bloodshot. The pupil is enlarged and the iris blurred. How do I treat this condition?—J. B., N. Y.

Answer: Bathe the eye with a 2 percent solution of boric acid, and follow with 1 drop argyrol (5 percent solution) three times a day. Do not permit her to rub and irritate the eye.

FUNGOUS GROWTH ON SKIN

Question: My two beagles were in perfect health until 2 months ago, when a small sore broke out on one dog's legs. Now each dog has about 20 spots, all deep-seated and with pus in them, which take off the hair around them. They reappear whenever they're pulled off. What shall I do?—M. C. C., Md.

Answer: It's very likely that your dogs have some fungous infection. Cleanse affected parts with a warm epsom-salts solution (1 tbsp. salts to 1 qt. water); then massage each sore gently to remove the pus, or have them cut if necessary. Once this has been done, you may apply ichthyol ointment (10 percent) twice a day. Always disinfect your hands after treating the animals.

SWOLLEN GLANDS

Question: My 4-year-old cocker spaniel seems to have swollen glands. At least, his neck is very sore and swollen at the base of the jaw. He still has a good appetite, but is very weak.—J. McD., Mont.

Answer: Apply warm and cold compresses alternately to the affected part 3 or 4 times daily. Then rub in camphorated oil. Give your dog milk and eggs every day. Also mix some broth with his meat, making it semi-solid. He will then be able to swallow it much more easily. Give him ½ of a 5-grain aspirin tablet every 4 hours, and ½ teaspoonful of brandy in 2 teaspoonsful of water or milk twice a day.

SHAKES HEAD AND SHOULDER

Question: My 5-month-old cocker spaniel seems to have St. Vitus's dance. She shakes her head and right shoulder, even when she is asleep. What would you advise me to do to help her?—G. G., N. Y.

Answer: Give her ¼ gr. phenobarbital every night for 2 weeks. Also, 5 gr. calcium lactate with ½₀ gr. parathyroid three times a day. The twitching may disappear or subside so as to cause the animal no discomfort. But it may take months, probably longer, before there is any improvement.

Feed her on rare beef mixed with stale whole-wheat bread and some cooked vegetables. Also milk, and a raw egg daily. If unable to get beef, you may substitute beef heart, kidneys, liver, poultry, or fish. Give cod-liver oil daily.

MANGE

Question: What do you advise for a bad case of follicular mange? I have tried everything I can think of, but nothing seems to help my dog.—J. G. D., Wis.

Answer: Apply the following mixture to the affected parts with cotton once a day: 1 oz. balsam Peru, 1 tsp. creolin, and sufficient alcohol to make 8 oz. Before applying the lotion, dab the affected parts with witch hazel. Keep your dog in sanitary surroundings, and bathe him every 2 weeks. Also, give him 1 tsp. cod-liver oil daily. Mange is difficult to contend with. It my take weeks, even months, to effect a cure.

SETTER'S NOSE RUNS

Question: My 10-month-old setter was treated for distemper and a bad cold within the last 3 months. He now seems perfectly healthy, except that his nose is continually running, occasionally giving forth a ropy green slime.—J. H., Pa.

Answer: This nasal discharge should disappear. Inject 2 or 3 drops of argyrol (5 percent) into the nostrils twice a day for a week; then continue, using mineral oil instead of the argyrol. Give the dog 2 tsp. of cod-liver oil with viosterol twice daily, and add 5 grains of potassium iodide to the drinking water once a day.

RHEUMATISM

Question: My 5-year-old varmint dog is in bad shape. He walks around with his head held about 8 in. from the ground, and can't seem to get it any lower or higher. His trouble seems to be in his neck or just behind his shoulders. Sometimes he can eat, other times he just walks back and forth in front of his food. Please tell me what I can do for him.—J. B. G., Mo.

Answer: It is likely that your dog has a rheumatic condition. Apply warm cloths to his shoulders and neck. An electric pad may be used. Give him half of a 5-gr. aspirin tablet every 4 hours. Give him a saline enema (1 tsp. salt to 1 pt. warm water) three or four times a week. Also, he should have 1 tsp. cod-liver oil daily.

PUP HAS RICKETS

Question: My 3-month-old hound pup stands drawn up all the time, and the upper joints of his legs seem to bend inward when he walks.—S. F. B., Va.

Answer: It's likely that your puppy has rickets, probably due to a diet deficiency. Give him 2 tsp. cod-liver oil with viosterol twice a day and add ¼ tsp. calcium lactate to his food twice daily. Give him 2 feedings a day of lean, chopped beef, raw or slightly cooked, plus some cooked vegetables and stale whole-wheat bread. He should also have a raw egg every day and milk twice daily. With this care, I believe the pup will be all right when he grows older.

SETTER SHEDS COAT

Question: I have an English setter that sheds the year around. It is impossible to get near her without becoming covered with hair. Also, when hunting hard, her kidneys act frequently, at times every 5 minutes.—W. K. A., N. C.

Answer: I advise you to groom the dog daily. Twice a week, sponge the coat with

4 tbsp. bay rum in a small basin of water, rub thoroughly dry with a Turkish towel, brush, and comb. Also, every two weeks, rub warm olive oil into the coat, allow it to remain on for an hour, and bathe the dog, using Castile soap or mild soap flakes.

The diet should consist of lean, chopped, rare beef daily (cooked lamb, mutton, beef heart or liver or head meat may be substituted). This meat should be mixed with stale whole-wheat bread and some cooked vegetables. Give a raw egg three or four times a week, and add 1 tbsp. cod-liver oil to the diet once a day. Exercise the dog regularly.

ELIMINATING TICKS

Question: The season before last, my Irish setter picked up some wood ticks. We got rid of them by having the dog dipped and the house—he has the run of it—fumigated with cyanide gas. Although I avoided the area where I believe my setter contacted the pests before, he has them again this season. Could small ticks or eggs drop off the dog and then develop later around the house? What do you recommend?—H. H. S., Mich.

Answer: It seems likely that there are ticks in the house, as well as outside in the shrubs and grass. They get into rugs, furniture, walls, and other parts of a house. You must first eliminate the vermin from your premises, or your setter will become re-infested. So if you want to rid your dog of ticks, you'll have to take heroic measures:

Examine him daily, removing and burning all ticks. Confine him to one room; put paper down, change it every day, and burn it. Examine your window sills, furniture, and similar places daily.

Once a week, sponge the setter's coat with 1 tbsp. of kerosene mixed in 1 pt. of milk. Let this preparation remain on 30 minutes. Then bathe the animal with Castile soap or soap flakes in water containing 1 tbsp. creolin.

Dust derris powder with 4 percent rotenone, into his coat twice a week.

DOSAGE OF WORM MEDICINES

Question: I usually have several dogs of all ages on my place, and would like to know the proper dosage of both roundworm and tapeworm medicines for pups and older dogs.—S. J. N., Mich.

Answer: For roundworms, I suggest the following effective mixture: 3 tbsp. castor oil, 1 tbsp. sirup of buckthorn, 16 drops oil of wormseed.

For puppies about 2 months old, give 1 to 2 tsp. of this mixture, according to the size of the breed. Very small pups should get even less.

Four-month-old pups, 2 to 3 tsp.

Six to 9-month-old pups, about 1 tbsp.

Dogs 1 year old or more, 1 to 2 tbsp., depending on size. Very large breeds require even more.

For tapeworm infestation, arecoline hydrobromide is usually given on an empty stomach, followed after an hour by a saline enema of 1 tsp. salt in 1 pt. warm water—more for good-size dogs.

For small puppies, give $\frac{1}{60}$ grain of the drug.

For good-size puppies, $\frac{1}{20}$ gr.

For large dogs, two $\frac{1}{20}$-gr. tablets.

Do not feed the animals for several hours after either treatment. Repeat the dosage in 3 weeks if necessary.

TREATING ASTHMA

Question: My 4-year-old beagle has what our local veterinarian diagnosed as asthma. Though the dog seems in good health and likes to get out and hunt, he has as many as four or five attacks a day, also some at night. They come on him suddenly whether he's resting, running, or sleeping. He will stretch his body out straight, then draw in air through his nose with a loud gasping sound. What can I do for him?—P. C. R., Mo.

Answer: I believe this condition can be corrected in time. Give the animal ¼ gr. phenobarbital twice a day for a week, then once a day for the same period. Apply a few drops of mineral oil in the nostrils twice a day. Add ¼ tsp. calcium lactate to the food once a day. Don't let the dog become constipated. Give him 1 tsp. mineral oil two or three times a week if necessary.

AGE FOR SPAYING

Question: I have just purchased a cocker spaniel, a female 4 months old. I am contemplating having the dog spayed when she is about 9 months old. Is this the proper time for such an operation, and will the dog necessarily take on weight as she grows older? Will the dog lose all desire to hunt.—A. D., Ontario.

Answer: I think it advisable to have the puppy spayed at 5 or 6 months of age. She will be coming in season at 9 or 10 months. However, if you wish, you may have her spayed when she is older. After this operation, there is a tendency for the animal to put on weight. You will have to watch her diet carefully and see that she receives plenty of exercise. It should not interfere with her hunting qualities.

BREEDING DIFFICULTY

Question: I have a 2-year-old foxhound bitch and want to breed her with my male beagle, but she snaps at him and won't let him near her.—C. P., Mich.

Answer: Try leaving the two dogs together by themselves for short intervals. The female sometimes snaps at the male but later becomes friendly. If this does not work, you might try to find another mate for her.

BRINGING A BITCH IN SEASON

Question: My black-and-tan hound is 2 years old, and a year ago she had a litter of pups. She has not been in heat since that time, and I want to breed her again. What should be done?—P. K., Ariz.

Answer: Have your local veterinarian give the animal some injections, or give her a 1-mg. tablet of diethylstilbestrol three times a day. Add ½ tsp. of wheat-germ oil to the dog's food once a day.

BREEDING A PUREBRED BITCH

Question: My uncle has given me a pure-bred hunting bitch, the daughter of a champion, and so I have a few questions to ask you. What is a stud fee? When would be a good time to breed my dog—she is 3½ years old—and what can I do to assure sound puppies?—R. T., N. C.

Answer: A stud fee is money paid the owner of a male dog for the service of that dog when mated to a female for the production of pups.

Since she is a mature dog, it will be O. K. to breed her any time she comes in season—which normally occurs twice a year.

The best way to insure sound pups is to give her lots of exercise and a well-balanced diet with plenty of proteins. Permit her to run free as much as possible while she is carrying her litter.

POOR LUCK WITH PUPS

Question: My pointer had a litter of six nice pups last year, but they began to ail and within a few weeks all had died. My veternarian said that the mother's milk was acid and the puppies couldn't survive. Do you think it advisable to attempt another breeding?—V. B., Conn.

Answer: You can breed your pointer again; it is not likely that she will have a recurrence of this condition. But if she does, take the puppies from her and obtain a foster mother, or feed them from a small bottle with a doll's nipple. Have the mother's milk analyzed if the pups do not thrive. At three weeks they will be able to lap milk and eat raw scraped beef.

SPECIAL PROBLEMS OF THE DOG OWNER

GUN-DOG FIELD TRIALS

Question: Our local club is planning a field trial for pointers and setters. It will be strictly for gun dogs, since many men who use their animals only for hunting will not enter them otherwise. Will you outline for us the general way in which the meet should be run and the standards for which points should be awarded?—E. C. B., N. H.

Answer: Field trials usually list three classes of entries—the puppy class, including dogs up to 1 year of age; the derby, of those up to 2 years; and the open stake, of all over 2. Those entered in the puppy class are not required to be steady to wing or shot, but in the other classes this is a major consideration.

Pointers and setters are judged on their obedience, their capacity to range and cover ground without back-tracking, and their ability to locate game. Their casts should be wide and free, but they should always keep their handler in view and remain alert to his whistle or call. (They have to remain within the course limits, illustrating the handler's control.) They must be stanch on point and steady to wing; they must never, under any circumstances, chase flushed game.

Two mounted judges usually keep score. If any dogs seem to rate exceptionally close the judges may demand that these contestants run the course again.

WHAT DOES REGISTRATION MEAN?

Question: Just what does a dog's registration mean? Is it just a come-on for gullible buyers, does it insure good puppies because of the selected stock from which the sire and dam descended, or does it mean something else?—K. P. Y., La.

Answer: Registration is by no means a come-on. It's the only method by which the traits of an individual dog can be known through the recorded characteristics and performances of its ancestors. This is the reason that so much effort has been expended in the breeding of dogs and in the preserving of pedigrees.

READYING DOG FOR SHOW

Question: I want to enter my pointer in a dog show to be held in our town in a few months. What are the main things to work on with the dog?—F. I., Va.

Answer: Simply put your dog in good physical condition, not too lean and not too fat, and brush him and groom him every day or two from now until the day of the show. Meanwhile, teach him to stand for you stylishly (look up some pictures of good show pointers and setters as a guide), and to walk and trot at your side nicely on a leash. That's all there is to it; the judge will do the rest. But the better he stands for inspection and the better he moves when on leash, the better will be your chances.

BUYING PUP BY MAIL

Question: Please give me some pointers on the best method of buying a pup by mail. Does the buyer have any protection against fraud?—T. B. P., Quebec.

Answer: Above all, deal with a reliable kennel which will guarantee you a good dog. Then if the pup you receive doesn't satisfy you, the kennel will take it back and refund your money. A kennel of this type will send you the registration papers, guarantee the health of the dog, and perhaps inoculate it against distemper.

To be doubly safe, incorporate these stipulations in your letter to the kennel. Keep a copy of the letter and also keep the breeder's reply. I doubt that you will have any difficulty if you deal with a reliable outfit.

ALL ABOUT FISHING

by Ray Bergman

HOW TO CHOOSE YOUR TACKLE

ROD FOR FLY AND BAIT COMBINATION

Question: What rod should I get for wet-fly and worm fishing for trout and bass? I can afford only one, and would prefer a steel rod since the streams I use are narrow and brushy. What line do I need?—E. J. H., Me.

Answer: I believe you could get along with an 8½-ft. steel rod—the new "bamboo-action" type rather than the old type. For a wet-fly line, either a level or tapered one in the very best grade you can afford. The size must be determined by the action of the rod you buy, but the tapered line should probably be at least H-C-H. For bait, the finer the line the easier it will handle. An H level probably would be best.

LINE FOR FLY FISHING FOR BASS

Question: What line should I use with a 7-oz. fly rod? I have a level E line now.

Also, what test leader should I use with the line—for both wet-fly and dry-fly bass fishing? What length should the leader be?—L. S. W., Tex.

Answer: You did not give the length of your rod, but a 7-ouncer would probably take a level C, or, at the lightest, a D. The E is a bit light for the best work, although it will be usable with limitations.

A good length leader for all-round bass fishing is 6 ft., although you could get by with 3 ft. or even less. A good weight for a level bass leader is .015. Personally, I prefer a tapered leader, 7½ to 9 ft. long, tapering from .019 to .014.

ALL-AROUND ROD

Question: What action and length fly rod would you recommend for both wet and dry-fly fishing for brook trout and browns, also with bait for brookies? The brook-trout streams I plan to fish are mostly brushy, while the brown-trout waters are fairly open.—A. Z. H., Pa.

Answer: Your best bet probably would be a medium-stiff dry-fly rod. The length depends on the degree of brushiness of the brushy streams, but inasmuch as a 7½-ft. dry-fly rod will do well on open streams and is also good on brushy ones, it would seem to be your best solution as a single all-purpose rod.

MINIMUM SPINNING OUTFIT

Question: I'd like to know what equipment I'd need for bass fishing in Louisianna. Many of my casting friends have wonderful luck with pork chunks weighing ¼ oz. Of course, I know I need a spinning reel, but is it necessary to buy a rod and the special line usually sold with it?—P. S. B., La.

Answer: Unless you have a light, limber bait-casting rod, one will be needed for the spinning reel. I have made out quite well using a 5½-ft., 6-oz. bait caster. However, it doesn't work as well as my regulation spinning rod, which is 7 ft. and 7 oz. You really need quite some whip in the rod, both to aid in the casting and for taking up most of the strain on the light line. For ¼-oz. lures you will need a very fine line—not more than 5-lb. test—and for this reason if no other the regulation bait caster is bad because of the line-breaking hazard.

SINGLE VS. DOUBLE-BUILT RODS

Question: I do most of my fishing with bait and flies in the Madison, Gallatin, and Big Hole Rivers around Yellowstone Park, where there are plenty of heavy, fighting trout, and in the last three years I have worn out two pretty fair rods. They didn't break—just became lifeless. Would a double-built bamboo rod stand up any better than a single-built of the same weight?—L. B., Mont.

Answer: I don't believe a double-built rod would be stronger than the equivalent in a good single. It's possible, since you use bait as well as flies, that one of the "bamboo-action" steel rods would be best for you. While you may not enjoy fly-casting with one of these as much as with bamboo, they do a good job and of course do not become lifeless in the way a low to medium-price split bamboo sometimes does under rigorous use.

BEST FLY RODS FOR BASS AND TROUT

Question: I have never done any fly fishing but plan to do so first chance I get. I gather that separate rods are advisable for bass, trout, and muskies. I am more interested in bass and trout than I am in

muskies. What kind of a rod, or rods, do you recommend?—R. T. H., Ill.

Answer: The following rods would make a good pair for bass and trout fishing: For trout, 8 ft.—about 4 to 4¼ oz. For bass, 9 to 9½ ft.—5½ to 6¼ oz.

The 9½-footer could be used for muskies although it is a trifle light to cast the necessary lures. Probably the best rod for such work would be 9½ ft.—7 to 8 oz. However, as a rule the fly rod isn't used for muskies—most anglers use a bait-casting rod, which is more satisfactory for the job.

PACK-TRIP TACKLE FOR TROUT

Question: My friend and I are going on a pack trip into the Kings River country of California, where we intend to fish. What tackle do we need?—L. M., Calif.

Answer: A fly-rod outfit with dry flies, wet flies, and perhaps some small spinners would be in order for any trout country. If you expect to fish in ponds it might be a good idea to take along a spinning outfit.

TACKLE FOR FLY CASTING

Question: I have done some bait casting and would now like to try my hand at fly fishing. As I don't know anything about it, I wonder if you'd be good enough to suggest the tackle required?

I'd be going after pickerel, panfish, and an occasional bass, and have been considering an 8½-ft., 5-oz. rod or a 9-ft., 6½-oz. rod. Are these the proper weights and lengths?

Could you also tell me what size of level line and what leaders to use? What flies are most reliable for the fish I've mentioned?—E. M., R. I.

Answer: Probably the 8½-ft., 5-oz. rod would be best for your purpose. This rod would, most likely, take a D level line, though the choice of line depends on the "feel" of the rod. The leader you use will depend on the fish you're after and the conditions you encounter. In a general way fine leaders are used for trout, heavy leaders for bass, and wire leaders for pickerel.

Streamer flies are good for pickerel, floating bugs work well on bass, and both wet and dry flies, as well as streamers, are good for trout.

OUTFIT FOR 1½ TO 5-LB. BASS

Question: What length and weight fly rod should I use with an automatic fly-weight reel? And what size line should I use for wet and dry-fly fishing? How about tapered lines—are they easier to cast, or what are their advantages over regular lines? All my fishing is for small and largemouth bass weighing from 1½ to 5 lb.—E. H. L., Wash.

Answer: The reel should be picked for the rod, not the rod for the reel. However, if the automatic reel has sufficient line capacity it will likely be suitable for the rod you need. My recommendation would be a 9 or 9½-ft. rod weighing from 6 to 6½ oz.

The size of the line depends on the length, weight, and action of the rod. It should be heavy enough to bring out the rod's action, but not so heavy that it kills it. For your purpose I would suggest either an H-C-H line or a D level line, and a 7½-ft. leader tapered from .019 to .014.

One advantage of a tapered line is the absence of an abrupt break in the connection between line and leader. Tying a leader to a level C or D line makes a poor connection which is troublesome in casting and often causes slack. Also, with a tapered line there is less strain on the rod when reaching out for distance—the heavy body of the line helps push out the lighter taper and the leader.

GEAR FOR BASS AND PANFISH

Question: Would my 9-ft., 6½-oz. fly rod with dry-fly action, and a level D line be any good for bass and panfish? If so, what type of reel should I use, and what lures are best?—E. B. S., Calif.

Answer: Your rod would be excellent for bass, and could be used for panfish, though somewhat heavy for sport with the latter. Any single-action reel that holds enough line would be O.K. A level D line would be satisfactory for fly casting. However, if you intend to fish with bait, I would suggest about a level G.

Any of the numerous bass plugs and streamers on the market would be in order, also spinners and fly-rod plugs. For the panfish, the same lures would be O.K., but the size should be considerably smaller. In flies and bugs I like hooks in the No. 2 size for bass, and No. 6 for panfish.

FLY TACKLE FOR CRAPPIES

Question: What size rod, and what type reel, line, and lures are good for fly-fishing for crappies?—M. L. H., Tex.

Answer: My choice for a crappie rod would be 8½ ft., 4 oz. The reel doesn't matter, so long as it balances with the rod, but for a line I'd prefer a double taper to a level one—an H-E-H tapered, or F level, should be right for the rod. These sizes are for American lines; the English run smaller and the proper size would be G-D-G or E. As for lures, any trout flies or lures are satisfactory.

TACKLE AND TECHNIQUE FOR NORTH UMPQUA STEELHEADS

Question: I want to do some summer fly fishing for steelheads in the North Umpqua River country in Oregon. I have fished that river a lot for mountain trout, but never for steelheads.

Since I understand you have taken steelheads from the North Umpqua, maybe you could give me some information as to the proper rod, reel, line, and leaders for these fish. I have been thinking about getting a 9-ft., 6½-oz. rod and a large fly reel. Does that sound O.K.?

Also, please tell me the flies to use and the technique involved. As you know, the river is unusually rapid, with many white riffles.—R. J., Calif.

Answer: The 9-ft., 6½-oz. rod you are considering would be satisfactory for steelheads. You will need a reel large enough to hold 30 yd. of fly-casting line and 400 ft. of about 12-lb.-test backing.

The principal method of fly fishing for steelheads is with wet flies. As a rule, the fly is cast across and downstream, and given steady jerks as it drifts. Always strike on the reel; otherwise your tackle is likely to break. The North Umpqua steelheads may take some dry flies, but they never did while I was fishing the stream. Use No. 4, 6, and 8 wet flies like the Umpqua, Cumings, Gibson Girl, Parmachene Belle, and Black Gordon (new and very good).

I never fished for small trout in the North Umpqua, confining my efforts to the large steelhead. The best fish I caught weighed 10¾ lb.

BEGINNER'S OUTFIT

Question: Would an 8-ft., 4½-oz. rod be good for a novice fly fisherman to use on trout? Would a 9½-ft., 5¾-oz. rod be suitable for bass bugs and bass flies? What size line should he use with it? What do you think about using automatic reels?—M. M., Ill.

Answer: Although I'd call an 8-ft., 4½-oz. fly rod pretty heavy for its length, it will do for trout. Try a 9½-ft., 5¾-oz. rod with an H-C-H line for bass bugs. I like a tapered leader for either trout or bass. The correct trout leader depends upon the wariness of the fish and the clearness of the water, but usually a 7½-ft. length tapered to 2X is satisfactory. For bass, a leader tapering from .019 or .020 to .014 is a good all-rounder.

The choice of an automatic or single-action reel depends upon your personal preferences; both sorts will do the job.

A GOOD ROD FOR BAIT FISHING

Question: I tried bait casting for several years, but had no luck. Probably I was doing something wrong, so until I can go out with a real fisherman and learn how to do it correctly I'm confining myself to trolling for wall-eyes and stillfishing for panfish. I have always used a 5½-ft. rod, but since the line often gets caught on the stern of the boat when I am trolling alone, I think an 8-ft. rod would be better. I use a multiplying reel. Can you give me any suggestions as to the best kind of rod for me?—A. P. C., Ill.

Answer: What I would consider your best bet for the bait fishing you like, using a multiplying reel, is a regular bait rod. This is, in effect, a heavy fly rod, with a bait-reel seat, and guides of a type which will keep the line from rubbing on the rod itself when the reel and guides are held on top, as would be the case when using a right-handed multiplying reel. Of course, it wouldn't be too serious if the line did rub on a steel rod, but it would if the rod is bamboo.

It is quite likely that it would be necessary to have such a rod made up. They were once very popular, but the main call today is for bait-casting rods, fly rods, and spinning rods.

ALL-AROUND OUTFIT FOR TEXAS

Question: Suppose you were 35, hadn't done any decent fishing in 10 years but loved that sport, lived near San Antonio, Tex., liked to eat fish but hated to dig bait, enjoyed fishing alone but hated to lug a lot of paraphernalia, what kind of fishing outfit would you select to last the rest of your natural life?

I'll be starting out new and haven't got enough time to learn by experience which equipment best suits my needs. I wish to learn a method of fishing to cover the widest territory with a minimum of equipment.—M. L. T., Tex.

Answer: Probably the best all-around outfit for your section would be a bait-casting rod and reel with an assortment of plugs. The principal fresh-water game fish in that region is the largemouth bass. I've also fished the Colorado below Buchanan Reservoir with flies and a fly rod, enjoying good results, particularly on white bass. In the lake and near-by ponds I've taken good bass with surface bugs.

Personally, I'd want both a bait-casting and a fly-rod outfit for bass fishing.

RIG FOR LAKE TROUT

Question: Perhaps you can make some suggestions that will help me with my lake-trout fishing. The lake where I fish is in Ontario, north of the Thousand Island section. The natives fish this cool, deep water by trolling a slow-moving silver wobbler which has a medium-size gang hook at the tail. They use copper wire for line, and a very large reel. Their all-metal poles are at least 8 ft. long.

When the trout are lying deep along the rocky bottom, some 350 ft. of the wire is let out. This results in lots of snags, lost lures, and broken lines. I'll appreciate your advice.—H. G., N. Y.

Answer: It occurs to me that the use of a Monel-metal line would help your lake-trout fishing. This wire is very tough; I use size .016, which is quite fine and enables me to use a smaller reel than would be possible when using copper wire. Also, Monel metal is heavy and sinks readily.

Only skill can prevent your getting caught on the bottom, but the finer the line the lighter the sinker, the less the danger of it.

TROUT TACKLE FOR LIVE BAIT

Question: For use exclusively on trout in small streams, creeks, and brooks—trout ranging up to 18 in.—what tackle would

you recommend? For bait I'll use salmon eggs, worms, grubs, grasshoppers, and creepers.—H. E., Calif.

Answer: It seems to me that the best rod for your purpose is an 8-footer of tubular steel, new style. This would handle all the baits you mention, and a spinner-and-worm combination besides. Personally, I should prefer a fine oil-dressed or "vacuum-finished" fly line in a small calibration (say G level, or I-G-I tapered). If this is unobtainable or the cost is too high, try one of the cheaper enameled lines in the smaller calibrations. Bait-casting lines are too soft and tangle too easily, when strip casting and retrieving —a technique that's necessary when using a fly rod for bait casting.

The question of reels is a matter of personal choice, unless you expect to fish for steelheads, which are of fair size and make long runs. In that case you'll need a substantially made single-action reel (*not* an automatic), with sufficient line capacity to take care of the situation.

OUTFIT FOR NEW YORK TROUT

Question: I intend to try fishing a small mountain brook, 60 mi. north of New York City, which contains only 7 to 9-in. trout and is grown over with brush and trees. If I use a 6 to 6½-ft. fly rod, weighing 2 to 3 oz., what size line is best? What patterns of flies?—P. N., N. Y.

Answer: It is impossible to make fool-proof recommendations for a line to fit any rod unless one knows the action of the particular rod. Generally speaking, a 6-ft., 2-oz. rod should take an H-F-H double-tapered or G level line, while a 6¼-ft., 3-oz. one would take an H-E-H taper or F level. However, much depends on the rod action. If very stiff, the lines must have sufficient weight to bring out the action. If limber, then the line should be lighter and thinner.

For brook trout in southern New York

I have always liked the following flies: Light Cahill, Campbell's Fancy, Orange Fish Hawk, Blue Quill, and Coachman, plain or Royal.

CASTING LIGHT LURES

Question: I want to assemble an outfit suitable for casting ¼-oz. lures 30 to 35 yd. for wall-eyes. Can I use my standard bait-casting reel? What kind of rod and line shall I buy?—H. V. C., Iowa.

Answer: To cast ¼-oz. lures 30 to 35 yd. necessitates a special outfit. You will need a free-spool reel (all the reel manufacturers make them) and a limber rod— one at least 6 ft. long and weighing between 4½ and 5¼ oz. Good rod makers produce these, but be sure you specify ¼-oz. lures in ordering one. The line should be light, preferably a 4-lb test.

FLY OUTFIT FOR OZARKS

Question: I am planning a week's fishing in the Arkansas Ozarks and want to buy a fly rod for it. Sections I will fish have mostly small streams, with brush along the banks. Would a 7 or 7½-ft. rod be best? What types of lures should I get for smallmouth bass and an occasional rainbow trout?—G. G. G., Okla.

Answer: A 7½-ft. rod is O.K. for brushy streams, provided you can wade them. If you must do your casting from the bank, with brush around you, then a longer and more powerful rod would be better. For smallmouths in the Ozarks surface bass bugs are effective. Streamers and bucktail wet flies combined with small spinners are also excellent. You can use 3 to 4½-ft. level leaders with these, but I prefer 7½ to 9-ft. tapered ones.

SWIFT-RIVER ROD

Question: I fish in swift rivers with rock bottoms for panfish, bass, fallfish, and chubs. I plan to buy a metal fly rod, 8½-ft. long, about 5 oz. in weight. Do you think this is a good choice? Is an automatic reel as good a choice as a single-action job for my use?—J. M. S., Va.

Answer: The rod you've chosen should serve you well for the fishing you plan to do. The reel is entirely a personal choice. I prefer the single action, but there are some mighty good fishermen who won't use anything except an automatic.

LEADER FOR PICKEREL

Question: I am planning to fish with flies in some ponds and streams where there are pickerel, pike, and some bass. What kind of leader should I use? Can I attach it to the fly with a snap?—J. H. G., Ill.

Answer: For pickerel or pike the only safe leader is a wire one. For bass I prefer gut or its substitutes, and a level leader would serve your purpose here. There are some flies you can attach to a snap, for instance: streamers and bucktails. However, I believe it is better to tie all flies directly to the leader.

TACKLE FOR COLORADO STREAMS

Question: For trout fishing in Colorado and Wyoming, what sort of tackle would you recommend?—C. B., Ariz.

Answer: The tackle used for stream fishing in Colorado and Wyoming is like that used in Pennsylvania and the Catskill Mountains of New York. I use either a 7½ or 8-ft. dry-fly rod, except when fishing the larger streams, when a 9-footer comes in handy.

The regulation dry flies are all in order: such patterns as Adams (a must for brown trout), Ginger Quill, Blue Quill, Royal Coachman, Gray Hackle or Bivisible. On the whole, the *size* of flies is smaller than it is in the East. No. 14 is very popular, and I have often found 16's and 18's a must.

For wet flies, bucktails are about as good as anything; but in this case *large* flies are often best.

FLORIDA BASS OUTFIT

Question: I am planning to fish for bass on the east and west coasts of Florida. What tackle, bugs, and plugs should I take along?—H. N., N. Y.

Answer: I have found Florida fresh-water bass fishing like that anywhere else, with surface lures which make a disturbance exceptionally productive. Your regular bass-fly rod and bait-casting rod should suffice, together with your regular assortment of lures.

ROD FOR BASS

Question: I was recently given an automatic fly-casting reel and should like to know the right kind of fly rod to purchase. I fish mostly for smallmouth and largemouth bass, though I expect to do a little trout fishing this year. I'd like to use the same rod for all my fishing.

Also, what kind of line would be best suited for my purpose?—B. L. W., Ohio.

Answer: Probably the best bet for you would be a 9-ft., 5½ to 6-oz. fly rod. Though this is a bit too much rod for trout, you mention that bass are your primary concern and trout a sideline.

A rod of this length and weight would probably take a H-C-H line. However, action has a lot to do with the right line, and it is best to check this with your tackle dealer when you buy your rod.

ALL-AROUND BAIT-CASTING OUTFIT

Question: I want an all-around bait-casting outfit for bass, pike, and pickerel, with the possibility of muskies in the offing. A man I used to know had a honey; he landed 6-in. muskies on it by being careful, yet could cast a wet fly and spinner with ease. What about a 5½-ft. tubular steel rod?—A. W. G., Pa.

Answer: A 5½-ft. rod with so-called bamboo action is a very nice rod. I have several and like them a lot. However, the bass weights in these are not very good

for muskies. You really need more heft to set the hook in a muskie than these rods have. On the other hand, you can get muskie-weight rods, but although you can cast ½ and ⅝-oz. bass lures with these, they are not at all well suited to the work. You have to decide which type of fishing is more important to you; if the bass, then the lighter rod can be made to do. I've never had any trouble landing muskies on a light rod, though I have had trouble hooking them.

FOR TROUT AND BASS

Question: What kind of fly outfit would you suggest that I buy to use on both trout and bass?—G. A. S., Wis.

Answer: When buying an all-around rod, you must pick one suitable for the most strenuous work involved—in your case, the bass fishing. Therefore I'd recommend a 9½-ft. fly rod weighing 5¾ to 6¼ oz. and the reel and line which fit it best. The line would probably be an H-C-H double taper. Then I'd stock up on both trout and bass leaders: the bass ones 4½ to 7 ft. and calibrating .017 in. level or tapered .019 to .015, the trout leaders 7½ to 9 ft. long and tapering from .016 to .008 or .007. These are merely general suggestions, and your local conditions may necessitate different tackle, but the above should give you an idea.

LINE FOR 5½-OZ. BAMBOO ROD

Question: Recently I became interested in the smallmouth bass in Otsego Lake, Cooperstown, N. Y. This lake, fed by many fresh-water springs, is very clear and, in places, very, very deep. There is little cover for fish other than some long water grass, lilies, and occasional windfalls along the rocky shore.

I have a 9-ft., 5½-oz. split-bamboo fly rod and a single-action fly reel. Can you suggest the proper line and leader for use with bugs and wet and dry flies? Also, how should the lures be fished in this clear water? Bass caught in this lake run from 2 to 9 lb.—C. R. S., N. Y.

Answer: It is rather hard to advise correctly on a proper line for a rod unless one can feel the rod personally. If your rod is stiff it should take an H-C-H; if limber, it might work best with an H-D-H. Your rod is on the border line for these two sizes. If it weighed 6 oz., I wouldn't hesitate on the H-C-H. If it weighed 5 oz., then H-D-H would probably be just right. What will be right depends on the action. Color of the line doesn't matter, but if you get a Nylon line be sure it is one size larger than silk.

A good leader would be one tapering from .019 to .014, and about 9 ft. long. Either floating bugs or wet and streamer flies may be used. But I would call surface lures the best bet for clear water.

FLY ROD FOR STEELHEADS

Question: I'm planning to fish for steelheads in the Santa Ynez River, Calif. Would a 6-oz, fly rod and a reel and line to balance be all right?—M. P., Calif.

Answer: That 6-oz. rod should be perfectly satisfactory, but since the fish sometimes run large be sure to have at least 300 ft. of backing line spliced to your regular fly-casting line, and a reel large enough to hold the whole business.

DRY-FLY ROD FOR WET FLIES

Question: Will a dry-fly rod handle wet flies satisfactorily?—W. M., Ohio.

Answer: A dry-fly rod will take care of wet-fly fishing well enough, although a wet-fly rod will not handle dries satisfactorily because it is too limber. If you fish both types of flies, the best single rod is a dry-fly model of moderate stiffness.

TROUT FISHING IN HIGH SIERRA

Question: What type rod should I get for trout fishing in California, especially in the High Sierra?—G. R. W., N. M.

Answer: My preference is a 7½ to 8-ft., 3½ to 4 oz. fly rod for the mountain streams. For the lakes, use a 9-ft., 4¾ to 5-oz. rod. A compromise would be an 8½-footer weighing about 4½ oz. These would be a little light for steelhead rods, which usually run about 6 oz. or more.

PROPER TROUT OUTFIT

Question: Do you think my trout-fishing set-up is O.K. for use with natural bait, flies, and occasionally spinners? I have an 8½-ft., 4-oz. rod, a good reel, and an 18-lb.-test level enamel line.—H. S., Ill.

Answer: Your outfit sounds suitable for the purposes you mention. If it works well, I see no need for any change.

You mention an 18-lb.-test fly line. Pound tests do not mean much as applied to fly lines. If your line is an F level it should be O.K. Of course, a tapered line makes for smoother delivery of the fly. A rod of the weight and length you give should perform well with an H-E-H line. It is, of course, impossible for me to be definite about matters like these when it's impossible for me to play the rod.

CHOOSING FLY RODS

Question: I have done a lot of river fishing and used a bait-casting outfit.

Now I have become interested in fly fishing and wish you would give me some advice about the proper rod to buy. Am considering a 9-footer weighing 5¾ oz. Is this right?—D. E. B., Calif.

Answer: The fly rod you're considering would be O.K. for bass fishing, but I wouldn't want it for trout fishing, except perhaps for steelheads. Of course I am going only by the weight, for I have no way to judge the action. For trout fishing the following lengths and approximate weights can be used as a guide: 8 ft.—3½ to 4¼ oz.; 8½ ft.—3¾ to 4½ oz.; 9 ft.—4½ to 5½ oz.

FACTS ABOUT BAIT

BAIT FOR OHIO WHITEFISH

Question: In several of the lakes around here there are whitefish, but nobody seems able to catch any of them. How do you take these fish?—J. C. L., Ohio.

Answer: The whitefish to which you refer is often very hard to take. As the mouth of the fish is tender and not very large, small hooks and bait must be used.

I have caught this species on small bits of minnows, little snails which had been removed from their shells, soaked pieces of wheat, and dough balls. The No. 14 dry-fly hook I used was tied on a fine leader. As the fishing was deep and on the bottom, I put a sinker on the line a few inches below the leader connection. This seemed to give good results.

BAIT FOR STURGEON

Question: Please tell me what sturgeon feed on and what is the best bait to use in fishing for them in Lake Erie and the Niagara River.—F. G. R., N. Y.

Answer: While there is not a great deal of information available on the feeding habits of sturgeon, they are said to feed mostly on small animals and plants which are sucked in through the tubelike mouth. Small fish also seem to form a considerable part of their diet and in the Columbia River they are known to feed on sardines, smelt, and other small fish. Lampreys are said to make excellent bait.

SUSQUEHANNA LURE SUGGESTIONS

Question: A friend and I are planning a fishing trip in Pennsylvania, preferably on the Susquehanna River. We believe there is bass fishing in that river, and trout in some of its tributaries. Would you please advise us as to the bait these fish will take.—H. R., N. J.

Answer: The following baits and lures are merely suggestions for bass and trout fishing in the Susquehanna watershed: Live baits for bass: hellgramites, minnows, and worms. Live baits for trout: worms and minnows. As for artificials, the bass will strike spinners and small plugs readily when they are active; both wet and dry flies will lure the trout.

FOOD FOR STORED BAIT

Question: I am keeping a supply of minnows in my cellar for future fishing. I have them in a barrel with a steady drip of fresh water, and feed them once a day with prepared goldfish food. They really go for this, but could you suggest some foods to vary their diet.—F. T., N. Y.

Answer: The kind of food necessary for minnows depends on the species, but most shiners and other minnows are more or less carnivorous, and finely ground meat of some kind would probably be the answer in your case. The most appropriate foods would be small crustaceans (Daphnia, etc.) and aquatic insects such as are usually found in small ponds and sluggish streams. These may be collected in a gauze dip net, and the crustaceans stocked in a rain barrel to maintain a steady supply.

PRESERVING BAIT

Question: What's a good recipe for preserving pork rind for bait, and for preserving minnows?—R. McK., Ontario.

Answer: The following instructions are more a guide than infallible recipes:

Cut pork rind to the desired size and shape, removing all skin. Place it in a 90 percent salt brine—heavy enough to float a potato. Leave the rind completely covered in the brine for at least 48 hours, until the brine strikes completely through it. Then remove the rind and drain it. You may bleach the rind by soaking it a few hours in diluted hydrochloric or acetic acid. This may be done either before or after curing. When well drained, pack in bottles with enough formaldehyde (10 to 20 percent) or sodium benzoate to cover it.

Pork rind may be preserved for bait by soaking it in a brine solution for 48 hours.

To preserve minnows, soak them in a fruit jar of water with 1 tbsp. formaldehyde added. You may also add 1 tsp. glycerine; this is not required, but some say it makes the minnows more attractive to the fish. After a few days pour off the water and refill the jar with another solution of the same proportions. If the minnows appear too hard, use more water; if too soft, more formaldehyde.

KEEPING SHINERS

Question: I have a large spring on my land in which I'd like to keep shiners for winter ice fishing. However, every time I put shiners in that water in the summer they develop a fungous growth on their bodies and die. What steps can I take to correct this?—J. A. G., Mass.

Answer: A thorough cleaning of the bottom of your spring might help, although the chances aren't any too good. Write to your state Department of Conservation for further advice.

WATERPROOFING MINNOW SEINE

Question: A minnow seine which I bought recently is untarred, and I'd like to do the job myself, to protect the threads.—M. R. G., Wis.

Answer: To waterproof your net, I should advise treating it with linseed oil. Soak the net in the oil for about ½ hour, then remove (letting all the oil possible drip back into the container, for use another time), hang outdoors, and allow to drain thoroughly.

KEEPING SHINERS ALIVE

Question: Please tell me if there is any way of keeping shiners alive for a number of days. I find that they do not last very long in an ordinary bait pail, and I wonder if there is any way I can keep them in the lake in front of my camp in Maine. As things are, I waste too much time looking for bait.—C. S. E., Mass.

Answer: Build a fine-mesh wire box—probably about a 3-ft. cube would take care of your needs—and sink it in the water. Cover the box with a solid, hinged lid which will cut off the direct rays of the sun. Do not put too many shiners in the box at one time, since this species of minnow is on the delicate side.

BEST PEN FOR MINNOWS

Question: Would galvanized iron make a good minnow pen or would it have a chemical reaction on the water? I want to make some sort of pen, equipped with running water, and keep minnows in it in my basement through the winter. What material do you think would be best for me to use?—P. K., Ohio.

Answer: A galvanized tank probably would be O.K., within limits, but the influence on the water of the acid used in soldering the joints, as well as the possible flaking of the zinc coating, will prevent it from being wholly satisfactory. A stone tank probably would be best. There are types of concrete which simulate soapstone and which have proved satisfactory. Some dealers keep their minnows in wooden tanks, and these too have worked out well.

No matter what material you select,

your use of running water will be a big help in keeping the minnows healthy.

HOW TO KEEP MINNOWS

Question: Do changes in water temperature affect minnows caught in one locality and kept in another for future use as bait?—W. A. W., N. C.

Answer: Yes, definitely. It's best to catch them in the same water in which you plan to use them. To keep them alive, place them in a wood-topped box made of fine-mesh wire, being careful to avoid overcrowding, and lower this into the water at a spot where there is some natural aëration. The wooden cover will block off the direct rays of the sun, which otherwise might prove injurious.

Minnows will live if kept in a wire mesh, wooden-topped box placed in an aerated spot in the water.

CATCHING AND KEEPING MINNOWS

Question: What is the best way to catch and keep minnows? I live about 75 ft. from a small river and want to store them there. Do rolled oats make good food for them?—A. M. R., Ark.

Answer: The seine is the only known method suitable for catching minnows in quantity. Use an umbrella net to get them from pockets between heavy weed growth. This is an umbrella-shape net which is baited with crumbs and lowered into a pocket. It is lifted when the minnows come over.

The river is your best bet for keeping them. Build a large wire box and avoid overcrowding. Rolled oats are good feed,

but pulverize them first. Dead insects or scraps of bread also can be used.

Decaying meat hung over the livebox attracts flies and breeds maggots, automatically providing food for minnows.

To keep minnows in a container a shorter period of time, follow the same idea of avoiding overcrowding. Six minnows to each gallon is about right. Sudden changes in water temperature when transferring them from the place where they were caught to the storage pail will cause heavy losses.

Small suckers and purplish-color chubs are much easier to keep than shiners.

KEEPING FROGS ALIVE

Question: Have had trouble keeping my frogs alive while fishing. Can you help me out?—F. K., Ill.

Answer: If you will keep your frogs in a well-aired container, with a top to ward off sunshine and with moist grass and a few soaked sticks inside, you shouldn't have any difficulty.

PLANT GRUBS AS BAIT

Question: A number of years ago I fished with a friend on a lake in Ohio. For bait we used reed grubs, purchased at a bait house. They were most effective on pan fish. Since then I have never again run across these grubs. They are found in the pith of certain reed stalks. Could you tell me what kind of reeds these are, and where they grow?—F. L. M., Pa.

Answer: The only plant grubs I ever fished with are found in the yellow pond lily (also called spatterdock). This is the common lily you see in nearly all lakes.

RAISING LIVE BAIT

Question: I intend to open a sporting-goods store, first starting out with live bait and tackle. What can you advise me about storing bait? I know how to catch it all right.—H. A. S., Mass.

Answer: The first requisites in keeping live bait are suitable tanks and a continuous supply of good water. Probably the best materials for making the tanks is soapstone, such as washtubs are made of, or wood. Metal is O.K., but galvanized iron doesn't have a good reputation. Sinking a box in the soil is about the best way to raise worms.

I would advise you to write the U. S. Bureau of Fisheries, Washington, D. C., and also the Superintendent of Documents, Government Printing Office, Washington, D. C., for a list of available booklets on the culture and care of live baits. One is the Propagation of Bait and Forage Fishes, which sells for 5 cents.

CARRYING WORMS ON LONG TRIP

Question: Last year I took some fishing worms along on a Canadian trip, driving about 300 miles in one day, and the next morning most of the worms were dead. I had packed them in fairly dry dirt in a pail, but found the dirt very soggy when I arrived. How can I avoid this on future trips?—A. C. McK., N. Y.

Answer: The best advice I can give you is to tell how I have carried worms. I packed a 20-lb. split-willow creel with slightly moist moss, gathered from rich soil where it grew long and thick, but with as much grit shaken out as possible. Then I put 150 worms on top and let them crawl in, removing those which stayed on the surface before starting the trip.

Aside from the packing, it may be that your worms were subjected to intense heat on the trip. Heat is the greatest killer of worms, and the soggy earth indicates it had something to do with this case.

PRESERVING NIGHT CRAWLERS

Question: There is an abundance of night crawlers in my yard after a rain. Is it possible for me to keep them in some kind of container for a month or two? What would you advise me to use in the container?—B. H., Pa.

Keep night crawlers alive by packing them in a large soil-packed box.

Answer: Sink a large box in the soil, preferably in the shade, and pack well with the soil in which the worms were found. The box must have drainage, but with the holes covered so that the worms cannot escape. Another method is to put them in a box of moss, keeping it in a cool place. The moss should be kept damp, *but not wet*. As injured or dying worms will cause others to die, look them over every few days, removing those which appear lifeless.

KEEPING HELLGRAMITES

Question: What food, if any, should be fed to hellgramites to keep them alive and lively? I have them on hand 3 or 4 weeks before I use them.—H. L. H., N. Y.

Answer: I do not know of any particular thing to feed hellgramites, but I have kept them successfully for 2 to 3 months by putting them in a damp stoneware tub well spotted with damp, rotted pieces of wood. Perhaps they get all the food they need from these sticks. It is necessary to dampen the tub frequently, being careful not to make the water so deep that it covers the food.

PAINT ON MINNOW BUCKETS

Question: Last year I bought a very good minnow bucket. When I took it out the other day I discovered that I had carelessly left some water in it, and that the bottom had rusted. I cleaned the rust off with emery cloth, and was preparing to do a paint job when a friend told me that minnows would not live in a painted container. Is he right?—C. B. M., Ohio.

Answer: It is a definite fact that minnows often die when left in a painted container for a period of time—such as between fishing trips. This happens even though they are supplied with running water. However, if you apply a good grade of enamel, and let it dry thoroughly before using, I doubt if it would cause minnows to die any quicker than normally.

FOOD FOR CRAWFISH

Question: Where I fish, crawfish are about the only thing the bass will take. I want to try to keep some of this bait alive for future use—can you tell me what to feed them?—J. W. R., N. Y.

Answer: While I have had no experience in keeping crawfish in captivity, I can tell you what they feed on. They lie in wait for small fish and eat them, and they eat all sorts of water insects. They also feed on dead plants and animal matter. I do know that if you bait the water where crawfish are plentiful, they will come to the spot quite readily.

NEWTS FOR BAIT?

Question: I have a lot of newts in my garden. Are they good bait for black bass and other fish?—J. W. J., Calif.

Answer: I've taken game fish on newts but I wouldn't call them effective bait. However, I haven't used them often enough to pass positive judgment on their taking qualities. Better try them and see what happens.

BAIT FOR ELUSIVE BASS

Question: Please tell me what tackle and bait (artificial or live) to use for some very elusive smallmouth bass. These fish

live in a small creek that has a sandy bottom, with rocks along the shore. A few of them, running up to 15 in., have been caught on night crawlers and crabs. I know the fish are there, but they won't bite.—R. J. F., N. Y.

Answer: Crawfish, hellgramites, nymphs, etc., would probably be the natural food for bass in the creek you speak of. I believe your problem is chiefly one of presentation. In such water, bass are likely to be wary, so that fine and far-off tactics will be required. The fish doubtless feed on the surface, especially during May when flies hatch or when insects like June bugs are plentiful.

BAITS FOR BLACKFISH

Question: I have had poor luck angling for blackfish in salt water, using sand and bloodworms. Are there any other baits for this fish that might bring in a more successful catch?—L. D., N. Y.

Answer: Calico, green, or blue crabs are often good. To prepare the bait, lift off the top shell, and break away all the legs close to the joints nearest the body. Then cut up the crab so that there is a leg joint on each piece. Thread the hook through the leg socket.

Fiddler crabs are good too. To bait up, simply pull out a claw and insert the hook in its socket. Hard or soft-shell clams are effective sometimes, as are shrimp in the summer months.

BAIT FOR CARP IN NEW JERSEY

Question: I find pickerel feeding near the shores of the Passaic River in New Jersey about the time the season opens each spring. Spawning carp come along about a week later and chase them. I'd like to catch some of these carp, since they spoil my pickerel fishing. I'd appreciate knowing the best type of bait to use and also best time of day to use it?—C. F., Va.

Answer: What works in one place may

not work in another. Probably the most popular bait is the dough ball, for which there are many recipes. One calls for two large potatoes, peeled and grated, ½ tsp. salt, 1 tbsp. corn meal, and wheat flour. Another requires ½ cup flour, ½ cup corn meal, a pinch of salt, and enough grated cheese to give scent and flavor.

In either case, mix the ingredients together, adding water to make a dough and a pinch of fluffed-out absorbent cotten to help stiffen the batter and hold it around the hook when ready for use.

If you use the potato mixture, cut the dough into balls about 1¼ in. in diameter; if you use the cheese batter, knead it into one workable lump. Now place in a kettle, the bottom of which has been lined with oiled paper to prevent sticking. Boil for 20 minutes (cheese mixture) or until the balls float (potato dough). Remove. Cut into pellets as desired.

Carp are wary, so fish as fine as you would for trout. The bait gives best results if fished on the bottom with a float. Morning and evening are good times.

CATFISH LIKE DEAD BAIT

Question: Do the blue (river) catfish strike more quickly at a dead minnow than at a live one?—O. C. McV., Mo.

Answer: Blue catfish often seem to prefer dead to live bait; in fact, they sometimes prefer the bait to be decidedly smelly. On some occasions, however, I've found live minnows best.

BAIT FOR CATFISH

Question: I read somewhere that a bait made of dough and chicken blood is good for catching catfish. Could you tell me how to make it? The best bait, I think, is worms. How can these be kept alive?—J. P., Ill.

Answer: Common catfish and bullheads will take worms as well as anything else. The fancy baits such as chicken blood

and the like are usually recommended for big channel cats, although other catfish will take them occasionally. I've always had good luck catching catfish on cut bait—minnows cut into chunks.

I do not have any recipe for a chicken-blood-and-dough bait, but it should be good. Chicken blood must coagulate before it can be used. Mixing it with dough might speed the process of getting it solid enough to be used on a hook.

To keep worms, put them in moss or soil which is kept damp—*not wet*—in a cool place. Avoid crowding and examine occasionally for sick, injured, or dead worms. All such should be thrown out, since it left they will cause more sickness and an increasing death rate.

BAIT FOR CHANNEL CATS

Question: Please tell me what baits to use for channel catfish.—F. M., S. D.

Channel cats can be caught with a variety of bait including minnows, crayfish and liver.

Answer: Any of the following are good baits for this fish: Minnows, crayfish, liver, beef, frogs, cheese, sour clams, chicken blood, jack-rabbit livers, chicken livers, Limburger cheese, and sometimes artificials like spinners and plugs.

BEST BAIT FOR EELS

Question: There are lots of eels in a nearby lake. What is the best bait, and when should I try for them?—J. S., N. Y.

Answer: Worms and cut bait are good for these bottom feeders. Eels usually bite best at night. Try for them wherever the bottom is muddy.

BAIT FOR GARS

Question: Do you know of any way to catch fresh-water gars? We have a stream nearby which abounds in them. I thought I might have fun catching them, and at the same time benefit sportsmen by ridding the water of these game-fish eaters.—G. W., Tex.

Answer: Gars will take minnows, cut bait, and shrimp. I have also taken them on plugs. However, they are cagy creatures, and it takes patience to get them to strike. Also, about the only way to hold a gar after hooking him is on a rigging which requires the fish to put its bill through a noose in order to take the bait.

WHAT BAIT FOR MULLET?

Question: I live near a canal that is loaded with mullet. While we do catch a few on a bamboo rod, using bread for bait, we think we should do much better. Can you suggest a different bait or method?—H. J. R., Honolulu, T. H.

Answer: The mullet is a bottom feeder, sucking in his food along with bottom muck. There are a number of different species, but they are hard to distinguish. Some are easier to catch with bait than others. Some anglers say they get best results with worms, others swear by dough balls. I can only suggest that you try various methods.

FLY LARVAE FOR BAIT

Question: I have heard of wigglers which are a good bait for panfish, and which are found in the mud bottoms of streams or lakes. Please tell me if these are the larvae of insects?—W. J. P., Ohio.

Answer: It is quite possible that the wigglers you speak of are the larvae of some species of crane fly. These are large, mos-

quito-like insects with very long legs. A favorite place for such larvae is among waterlogged sticks and leaves which catch here and there in riffle-filled brooks. Others live in very rapid water, still others are found in springs, and some are only semi-aquatic, living in moist places in meadows, shady woodlands, damp moss, and decaying wood. Or sometimes they are found in the decayed underwater debris and leaves along lake shore. They make good bait for trout as well as panfish.

BAIT AND LURES FOR PANFISH

Question: We have several new lakes near by, stocked with crappie, perch, and bluegills. What baits and lures, and what weight fly rod should I have to fish for them?—K. W., Kan.

Answer: These panfish will respond to a variety of lures and baits. Perhaps the most generally used are worms, tiny minnows, grasshoppers, and grubs of various kinds, but they will also strike small spinners and fly-rod plugs. The bluegill is particularly good on flies too. I would prefer a limber rod for this work, say 9 ft., 4 oz., but any good rod not too strong will serve. Too heavy a rod will kill much of the sport of playing the fish.

NEW YORK SHORE FISHING BAITS

Question: Can you recommend baits for fishing wall-eyed pike in the Mohawk River, N. Y.? Using night crawlers, I can generally catch a wall-eye or two, but the usual run are carp, suckers, etc. I usually fish from a sunken barge along the shore as I do not have access to a boat, and I am not sure about casting because it takes about 1½ oz. of lead to keep a bait on the bottom in the face of the strong current.—D. F. G., N. Y.

Answer: Due to the difficult conditions for fishing you describe, which would make artificials a poor bet, the only thing I can recommend is minnows. These are about the best live bait for wall-eyes. Use a heavy sinker that will hold when sunk to the bottom, attaching a hook with 9-in. gut snell about 1 ft. up the line from the sinker.

BAIT FOR SUCKERS

Question: What are the best artificials and natural baits for suckers especially during July and August?—M. N., N. Y.
Answer: About the only way you can catch suckers—especially in summer—is to sink a piece of bait in a hole where they feed, and wait. Small worms would perhaps be as good as any bait, and the hook should be small.

Suckers bite best in the spring when making their spawning runs. As a rule they will not take artificials, although I have caught quite a number on wet flies when fishing at night for brook trout in spring holes. Once I took a double. Of course, there are many varieties of suckers, and some varieties bite better than others do.

EARLY-SEASON STARTERS FOR TROUT

Question: What would you recommend as early-season starters for trout—streamers or worms? What pattern would be the most effective?—A. D. H., N. Y.
Answer: Both worms and streamer flies are good as early-season starters. Sometimes, if the season is warm, small black or blue-gray wet flies are most effective. As far as I'm concerned, however, there just isn't anything more killing for trout than a worm until around May 15 or after.

BULLHEADS AS TROUT BAIT

Question: Have you ever heard of using small bullheads as trout bait? A veteran fisherman favored it.—N. B. W., N. Y.

Answer: While I have never tried them I see no reason why bullheads wouldn't make excellent trout bait. Bullheads are very plentiful in many northern trout ponds and lakes, so no doubt they are gobbled up by large, cannibalistic brookies. I have found small bullheads in the stomachs of trout I have caught on flies.

TOUGHENING CRAWFISH TAILS

Question: I sometimes use crawfish tails for bait but have trouble keeping them on the hook. Is there a way of making them tough?—H. L. S., Ohio.
Answer: I've never tried to harden crawfish tails, but you might try the minnow-preserving formula: 1 oz. formalin, 6 oz. glycerin, and 40 oz. water. After a month or 6 weeks, remove bait and keep in strong brine. This brine will remove the formalin flavor which, some claim, the fish do not like.

PRESERVING SALMON EGGS

Question: How can I preserve salmon eggs for bait? Will the same method do for others fish eggs also?—H. C. H., Calif.

To preserve salmon eggs, sprinkle them with formula given below and pack in fruit jars.

Answer: Use eggs less than 24 hours old only; older ones will turn dark. Pack 10 lb. of rolls or clusters in fruit jars or a wooden tub, sprinkling over them, as you put them in, the following mixture: 1 tbsp. saltpeter, 1 tbsp. sugar, 1 tbsp. benzoate of soda, and 1½ lb. ground rock salt, well mixed together. This formula should be suitable for other fish eggs, too.

FACTS ABOUT ARTIFICIAL LURES

ARTIFICIALS DISCOURAGE BAIT EATING FISH

Question: I have been able to catch a few good-size pickerel, perch, crappies, and bass at an artificial lake in these parts, but I am much annoyed by small fish stealing my bait or gradually tearing it to pieces.

Where I fish the bottom is rocky, at least near shore—5 ft. out it becomes quite deep. At times, by using a casting rod and getting the bait out as far as possible, I've caught some nice bullheads and wall-eyed pike.

What equipment (hooks, bait, etc.) do you think I should use? So far I've been using worms and minnows.—K. B., Mich.

Answer: When fishing where small fish are plentiful one is bound to catch them oftener than big ones—especially when bait is used. A larger hook would prevent you from hooking so many smaller specimens, and make it easier for you to unhook those that did get caught, but it would not help in the loss or mutilation of your bait. Of course, there are often spots which contain mostly large fish, but one can find this out only by experimenting in different locations.

Personally, I would try artificials rather than live bait. Fair-size floating bugs often catch large panfish. Plugs are perhaps best for large bass; bass bugs and flies also take their share, but are likely to take a lot of small stuff too. Spoons are good pickerel lures, and sometimes a trailer of pork rind on a spinner does things to them.

The size of the hook depends on the bait you use. Average hooks for panfish run from No. 6 to 10, and for bass from No. 2/0 to 2. The larger sizes are best for large baits, the smaller for small baits. Regular-shank hooks are perhaps best for all the fish you mention except pickerel and wall-eyes. This is only because these two species have sharp teeth which cut line or leader.

BUGS FOR DIFFICULT WATER

Question: The water we fish is of two types: backwaters with lots of lilies and weeds, and a river with plenty of brush along the deep side. Plugs and bait aren't so good for bass here. Could bass bugs be used, and what types? Would trout tackle be suitable?—D. B., Calif.

Answer: The waters you describe should be good for bug-fishing. There are many manufacturers making good bass bugs. Get some of the spreading-wing type, some plunkers, and some which imitate frogs. While you can use a trout-fly rod for bass bugs, it's likely to be too light for this sort of work. The best outfit would be a 9½-ft., 6 to 6½-oz. rod, an H-C-H line (the best floating type possible to get), and a leader 7½ to 9 ft. long, calibrating .019 to .014.

CROSS-COUNTRY TROUT LURES

Question: This summer I hope to take a motor trip across the Eastern United States and Canada, passing through Indiana, Michigan, Ohio, Pennsylvania, Ontario, Quebec, and Maine, and stopping to fish for trout. What flies would cover my needs?—R. W. W., Iowa.

Answer: The following assortment should take care of you in all of the territories mentioned:

Dry flies—White Wulff, size 10; Blue Quill, 12, Light Cahill, 12 and 14; Royal Coachman, 10 and 12; Multi-color Variant, 12; Quill Gordon, Adams, Brown Spider, and (for Pennsylvania) R. B. Fox.

Wet flies—Blue Dun, sizes 8 and 12; Royal Coachman, 8 and 12; Campbell's Fancy, 8 and 12; and (for Canada) Parmachene Belle, 6 and 8; Montreal, 6 and

8; and Silver Doctor, 6 and 8.

Also a few bucktails, such as brown and white and also black and white. Of course, there are many other flies I could suggest, but these should be sufficient for most conditions.

PLUGS FOR TROUT

Question: There is a stream in my locality which has been stocked with a large number of big browns and rainbows. I'd like to try for 'em with plugs; what kinds should I use?—A. A., Pa.

Answer: Generally speaking, you should use small plugs for trout—in the ¼-oz. class or smaller. But I have heard of large trout being taken on regular, bass-size casting plugs. In Hebgen Lake, Mont., and other Western waters, many trout are caught with bass plugs and spoons.

Personally, I use a spinning outfit for bait-casting for trout. Of course, with the small fly-rod plug, I use a ¼-oz. sinker on the line or leader about 2 ft. above the lure. This same principle can be applied to the regular bait-casting outfit, the only difference being in the weight of sinker used.

WOOLLY WORM FOR TROUT

Question: I have heard a lot about a lure for trout called the Woolly Worm. How do I tie this pattern?—E. S., Mass.

Answer: The lure as originally designed is tied on a No. 6 or 8 medium-long or long hook as follows: *tail,* fibers of guinea-fowl feather; *body,* black silk chenille (not too thick); *hackle,* Plymouth Rock saddle, tied along the shank in eight turns so that the hackles point forward; *ribbing,* oval silver tinsel.

MARABOU FLY FOR TROUT

Question: A lake I fish is filled with Eastern brook trout, but I can't find a fly to interest them. When I've opened the few I've caught with bait I've found them to contain small minnows about 1 in. long, resembling small stickle-backs. What fly can I use?—L. W. M., Alberta.

Answer: A 1-in. long Marabou fly ought to help. When the trout are taking minnows, the answer should be a minnow-imitation fly plus careful fishing, so the fish don't get suspicious. If you haven't tried angling for them after dark, give that a whirl.

PLUGS AND BUGS FOR WISCONSIN BASS

Question: What kind of lures are best for Wisconsin black bass?—R. G., Wis.

Answer: Both plugs and bugs are good for bass in your section of the country. In the lakes near Chetek I've had good luck with perch-finish plugs, both surface and underwater, and with hair frogs.

FLY SIZES FOR EASTERN STREAMS

Question: What is the best size to use on these flies for brook trout in Eastern streams: Royal Coachman, Goldrib Hare's Ear, Cahill, Brown Bivisible, Wickham's Fancy, Pink Lady, Beaverkill (male and female), Whirling Dun, Pale Evening Dun, Gray Drake, and Ginger Quill?

What are some of the best takers among wet flies for this use?—F. J. B., Pa.

Answer: Sizes 10, 12, and 14 will meet most Eastern conditions and all patterns mentioned are good.

Among many fine wet flies are the first two you specified, tied wet, plus the Coachman, Quill Gordon, Blue Quill, Orange Fish Hawk, Campbell's Fancy, Queen of Waters, and Leadwing Coachman. For Northern brook trout, try Parmachene Belle, Montreal, Professor, and Grizzly King.

GOOD FLIES FOR CALIFORNIA

Question: Please recommend some flies for trout streams in northwestern California.—W. K. W., Calif.

Answer: For dry flies, try the Black Gnat, Ginger Quill, Blue Quill, Quill Gordon, Adams, Badger Variant, Royal Coachman, and Pink Lady. For wet flies, try the three first named above; also Pink Lady, Royal Coachman, or the nymphs with dark backs and yellow bellies.

BUGS FOR FLORIDA STREAMS

Question: What is a good fly-rod lure for bass and trout in Florida?—B. N., Fla.

Answer: Any standard bass bugs will do. Why not write several leading firms for catalogues and choose an assortment? Include a bug which pops or creates some other disturbance when jerked, a bug with spreading wings and either a cork or deer-hair body, a minnow made for a flyrod (such as a feather minnow), and some small spinners with fly tailers.

GOOD WET FLIES FOR KANSAS BASS

Question: Please name some good weighted flies for catching bass in Kansas lakes.—F. N., Kan.

Answer: Good standard wet flies for bass include: Scarlet Ibis, Silver Doctor, Parmachene Belle, Polka, Montreal, Seth Green, Lord Baltimore, Oriole, Rube Wood, and Professor.

WET FLIES BEST IN MAINE

Question: I'd like your advice on wet and dry flies for use in Maine.—F. G. C., N. J.

Answer: On the whole, wet flies are more useful for Maine trout fishing than are dry flies. Popular patterns of long standing in that state are: Parmachene Belle, Montreal, Silver Doctor, Black Gnat, Brown Hackle (red tag), Black Ghost streamer, and Edson Tiger Bucktail. Sizes 6, 8, and 10 cover the general range.

FLIES FOR BROWNIES IN MASSACHUSETTS

Question: Can you give me any suggestions as to flies and streamers that will work for brown trout here in the Massa-

chusetts area?—C. H. D., Mass.

Answer: My favorite brown-trout flies are Royal Coachman, Cahill, Light Cahill, Quill Gordon, Ginger Quill, Light Hendrickson, Dark Hendrickson, and Adams. Any minnowlike streamer or bucktail fly will give good results.

MICHIGAN FLIES FOR MAY

Question: What type of wet flies should I try for trout in Southern Michigan in May? Are nymphs good for early-season fishing?—F. A. B., Ind.

Answer: For the fishing you describe I'd prefer bucktail or squirrel-tail and streamer flies to regular wet patterns. The nymph is used for early fishing, but I like to save it until after the waters reach normal summer flow.

PATTERNS FOR MEXICAN TROUT

Question: What are the patterns for trout fishing down here in Mexico, for both streams and lakes?—B. M., Mexico.

Answer: I would say that any of the standard wet and dry flies, such as Royal Coachman, Ginger Quill, brown and gray hackles, Wickham's Fancy, Blue Quill, Grizzly King, and Professor would do a satisfactory job. I've used them successfully everywhere I've fished.

MICHIGAN FLY PATTERNS

Question: What flies are best for trout in southern Michigan?—N. F. S., Ind.

Answer: A few patterns I have found good in Michigan are: Adams, Madsen, Coachman, Spent-Wing Royal Coachman, Ginger Quill, and Blue Quill. Streamers are very good, too, including bucktails and feathers. Of course, there are many other good flies.

OUTFIT FOR NORTHERN PIKE

Question: I am planning to go fly fishing for Northern pike on Basswood Lake, Minn. I like to tie my own flies. Can you tell me the ones to use—and should I use a spinner, and what size? Also, what size gut leader? I have two fly rods, a 3½ oz., and a 6 oz. Which should I take on this trip?—F. E., Ohio.

Answer: I had great luck one year on Basswood Lake, using regular cork-body bass bugs—floaters. However, I used gut and imitation-gut leaders and the loss of bugs was scandalous. The pike ran large; they swallowed the bug and cut the leader. At another time I tried it with fine wire leaders, but the fish wouldn't take the bugs for a darn unless they were on gut. The reason, of course, was the difference in action. The wire, even though fine, sank the bugs a bit and made them too stiff and lifeless. This was before Nylon. It may be that pike would have a tougher time cutting this slippery material than they did the gut. But watch your knots.

I've also taken plenty of Northern pike on a spinner-and-fly combination. On this a wire leader is O.K. I have never found the fly pattern important, but the largest-size fly and spinner that will work on your rod would be in order. I would advise the 6-oz. rod for that lake.

FLIES FOR MINNESOTA FISHING

Question: Which wet and dry flies are best in Minnesota for brown, rainbow, and speckled trout.—E. M., Minn.

Answer: You can't go wrong with the following trout flies: *Dry*—Brown and Gray Bivisibles, Royal Coachman, Blue Quill, and Ginger Quill, in sizes 10, 12, and 14. *Wet*—G. R. Hare's Ear, Royal Coachman or plain Coachman, Blue Quill or Dun, Ginger Quill, and Parmachene Belle—the last named for brook trout especially.

Of course these are simply fundamental patterns which will serve most purposes. It would be impossible to tell you of all the patterns necessary to meet the various types of conditions.

DRY FLIES FOR NEW JERSEY

Question: As I am green at fly fishing, I would like your advice on the patterns to use in New Jersey.—W. D., N. J.

Answer: Here are the patterns I like for New Jersey waters: Light Hendrickson, Royal Coachman, Ginger Quill, Light Cahill, Blue Quill, Quill Gordon, Queen of Waters, Dark Cahill, and Campbell's Fancy or Gold Body Cahill.

As a matter of fact, these are excellent patterns for most any waters where trout rise for dry flies.

NEW HAMPSHIRE BASS BUGS

Question: What type of bass bugs, dry flies, and leaders do you recommend for smallmouth-bass fishing in northern New Hampshire?—A. M. A., Mass.

Answer: I'd suggest the following general types: spread-wing bugs, frog designs, popping types, and bugs that simulate minnows; in dry flies, a pattern such as the Wulff in white and gray, and the Royal Coachman, all in No. 2, 4, and 6 salmon sizes; in leaders, 7½ or 9-ft. tapered ones, running from .019 in. to .014 or .013.

DRY PATTERNS FOR NOVA SCOTIA

Question: I would like the names of about two dozen dry flies for use on trout in the Margaree River, on Cape Breton Island, Nova Scotia.—B. R., Nova Scotia.

Answer: I hardly believe you would need so large an assortment of patterns to fish in your country. I would advise the following: White Wulff, Gray Wulff, Royal Wulff, Pink Lady Bivisible, Brown Bivisible, Greenwell's Glory, and Professor. Of course there are many others, but I have found this list will do a good job.

PENNSYLVANIA PATTERNS

Question: What fly patterns are good for trout in central Pennsylvania in May and June?—J. A. F., Pa.

Answer: Patterns used by good anglers in this region generally include: Ginger Quill and Quill Gordon, in sizes 14 and 16; Madsen, Gold-Ribbed Hare's Ear, Blue Dun, Badger Spider, Multicolor Variant, and Pale Evening Dun, all in size 14; Black Quill in 16 and 18; and Dark Hendrickson in 14, 16, and 18.

FLIES FOR QUEBEC

Question: What trout flies do you recommend for the streams of Quebec during the early summer? What flies are good for smallmouth bass?—D. V. A., Kan.
Answer: The favorite trout flies for Quebec are: Montreal, Silver Doctor, Parmachene Belle, Brown Hackle, Professor, and Black Gnat. For bass, any good floater with spreading wings is excellent, or (underwater) a streamer or bucktail attached to a spinner.

WISCONSIN FLY SELECTION

Question: What are the best-producing trout flies and bass fly-rod lures for Wisconsin?—E. H., Wis.
Answer: I've had good success with Wisconsin trout using Adams, Blue Quill, Royal Coachman, and Campbell's Fancy, and bucktail streamers. For bass, any surface bugs should work; my favorites for your state are frog types and spread-wing bugs in various colors.

COLORS OF FEATHER MINNOWS FOR BASS

Question: What color feather minnows would you recommend for catching largemouth bass?—A. K., Mich.
Answer: My own choices are gray, white-and-red combinations with white predominating, and the plain, dark body hair of a deer.

SURFACE PLUGS FOR BASS

Question: What plugs should I try in a good-size lake varying in depth from 3 to 18 ft.? I just can't seem to catch bass the way my friends do.—T. M., Jr., Tenn.
Answer: If you haven't a surface plug, try one. The darting and plunking designs are good. Of course, you must manipulate these plugs so they'll do the work they're supposed to, combining twitches and jerks with your reeling.

FLY FOR BASS IN SLUGGISH STREAM

Question: What type of fly would you recommend for black bass in a comparatively sluggish stream? How should it be handled?—K. D., Ill.
Answer: My best suggestion for a bass fly in a sluggish stream is a floating bass bug. This should be fished very slowly indeed—a slight twitch every minute would be better than continual excessive movement. Watch a large bug when it falls alive on the water and try to imitate it. Also, you might try streamers and bucktails, which more or less imitate minnows, and must be fished so that they dart through the water in an erratic manner.

PLUGS FOR WHITE BASS

Question: I know where there are plenty of white bass, but seldom catch one. Will they strike a plug?—A. R., N. C.
Answer: When white bass are in the mood they will take artificials readily, especially deep-running plugs of a pearly finish, spinners, and darting or wobbling spoons. However, these fish seem to take only at certain periods; the rest of the time they seem diffident and uninterested.

WET OR DRY FLIES?

Question: Which will take the most largemouth bass and pan fish—wet or dry-fly methods? In fly-fishing at night for crappies, how can one set the hook when one cannot see the strike?—F. A. B., Ind.
Answer: I'd prefer wet flies for pan fish, and floating bass bugs for largemouths, as far as the largest catch goes. I've always

had my best luck fly-fishing for crappies when using wet flies, but have found small live minnows even more effective. At night, the fly should be kept moving, even if only the slightest bit, so that the line is always taut. Then one has no great difficulty in setting the hook in any striking fish which is large enough to be worth catching.

FLIES FOR BLUEGILLS

Question: How soon after the ice goes out will bluegills take flies. What flies do you recommend, and how should they be worked?—J. B., N. Y.

Answer: Bluegills will usually take a fly as soon as they come into the shallow parts of a lake to forage. I've taken them in upstate New York right after the ice went out. However, it sometimes is poor fishing until the sun has warmed the water. I usually like flies in sizes 8, 10, and 12. Yellow and black flies are excellent, also small streamers of minnow type, and nymphs. A slow jerk is best for the regular wet fly, a still-slower jerk for nymphs. With the minnow-type streamers, imitate as nearly as possible the darting action of a wounded minnow.

LURES FOR CRAPPIES

Question: So far I have been unable to catch any of the large crappies in our lake. What are the best artificial lures for this fish?—J. L., Miss.

Answer: Small spinners, and flies. Crappies feed on minnows, so any artificial bait that imitates these small fry should prove to be effective. I've also taken this species with regular trout nymphs in No. 8, 10, and 12 sizes, and mostly of a brown-and-yellow coloration.

COLOR FOR CRAWFISH PLUG

Question: I'd like to include a small crawfish plug in a set of lures I am making for use with a spinning outfit; but I don't know what color to make it. While most live crawfish are a muddy brown, the crawfish found in the stomachs of our local bass are almost invariably either bluish or greenish. Do the bass prefer crawfish of these colors, or does digestive action bring about the change in color?—W. E. D., Ill.

Answer: It's quite possible that the digestive juices of the bass tend to change the color of the crawfish, but I would expect a fading rather than a distinct change of hue. I have seen bluish and greenish crawfish, as well as brownish and reddish ones—all with faint suggestions of color rather than vivid shades. Your finding those two colors in the bass would seem to prove that they were taking those colors. Incidentally, I have had very good luck with a pale green crawfish plug.

ARTIFICIALS FOR SUMMER FLOUNDERS

Question: Many times I've heard anglers speak of catching flounders on metal squids. Do they mean summer or winter flounders? I once caught a summer flounder (fluke) on Long Island's South Shore, on a metal spinner.

Do winter flounders sometimes break water chasing small fish?—N. M., N. Y.

Answer: Summer flounders have been taken on metal squids and on all sorts of artificials. I have never known of winter flounders being caught that way, nor have I heard of them breaking water. However, the summer flounder is often known to leap and chase minnows just the way a trout does.

LURE FOR MUSKIES

Question: What is a good bait-casting lure for muskies? Although I've never fished for them, there are a lot of them here and I am tempted to try my luck at catching them.—J. B. C., Wis.

Answer: Any of the standard plugs in

muskie size are O.K. Propeller-headed plugs, spoons and spinners of medium and small muskie size are also good.

THE DOPE ON BAIT-FISHING FOR PAN FISH

Question: Is it advisable to use cork and sinker when bait-fishing for crappies, bream, and other pan fish with a fly rod? Will a small shore-minnow plug be as successful as live bait? Is a fly better for pan fish than a plug?—J. W. P., N. C.

Answer: A cork and sinker may be used with a fly rod, but you must use judgment and avoid excessively heavy weights, also learn how to handle this rig without injuring the rod. There is no general rule for pan-fish lures: sometimes artificials work as well as or better than live bait, but at other times bait is a necessity. The same applies to small plugs and flies. I prefer flies, but they aren't always the best.

LURES FOR NEW YORK PICKEREL

Question: I am strictly a fly-rod fisherman —for bass, trout, and panfish, but this year I intend to take a crack at the local pickerel. To the best of my knowledge they run from legal size up to 24 in., and I would appreciate any tips on the bugs or flies to use.—R. H., N. Y.

Answer: Basically, pickerel are minnow feeders, so any lure that looks like a minnow would be the best bait. This means streamers and spinners rather than floating bugs, although the latter sometimes work. Probably the one best lure for pickerel, which can be used on a fly rod, is a spinner and fly combination; or spinner and pork rind (perch belly can also be used).

LURES FOR WEST COAST STEELHEADS

Question: The annual run of steelheads is on full blast right now, but they absolutely refuse any kind of a fly. The old-timers use salmon eggs—legal here on the West Coast—as the steelheads won't look at anything else. Could you advise us on these stubborn steels?—J. S., Calif.

Answer: There are places where flies do not work. Perhaps you are not fishing them deep enough. Sometimes, when fished with a natural drift, the same as bait, they will produce when regular wet-fly methods fail. I have always found flies satisfactory in fishing for steelheads, my favorite patterns being Umpqua, Cummings, and either a Black Gordon or a Black Coachman.

RAINBOW LURES

Question: What are the best baits and lures and the three best wet flies for small rainbow trout? What periods of the day are best for fishing?—H. E., N. C.

Answer: As a rule, rainbows will take spinners, flies, worms, minnows, grasshoppers, helgramites, and many other baits. For myself, the three best wet flies have been Royal Coachman, Campbell's Fancy, and Gray Hackle Peacock. There is no best time of day for the entire season. You will discover the best times in your stream by fishing it all through the daylight hours over a period of weeks, and comparing notes.

DESCRIPTION OF IRRESISTIBLE FLY

Question: I would like to tie some Irresistible flies. Will you kindly let me have the description?—S. T. N., Ill.

Answer: Here is the description of the Irresistible fly: wings and tail—speckled brown body hair of deer; body—gray body hair of deer, clipped to make a tapered and rather thick body; hackle—blue-gray. Use hook sizes No. 10 and 12.

MAKING VARNISH FOR FLIES

Question: How can I make a varnish to secure the head windings of flies? What is a good color preservative for the silk windings of a rod?—J. A. S., Fla.

Answer: Either model-airplane cement or nail polish will make head windings fast and somewhat impervious to wear on flies. Collodion will prevent silk from changing color.

MAKING DRY-FLY OIL

Question: How can I make a good dry-fly oil?—B. C., Utah.

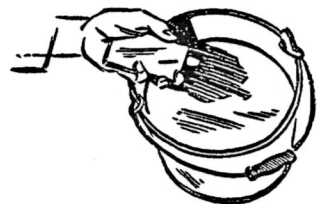

A mixture of paraffin and gasoline produces a good dry-fly oil.

Answer: Dissolve ¼ cake commercial paraffin wax, obtainable at any drug or grocery store, in either gasoline or lighter fluid for a good dry-fly oil.

BEST WOOD FOR PLUGS

Question: I would like to make some red-and-white surface plugs with a spinner. Can you tell me the kind of wood to use, and also the kind of paint? In the past I have tried to refinish old lures with enamel, but the results were poor. Perhaps varnish should be used over the enamel.—T. DeV., Ind.

Answer: Probably the best kind of wood to use for a surface plug would be white cedar. Of course, balsa wood floats very well indeed, but it is too light for casting.

Most of the amateur plug makers I know use a du Pont lacquer for the paint job. No varnish is used over this.

ARE FLIES PATENTED?

Question: I have been selling (wholesale and retail) bugs and flies for trout and bass. Many of the patterns are original; others are not. Am I infringing on patent rights by manufacturing and selling these flies, or can I legally make all flies described in books on fly tying? Also, can I legally sell snelled hooks (buying the hooks and snelling them)? I would appreciate any information you can give me on this subject.—W. N. F., N. Mex.

Answer: There are few patents on flies, and they apply only to the hook. Anyone can make and sell any standard fly pattern, either wet, dry, streamer, or bucktail. However, every maker of flies must pay an excise tax (10 percent of the selling price) on all he sells. This must be paid to the Collector of Internal Revenue once a month.

As far as I know, there are no restrictions on snelling hooks for resale, either from the tax or the patent standpoint. The excise applies to flies, rods, reels, creels, fly boxes, and all similar merchandise, but does not apply to hooks, leaders (Nylon or gut), etc. However, if a fly is made on a snelled hook it constitutes a lure, and is taxable.

FLY-FLOATING FORMULA

Question: Please give me a formula for keeping dry flies afloat during a day's fishing.—F. G., Jr., Mass.

Answer: To 1 pt. gasoline or carbon tetrachloride add 2 oz. of paraffin, flaked as thin as possible, and dissolve in the heat of the sun only.

PRESERVING BUCKTAILS

Question: Will you please tell me the proper method of preserving bucktails so that they may be used in the making of fishing lures? I know that there is a simple method of tanning them which is effective for a short period of time, and this, I am sure, will be sufficient for my purpose.—A. A. M., Pa.

Answer: Here is an excellent formula for preserving bucktails. It was given to me many years ago by a taxidermist of the

American Museum of Natural History, and I still have the first bucktail I cured by his method:

2 oz. alum
1 pt. water
½ pt. salt

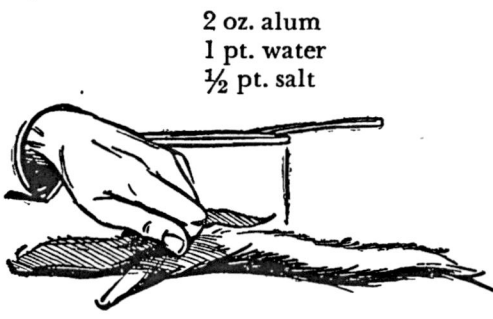

An excellent formula for preserving bucktails contains alum, water and salt.

Boil, cool, and apply to the hide with a rag. If redness persists after the first application, continue to apply until the hide takes on a whitish or cream color. This preservation not only does a good job of curing the hide, but it keeps the hair tight—which is more than can be said for some preservatives.

WHY FISH TAKE RED-AND-WHITE PLUGS

Question: I have six bass plugs in various colors and have offered them all to the fish in a near-by lake but they reject all but the red-and-white ones. Why is this? Aren't fish color-blind?—W. R., Pa.

Answer: In my estimation fish are not color-blind, and the fish you speak of probably take only the red-and-white plug because they prefer that combination. As far as plugs go red-and-white is universally a killing combination. However, in most cases where red-and-white plugs are considered the only thing to use, I have found the bass will take a plug which represents minnows and other small fish that they feed on. For instance, the plug with yellow-perch finish is often tops in waters where small yellow perch are in evidence.

DYEING FLY MATERIALS

Question: My fishing partner and I have been trying to dye deer hair for tying flies and haven't had much luck. What's the best way to dye both bucktail and feathers?—G. A. McC., Mich.

Answer: To dye deer hair, first wash it with soap chips, then put it in a boiling solution of good-quality dye (I use an imported coal-tar-base dye) for a short time. The timing you'll have to experiment with yourself; I've had the hair take dye in one 3-minute boil, and in other cases have had to give it a dozen such treatments or leave it to soak overnight. Dyeing feathers is a matter of experiment, too; I treat each job as a new problem. But good dye is especially important with feathers, and they should not be boiled, or they will lose their luster and (in the case of dry-fly feathers) their stiffness.

MEANING OF QUILL AND PALMER

Question: Would you please inform me what the words "quill" and "palmer" mean when they are used in the names of flies.—W. H. S., Nova Scotia.

Answer: Quill means that the body is made from the stripped quill feather of some bird—for instance, a spine from the eye of a peacock feather, which has had all the fluff or nap rubbed off. The quill is wound on the hook so that the dark line on one side makes the body striped. Palmer, on the other hand, means that the hackles of the fly are tied the entire length of the hook shank.

MAKING BASS BUGS

Question: I want to make my own bass bugs. Where can I get the necessary materials to do this?—C. L. S., Ark.

Answer: I suggest that you write to the firms which advertise fly-tying materials. Some of them also furnish pamphlets on the making of flies and other lures.

TROUT AND PICKEREL LURE

Question: What is the best bait for trout and pickerel in fishing a large pond from the shore?—W. W. G., Mass.

Answer: A spoon probably is best. If the trout take flies, use them. Worms, minnows, and flies which imitate minnows also are good for trout. In general, the same is true of pickerel, except that they do not accept worms readily unless the live bait is preceded by a spinner.

FLIES FOR CATSKILL TROUT

Question: We are planning a trout-fishing trip to the Catskill Mountains of New York. What are some good flies to use?—H. B., N. J.

Answer: In both dry and wet flies: Light Cahill, Quill Gordon, Royal Coachman, and Ginger Quill. In wet: Gold-Ribbed Hare's Ear, Campbell's Fancy. In dry: Brown Bivisible. Good sizes for all are 10, 12, and 14.

FLIES FOR CONNECTICUT

Question: I tie my own flies, and would like to know some trout patterns for Connecticut waters.—J. C., Conn.

Answer: Here are a few patterns which are particularly recommended for Connecticut: Housatonic Quill, Royal Coachman Fan Wing, Quill Gordon, Light Cahill, Light and Dark Hendrickson, Green and Yellow May, Brown Spider, G. R. Hare's Ear, Black Angel or Gnat, and R. B. Nymph (olive).

BASS WILL TAKE GIANT-SIZE PLUG

Question: To settle an argument, will bass as small as 10 in. take a 6¼-in. plug? I've made the plug; it has a large lip about ½ in. from the front, a propeller in the back, and three trebles. It rides about ½ in. out of the water, has an excellent action, and creates a loud disturbance.—C. E. K., N. Y.

Answer: Small bass definitely will take such a lure, perhaps even more readily than will larger fish which might regard it with suspicion. The lip and propeller should make it attractive—but if the lure were smaller it probably would be even better than it is now.

FLY ASSORTMENT FOR TROUT

Question: I should like to know what flies—both wet and dry—are needed to make up a well-rounded collection of trout flies. I own a 9-ft., 6-oz. rod and wonder if it would be suitable for trout fishing.—R. F., Pa.

Answer: Here is a list of good fly patterns for general use, either wet or dry: Ginger Quill, Blue Quill, Gold-Rib Hare's Ear, Royal Coachman, Bread Crust, Campbell's Fancy, Pale Eve, Dun, Dark Hendrickson, Light Hendrickson, and Light Cahill. Of course, there are many others but this list is quite adequate.

A 9-ft., 6-oz. rod is rather heavy and perhaps somewhat stiff for trout fishing. It would be all right for streamers and spinners in bug water but not too satisfactory for dry and wet fly fishing in medium to small streams. Naturally it can be used for this purpose, anything can, but the right gear for the particular work is always the best.

WET-FLY ARRANGEMENT

Question: Please explain the manner in which a three-fly cast is made up for wet-fly trout fishing? How far apart should the flies be?—M. C. C., Mich.

Answer: While there isn't any standard spacing for the loops on wet-fly leaders a good distance for them to be apart is about 3 ft.

BEST WOOD FOR PLUGS

Question: What is the best wood to use in making casting plugs?—W. H., Mass.

Answer: Cedar is the best wood for plugs.

HOW TO IMPROVE YOUR FISHING

FISHING WEED FILLED POND

Question: There is a pond near my home that abounds with both bass and panfish, which can be easily seen as the water is clear the year round. However, there is an abundance of water vegetation such as pondweed and cat-tail, which makes fishing extremely difficult. What is the best way to fish this pond?—K. G., Ga.
Answer: In a moderate amount of weeds, weedless lures and hooks might be the answer. If the vegetation is just too heavy, there isn't anything you can do about it.

Where the fish are in the habit of surfacing, they can be taken with surface lures, either bugs or plugs. The chances are that most of the fish will be in the shallows among the weeds. If you do fish in the deep part, use worms or minnows and let your bait go far down. You do not mention the panfish species. Some of these like deep water at certain times of the year.

KEEPING INJURED MINNOWS FROM DIVING

Question: I have trouble keeping injured-minnow plugs from diving when jerked on the retrieve, if attached to a cable leader. And if I don't use such a leader I lose plugs.—J. M., Pa.
Answer: Unfortunately any wire leader or trace will spoil the action of these sensitive plugs; even a too-heavy line or a loop connection with the line will ruin their effectiveness. There's nothing you can do about it except to make sure that the end of your line is not frayed or rotted before you tie the plug to it and then hope for the best.

STRIKE HARD WITH BASS BUGS

Question: Why do I lose so many bass—both large and smallmouth—when I seem to have them hooked solid on various types of bass bugs which have ample-size hooks?—F. M. P., Ill.
Answer: You probably lose the bass because you are not setting the hook over the barb. It takes a mighty hard strike with a stiff rod to set home a bass-bug hook, especially if it is larger than No. 2. Perhaps your rod is too limber. However, in addition to striking with the rod one should also strike by pulling the line. There's a knack in this, but it is easily mastered with practice.

USE OF ANTI-BLACKLASH REELS

Question: I want to buy a bait-casting outfit, including a good reel. Is it true that some reels don't need to be thumbed when you cast? Don't you use your thumb to stop the plug and make it land where it's wanted?—B. H., Calif.
Answer: Anti-blacklash reels can be set so that one does not need to use the thumb when casting. It is done by a retarding brake action that can be adjusted for lures of different weights. You may release the spool from any retarding action if you wish to cast without it.

Of course, when using reels that do not have this feature, it is necessary to use the thumb for braking.

FLIES TWIST LEADERS

Question: In fishing with fan-wing and bivisible flies, I find that both seem to have a sort of propeller effect when cast, and twist the leader so much that when the fly is laid down, the leader loops up into flat coils lying on the water. Almost every time a fish strikes, he pulls the loops straight, kinks the leader, and snaps it off. This happens even with new leader material.—R. B., Ill.
Answer: I can understand your fan-wing trouble, but not the bivisible. Fan-wings will twist a line every time unless the

wings set just right. When tied perfectly they will not turn, but if a fly tyer took time to make each individual fly perfect in this respect the cost would be so great that only a very few anglers would buy them. However, when using a No. 10 or larger fan-wing, especially if it is tied rather large, you should use a quick-tapering leader—say from .017 to .009 or .010 in. This helps prevent the twisting.

I've never had this trouble with bi-visibles unless I happened to be using gut too fine for the bushy ones. When the leader is right, they should cast O.K. I prefer my bivisibles a bit sparse and with hackles not too wide in the spread for the hook size. Also, fine-wire hooks help.

QUARRY FISHING

Question: Near my home there is an old quarry with a lot of fish in it, but few of them are ever caught. There are bass, sunfish, catfish, yellow perch, carp, and suckers. Trout were stocked there several years ago. The shores are mostly bare, steep rock, except at one side where there are several trees. The water is deep and the bottom, as far as we know, is rocky.

What do you think would be the best bait to use on this water?—R. Z., Pa.

The best quarry fishing according to the experts is from dark to midnight in the dark of the moon on a rising barometer.

Answer: Judging from my own experience and what I've learned from old-time, successful quarry fishermen, the best fishing is from just about dark to midnight in the dark of the moon and on a rising barometer. The best artificial lures seem to be surface plugs, color unimportant, or good live baits such as hellgramites, crawfish, and minnows.

RETRIEVING LURES TOO FAST

Question: I have fished a small, shallow, weedy lake for a good many years with very little success. Others have fished this same lake with much better luck. Many of them have used inexpensive lures while I have used only the best. I sometimes have the feeling that I might be reeling in my lures too fast. I should appreciate it if you could give me a few pointers on handling lures so that I might have a much more successful fishing season.—J. S. N., Ill.

Answer: Yes, it is possible to reel a lure too fast. Each lure should be used to bring out its individual action, and this varies with the different baits. In my own experience I found that I had the best luck with baits which had good action when reeled at moderate speed. However, at times just the opposite has been true.

If you haven't already tried surface plugs, they might surprise you. Work them slowly. The best way to use a surface plug is to let it lie still for a moment or two and then to twitch it. Do not reel in a surface plug at a steady rate of speed unless the one you happen to be using is one designed to be handled in that manner. Usually manufacturers give instructions in the boxes regarding the use of the different lures.

THE PROPER SPINNING TECHNIQUE

Question: I have just purchased a new spinning outfit and am having a tough time learning to cast with it. I get one good cast and ten bad ones. My line constantly bunches and knots on the spool. At present I am using a 7-ft., 5-oz. rod and a 5-lb.-test Nylon line.

I'd certainly appreciate any advice you could give me concerning the right use of this equipment.—J. R. B., Pa.

Answer: It is rather difficult to prescribe for your trouble without watching you work but here are some suggestions:

Do not use force in your cast. It is not necessary. You need only enough snap to start the lure traveling. If your line is correctly spooled and not twisted, it should be almost impossible for you to have a backlash.

Be sure to set the reel correctly when making the cast. After catching the line with the forefinger, the handle should be turned back about three-fourths of a turn, and then the release pushed. The rod should be grasped at the reel, the upright of the reel being in position between the first and second fingers—or even the second and third fingers if it works easier for you that way.

The fact that your line knots and bunches makes me think that perhaps you are using a lure which twists the line. When fishing, be careful about lures which always run in the same direction (spinners, Devons, etc.) for once such lures twist the line it is next to impossible to cast and just about impossible to get the line free from the twist.

HOW TO FISH FOR PIKE IN DEEP RIVER

Question: I fish for bass and pike in a river about 15 to 25 ft. deep in eastern Kentucky, using artificials altogether. There are some Northern pike in this river, but very few are taken. Would trolling or casting be good for these pike, and what baits are best? How far from the bank should I troll? How fast should I retrieve when casting? What seasons are best for pike?—C. L., Ky.

Answer: As a rule, Northern pike will strike any of the artificials which are used for bass. It is unlikely that there would be a large number of pike in your waters, which would account for the few taken. I would guess that in the river described they would be found anywhere from close to the bank to about 20 ft. out, and it would be a good plan to float along some distance out, casting close in toward shore, then troll along fairly near it afterward. I have my best luck with pike when using a fast retrieve with the plug, whether surface or underwater. However, when using a spoon, I prefer a speed just high enough to make the lure work properly. As to seasons, I have found Northern pike ready strikers where the water is suitable for them and they are plentiful, except when the water gets too warm or when it blooms.

STRIKE QUICKLY ON ARTIFICIALS

Question: Here's something that puzzles me: When I'm fishing for bass with frogs or minnows, I let the fish run a little with the bait before striking him. Should I do the same with plugs or fly lures that imitate live baits?—L. C., Ohio.

Answer: No. Once a fish feels the wood or feathers and the hooks on an artificial bait, he's pretty sure to spit it out as quickly as possible. The sooner you strike the better, once you feel or see the bass grab your lure.

CATCHING LAKE TROUT IN SPRING

Question: I am planning to fish for lake trout as soon as the ice goes out. The only way I have caught them before is by trolling deep, in summer. Should I use the same method or a different one for the early fishing?—T. B. P., Ontario.

Answer: Whenever I have fished for lake trout in the spring they have been near the surface, and I have caught them on my regular bass casting outfit, using a wobbling spoon. However, live bait is also good, and so are spinners and translucent spinning minnows. Usually the fish are found near rocky reefs or shores having deep water fairly near.

CATCHING GAR ON ROD AND REEL

Question: Having heard that it is possible to take gar on rod and reel, I'd like to know what sort of outfit is used, especially the hook required. I have never been able to catch them on a regular hook.—G. T. M., Tex.

Answer: One method by which anglers catch gar is to make a rigging with a noose. It is so arranged that to take the bait the gar has to stick his bill through the noose. In some parts of the South where these pests are very plentiful, I have often caught small ones on plugs and flies. However, the large specimens seem to be very cagy, and I've never had one hit an artificial. Occasionally a big one is taken on a trotline and sometimes with bait on a regular hook, but I believe the noose arrangement is best.

POINTERS ON WALL-EYE FISHING

Question: For Minnesota wall-eyes, is it better to fish deep? And if artificial plugs are used, how does one get them to go deep?—H. A. J., Iowa.

Answer: On the whole, wall-eyed pike are caught in water of fair depth, say from 20 to 30 ft. However, when the water gets cool, and in some places during the early morning and evening, they are often caught while casting the shores for bass and Northern pike.

June Bug spinners are often used; these revolve at slow speed and, when baited with minnow or worm, readily sink to fair depth. However, a sinker is often needed to get them down where the fish are.

Plugs too can be weighted. As a matter of fact, the sort which floats when not in action creates a most attractive lure for deep-feeding fish, if weighted with a sinker placed a foot or two above the plug. Use a sinker heavy enough to get the plug down.

FLOATING DRY FLIES

Question: As a beginner at fly-fishing, I'd like to know whether a dry fly will float on the surface at all, or is there a drying process which must be followed after each cast? How is a water-repellent solution applied to flies?—D. K., Ind.

Question: To be fished correctly, dry flies should be floated on the surface. But because the best flies cannot be made of floating material, one must dress them with a special floating substance, and also shake off the water by false casting after each retrieve. Water-repellent solutions are applied in different ways, some by brush and some by dipping. You will find instructions on the solution you buy.

TROUBLE WITH SPINNING ROD

Question: I have tried three kinds of line, and still can't do anything with my spinning outfits. On my last fishing trip I decided to give it another try and, using a Devon minnow, 50 ft. was all the distance I could get; and the minnow hit the water with such a splash it probably scared away all the trout. I can cast a fly 80 ft. with my fly rod. Could you give me any pointers?—V. M., Quebec.

Answer: You might be trying to cast with a lure that's too light. It may well be that your outfit won't work properly with a lure that weighs less than ¼ oz.

Of course, the lighter the line the more distance you can cast. However, in this respect, I have found that a 5-lb.-test Nylon is about as near right in all respects as any I have yet used.

TROLLING WITH BAIT

Question: How fast should dead frogs and minnows be trolled, when fishing for bass and pickerel? When should I set the hook?—R. A., N. Y.

Answer: Move very slowly: not faster than 1 mile an hour. If you place the hooks in the bait in such a way that no matter how the fish strikes, one will be in its mouth, then strike at once. But if fishing live bait with a single hook, it's usually necessary to let the fish have the bait for a moment or so before you strike. But there's no positive rule about this.

SOUNDS THAT FRIGHTEN FISH

Question: Will using the click on my fly reel scare trout away?—T. B., N. Y.

Answer: The click does not scare trout; in fact, talking or any noise confined to the air can be indulged in without any harm to your fishing. It's vibrations which may carry through the water which you must avoid. You could yell at the top of your lungs and a fish would not hear you, but the same fish would be frightened if you stamped your foot.

METHODS OF CATCHING PICKEREL

Question: What is the best method of fishing for pickerel? I am a complete newcomer to the sport of fresh-water fishing.—H. F., N. Y.

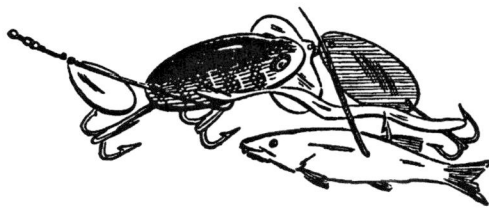

A good choice of bait for pickerel includes minnows, bass lure, spoons and pork rind.

Answer: Pickerel may be caught with minnows; with bass plugs and other bass lures; by trolling with spoons; and in many other ways. One excellent method is to work a piece of pork rind erratically over the surface of the water. This is called "skittering." Years ago we used to use perch belly—cut with the pectoral fin heading the slice, which tapered back about 4 in.—for the same purpose.

WORKING ARTIFICIAL FROG

Question: When fishing with a live frog, I let the fish run before striking. Should I do the same with an artificial frog bait, or strike at once?—H. P., Wis.

Answer: With any artificial frog it's necessary to strike immediately. If the fish is allowed to take the lure he'll spit it out unless the hook is set at once. While the fish may be fooled by the looks or action of your artificial, he knows as soon as he takes it in his mouth that it's a fake.

WORM-FISHING TACTICS

Question: At the stream I fish there is a deep hole where trout stay. How should I fish this with a worm? What leaders and hooks should I use?—T. F., N. Y.

Answer: I would fish a deep hole by casting the worm where the current leading into the hole would carry it down to where the fish lie, letting it travel over the bottom until I got a strike or the worm got lodged on bottom, in which case I would retrieve it gently, let the pool rest awhile, and then repeat the drift. I use a 6-ft. leader for baiting, one tapering from .14 to .010 in.—or lighter if the water is extremely clear and the trout wary. Hooks may be No. 8 to 10, eyed, not snelled, and tied directly to the leader as you would an eyed fly.

SPINNING EXPLAINED

Question: I hear a lot of fishermen talking about spinning, but I am not clear as to just what they mean. Would you please explain this?—M. T., Ohio.

Answer: Spinning is really a supplementary method which bridges the gap between bait and fly casting but does not take the place of either. The rod is 7 ft. long and reasonably limber and could be used in a pinch for fly casting. One could, if necessary, use regular bait-casting plugs with it too, but I wouldn't call it really satisfactory for either.

LINE SNAPS LIKE WHIP

Question: I am trying to learn fly casting, but my line hits the water both in front and in back of me every time I cast, and snaps like a whip.—A. J., Ontario.

Answer: I suspect that your line is too light for your rod and doesn't develop enough momentum on the cast to stay in air. Also, the fact that you snap the line shows that you are using the rod like a whip instead of giving the line time to almost straighten out in back before starting the forward movement.

DISTANCES FOR FLY CASTING

Question: What is a good casting distance with the fly rod?—J. A. H., N. Y.

Answer: In general, the distance ranges from the nearest point to which you can cast without scaring the fish, to perhaps 60 ft. Of course, many anglers can fish at longer distances. In tournament fly casting, 100 ft. is quite common. In 1944 a new world's record for distance—192 ft. —was hung up with a salmon fly.

CATCHING ELUSIVE LUNKERS

Question: I've spent my last two summer vacations fishing an artificial lake at Table Rock State Park, S. C. The creek which feeds this lake has long been inhabited by native trout, and the lake itself has been stocked with several thousand rainbows as well as bass and blue cats. Folks tell me they've seen bass and trout as big as 24 in. in the lake, but I've fished two weeks steady at all hours in mid-July and have never connected with anything bigger than a 14-in. bass. I've used everything I could think of, including plugs, worms, and live minnows. What do you think accounts for my in-

different luck? No motorboats are allowed on the water, the bottom has an abundant growth of weeds, and, to the best of my knowledge, there are no underwater springs.—R. McD., S. C.

Answer: Lake-dwelling rainbows often make poor sport for fishermen because they stay in the deep water during the summer. Of course, deep trolling will sometimes bring results. If there are streams running into the lake which will float decent-size fish, there should be a rainbow run sometime between November and April 15, according to water temperatures and the strain of the rainbows.

Have you tried fishing for those big bass with surface bugs? When bugs are fished as they should be—and in places where the fish are—they are mighty effective.

CATCHING FEEDING FISH

Question: The lake on which I fish has a great many crappies in it. In the evening, just at sundown, they rise and feed exclusively on mosquitoes that are hatching among the weeds. I have tried many kinds of flies, but with only fair success. When the fish are feeding this way the water fairly bubbles with them as they hit the mosquitoes just as they leave the surface. On examining the throat of a freshly caught crappie I found a dozen mosquitoes. Can you suggest the right kind of fly to use?—C. A., Pa.

Answer: What you describe is definitely a selective rise, and these always break an angler's heart whether the fish be trout or panfish. Apart from the possibility that some special technique in handling a fly would bring a bit better results, there are only two suggestions I can make —and I'm not at all sure they'll work.

First experiment with an artificial that imitates the natural, hatching mosquito as closely as possible in size, color, and delicacy. Second, also try something *en tirely different*—something flashy and exciting, such as the fan-wing Royal Coachman, for example.

Candidly, in my opinion, the toughest time to catch fish is when they are simply boiling on the surface of the water. I doubt if fish are ever really fooled into believing that our flies tied on hooks and attached to leaders are the insects we think we are imitating. But fish are greedy. When there is enough food around to make them interested but not surfeited, the anglers' flies come into their own. When fish can take the real thing easily and in quantity, as in the case of large mosquito hatches, they are exceedingly hard to catch because they can get *all* they want of what they know is exactly *what* they want.

TEMPTING YELLOW PERCH

Question: Near my home on Long Island there is a lake containing some large yellow perch. So far I've been unable to make any of these big ones strike either worm or fly. What will tempt these panfish?—W. V. K., N. Y.

Answer: Try fine tackle and make long casts with a fly rod, using a nymph or wet fly. If you have spinning tackle, you might tempt them with a spinner or a small plug.

But as yellow perch are primarily fish eaters, there isn't a better bait for them than a minnow.

BASS WON'T BITE

Question: Near my home is a small lake about 2 x 4 city blocks and 80 ft. deep at its deepest point, and stocked with bass each year. These fish will not take a plug, fly, or other artificial lure and only a few have been caught with worms or minnows. I have been told that because the lake is so deep the bass won't rise; also that they are not biting because of the swimming permitted in one section of the water. Why do you think these bass don't bite?—M. T. R., Calif.

Answer: The swimming may bother the fish while actually in progress, but should ordinarily have no aftereffects. Have you tried the shallow parts after dark, or fished all through the night to see if they would bite then?

When the fish are in deep water, a natural bait will work best.

PLAYING FISH

Question: Much has been written about the art of casting, but darn little about playing the fish. Recently I read that in playing one the line should be stripped from the reel; but since the rod is usually held in the right hand, how should the line be reeled back on so as not to get all tangled up?—A. F., N. Y.

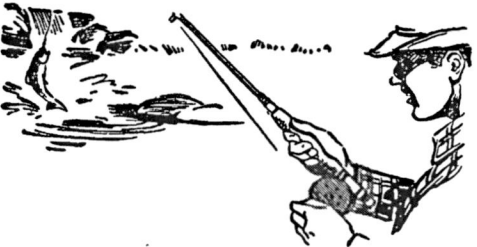

When playing large fish, reel in the slack and let the fish play against the reel.

Answer: In fishing with the fly rod small fish are usually played by stripping the line by hand. This is not so good, however, if the fish happens to be a large one. If a fish makes a fast run when the line has been stripped in, the loose coils might jam in the guides of the rod and cause a break somewhere. When playing a large fish, reel in the slack (provided the fish doesn't run it out at the beginning) and from then on let the fish play against the reel. Personally I use my left hand for reeling in, so that even though I cast with my right hand I do not need to change the rod to my left in order to play the fish. If you both cast and reel with your right hand, then you must shift the rod to your left hand when playing a fish from the reel.

MUSKIES BY FLY ROD?

Question: A friend of mine says muskies have been caught on 5½-oz. fly rods, using D level line, with 24-lb. leaders. He also claims they have been taken by casting with a fly and a muskie plug. I say you have to troll to get muskies. Can you settle the question?—C. B. O., Wis.

Answer: Muskies are taken both by casting and trolling. Spoons and plugs are the usual lures. A heavy fly rod, say a 9-ft., 7-oz. job, with a spinner trailing a single-hook fly, may take muskies, but this is not really fly fishing.

CAN'T CAST LURES

Question: I have caught many bass and bluegills on live bait with my 9-ft. tubular steel fly rod, but I can't cast a fly or bass bug with any degree of success. The rod flexes back to perpendicular too fast and the line doesn't shoot smoothly through the guides. I can find no sign of roughness on the guides and have been careful to keep the line clean and treated with a good dressing.

The automatic reel balances with the rod. I have been using a size D level Nylon fly line. Would a larger size help bring out the action?—M. R. L., Iowa.

Answer: For one thing, your line probably is too light for the rod. Nylon lines should run a size heavier than silk ones. Apart from that, it is impossible to analyze your difficulty without feeling the outfit and watching you use it. However, maybe these suggestions will help:

Remember, the pick-up of the fly or bug for the backcast is important. It must come quickly and cleanly from the water with enough snap so that it carries out in back of you to the limit of the length of line you're picking up.

To help the forward cast, watch the line and fly as you make the pick-up. When they are about to straighten out in back, make your forward cast. By watching this, you will be able to spot any errors in technique.

GETTING THE BIG ONES

Question: A near-by lake is filled with fine panfish, some bass, pike, and pickerel. The water is clear, and I can see the fish go after my fly when I cast. So far, however, I have caught nothing but very small sunnies, since they are more active and less wary and hit the fly before it gets down to where the big fish are. I have tried weighting the leader and casting in water so deep that I can't see the fly or the fish. The answer is the same —a lot of fish, but all small.

Would using a larger fly help get the big ones?—A. C. M., N. Y.

Answer: The only suggestion I have to offer is the one you make yourself—use a larger fly. Then if you get to distinguish between a small fish and a big one by the way they hit, so that you don't do a lot of unnecessary striking, there is a possibility that you might connect with some of the larger fish.

Even when fishing with worms one finds the big fish getting to the bait only after the babies have chewed it unmercifully. For that reason, when I fish with worms for panfish I usually use a big gob. I do not catch many small fish by doing this, but I get more good ones.

ON TAKING QUARRY BASS

Question: Kindly tell me what tackle you consider best for fishing for bass in a quarry.—D. L., Ohio.

Answer: Quarry-bass fishing is best on a dark night on a high barometer, or, better still, a rising barometer.

A bait-casting rod and plugs will do a good job. Live bait is also O.K.

FACTS ABOUT TACKLE

WIRE LEADER FOR PLUGS?

Question: What kind of wire leader can I use when plug casting for bass and pike? The ones I've tried seem to make bass plugs run nose downward, and spoil their actions.—G. S., Minn.

If some plugs won't take wire leaders, just tie the plug directly to the line.

Answer: You had just better forget about trying to use wire leaders with plugs that won't take them. The action and balance of many plugs is so delicate that added weight in front will make them ineffective, and about all you can do is tie them directly to the line and hope for the best —first making sure the line is strong by breaking off any frayed and rotted portions. You'll lose some plugs, from time to time, but you'll get more strikes.

LEADER LENGTH FOR SPINNING

Question: What length and thickness of leader do you recommend for spinning with 3 and 5-lb.-test lines?—H. M., Mass.

Answer: Except to save wear, there is no real need for using a leader with such light lines. However, I have used gut for this purpose, in lengths from 18 to 24 in. A leader calibrating about .009 in. will suit the 3-lb.-test line; and .011 in. gut will be right for the heavier one.

SLUGGISH LINE

Question: Recently I purchased an 8½ ft., 4¼-oz. rod of excellent make, which

I intend to use only for fly fishing for trout. I matched it with an H-D-G torpedo-head line, but with this line the action seems sluggish and soft. Would a double-tapered line work better, and if so what size?—R. B., Conn.

Answer: While it is most difficult to tell just what line is best for any rod without having the rod to cast, I have noted a tendency for torpedo-headed lines to make a rod feel sluggish as you mention.

It may be that a double-tapered line would work best. I prefer the double taper, except on occasions when long distance is necessary—something not usual when trout fishing in Eastern waters.

SYNTHETIC VS. NATURAL GUT

Question: Do you prefer a silk or a Nylon line for dry-fly fishing? Does a double-taper line make a soft delivery easier than with a torpedo head? Is Spanish gut superior to Nylon?—J. B., Minn.

Answer: A Nylon line is very satisfactory for dry-fly fishing because it floats better than silk, although the finish doesn't last so well. It is best to get Nylon a size larger than silk, for it is lighter in weight than silk of the same calibration.

I feel the double-taper job is much the best for ordinary fishing, say up to 50 ft. For longer casts the torpedo head is best.

There is much argument between the users of new synthetics and natural gut. Nylon has won many followers, particularly for stout sizes, but a number of fishermen who were enthusiastic at first have returned to gut in the belief that it works better when using small trout flies and finely calibrated leaders.

CASTING LIGHTWEIGHT PLUGS

Question: Last season I had good luck with midget bass plugs—¼ to ½ oz.— but couldn't cast them more than 15 or

20 yd. with my rod and reel. What kind of outfit should I have?—A. B., Pa.

Answer: For plugs weighing ½ oz. or more, the average bait-casting outfit should work, but for the ¼ and ⅜-oz. lures you'll need a free-spool reel with an aluminum spool built up to large diameter with a cork or balsa-wood arbor. The line should be light—not over 6-lb. breaking strength—and the rod about 6 ft. long and weighing about 4½ oz. This is if you use regular bait-casting methods. The spinning rod and reel are also exceedingly good for this work. For your purposes, the 7 ft. spinning rod is right.

AUTOMATIC VS. HAND REELS

Question: Would you say that automatic reels are as serviceable for fly-fishing as the hand types?—J. D. W., Pa.

Answer: Automatics serve a need in that they take care of slack line by a mere touch of the finger. Many anglers think there is nothing like them. However, it must be pointed out that they are very much mechanical contrivances, and the more mechanical a device is the more likely you are to have trouble in the "engine room."

DIMENSIONS FOR SPINNING ROD

Question: I've had some success building my own rods, and now I want to make a spinning rod. Can you give me some average specifications?—P. W. H., Conn.

Answer: The best length for such a rod is 7 ft., with the weight from 5½ to 6 oz. Make the grasp long—15 to 18 in.—so that you can compensate for lure weight. The reel is attached by means of two loose rings on the grip.

Unofficially and unscientifically, the bamboo should taper from .275 to .095 in. The guides should be like those found on bait-casting rods, with the first one on the large side; the others of light weight and decreasing in size toward the tip.

REEL FOR LEFT-HANDER

Question: I am contemplating buying a new bait-casting reel. Trouble is, I am left-handed, which has always been a curse when buying sporting goods to fit; they are higher priced and harder to get. In the past I have used a right-handed reel, and so haven't had to change hands to reel in. Would I be able to cast farther or better if I got a left-handed model, or will another right-hander do just as well? —M. G. D., Kans.

Answer: I see no reason why a right-handed reel will not cast just as well when operated with the left hand as it will with the right. In fact, by casting with one hand and reeling in with the other, without changing hands, you have an advantage in instant control of your lure after it strikes the water. I know several excellent fishermen who handle their outfits as you do.

WOOD FLY ROD

Question: I have been thinking about making a fly rod out of wood. I can get hickory or lemonwood in these parts— do you think either would be practical for this use?—I. E. S., Tex.

Answer: Candidly, wood doesn't make a very satisfactory fly rod. Split bamboo and steel are the best materials. However, if you are set on using wood, the kinds you mention are about as good as any domestic species.

SINGLE OR DOUBLE-BUILT ROD?

Question: I want to buy a good rod. Would you please compare the relative merits of single-built and double-built bamboo rods?—G. S., Mich.

Answer: I do not see any advantage in double-built construction when it comes to fly rods. There may be some strength gained in a heavy rod, such as one for salt water, because in such cases it is hard if not impossible to get bamboo thick enough to make good joints. Of course, most of the better fresh-water fly and bait-casting rods are single built, and the tips of double-built rods are also single built since a double thickness would not be practical in such fine joints. If you get a rod of good make you need not worry about either construction.

RIGHT LINE FOR A FLY ROD

Question: Please tell me if an H fly line 14-lb.-test, fits my 9-ft., 6-oz. rod. The rod seems to have plenty of action, and even a 6-in. brookie will bend it. The fishing-tackle dealer in my town advises me to use an H-D-H, but I have no trouble in getting my line out, and it casts average distances easily without much wrist effort on my part. I seldom have to use more than 15 ft. of line and leader.

What is the best type of reel for me to use with this rod?—C. S., Mass.

Answer: If you can cast well with the line you have, I see no reason why you should use something else. As a matter of fact, the finer the line one can use, the better it is as far as fooling the trout is concerned. The only reason for weight in a line is to bring out the action of the rod. Normally, a 9-ft., 6-oz. rod would require an H-D-M or an E level, just as your dealer says, but if you make out with what you have, of course that is the final answer.

The reel for a fly rod is relatively unimportant. Any single-action reel of average capacity and narrow spool is O.K.

WHICH STEEL ROD IS BETTER?

Question: Which type steel rod is best: tubular or solid?—J. D., Calif.

Answer: I like the tubular construction best because it makes a lighter and faster rod. However, solid steel rods are tougher, and many of my friends prefer them. Moreover, they do just as good work with them as I do with a tubular. In either case, the better the grade, the better the rod will perform.

I'd say the preference, if any, is largely a matter of personal adaptation.

COMPROMISE FLY ROD

Question: I am trying to decide between a 9½-ft., 6-oz. rod and an 8-ft., 4-oz. rod. I would like to use dry flies, and also streamers and spinners, but I have heard the latter are too heavy for a 4-oz. rod. Could I use dries on the 9½-footer with any great success?—W. P., Jr., Pa.

Answer: You can use both dry flies on the 9½-ft. rod and streamers and spinners on the 8-ft. rod. However, the 9½-footer would be a bit too much rod for delicate trout-fly fishing. Why not compromise on a medium-action 9-ft. rod, say one about 5 to 5¼ oz. that is neither excessively stiff nor yet like a willow wand? This should be your best bet.

INEXPENSIVE PLUGGING TACKLE

Question: I want to buy a serviceable plug-casting rod and reel, but my means are moderate. Would an inexpensive reel and a steel rod do?—J. M. N., Pa.

Answer: You would probably be well satisfied with one of the "split-bamboo-action" steel rods now made by various manufacturers. I'd recommend one of the lighter weights in a 5 to 5½-ft. length. You may now purchase excellent bait-casting reels that are not too expensive. For line, get hard-braided waterproof silk, which casts very nicely after it is broken in and wears well. A 15-lb. test is heavy enough for anything you are likely to use the line for; in fact, I would prefer 12-lb. test for everything but muskie fishing.

LINE FOR BRACKISH WATER

Question: We anglers who fish with flies in the tidewater streams along the California coast are having trouble finding lines that will cast long distances and yet hold up in salty water.—H. T., Calif.

Answer: I can readily imagine your troubles with fly lines in brackish water. I've had the same experience, and it doesn't matter much what line you use. However, if you keep your line well greased with a line flotant it does help considerably. Never put a line away over-night without washing it in fresh water.

FLY LINE FOR LONG CASTS

Question: Should I use a tapered or torpedo-head line for maximum distance in fly casting? At present I am using a size D level line on my 9-ft., 5¾-oz fly rod, and 55 to 65 ft. seems to be my limit. Would a tapered leader also improve my distance casting?—J. E. K., S. C.

Answer: I couldn't prescribe the exact best line for your rod without having it in my hand and trying different lines on it. However, I would say that a torpedo-head, bug-taper, or three-diameter line— whatever you want to call it—would be best for distance. It should be heavy enough in the casting part (even though light at the very tip) to produce maximum action, and light enough on the back end for the heavy part to pull the lighter section out well on the "shoot"— the moment when the forward cast exerts its greatest influence. As a guess, I'd suggest a short G fly end, a C heavy part, and an H running part or back end. However, most tournament men continually experiment with lines for their particular rods, cutting and splicing to get what they want, and even though commercial lines are designed from such experiments they must naturally be average types—not necessarily right for your particular rod. A tapered leader conforming to the line you use will be of advantage in straightening out the cast, but beware of getting one too heavy at the line end or too light at the fly end.

FLY-ROD OUTFIT FOR BEGINNER

Question: I am about to try a fly rod for the first time. What type rod and line would you suggest?—M. F., Mich.

Answer: If you are going after trout, as I assume, you'll find an 8 or 8½-ft. rod, weighing from 3¾ to 4½ oz., your best bet. A double-tapered line is to be preferred but a level one will do. The size of the line will depend upon the length, action, and weight of the rod.

STEEL VS. BAMBOO FLY RODS

Question: I am planning to buy a new 8½-ft. fly rod for more or less all-round use. I have never used anything but a bamboo rod, but now I am debating the relative merits of a bamboo and a tubular-steel rod of good make. What is your opinion on this subject?—J. S. D., Pa.

Answer: It is rare that a person who has been accustomed to using split-bamboo fly rods ever forms an affection for a steel rod, regardless of the relative merits of the two.

Steel rods of the new lightweight construction will cast just as sweetly as a split bamboo and will not lose their power with use as will bamboo. Another factor in favor of the steel rod is that if you like the action of any particular one, it can easily be duplicated—something that is difficult to do with split bamboo. On the other hand, the action is different from that of bamboo, and one has to learn to like it. In addition, I've heard many reports of sudden breakage of steel rods, and the line makes a metallic sound when being cast.

I often use a steel rod and like the way it performs, but my first love is still the split bamboo. There is room for both in any enthusiastic angler's life.

SPINNING-REEL FISHING

Question: I am interested in spinning-reel fishing, and would like to know what type of reel, plug, and line should be used.—T. B., Conn.

Answer: The spinning reel is altogether different from the conventional type of fishing reel. The spool does not revolve, the line simply flowing from it. Because the line runs free—without the drag caused when casting necessitates the spinning of a spool—it is possible to throw very light lures. When reeling in, a fingerlike attachment re-winds the line on the spool.

With the regular bait-casting reel, the free spool is best for light lures. One can become quite proficient with a light line, casting lures as light as $\frac{1}{4}$ oz. The bait-casting reel, however, doesn't work so well on light lures as the spinning reel.

TACKLE FOR HEAVY ROD

Question: My fly rod weighs 7¾ oz., is 9 ft. long. Would you advise me to get a level, tapered, or torpedo-head line, and what size? Also, what kind of plugs and lures would be best for my rod (I have some spinners). I would want a plug that makes a popping noise.—S. M., N. J.

Answer: If you want distance, get a torpedo-head line; if you want delicacy, get a double-taper. A rod the length and weight of yours should require an extra-heavy line—I should say a G-B-G double taper or a G-A-F torpedo-head. This is only a guess. The average 9-ft. rod takes an H-C-H or G-B-F, but the weight of yours denotes great stiffness.

Your rod is a fly rod and you should use fly-rod lures with it, not plugs. You can use your spinners, and you can get popping bugs instead of popping plugs if you like this action.

BARBLESS HOOKS

Question: Where can I obtain barbless hooks? Our local sports shop doesn't have them.—J. A. F., Wis.

Answer: Any large sporting-goods house should be able to supply them. However, a pinch with a pair of pliers will flatten or break the barb on a regular hook and make just as good a job as you could wish. I now use nothing but a pinched-down barb on a regular hook myself.

HOOKING MINNOWS

Question: What is the proper way to bait the hook with a minnow, and how often must the bait be replaced?—R. S., Mich.

Answer: There are a number of ways to hook a minnow, depending on conditions. Generally speaking, when trolling or fishing in fast water hook the minnow in the lips, but when stillfishing in a lake hook the minnow near the dorsal fin, being careful not to strike the backbone. When trolling or fishing where current will cause action, a dead minnow often works as well as a live one, but when stillfishing a minnow becomes pretty useless as soon as it loses its pep.

SUCKER HARNESS FOR MUSKIES

Question: What are the different methods of harnessing or tying on suckers for muskie casting.—W. P. C., Wis.

Hook a live sucker through both lips and cast it this way for best results.

Answer: One way of hooking up a sucker for trolling or casting is to take a wire snelled hook, loop it through the gills and around the snout, then impale the hook through the tail. You may also simply hook a live sucker through both lips and cast it this way. I prefer this latter method, if the bait is alive.

MEANING OF PARABOLIC ACTION

Question: Just what is meant by "a rod with parabolic action"?—C. L. M., N. Y.

Answer: This is a rod in which the action is distributed through the butt and the middle of the rod rather than confined to the tip. To be truly parabolic, the rod's middle joint must be on the limber side—too much so to suit me. I prefer a modification of this rod, with the action fairly evenly distributed from the top of the grasp to the tip. However, a real parabolic-action rod will cast a long line.

TAPERING LEADERS

Question: When tying tapered fly leaders, how should I grade sizes of gut down from the largest?—J. L. D., Calif.

Answer: The process of tapering leaders is very simple, the principal thing being to keep the reduction of size from strand to strand as uniform as possible, for too much difference between joined sizes makes for both weakness and poor performance. Take the 7½-ft. dry-fly leader tapering to 2X at the tip, tied from 16-in. strands. If you can tie your knots closely enough you may make this with six strands, calibrating .016—.014—.012—.010—.009—.008 from base to tip. However, because it is difficult to tie knots with so little waste, and because in Spanish gut lengths of 16 in. are rare in the larger sizes, it probably will be better to use seven strands instead of six, making the extra one either .011 or .009 and fitting it into its proper place in the series. The same process of grading applies to leaders of other lengths: for a 7½-to-9-footer you can start at the base with .017 or .016, for a 12-ft. leader .017 is best, and for 15 and 18-footers start with .018 or .019.

DYEING NYLON TIPPETS

Question: After some trouble I have managed to acquire several dozen Nylon leader tippets. Unfortunately, they are white, which, I am afraid, will cause them to reflect too much light. Is there some way of dyeing them green or mist color to match the color of my leaders?—L. H., Wyo.

Answer: To dye Nylon a mist color takes quite a bit of experimenting. The basic dyes to use are methylene blue and aniline violet. Use very little dye, and the water must be hot for it to take.

ATTACHING LEADER

Question: I would like to use a leader in bait casting for bass. What attachment can I use for line and leader that will pass through the guides with the least difficulty on the cast?—G. R. S., Pa.

Answer: If you will splice a loop in the end of your line, then join this to the loop of the leader without tying any knots, it will help considerably. This joining is done by slipping the leader loop over the line loop, bringing the tip of the leader up through the line loop, and then pulling the entire leader through after it, leaving the two loops interlocked.

REVIVING LEADERS

Question: I used to know of a glycerin formula to revive leaders, but now I've forgotten it. Do you know of any using this ingredient?—M. G. P., N. Y.

Answer: Here's a good one: add ¼ tsp. baking soda and 1 oz. glycerin to 4 oz. distilled water.

FLY-LINE CALIBRATIONS

Question: What are the thicknesses of various sizes of fly-casting line, in thousandths of an inch? Are these standard with all manufacturers?—R. R. E., Ind.

Answer: The lines of different manufacturers differ in thickness. Here are the calibrations I have on my records: G—.032 to .034; F—.035 to .037; E—.038 to .040; D—.041 to .043; C—.044 to .046; B—.047 to .050. These are decimal parts of an inch.

HOW TO SPLICE LINES

Question: How do you attach a fly-casting line to backing?—R. B. B., Utah.

Answer: Fray out the ends of both lines for 1 in. or more, overlap the loose fibers, and wrap them tightly with silk. Finish the splice with varnish or shellac.

PROS AND CONS OF LINE COLOR

Question: I have had some heated arguments about the most effective color for a fly line. I am not in favor of yellow or orange because bright colors are more noticeable, and might tend to scare the fish away.

Also, most persons recommend a line that will balance the rod. I prefer the lightest line possible. I fish mostly in small streams where long casts are not necessary. Besides, I use bait as often as a fly, and a light line produces less strain on the rod in bait casting—but will still handle a fly for short distances.

What do you think?—R. T., Tex.

Answer: It is doubtful whether this difference of opinion regarding line colors will ever reach a single conclusion, no matter what arguments are given on either side. Some experts prefer the lines you dislike—on the theory that the fish see the line against the light; therefore a light line is less noticeable than a dark one, and, in addition, a light line is translucent rather than opaque.

The opposition claims that a dark line matches the bottom better than a light line, does not catch the light rays, and so is less noticeable. The same arguments pertain to leaders. For my part, I believe both light and dark are needed, depending on conditions at the time of fishing.

There's no doubt that the smaller the caliber of the line the less noticeable it is. For fly casting, though, the size of the line is determined by the rod. It must be heavy enough to bring out the rod action; otherwise it will be difficult to handle the fly properly. However, if you can handle the fly properly with a very light line, then it is certainly all right to use it. With bait, of course, the finer the line the better the results.

LINE SIZES

Question: Please tell me what the approximate diameters of the different sizes of lines are?—J. R. U., N. Y.

Answer: Here are the usual calibrations, though they may vary .001 in. in either direction: H—.028 in., G—.033, F—.036, E—.039, D—.042, C—.045.

MEASURING LINE STRENGTH

Question: How is the strength of a silk or Nylon casting line measured? That is, when they speak of an 18-lb. test line, do they calculate by the number of strands, tensile strength, or how?—E. G., Okla.

Answer: An 18-lb. test line is one which will break, when new, if called upon to lift that much dead weight, though it can handle far more weight when the rod is brought into play.

SINKING LEADERS

Question: What can I do to make my dry-fly leaders sink?—H. D. S., Mich.

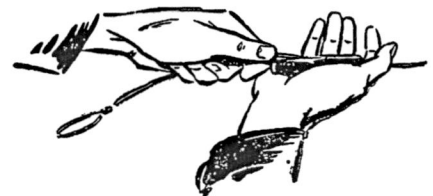

Frequent applications of pumice soap make dry-fly leaders sink.

Answer: No matter what preparation you use, your leaders will need frequent applications, especially if they are kept in the air a lot as in dry-fly fishing. Try pumice soap. Some other soaps will work too; so will mud. Remember Nylon will not sink so readily as silkworm gut.

TACKLE CARE, REPAIR AND CONVERSION

CARE OF TACKLE

Question: I am 17 years old, just starting as an angler, and have been given a fly rod, reel, and line. How shall I keep them in the peak of condition?—H. H., Mo.

Answer: Keep the rod waxed with a good furniture polish, and see that it is dry before putting away. Keep the reel well oiled and free of grit and grease. See that the line is dry, and store it in a cool, dry place. Put plenty of moth preventive in your flies so that they do not get ruined. And keep your leaders in a cool, dark place.

LEADER PRESERVATIVE

Question: What can I use to soften and preserve leaders?—R. C. A., Ohio.

Answer: A good formula for this purpose is 4 oz. distilled water, 1 oz. glycerin, and ½ tsp, baking soda.

STRAIGHTENING GUT LEADERS

Question: Can you tell me any method for getting Spanish-gut leaders to straighten out quickly when taken from the leader box?—F. W. A., Mont.

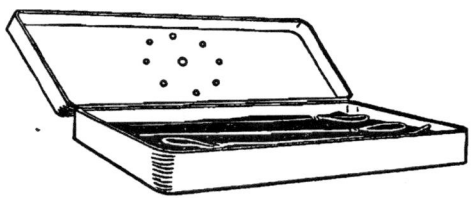

Good Spanish gut will straighten out as long as it is well soaked.

Answer: Good-grade Spanish gut should straighten out O.K. as long as it is well soaked. It is all I use for dry-fly work, and I have no trouble in this respect. Of course, it must be well wetted before use. If you are having trouble with the gut you have, try wetting it thoroughly, then stretching it out to dry. Wet it thorough-ly again for use, and it will be O.K. If not, the fault is in the gut.

GREASING LINE AND LEADER

Question: When should I grease my line? My leader?—R. R. R., Ill.

Answer: Grease your line only when you are fishing with a dry fly or floating bug. Grease your leader only when you're fishing a sinking lure and want to control its depth; in which case the leader is greased from the line end out as far as you want it to float, and from there to the tip is treated with a sinking agent.

REPAIRING ROD TIP

Question: Will you please tell me how I can replace the tip of a dandy fly rod which I received as a gift? The original tip is broken, and the maker of the rod is no longer in business.—E. H. L., Me.

Answer: Any rod manufacturer can make a joint for a rod of another make. Of course, you'll have to send him the rod, but this is usually necessary even if the joint can be obtained from the original maker. I suggest that you ask your sporting-goods dealer to send it to the company that supplies him.

WANTS TO ALTER BASS ROD

Question: I own a 77-in. medium-stiff bass rod, and would like your opinion about cutting it in two so as to make it into a two-piece rod. Would I be taking a chance on spoiling the rod, and do you think I could do the job myself? I am only 13 years old, but I'm handy with tools and know just where I'd cut the rod and attach the ferrule.

I just caught my first trout, a 10-in. rainbow, and am I proud!—L. S., Conn.

Answer: While it is possible to cut a rod in half and make it into a two-piecer, I certainly wouldn't advise it. If you have a good bass rod, keep it just the way it is. And by all means, don't try to do the work yourself; only an expert workman of long experience could make a satisfactory job of it.

DON'T THIN BAMBOO TIP

Question: I have a 6-ft. rod tip of good quality bamboo (six strips forming a hexagon) but of fairly heavy build. Is it possible to thin this bamboo down to make it lighter and have more whip to it, without spoiling it?—K. G., Del.

Answer: You cannot make this tip lighter without ruining it. The outside part of bamboo is the strongest and hardest. Taking this off would spoil or at least greatly weaken the rod. Don't do it!

CUT DOWN FLY ROD?

Question: My 9½-ft. fly rod is just a little too limber to suit me, and is too long for the type of fishing I do. Will it ruin the rod if I cut 4 in. off each section at its upper end?—D. G. F., Wash.

Answer: It is sometimes possible to cut down a rod satisfactorily—but not without first calibrating its taper, and considering other factors which indicate probable success or failure.

I once shortened and stiffened a fly rod by cutting 1 in. from both ends of each section. The taper was so slight at these points that the ferrules fitted well on the bamboo after the shortening.

I'd suggest you send your rod to an expert rod maker, or to the original manufacturer for the best results.

TO STRAIGHTEN FLY ROD

Question: How can I straighten the tip of my bent fly rod?—E. C., Ark.

Answer: Send it back to the manufacturer, if it is badly bent. If not, hang it for the winter with a weight attached. If it straightens too easily, it probably has gone soft and will bend again soon. To

try to straighten it by means of heat is tricky business, and for experts only.

To straighten a fly rod, attach a weight to it and hang for the winter.

CONVERTING BAIT ROD TO FLY ROD

Question: Would it be possible to convert an 8½-ft. bait rod of split bamboo to a fly rod?—D. I., N. Y.

Answer: If your rod is on the limber side, it might make a fair fly rod, although it would be heavy. You'd have to switch the reel seat from the top of the grip to the bottom.

REWINDING AND REFINISHING ROD

Question: I have a 5-ft. bamboo rod tip that I wish to rewind and refinish. Will any good silk thread do for binding? Should I use a silk-color preservative? How should I apply the finish? How many guides are best for a 5-ft. tip, and will extra bindings between them help, especially on a surf-casting rod?—G. K., N. Y.

Answer: Yes, any good silk thread will do. You may use a color preservative on the silk, but I do not recommend it. The preservative dries brittle and does not make as lasting a job as varnish. The rod should have about three coats of varnish;

the first two are rubbed down, after drying, with rottenstone, the last may be rubbed slightly, and then waxed. Use best-grade spar varnish. I would recommend four guides and the tip top for a 5-ft. rod tip, assuming that the length of grasp is not included in the 5 ft. Extra silk bindings do not add any strength to the rod, but do slow up the action to a certain degree.

REVARNISHING A ROD

Question: How often is it necessary to varnish a rod? Also, how do you prepare gut leaders for use.—W. V., Iowa.

Answer: You should not revarnish your rod as long as the finish remains unchecked and is not worn through. Varnish will only add weight without being of any benefit. When slight scratches occur touch up the affected parts with a bit of spar varnish and rub it in with your finger. If the entire finish is in poor condition, it is best to remove the old varnish and start a complete revarnish job from scratch.

Natural gut leaders need only to be moistened in water to prepare them for use. The new American synthetic guts do not require moistening. Carry natural gut between two pieces of felt, or two blotters, thoroughly moistened and placed in a waterproof container.

WHY VARNISH GETS LUMPY

Question: In rewinding and varnishing rods, lumps frequently appear in each coat of varnish which, incidentally, I apply with my fingers. Can you tell me the cause of this?—H. F. S., Mich.

Answer: Assuming that you are using the right amount of varnish—not too much —and rubbing it in properly, it is possible that you are doing the job where the temperature is too low. You'll find that varnish goes on best at a temperature of at least 75 degrees F.

REMOVING ROD VARNISH

Question: Can you suggest a way to remove the varnish from a split-bamboo fly rod without disturbing the windings? The rod has had several coatings of varnish, which is now so thick that it breaks off in spots.—P. R. W., Pa.

Answer: The professionals use varnish remover for refinishing a rod. The only alternative is to scrape the rod with a dull knife or piece of glass. When using the remover, do so sparingly, and be sure all action due to it has stopped before you revarnish. For complete revarnishing you should apply at least three coats and be sure each one is well rubbed down and thoroughly hard before applying the next. After that, apply good furniture wax after each few days' use. (Too frequent varnishing is never good, as you know from experience.) You may possibly save all the windings, or you may find a lot of them need replacing when you get the varnish removed.

FINISHING BAMBOO RODS

Question: I am refinishing my bamboo rods, removing the varnish down to the bare wood. This leaves them the natural bamboo color, like straw. Do you know of any method by which I can give them the brown color of Tonkin cane or the brown that is the natural color of Calcutta rods?—J. E. G., N. J.

Answer: The permanent brown color given some bamboo rods is achieved through a heat process which is a commercial secret. The finish can be made a bit darker, however, by the application of a stain before revarnishing the rod.

REFINISHING STEEL RODS

Question: One of my steel casting rods needs revarnishing. What kind of varnish should I use, how should I put it on, and must I scrape off the old coat before applying the new?

My other steel casting rod has a slight bend in the middle. Is there any way I can straighten it? Also, will you please suggest a few fly patterns which pickerel will take?—L. S., Wis.

Answer: I'd advise you to get the varnish from the maker of the rod. The finish on steel rods is different from that on bamboo, and you can't expect to do a perfect job at home. For best results, however, apply the varnish with your finger, in a dust-free room having a temperature of at least 75 degrees. If the old finish is very bad it's best to take it all off, but if it is bad only in spots you might just touch up the spots.

If your bent rod is a tubular one the chances are that it will buckle if you try to straighten it.

Generally speaking, bright-colored flies are best for pickerel; white-and-red combinations are especially good.

POLISH ON STEEL ROD?

Question: I have a new steel fly rod, and wonder if I should use wax or auto or furniture polish to keep the finish in shape.—H. M. F., Ohio.

Answer: The steel rod needs no waxing. As long as the surface remains intact it isn't necessary to use anything. However, if you should crack the finish in use it would be wise thereafter to rub the rod frequently with an oily cloth.

STRAIGHTENING BENT ROD JOINTS

Question: I have a 9 ft. split-bamboo fly rod. The last section somehow got bent, and I would like to know how to straighten it.—A. J. P., Mont.

Answer: Straightening a rod joint is a ticklish job. If the set is permanent—that is, if it stays as is and can't be straightened by careful pressure—then the joint is O.K., and has simply been overstrained. To straighten, it is necessary to heat, and when hot the joint

should be held straight by mechanical means until cool and for at least 8 hours afterward. I have seen joints straightened by tying to a steam pipe. In any straightening process care must be taken that the rod joint does not become overheated. If it is, the joint will be ruined.

A bent rod joint can be straightened by heating it and then holding it straight by mechanical means for 8 hours after it has cooled.

If you can bend the joint back straight without any heating then the joint has gone soft and there isn't anything you can do about it except straighten it every time it gets so it bothers you.

CARE OF A STEEL ROD

Question: I was recently given a fine solid-steel bait-casting and trolling rod. An angling friend tells me I should scour the rod with steel wool, wash it thoroughly with soap and water, dry it, and coat it with rust-preventing oil after each use. Is this necessary?—J. R. C., Conn.

Answer: I definitely see no reason for scouring your new rod with steel wool. In fact, I strongly advise against doing so. The use of oil after each use is a good idea, but it is not necessary unless the rod is checked or chipped.

DOES RAIN HURT FLY RODS?

Question: Recently my brother and I bought new fly rods. Both were quite expensive, but his has only a few windings on it. In your opinion does that mean that my brother's rod is weaker than mine? Also, will using these rods in the rain cause them to warp or come apart where the strips of bamboo are glued together?—H. K., Ohio.

Answer: Nearly all good rods are made with windings only at the guides. Other windings are not necessary, so your brother need have no worry on that score. Rods so wound have given me more than 30 years of service.

Any split-bamboo rod that's worth anything at all will not be injured by being used in the rain. The varnish protects it, and anyway, water will not penetrate properly glued joints unless, of course, the rod is exposed to it for considerable time. However, never put your rod away wet or in a damp case. I further protect my rods by waxing them with solid furniture wax. This keeps revarnishing at a minimum.

TO SEPARATE ROD SECTIONS

Question: Last winter when storing my favorite rod, a light two-piece beauty, I applied a lubricant and joined the sections before putting it away.

Upon taking it down to use, I found that the parts stuck together as tight as if they were glued. I've heated the parts, and twisted them, without avail. How can I get them apart?—P. B., N. Y.

The combined pull of two persons' hands on a rod will separate the rod sections.

Answer: Try to pull the rod apart with the aid of another person. Stand facing each other. You place your hands on each side of the stuck joint, and have your companion place his hands over yours.

Then apply the force of your combined pull. In this way the strain will be equalized, and you may be able to separate the two pieces. Use only a straight pull. If the rod is split bamboo the worst thing you can do is to twist it.

If this does not work, I would advise taking it to a dependable sporting-goods dealer who can handle the job.

Never put your rod away again in one piece. And never use excessive grease on the ferrules. The natural oils obtained by running the ferrules through your hair or along your nose are just about right for the purpose.

CRACKED ENAMEL ON GUIDE WINDINGS

Question: Can you give me any information regarding cracked enamel on the guide windings of my fly rod? What can I do to prevent it?—J. L., N. Y.

Answer: Cracked guide windings are caused by the lacquer so many makers use to make a snappy-looking job. If you rewind and don't use lacquer or color preservative, you'll find that the cracking won't occur again.

COLOR PRESERVATIVES FOR ROD WINDINGS

Question: What inexpensive formula can I use to preserve the color of rod windings when revarnishing?—H. S. J., Wis.

Answer: Why use preservatives at all? If you experiment with different-color silks and use nothing but the best-grade varnish, you can get good colors and have a more lasting job. As a rule, you need brighter and lighter colors to get the right effect when varnished, if you aren't using preservatives.

BLUING FERRULE

Question: What can I use to blue the ferrules on a fly rod I'm making, and how do I apply it?—R. K., Tex.

Answer: The chemical processes used for bluing gun barrels work only on steel, and are no good on nickel-silver ferrules.

For ferrules you want the gun bluing which is a lacquer enamel, like fingernail polish. It requires some skill to get it on smoothly. You might try dipping. First roughen the ferrule with fine emery paper to get good adhesion.

WATERPROOFING FISH BAG AND NET

Question: How can I waterproof my fish bag and landing net?—F. W. R., N. Y.

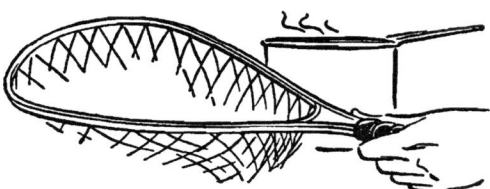

Fish bags and nets can be waterproofed with a home-made solution of beeswax and turpentine, but factory-made dope is better.

Answer: I'd use a solution of genuine beeswax dissolved in turpentine. Heat 1 qt. turpentine in a container set inside a tub or pail of boiling water. Do this away from any open flame—never attempt to heat turpentine over a flame. Shave the wax into the warm turpentine and stir until dissolved. Then paint it on the fish bag while it's still warm. To treat a mesh net, soak it in the mixture for a few minutes, shake dry, and hang up in the sun.

If you can't get beeswax you may substitute ordinary paraffin, although the wax will be more flexible and satisfactory. The drawback to paraffin is that it makes any fabric stiff in cold weather or cold water.

This is about the best home treatment I know. Generally it is far better to buy a factory-made dope and apply it accord-

ing to directions. Cost is not much greater—and the mess is certainly less.

BACKING ON REEL

Question: When is backing necessary on a fresh-water reel? What type line is best for this purpose?—D. I., N. Y.

Answer: Backing is used on a reel only when necessary to build up the height of the line for casting, or to provide running line for playing large, far-dashing fish such as salmon and steelhead trout. Use 10-lb. Nylon braided casting line, 6-thread linen line, or any strong but thin line not greatly affected by dampness.

PRESERVING COLOR OF WRAPPINGS

Question: How can I prevent the wrappings on my fly rod from changing color after they are varnished?—C. C., Mich.

Answer: Before applying varnish to wrappings, they should first be coated with some color preservative made with a collodion base. Many people use clear nail polish for this job.

By using light-colored silk and regular varnish, you can get a fairly good effect if you prefer bright colors on a rod. To guide you, get a stick that is about the color of your bamboo, then wind it with various threads to see how they will react when varnished.

STORING A FLY-ROD LINE

Question: What is the best way to store a double-tapered fly line?—A. L. M., Fla.

Answer: Make one large coil of the line and place it in a perforated paper bag or similar container through which air can circulate. Store the line where it will not be subject to intense heat or dampness.

USING FLY-LINE DRESSING ON CASTING LINE

Question: Is it possible to use fly-line dressing on a silk or Nylon plug-casting line? Would the use of such dressing cause deterioration?—M. S., Mass.

Answer: I have never tried using fly-line dressing on a casting line. However, there is nothing in any fly-line dressing with which I am familiar that would injure the bait-casting line.

Treating the line with the dressing might cause some trouble in casting until all the excess grease was either absorbed or otherwise dissipated.

WATERPROOFING COTTON LINES

Question: What is the best way to waterproof a cotton trot-line?—O. C. W., Ark.
Answer: A thorough dressing with linseed oil will waterproof this line.

REMEDYING STICKY FLY LINES

Question: I applied too much dressing to my fly lines and they turned sticky; a condition I've been unable to correct by working them with my hands. What do you suggest?—O. H. K., Mass.

Sticky fly lines can be remedied by uncoiling the lines, placing them in a dish and dusting with talc.

Answer: This is a very difficult condition to remedy without taking off the old finish and putting on a new one—something best left to the professional.

However, you can uncoil the line, place it in a dish standing on newspaper, and dust liberally with talc. Let it lie in this powder for 24 hours, then rub down with more powder and a soft rag. Finally rub with paraffin wax.

Or, if the line has a linseed-oil finish, bathe it in limewater for an hour, moving it every few minutes so that the liquid will reach all parts. A powdery deposit

then will replace the sticky coating and can be wiped off when the line dries. Then stretch the line, polish with a fine abrasive, and finish off by rubbing with paraffin wax and chamois.

PRESERVING TROT-LINES

Question: What can I use on trot-lines to make them water resistant?—C. A. B., Kan.
Answer: The only preservative I know of for trot-lines is linseed oil, which does make them somewhat water resistant for a time. Many men use tarred lines, but I've never seen these last very long. They do not even seem to last as long as a good linen line without dressing.

STORING FLY LINES

Question: What is the best way to store fresh-water fly lines here in Florida, to keep them in shape for my next trip north?—E. K., Fla.
Answer: About the safest way for you to keep fly lines, in your location, is to coil them loosely in large coils and hang them in the coolest, dryest place possible—one where they will get plenty of air.

CARE OF CUTTYHUNK LINE

Question: My cuttyhunk line becomes water-logged after I use it a few times. How can I prevent this?—F. M. R., Kan.
Answer: Give it a bath or two in either linseed oil or melted paraffin. If you use the former, be sure to rub off all excess oil; if the latter, polish down well. Frankly, it takes a lot of work to do a good job in either case.

SHORTENING TAPERED LINE

Question: The taper on an H-E-H line I have strikes me as being much too long for good casting at short distances. How much would you recommend cutting off?—E. W., Mass.
Answer: There is only one safe way to tamper with the tapered end of a line.

That is to take off only a few inches at a time, trying it after each cut, until it casts as you want it to. Length of taper varies with the make; some manufacturers purposely leave considerable level line on the end, so that the user can cut this to suit. Rarely have I found it necessary, however, to cut off more than 3 ft. of any new line I have bought.

Of course if the line is too light for the rod to begin with, you may have to take all the taper off to make it perform in a satisfactory fashion.

REFINISHING LINE

Question: Last October I had a fine week of steelhead fishing on the Rogue River in Oregon, marred only by a little trouble caused by bad finish on my lines. If I were not very careful they would stick and pile up at the stripping guide. Could you tell me how to put a hard finish on my lines?—F. A. B., Calif.

Thoroughly rubbing a line with paraffin will give it a hard finish.

Answer: If the line isn't too bad, rubbing it with paraffin might help. Melt the paraffin to apply it, then rub, and rub some more. If this doesn't work, try graphite. Although this latter is messy, it does make a line shoot.

WATERPROOFING LINEN LINE

Question: I intend to do considerable fishing with a linen thread. How can I waterproof it.—S. S. P., Nebr.
Answer: The only satisfactory treatment

I have found for waterproofing a linen line is a paraffin bath followed by a thorough rubdown. The rubbing is very important. However, some prefer a linseed-oil treatment. Personally, I believe it would be better to buy the regular prepared waxed thread.

KINKS IN NYLON LINE

Question: My Nylon lines, which I use for bait casting and trolling, kink continually—something my silk ones never did when I used the same methods and lures. What can I do to correct the situation?—E. J. D., La.

Answer: Write the manufacturer for suggestions. Your trouble may also be due to the lures you use. Some do twist lines more than others, and you might try using a keel between the lure and the line. This is a small metal plate which hangs down like a boat keel, with a swivel above and below it, and does not revolve with the lure, thus keeping the line straight. However, if the line has a twist in it to start with, nothing much can be done with it.

CARE OF BAIT-CASTING LINES

Question: While on a recent fishing trip my friends and I had some discussions as to the proper care of 24 and 30-lb.-test silk lines. There seemed to be two theories—one that they should be dried every day after being used, the other that they should be dried only at the end of the trip, before they are put away. Which is the better method?—F. G. H., Ohio.
Answer: In my opinion, even though I must admit I don't always practice what I preach, it is best to dry the line at the end of each day's fishing. However, on a 3 or 4-day trip, I really believe that a thorough drying before putting the line away would be sufficient safeguard against deterioration. At least, that's been my experience.

SPECIAL PROBLEMS OF THE ANGLER

YOUNGSTERS AS ANGLERS

Question: How old do you think a child must be before he can really learn to use a casting outfit?—W. W., Tex.

Answer: Generally speaking, about 9 years old, although some youngsters might learn earlier.

CARE OF FISH IN CREEL

Question: Please give me some tips on keeping fish in a creel.—H. L., N. C.

Answer: Usually grass or some other vegetation is put in the creel to provide a sort of bedding for the fish. While some authorities are against wetting the fish, once in the creel, I have found that an occasional dip in cold water helps keep them fresh. Wash the creel out after each trip to keep it clean and sweet.

LAKE BLOOM

Question: Last year, from September 19 to October 2, I fished a lake in northern Wisconsin that was blooming. What time of the year does lake bloom begin, and when does it stop? How does it affect fish?—A. W. J., Ill.

Answer: Lake bloom depends on the individual lake, and the season. As a rule, lakes start blooming in August, and the condition often lasts 2 months or more. I have found lakes in northern Wisconsin blooming in late September. Generally speaking, bloom tends to slow down fishing, although this doesn't always hold true. For instance, one year we had marvelous fishing in Mud Lake, Wis. The bloom was very bad. Naturally it affects the proper working of some lures, bothers the fish by getting in their gills, and is otherwise objectionable.

DRAINING LAKE

Question: We own a man-made lake which is inhabited by goldfish. Last year we had it stocked with trout but there

are now none left to speak of. We think the goldfish are the cause of this. We would like to drain the lake but are afraid of losing all the fish. What advice can you give us?—F. M., Jr., S. C.

Answer: The only practical way I know to rid a pond of objectionable fish is to drain it. If you desire to save some of the desirable fish it may be possible to drain to a certain point and then do the elimination by seining.

Probably the best way to save the trout would be to build an enclosure of galvanized screening in the partially drained pond, and segregate them in it. If there are very few trout, however, they could be kept in live boxes. Incidentally, do your draining when the weather is cool and the water cold.

It may be, of course, that your pond is not suitable for trout, but would be better for a species which would feed on the goldfish—such as bass. This could be determined by having a fish conservationist experienced in such work make an analysis of the water.

RIDDING LAKE SHORE OF WEEDS

Question: The water near my camp is very weedy. Is there any way to kill or remove the weeds?—V. E. S., N. Y.

Answer: The most effective way to control weeds is to pull them out and drag ashore all floating masses. Use a seine or a drag of fine-mesh poultry netting.

Copper sulphate is one of the most common compounds used for killing weed growth, but it should never be used in fish ponds except under supervision of the proper conservation authorities.

TO REMOVE LAKE MOSS

Question: A friend of mine has a 100-acre lake which contains a great quantity of moss. Is there any way to eliminate this

without injuring the fish?—R. S. S., Ark.
Answer: Chemical compounds are sometimes used—copper sulphate, for example. However this should never be done except under the supervision of a state conservation expert in order to protect fish life.

Moss is most effectively removed by raking it out as it approaches the shore.

One good way to remove moss is to rake it out when it comes near shore; or to wade or go out in a boat, gather the growth up, and haul it ashore.

REFINISHING MOUNTED TARPON

Question: Several years ago I had a tarpon mounted, but now the color is turning dark and showing what seem to be small blood streaks. What kind of paint restores the natural color?—O. H. I., Ill.
Answer: A taxidermist tells me that the dark spots were caused by failure, when the fish was mounted, to remove all the fat from the skin. This works its way through to the surface after a few years, rotting the skin. However, if painted and varnished over, it may hold for a while.

Remember that blending tints and painting a mounted fish requires considerable experience. Use tube colors ground in oil and mixed with turpentine to paint out the spots, then varnish the entire fish.

GOOD FISHING TOWNS

Question: I'd like to move to some place where there's good fishing and hunting, and where the climate is not too severe,

neither damp nor cold. Any small town in the Pacific or Rocky Mountain states would suit me, if it fills the bill. Any suggestions?—F. W., Fla.
Answer: Here are a few places you might consider: Livingston, Mont. (this is excellent); Rock Springs, Laramie, and Cody, Wyo.; Roseburg, Ore.; Fort Collins and Craig, Colo.; Bishop, Dunsmuir, and Redding, Calif.

There are many more, but these should keep you occupied for a time. They are all towns of more than 1,000 and less than 15,000 population.

SMALL WOUNDS KILL BROOKIES

Question: Is it true that if you land a brook trout which is bleeding anywhere, it will die even if put back in the water, no matter how small the wound?

Is it good practice in wet-fly fishing to place a dropper fly 2 or 3 ft. above the tail fly? I was out with a guide who claims it is essential. He says if the dropper is made to bounce along on the surface it attracts fish, even though they may often strike the tail fly.—W. H. S., Nova Scotia.
Answer: While I haven't made exhaustive tests, such experiences as I have had indicate that the slightest bleeding does prove fatal to brook trout.

A dropper fly used as you mention is mighty good wet-fly practice. Aside from being used to skitter across the surface, it acts differently than the tail fly under the simple retrieve.

BIGGEST BASS

Question: What was the weight of the largest fresh-water bass ever caught in the United States, and where was it taken? I specify fresh-water bass rather than large or smallmouth bass because that is the way I'd like to have the question answered.—J. F. T., N. C.
Answer: According to the records, the largest fresh-water bass ever caught in the

United States was a 22-lb. largemouth, caught in Montgomery Lake, Ga. in 1932.

Just as a matter of interest, the largest smallmouth to be caught in this country was a 14-pounder. It was caught the same year at Oakland, Fla.

YEARLING TROUT CONTAIN EGGS

Question: One 8-in. and two 6-in. native brook trout I caught had two strings of tiny eggs inside the abdomen when I cleaned them. I have heard that 3-year-old trout spawn in cold streams, but these fish seemed to be a lot younger than that. Can you tell me why they contained eggs?—C. S., Mass.

Answer: According to the U. S. Fisheries Commission, yearling brook trout will produce from 150 to 200 eggs. Your fish apparently were in this category.

WILL FISH FROZEN IN THE ICE REVIVE?

Question: Will fish which are frozen in the ice of lakes and streams revive when the ice breaks up in the spring? Is it possible to cut out a fish so frozen, put it in warmer water, and have it come back to life?—L. W. K., Wis.

Answer: There is no doubt that fish which are frozen in the ice of streams or rivers will revive when put back into warmer water. I have tried it out myself. However, there is a time limit on such a process and no fish will live if frozen in solidly for a long period.

In lakes which freeze to the bottom, many fish die in the course of the winter. Sometimes well-stocked lakes suddenly become fishless after a severe winter. Catfish and eels usually survive such ordeals better than the popular game fish.

SIZE OF BASS AT VARIOUS AGES

Question: What is the average length and weight of bass at 1, 2, 3, 4, and 5 years? There's a lake near here which has been stocked with fingerling bass and I want to know how long it'll take them to reach decent size.—A. H. K., Jr., N. J.

Answer: There doesn't seem to be any data available on the average size of bass at various ages. For one thing, locality and food varies the size greatly. The only dope I have is that an average bass of 5 or 6 months runs between 4 and 8 in., and that under some conditions a bass has been known to attain 1 lb. 9½ oz. in less than 18 months.

DO BASS HIBERNATE?

Question: Some of my friends say that bass fishing is over for the year when cold weather arrives; others claim you can catch bass all winter. Then I read a newspaper article saying bass burrow into the mud when the temperature drops below 50 degrees F. What's the true story? Can you, or can't you, catch these fish in the winter?—C. E. V., Ky.

Answer: Usually bass hibernate when the temperature gets below 50 degrees. This doesn't mean that they go to sleep; rather that they pass the winter in deep water, sometimes hidden under rocks or logs, or buried in mud or under weeds.

Occasionally a bass is taken through the ice—then the argument starts again. Leading authorities say this species definitely does hibernate—the occasional one caught being the exception.

Several other fish are active, however, and provide sport all through the cold months. Yellow perch and pickerel will go for minnows and spoons; wall-eyes and pike will be on hand, and sunfish too, in some localities.

CATCHING THE GASPERGOU

Question: Is the gaspergou a game fish? How can it be caught?—J. D., N. Y.

Answer: The gaspergou is considered a game fish by some authorities, but the average sportsman does not fish for it.

It's widely known as the fresh-water drum, but different states know it by various names; for instance, it's called the sheepshead in Nebraska and Minnesota, the drum in Tennessee (where there is no closed season), the gaspergou in Louisiana, and the crocus, croaker, bubbler, perch, gray perch, and thunder pumper in other sections.

This is one of the largest of our fresh-water fishes, reaching a weight of 60 lb. It's fond of mollusks, mussels, and crustaceans, occasionally eats other fishes, and is usually found along muddy bottoms, where it feeds. It may be taken with a hook and line, fishing a small bait on the bottom of the water.

FISHING IN LAURENTIDES PARK

Question: Are the black flies really bad in the Laurentides Park area of Quebec in late June and early July? And what will the fish there bite on?—C. P. L., Va.
Answer: Black flies are still bad there in late June, but in July they start to disappear and by August they are practically gone. They bother some unfortunates very much; others they seem to let alone.

The fishing is entirely for Eastern brook trout. As a rule they like large, bright-color wet flies such as Parmachene Belle and Montreal; I've also had good results with the sort of bucktails used for steelheads in California and Oregon.

WHAT'S A JACKFISH?

Question: There is a fish here in Arkansas that we call the jackfish. I've tried to learn all about him, but have not succeeded. He looks like a Northern pike. Not having counted his cheek scales, I cannot give any details, nor do I know how large he grows, but I haven't seen any specimens above 3 lb.—P. S., Ark.
Answer: Although, without a more complete description, I cannot be sure of the identity of the fish you refer to, I suspect,

because of geographical location and size, that it is a pickerel.

I have heard pike, pickerel, and walleyes all called jackfish. If you are sure that the fish is of the pike family, you can easily establish its species. On the pickerel, both cheeks and gill covers are scaled. On the pike, the cheeks are entirely scaly, and so are the upper gill covers, but the lower gill covers are bare.

DO SUCKERS JUMP?

Question: Do you know whether or not suckers jump, and if so—do they clear the water?—R. H., Wyo.
Answer: I have never seen a sucker make what could really be called a jump when hooked, but I have encountered specimens that broke water while fighting.

I have also noticed that these fish will break the surface when on their spawning runs. But generally they are fairly sluggish and stay close to the bottom.

HOW TO IDENTIFY BLACK BASS

Question: Recently I caught a black bass that went better than 5 lb., but I'm not sure whether it is a largemouth or smallmouth. How can I tell?—K. D. K., Ohio.
Answer: When its mouth is closed, the end of the maxillary or upper jawbone of the smallmouth is in a direct line with the center of the eye. A largemouth's maxillary goes past the eye.

The smallmouth has about 11 rows of scales, counting from the center of the back, just ahead of the dorsal, down the side to the lateral line. The largemouth has only about 7 such rows.

DO FISH SMELL OR SEE BAIT?

Question: Do fish smell the bait or do they see it?—H. T. B., Jr., N. J.
Answer: Fish feed from sight, smell, and taste. Game fish such as trout and bass take food mostly by sight. However, catfish do their feeding by taste and smell.

HOW LONG FOR BASS TO MATURE?

Question: When a lake is stocked with bass fingerlings, how long does it take the fish to mature?—S. J. N., Ill.

Answer: The growth of bass from fingerlings to adult size varies. As a rule they mature in about three years. However, anglers have been known to get them as large as 1 lb., 9½ oz. in less than 18 months. Some grow faster than others and fingerlings starting out at the same time will not attain the same size within the same period.

PICKEREL'S FEEDING HABITS

Question: Last July I caught a number of pickerel in a mountain lake which had a fair number of lily pads. In August the number and size of the pads increased and the fishing fell off. Do the fish feed on the roots or some other underwater portion of the plant?—A. L. F., N. Y.

Answer: I would not subscribe to the plant-feeding theory. Pickerel, as soon as they reach any size, feed on other fish that are available. They may try to get bugs or grubs on the stems of the plants, but it seems more likely they are after smaller fish which, in turn, are trying to get these bugs. Pickerel and all members of the genus *Esox* get off their feed in the summer. This may be due to tooth trouble or possibly the enervating influence of the warmer water.

WORLD'S RECORD TROUT

Question: Please tell me what the maximum recorded weights, lengths, and girths are for brown, brook, and rainbow trout?—E. A. L., N. Y.

Answer: The largest recorded brook trout weighed 14½ lb. and was taken from the Nipigon River, Ontario, in 1916. The world's record brown trout was taken from Lock Awe, Scotland, in 1866, and weighed 39½ lb. The champion rainbow, hauled from the Skykomish River, Washington, in 1914, was 42 in. long and weighed 26½ lb. These figures go up to 1936; I have no later records which are authentic. No girths are given in my source material, and only one length—that of the rainbow.

BOWFIN, ALIAS GRINDLE

Question: In the bayous of Arkansas I caught a fish the natives called grindle. It resembles the dogfish in Michigan, except for a slight variation in marking. What is it?—A. M., Mich.

Answer: The fish you caught was probably a bowfin, which, in some sections of the country, is also called grindle or dogfish. Its markings may vary somewhat in different waters. It is often a ready biter and a hard fighter but is good for nothing when caught.

WEIGHT OF CUTTHROATS

Question: A chap I know claims he caught a 14-in. cutthroat trout weighing 12 lb. Have you ever heard of such a monstrosity?—W. D., Ark.

Answer: A 14-in. cutthroat could not possibly weigh 12 lb. There isn't any fish I know of outside of the large salt-water species, whose weight will run more than a pound to the inch. For example a shark 11 ft. 6 in. long has been known to weigh 798 lb. The girth of this fish was 6 ft. 2 in.

Fresh-water bass run heavier to the inch than trout. Here are the measurements of a brook trout I took a short time ago: Length 21¹⁰/₁₆ in., girth 12⅜ in., weight 3 lb. 11 oz. And here's how a steelhead which I caught quite recently measured up: Length 31¾ in., girth 15⅜ in., weight 10¾ lb.

LOCATIONS FOR WHITEFISH

Question: I am interested in fishing for whitefish. Could you please tell me which of the Great Lakes and also which lakes in the Adirondacks are best for this type of fish.—C. M., N. J.

Answer: The only Adirondack lake on which I have fished for whitefish is Lake Clear. They are abundant in Lake Champlain, N. Y., and in the Great Lakes—Erie, Huron, Michigan, and Superior.

I have taken quite a number in Lake Otsego, N. Y., where they are landlocked and known as Otsego bass.

SPAWNING OF TROUT

Question: When do rainbow, brook, and brown trout spawn?—L. W., Colo.

Answer: Rainbows, in most cases, are spring spawners. However in my own observation and on checking with hatcheries, the range actually seems to be all the way from late fall to the middle of spring. Of course all spawning is governed by water temperature, so that the time varies according to locality, type of water, altitude, and other factors.

Both brown and brook trout spawn most commonly in the fall. In their case, too, the actual time is regulated by water temperature. Generally the period is from September through February.

In Quebec, where I've done a lot of brook-trout fishing, spawning starts as early as September 15, and even earlier than that in higher-altitude localities. Most of the spawning in this country is finished by October 31. However, I've noted brook trout spawning in October and November in the Adirondacks of New York state. Some people believe that both brooks and browns start as early as mid-August, but I've never seen it until late in September and thereafter.

DETERMINING FISH'S AGE

Question: How can scientists determine the age of a fish?—R. R. R., Kan.

Answer: This is done by reading the growth line in the scales, just as the age of a tree is determined by similar lines in its stump. With fish, you need a strong microscope—and some technical knowledge—to do the job right.

PICKEREL AND WALL-EYE SAME?

Question: Are the pickerel and wall-eye pike the same fish?—T. B., Manitoba.

Answer: No, they are two entirely different fish. The pickerel belongs to the pike family, genus *Esox*. The wall-eye is a perch, another common name for it being pike-perch.

BEST TIME FOR YELLOW PERCH

Question: How early in the year do yellow perch first start biting well? What fly-rod lures would you advise me to use for them?—R. V. C., N. Y.

Answer: I have often caught yellow perch as soon as the ice leaves a lake in the spring, but on the other hand I've often fished for them at this time without success. There aren't many periods when they can't be taken if one knows how, either through the ice in winter or by regular fishing in other seasons, except that during the spawning season they will not strike very well if at all. I would say that a small spinner is the best artificial for yellow perch.

STEELHEAD OR RAINBOW?

Question: A buddy and I have been having quite a controversy over the relationship of rainbow and steelhead trout. We would appreciate your opinion on this subject.—R. T., Tex.

Answer: Here is the latest dope I have—in the simplest manner. The steelhead is a rainbow which goes to sea for part of its life, and returns to spawn in fresh water. Or, you might call the rainbow a landlocked steelhead. A prominent authority on the subject recently gave about the same opinion, as follows:

"The only difference between a steelhead and a rainbow is that the steelhead goes to salt water, and the rainbow does not. The adult steelhead is a trout which has spent part of its life in the ocean. While there, it grows faster, as is always the case with such life. Young steelheads are the young of these fish. Steelhead streams are those which contain a majority of fish of this type. However, they may also contain trout which have reached maturity without leaving the stream. It may be that the hatch from eggs of this latter type can become migratory."

BLACK BASS MISNAMED

Question: There is a little controversy down at my shop as to whether or not the sea bass belongs to the black-bass family. What is your opinion?—F. U., Ill.

Answer: The sea bass does not belong to the black-bass family. The sea bass is a bass but the black bass is a sunfish. Most of the bass family are marine, the two notable exceptions being the white bass and the yellow bass, both of which are found in fresh water.

SIZE OF CATHERINE CREEK RAINBOWS

Question: I'm having a job persuading some friends that rainbow trout as large as 15 lb. have been taken from Catherine Creek, near Elmira, N. Y. Can you give me some figures?—R. R., N. Y.

Answer: Here are some Catherine Creek rainbow records which will enable you to talk turkey to those skeptics: April 8, 1939, a specimen weighing 17 lb. 6 oz. was caught by William Toopke, while on April 13, 1941, Grant Carpenter took one which weighed 15 lb. 2 oz. The world's record rainbow is 26½ lb., caught by A. A. Cass in the Skykomish River, Wash., in 1914.

RECORD SMALLMOUTHS

Question: Will you please tell me the weight of the largest smallmouth bass caught during the 1943 fishing season?

Also, the all-time record?—D. B. M., Pa.

Answer: The largest recorded smallmouth for 1943 was 7 lb. 5 oz.—caught at South Two Lake, Wis. The largest ever recorded weighed 14 lb., and was caught at Oakland, Fla.

BASS CAUGHT IN SHALLOWS

Question: Do you believe that bass move to deep water between 8 A.M. and 5 P.M. because of the lack of oxygen in shallow water?—B. H. H., Ind.

Answer: While a lack of oxygen would cause fish to move from place to place, I hardly think it would account for such a steady movement as you describe. I have caught many bass in warm lakes in the middle of the day and in water so shallow that I could see the wake they made when scared.

TEMPERATURE FOR BROWNIES

Question: What is the warmest water temperature in which brown trout can live?—A. B. D., Mich.

Answer: In some places, I have taken brown trout with a dry fly when the thermometer showed a water temperature of 80° F. They will do all right in 75° F., provided food and oxygen content are O.K.

HOW TO SMOKE FISH

Question: What method would you advise me to use for smoking trout, salmon, and whitefish at home?—L. H. H., Ore.

Answer: First make a brine solution strong enough to float a potato. Soak 1-lb. fish for 12 hours, those up to 2 lb. for 24 hours, and larger ones for 48 hours.

Then hang the fish in a smokehouse—which can be a small room or shed—so that they will be exposed to plenty of smoke, but not the heat of the fire. This should be made of sawdust and green wood, such as hickory, poplar, or birch.

Smoke 1-lb. fish for 24 hours, specimens up to 2 lb. for 48 hours, and anything bigger for 96 hours.

SCALE FISH PROMPTLY

Question: Isn't it unnecessarily cruel and uncalled-for to scale fish alive? Please tell me what you do with fish after you catch them.—G. S., Mont.

Answer: Personally I always kill my fish before cleaning. In fact, unless the fish can be put in a suitable live box, I kill them as soon as landed. I believe that fish so killed taste better than those which flop and gasp to their end.

LARGEST MUSKIE

Question: My friend claims that a 102-pound muskellunge has been caught in the United States. I say that the largest was not more than 76 lb. Hope you can settle this for us.—C. Z., Va.

Answer: According to the records, the largest muskie taken on rod and reel weighed 62½ lb. It was caught in Lake St. Clair, Mich., in 1940. The largest taken by any method weighed more than 75 lb., and was caught in Minocqua Lake, Wis., in 1906.

SIZE OF LAKE TROUT

Question: I got into an argument with two boys about the size of lake trout caught in upstate New York. I said lakers come bigger than 20 lb., while they claimed this species doesn't exceed the 10-lb. mark. What do you say?—M. S., Va.

Answer: You are right. The largest laker I can find listed as caught by rod and reel dragged the scales down to 47½ lb. I have taken such fish up to 25 lb., and I believe all the Finger Lakes produce specimens every year that exceed 20 lb.

FISHING BY BAROMETER

Question: Last September I happened to notice the barometer reading when I caught bass. The barometer was standing at the same place in November, but the bass seemed to be deeper. Isn't the barometer accurate for judging how deep to fish?

Also, do you think bass and pike would strike artificials here in eastern Kentucky in November and December?—C. L., Ky.

Answer: On the whole, fish are inclined to go deeper on a falling barometer. However, not always. In the case you mention, no doubt the fish were down because the water was colder. Bass definitely go deeper when the water gets colder, and if it gets too cold they go into hibernation and practically cease biting.

I'm not sure just what fish you mean by "pike." The common pike, *Esox lucius,* and the pickerel of the same family are cold-water fish. One is likely to find them in either medium-deep to shallow water, according to the food supply, all through fall and winter. The pike-perch or wall-eyed pike, *Stizostedion vitreum,* is a deep-water fish at all times except when coming to the spawning beds, which usually occurs in the spring.

CROAKER AND KINGFISH

Question: Can you tell me the correct names of two fish we catch in Barnegat Bay, in south Jersey? First, the kingfish. I understand kingfish become very large, but the ones we catch weigh from ¾ to 1½ lb. Are these fish really kingfish or are we calling them by a local nickname?

Second, I have never seen reference made to a croaker in any magazine or book, but we catch a fish which we call by that name. Perhaps we call it that because it croaks; but doesn't it have a particular name of its own?—H. A. W., N. J.

Answer: As far as I can ascertain you are calling those fish by their correct names. The kingfish you catch is of the genus *Menticirrhus gill,* which has nine species, occurring all along the Atlantic, Pacific, and Gulf Coasts, particularly along sandy shores. The other kingfish, *Scomberomorus cavalla,* is also called cero, and cavalla. It may reach a weight of 100 lb., and usually goes only about 10 lb. It ranges as far north as Cape Cod, Mass., and south to Brazil and Africa, but is common along our southern Atlantic Coast and among the Florida Keys.

The name croaker is correct for the other fish you mention. There are some 30 genera and 150 species.

FRESH-WATER CLAMS AS FOOD

Question: Are fresh-water clams worth anything as food? I have a feeling they're not fit to eat, but would like to know definitely.—E. B. C., Mich.

Answer: Fresh-water clams, or mussels, are not considered especially palatable. However, they are edible. Select the smaller ones for the best flavor and greatest degree of tenderness.

After thoroughly scrubbing 4 doz. mussels, boil them in about a quart of water until they open, then carefully strain off the broth. Fry the mussels in butter—if you have any—adding some minced onion for better taste. Fry until lightly browned. Now mix with the broth, adding rice or noodles, and season. This is just the general idea.

IDENTIFICATION OF STONE CATS

Question: What kind of fish is a "stone cat," and where is it found?—M. F., Tex.

Answer: The true stone cat, or little yellow cat (*Noturus flavus*) attains a length of a foot or more and is found from the Great Lakes region westward and south to Montana, Wyoming, and Texas. It is especially common in the West.

Related to this catfish and often called "stone cat" are about a dozen varieties belonging to the genus *Schilbeodes.* These are known as mad toms in many places and are very small, none exceeding 4 in. in length. They live in the shal-

low water of lakes and streams and hide under stones and other objects which might provide protection. Their range extends from Vermont to Florida, west to the Dakotas and south to Texas. They are often used for bait.

RIDDING LAKE OF REPTILES

Question: There is a 6-acre lake on my property which is stocked with perch, bream, crappies, and sunfish. Trouble is it also contains a tremendous number of turtles and snakes. How can I get rid of these reptiles?—G. F. N., N. C.

Answer: I know of only one way to get rid of snakes, and that is to shoot them. The turtles, however, may be trapped in any of several ways. One of the best methods is to sink a water-tight barrel in the lake so that about one fourth of it is above the surface. Then balance a cleated board on the rim of the barrel, its long end extending into the water of the lake. The cleats are to help the turtle climb up the board. When the turtle passes the barrel rim its weight overbalances the board and drops it into the barrel. The cleats, therefore, should be on the long end of the board only. The bait which can be either a piece of ripe meat, a chicken head, or a fish, is nailed to the short end of the board.

Worms attack bass, bluegills and white perch.

WORMY PANFISH

Question: Is it possible for bass, bluegills, and white perch to be wormy? Last season every fish I caught had little black specks all through the flesh. What do you think about these spots?—P. B. W., Me.

Answer: Both bass and bluegills definitely get wormy on many occasions, and there are a number of different parasites which attack them. There isn't any doubt in my mind that they would also affect white perch. The ones in your fish were probably some species of black grub.

BASS VS. BREAM

Question: I own a deep fish pond. Almost every kind of vegetation grows in it—cat-tails, willows, and many species of water plants. Moss has now spread over the bottom of the pond also. The pond always has plenty of fresh running water, being supplied by seven springs. I stocked it with bream, catfish, and bass by seining a nearby pond. I also introduced a supply of top minnows for feed.

We waited for three years before starting to fish it. At first we caught some fine bream, but now they never get much bigger than fingerlings. The bass seem to be the only fish that are attaining any size. What can I do to make the bream grow large?—T. C. K., Ga.

Answer: While I hesitate to pass an opinion without having had a chance to study your pond, my guess would be that the bass are keeping the bream population down. I remember a somewhat similar case in the Adirondacks. A lake, originally abounding in fair-size sunfish, was stocked with trout. The trout became large but, after a number of years, one never could see a sizable sunfish.

If you feel that the weeds and moss are becoming harmful, get the opinion of your conservation commission.

DON'T PUT CRAPPIES IN TROUT STREAM

Question: I own a small stream that, in the spring, contains a good many brook, rainbow, and loch leven trout. However,

when the water gets low, the fish move downstream and I find a vast quantity of 2 and 3-in. chubs. Would it be wise to plant a few crappies to clean up these chubs?—L. L. J., Wyo.

Answer: Don't, by any means, put crappies in your trout stream. The fact that the trout move downstream when the water gets low is something that can't be helped by adding another species of fish —especially an alien—to the water. The small chubs don't hurt anything. In fact, they provide food for your trout.

STOCKING ARTIFICIAL PONDS

Question: Our local Lions Club has three artificial lakes or ponds, about 70 acres each, which, at high water, are connected by a small shallow stream. The deepest of these ponds has been stocked with largemouth bass and bullheads; the two others have not been stocked at all. Can you tell us what fish to put in the shallower ponds (they are about 8 ft. deep), or should we confine our stocking operations to the pond which contains the bass and bullheads?

This stocking business is all new to us, and we would appreciate any information you can give us.—C. E. L., S. D.

Answer: Before doing any more stocking you should ask the advice of your state Department of Game and Fish. The water should be tested, and other important factors about the ponds determined.

Assuming that your ponds are suitable for bass, a good combination fish would be the bluegill. However, if panfish are not wanted, then by all means stock some minnows. The golden shiner is very good; so is the blackhead minnow. The latter, though, is small and weak, and so easily caught by the bass that frequent restocking may be necessary.

Forage fish—minnows and bluegills—tend to prevent cannibalism among the bass. Perhaps even more important, they change certain forms of plant and animal life, which the bass won't eat, into food which they will eat. This, of course, increases the food supply in the manner that nature intended.

POOL FOR BREAM AND PERCH

Question: I've been raising minnows in a pool, 18 ft. wide and 2 ft. deep, in my backyard. Do you think I could raise bream or perch?—C. M. H., S. C.

Answer: You probably could keep a limited number of bream and perch in your pool. Be sure to provide suitable shallow-water weeds such as the arrowhead or pickerel weed. These will purify the water, furnish shade (which helps keep the water cool), provide food and shelter for those forms of insect and animal life which may be eaten by your fish, and add to the attractiveness of the pool.

Be sure to avoid aquatic plants which may become noxious such as the water lily, lotus, coontail, and cattail.

PUT BASS IN TROUT STREAM?

Question: Though we have plenty of good trout fishing, our club would like to stock our stream with bass. To begin with, it is literally alive with aquatic life —fresh-water shrimp, hellgramites, and many other bugs and nymphs. Also there is an endless supply of minnows, shiners, and suckers.

The water never gets warmer than 60 degrees—maybe 65 on rare occasions— even then the fish can reach 55 or 60-degree water within 25 ft. The stream dries in a few places in the very hot season, though there are spring-fed holes 2 to 12 ft. deep. These holes never get very warm.

Experienced bass fishermen tell us that largemouths are not the fish for it. We'd like your advice.—J. B. R., Mont.

Answer: It isn't good practice to make stocking recommendations without having a complete survey of the situation.

From what you say, however, the water is a trifle too cold for bass. I certainly do not recommend largemouths. The smallmouth might do O.K., but, in water that never tops 65 degrees, it is very doubtful.

However if the stocking of bass doesn't interfere with your trout, it might be worth while to try a test planting—with the consent of your state authorities.

PROMOTING GROWTH OF FISH FOOD

Question: We have several small lakes in the vicinity of our boy-scout camp high in the Cascade Range near Mt. Jefferson, Ore. We'd like to know of a process that promotes the growth of fish food in ponds and so enables them to be stocked. Can you give us any information on this subject?—L. L. L., Ore.

Answer: An excellent bulletin on making ponds suitable for fishing is—Management of Small Ponds for Food-fish Production in New York State, by C. Willard Green. It is issued by the Conservation Department, Albany 7, N. Y.

Your ponds may not be suitable because of location, character of bottom, and other factors. However, the bulletin should help considerably in deciding what to do.

BASS IN PICKEREL LAKE

Question: A friend of mine has a small lake in eastern Pennsylvania which has plenty of pickerel, perch, and shiners, but no bass. Could bass be planted, or will the pickerel kill them? Where could I get them?—J. S., N. Y.

Answer: Bass can well take care of themselves; in many cases I have known them to cut down the pickerel population. However, I wouldn't advise stocking with fingerlings. Start with adult bass, at least 1½ to 2½-pounders. As for obtaining them, if you can't locate some for sale, why not get permission to catch some in another lake and transplant them? The

Pennsylvania Conservation Department will give you good advice about this.

STOCKING POND WITH TROUT

Question: I have a pond in Michigan that I would like if possible to stock with trout. It is spring fed, muck bottom, 70 to 80 ft. deep, with very cold water, and now offers fair bass, panfish, and pike fishing. What would you advise me to do about this?—M. W. V., Mich.

Answer: As your lake is already producing bass, pike, and panfish, it would be my advice to concentrate on bettering the fishing in these species. If you are set on stocking with trout, then you will first have to get rid of the other fish, and this should be taken up with your Michigan Department of Conservation.

STOCKING SMALL BROOK

Question: My family owns a brook on Long Island, N. Y., which is about 1 ft. deep in some places, and a few inches in others. My friend and I would like to know if any kind of game fish would be suited for this brook.—N. T., N. Y.

Answer: Your brook seems a bit small for much more than minnows, according to your description. Of course, some small brooks can be made suitable for a limited number of fish by building wing dams, etc., which form holes and make for more depth in certain places. A brook of this size naturally suggests trout, but whether or not yours is suitable would have to be determined by careful examination. For one thing, the water should not go higher than 65 degrees temperature in the hot months, although in larger streams 70 degrees is all right.

KEEPING GAME FISH

Question: I have been thinking of stocking my two cement pools, each 10 ft. in diameter and 3 ft. deep, with game fish— maybe bass or trout. Can you tell me whether mixed fish of such types will live together? If so, what should I feed them and would they be edible?—G. I., Calif.

Answer: Stocking pools in this manner brings up many problems, including a number of a local nature. I should advise you to contact your State Division of Fish and Game for detailed information.

STOCKING LAKE WITH DRUMFISH

Question: What do you think of stocking an 18-acre lake with 12 to 15-in. drumfish? This lake now has bass, bream, and crappies. Are drums good eating, will they take a hook, and do they propagate in clear water?—R. H. W., Ky.

Answer: I would not stock a pond containing bass, bream, and crappies with the fresh-water drum (*Aplodinotus rafinesque*). It feeds on the bottom, mostly on crustaceans and mollusks, and would deplete the food supply of the other fish without providing any sport.

TAGGING FISH

Question: How do I go about tagging fish for identification?—J. W. K., Wis.

Fish can be marked by clipping a notch in one or more of the fins and making a record of the marking.

Answer: Write the conservation department in the state where you intend to do the tagging; it may be able to supply you with special tags as well as information. I mark fish by clipping a notch or punching a hole in one or more of the fins and making a record of the markings.

ALL ABOUT CAMPING

by Maurice H. Decker

HOW TO CHOOSE YOUR CAMPING EQUIPMENT

CHOOSING CANOE FOR 4-WEEK TRIP

Question: My partner and I are going on a four-week canoe trip. What type of canoe should we get? We want one that will take a fair load and still be safe, and not too heavy on portages. What mileage should we make daily, generally speaking?—L. E., N. Y.

Answer: An 18-ft. guide model would probably be the best canoe for a four-week trip. It will hold as much as 1,000 lb., but prudent canoeists never load it so heavily. I believe a safe limit would be around 600 lb., this including campers, supplies, and outfit. You should be able to cruise about 25 miles a day if there are few portages; longer daily trips are hard work. With frequent portages, your mileage will be cut to probably no more than 10 or 12 miles a day.

CANOE-CAMP OUTFIT

Question: I'm planning an extended lake-and-river canoe-camping trip in my 15-ft. canoe, which is extra wide and extra deep, and will be powered with a 9 horsepower outboard. Will you give me your ideas on a camping outfit?—R. E. M., Ohio.

Answer: I'd suggest a lightweight camping outfit for your 15-ft. canoe. Your tent can be around 5 x 7 ft., weighing not more than 10 lb. The best bed would be a medium-weight sleeping bag. One of the light ¾-length air pads used as a mattress under the bag will add to your comfort. Or you can use a heavier, less comfortable camp mattress stuffed with cotton or kapok. In place of the sleeping bag you could probably use three heavy single blankets of wool. Sleeping equipment, of course, must be adjusted to the season of the year.

Other useful items are a light camp ax, knife, compass, light cooking kit with a kettle, a pot for coffee, and a small skillet. I like a canvas water pail and wash basin for canoe trips. They are just as handy and useful as the metal containers and fold up compactly. A waterproof match box, small first-aid kit, flashlight, and a couple of candles for emergency light (and for starting fires under bad conditions) will about complete your outfit.

PREPARING FOR A HIKE TO ALASKA

Question: I'm planning a 6-month hiking trip to Alaska next summer. I'll get into a settlement once every 10 or 15 days. I will appreciate your advice on itinerary, equipment, and any other suggestions, bearing in mind that I have only $1,200 to spend.—R. M. T., La.

Answer: My advice is not to make this trip alone. Take a companion so the weight of your equipment can be divided between you. And even so, such a trip is a big undertaking. There's plenty of wasteland along the way and you're liable to get sick of the monotony and hard work involved. The supply problem will be a tough one; in some of the northern sections the mosquitoes are so bad that a white man can hardly endure their attacks; and there's a real danger that you'll get lost. However, if you're determined to try it, take a few practice hikes of a couple of hundred miles each in southern Canada before you tackle the Alaska trip.

Perhaps you can follow the Alaska Highway, although the problem of supplies will still be present. Even motorists are advised to keep several days' supply of food on hand when they travel that road, and since an auto will cover 20 miles to every mile you make, you can see what you'll be up against. You'll have to take all necessities, while at the same time trying to keep your load manageable. The question of what rifle to take is an important consideration; the answer depends upon your skill. If you can approach close to big game, a .30/30 will be a good bet because its ammunition is generally available. If you're not a skilled stalker, a .30/06 will be better. A light shotgun is O.K. for killing small game, and an over-and-under combination is good if you can aim the rifle barrel accurately enough to bring down a deer at 200 yd.

You'll likely find costs high. Your $1,-200 may be enough for bare living expenses, but food probably will continue to be high and scarce in that section for some time to come. Read all the camping books you can find—and get ready for a

tough grind. A friend of mine, an experienced woodsman, made a similar trip —but although he'd spent most of his life trapping and hunting in the wilderness, it took him more than 6 months to complete the hike. And he suffered some terrible hardships on the way.

BEST BED AND STOVE FOR WINTER CAMPING

Question: During the winter I plan to spend two weeks camping. What type of bed is best for cold weather? Since I've been told that a camp stove used in a tent may cause asphyxiation, I'd like to know if there is a safe type to use.—G. F., Mass.

Answer: A bed for winter camping should lie flat on the floor, lest cold air get underneath and chill the sleeper. The best combination is a down-filled sleeping bag on a ¾-length air-pad mattress; this would be very warm, very light, and quite compact to carry to the camp site. If you want something less expensive you could procure a kapok or cotton mattress, camp style, and four heavy woolen blankets.

By all means use a wood-burning tent-heating stove. Install a metal and asbestos outlet in the tent through which the smoke pipe is passed. There is no danger in using a wood stove that has an outside exhaust, but there is definite peril in using a gasoline heater. Some of the wood-burners have a cooking surface, others have not.

EQUIPMENT FOR WISCONSIN CANOE TRIP

Question: Three of us, 18 to 19 years old, want to take a 2-week canoeing and fishing trip on the Menominee River in Wisconsin. What should we take along in the way of equipment?—H. H., Wis.

Answer: Three is rather an awkward number for a canoe cruise since most sizes of canoes are made for only 2 persons and their equipment. That means you'll need a larger craft—at least an 18-footer with plenty of beam. The right sort will weigh a little more than 80 lb., so pick out a route with as few portages as possible.

Your tent should be light, to keep the canoe from being overcrowded or over-loaded. Three persons need one at least 7 x 7 ft. in size. Or you could use two or three small pup tents.

Each of you should have at least two heavy single blankets, and three are better. If you can get air-mattress pads of the short ¾ length you'll be much more comfortable. Lacking air pads there are kapok and cotton-stuffed pads with waterproof bottoms that you can lay directly on the ground.

For cooking, a small folding grate is helpful. Cooking kit should contain a coffeepot, boiling kettle, skillet, and cup, plate, and cutlery for each of you. Take a half-length ax for chopping. Each of you will need a waterproof box for matches, a knife, and compass. A map of your route also is needed.

Wear pants of khaki or any stout cloth, light flannel shirt, felt hat, and comfortable well-oiled low shoes. Also take a sweater for cool evenings and a lightweight rain shirt for bad weather. Advisable also are first-aid kit, a change of underwear, and an extra shirt for each of you. Two pairs of socks apiece will see you through. It's better to wash clothing en route than to overload the canoe.

Plan your route so you can renew the grub supply often, so that you won't have so much weight to carry in the canoe.

ADIRONDACKS CAMPING

Question: What clothing should we wear and what equipment is needed for camping in the Adirondack mountains of New York?—L. G., N. J.
Answer: Time of year and whether you travel on foot, by auto, or canoe all are important in advising you, and this information you omitted. Assuming that you will go in summer, provide pants of khaki or some similar cloth that not only wears well but is comfortable. Take a light wool shirt, 2 suits lightweight underwear, a jacket or sweater, and rainproof coat or jacket. If the trip is to be a long one, take along 1 extra pair of pants, 1 extra wool shirt. Take 2 pairs heavy cotton socks, and an old felt hat with wide enough brim to shed sun and water.

For travel by canoe have soft-soled moccasins or similar shoes. If you expect to do any mountain climbing, the shoes should be about 8 in. high. Bird-hunting or hiking shoes are entirely suitable.

Size of tent depends on number in your party. A 5 x 7-ft. model will do for two if a light outfit is needed. One 7 x 7 is better if your route doesn't require hiking or carrying over portages.

Three single blankets are needed for each man, a cotton or kapok or air-filled mattress to lay under the blanket bed, a stove or grate, necessary service pieces, and a nested cooking kit that's not too heavy. For two men a skillet, cooking pot, and coffeepot can be made to do. Each of you needs a stout knife, waterproof match box, and compass. Other necessities are a camp ax, a folding canvas water pail and washbasin, small first-aid kit, map of the country in which you're to camp, and repair materials such as small wire, cord, tacks, screws, and a few nails. Safety pins come in very handy.

EQUIPMENT FOR CANADIAN CANOE TRIP

Question: What equipment should two men take on a summer canoe-camping trip on the Albany River in north-central Ontario?—R. M., Ill.
Answer: If you are going for not more than 10 days a 17-ft. canoe will serve, but if your trip will last longer than that, use

an 18-footer. Take a 6½ x 8 or 7 x 7-ft. tent, a cooking kit for two, a light folding grate, a canvas water bucket and washbasin, a first-aid kit, and some canoe-repair material. Each man should have three single lightweight blankets or a sleeping bag and mattress.

Wear felt hats and take a sufficient number of medium-weight wool shirts, a khaki-color cotton shirt, khaki pants, both cotton and wool socks, lightweight underwear, rubber-bottom low shoes, a sweater, and a waterproof coat. Be sure to carry an ax, a knife, a compass, and a waterproof matchbox.

EQUIPMENT FOR BACK-PACK TRIP

Question: What equipment will I need to make a pack trip on foot, doing some bear hunting, in the remote sections of Arizona?—J. W. T., Mich.

Answer: If the trip will take you into the mountains in winter or spring, carry a fairly protective outfit, including a light hiker's tent, fitted with a floor and mosquito curtains. You can get along with less protection in warmer seasons and in other parts of the state.

Take a medium-weight sleeping bag, with light ¾-length air mattress. Your one-man cooking set should include a coffeepot, small kettle for spuds, frying pan, cutlery, plates, and cup. A canvas washbasin and water pail are musts. Carry a compass, knife, and waterproof matchbox with your maps.

Take a few first-aid supplies, a camp ax, and, if you have room, a folding grate. If the country is new to you, make short trips at first, using a town as a base. As your experience grows, you can add the equipment you need.

Later on, when your outfit has grown in size, you might buy a burro to carry the load and leave your hands free for the rifle. Carrying a pack is hard work no matter how much experience you have had.

TENT PROBLEM FOR LARGE PARTY

Question: Sixteen of us are planning a deer hunt this fall in the Adirondacks of New York, and we are considering the use of one 18 x 24-ft. tent to house the whole party. What do you think of the idea?—A. R., N. Y.

Answer: Such a large shelter will be quite high and will require long, heavy poles for support. Because of the large area covered, you may have trouble finding a smooth enough piece of ground on which to pitch the tent. Moreover, a shelter of this size will have to be made of heavy canvas, so that its weight and cost will be considerable.

For these reasons I'd suggest you use four smaller tents. Lastly, the 18 x 24-ft. model will provide a space of only 3 x 9 ft. for each hunter.

EQUIPMENT FOR HIKING TRIP

Question: Another 16-year-old boy and I want to hike over part of the Long Trail in Vermont. We'll be gone about 3 days and will cover some 50 miles. We won't need a tent—shelters are placed at convenient intervals—and we want to travel as light as possible. What equipment do you suggest we take?—A. B., Vt.

Answer: *Bedding*—At least three, and possibly four, blankets weighing from 4 to 4½ lb., depending upon the season. If the shelters lack board floors, take a waterproof tarp to place on the ground and keep your blankets dry and clean. Since you will travel light and probably won't want to carry an air mattress, gather evergreen boughs at night to make a padding between the ground and the blankets—otherwise you'll probably find it difficult to sleep.

Cooking kit—This will depend upon how much cooking you do. If you're going to prepare vegetables, take two kettles with lids. Use one kettle for boiling and the other for fixing hot drinks. For a lighter outfit, take a single pot. In either case, each man will need a frying pan, plate, cup, and cutlery.

Camp articles—Carry a small ax for cutting kindling and fuel, a canvas pail to pack water, a canvas washbasin, simple first-aid necessities, and a toilet kit.

Personal articles—Each man should pack a pocketknife, compass, waterproof matchbox, and flashlight. Also take an extra suit of underwear and a spare pair of socks. You can use the underwear in place of sleeping garments.

Miscellaneous—Be sure to take a watch and a map of the trail. Each hiker will want a canvas packsack to carry his share of the equipment and grub. And don't overlook the little things—an extra pair of shoelaces, for example. Wear comfortable shoes, a medium-weight flannel shirt, stout cotton pants, a waterproof or water-resistant jacket, and a soft felt hat.

EQUIPPING STATION WAGON FOR CAMPING TRIPS

Question: Although I am a novice, I plan to devote the rest of my life to fishing and hunting and am buying a station wagon which I want to equip for long trips. What type sleeping bags would you recommend for my wife and me; what type tent for semi-permanent use and what other equipment should we buy?—R. S., Calif.

Answer: You could possibly have your station wagon equipped with removable beds, but this wouldn't be worth the trouble and expense involved if you plan to use a tent and sleeping bags. Take a 7 x 8-ft. auto or umbrella tent and a nested aluminum cooking outfit for two, including plates, cups, bowls, frying pan, coffeepot, boiling kettles, and cutlery.

Buy a fuel-oil stove with a separate folding oven to fit on top—you can use the stove often to dry out your tent, so long as you are careful not to close the tent tightly at the time. If you plan to camp in cool weather take a small heating stove too.

Provide medium-weight sleeping bags and an air mattress for each. Consult various manufacturers for the proper-size bag in relation to each size.

EQUIPPING CANOE FOR TWO

Question: My friend and I are planning to go on a 10-day canoe trip. What pans, kettles, etc., will we need? There is no thwart on our canoe. We will meet some rough water. Do you think it advisable to use leeboards? We are going to paddle —not sail. The canoe is a standard 16-footer. Will it hold two people and about 75 lb. of baggage?—R. L.,.Manitoba.

Answer: You should have a 4-qt. kettle or pot with lid, for vegetables and stews, a 2-qt. pot for making coffee and tea, and an 8-in. frying pan. Add to these pieces one small mixing bowl and the necessary cups, plates, knives, forks, and spoons and you'll have a serviceable outfit.

I don't think leeboards are satisfactory when paddling. I would not take them. You could easily put in a cross brace, making it from stout wood like spruce or oak, and screwing it to the gunwales of the canoe.

Your 16-footer should carry two men and an outfit of 75 lb. if it has a reasonably wide beam.

EQUIPMENT FOR CAMPING IN THE PLAINS

Question: It is my plan to spend several months roaming and camping in the outdoors with as little civilization about as possible. Texas appears to be the ideal state for it, having ample grazing and a mild winter. How much should a cow pony and burro cost me there? What equipment do I need?—P. K., N. Y.

Answer: Yes, there is plenty of room in Texas, especially in the northern and western areas. However, there is also very little water in many localities, and that makes it a difficult country to camp in, especially for strangers who are not acquainted with the different sources of water. If you decide on Texas, I'd suggest you make very short trips out of your headquarters at first.

I would suggest that you check with several dealers on the cost of ponies and burros. There are, of course, cheap animals to be had, but I would rather pay a good price and get a sounder beast. You'll need a small tent, bed roll and blankets, air mattress or camp mattress to place beneath the bed roll, cooking kit, pack saddles, picket ropes, hobbles, and picket pins. Your animals will have to graze during the night in order to obtain enough food. You should have also a snake-bite kit, provisions, water bags and canteen, short ax, compass, waterproof match box, maps, good stout riding clothes, and a saddle slicker. After you have made several short one or two-day trips from your selected headquarters you'll know what items must be added.

TRACK-TRAIL PACK

Question: I would appreciate your advice on what equipment and supplies a hunter should carry when he is tracking game in deep woods.—L. H. P., N. H.
Answer: The equipment carried by hunters when they leave headquarters or a base camp to trail game is usually restricted to a few articles that should prevent them from becoming lost, and emergency rations and equipment in case they should do so. In the first group the "musts" are a compass, and a map (either purchased or homemade) of the country that's being hunted. The materials which will sustain a hunter in the bush for a short time are matches in a waterproof box, a good knife capable of cutting kin-

dling, and a few emergency foods—sandwiches made up at the base, or such items as uncooked bacon, cheese, salami, bread, and tea. Chocolate is also very nourishing. All these foods are light in weight in comparison with the calories they supply.

Now when a hunter leaves his base with the deliberate intention of spending two or more days on the trail, of course he'll need more equipment: a light, waterproof tarpaulin for shelter, a down sleeping bag or heavy blanket, a short ax to cut shelter poles and firewood, a folding mess kit, and more food.

CHOOSING THE RIGHT TENT

Question: A friend and I are planning a camping trip of about a month's duration and are a bit puzzled as to what type of tent to take. This will be our first trip, and any advice you will be able to give us would be appreciated.—G. F. P., N. Y.
Answer: The proper choice of a tent depends on the type of trip you are planning. If you are traveling by canoe, you would need a moderately heavy tent about 6 x 7 ft. in size. If you will be hauled in to the site and plan to stay there during the entire month, then you could use a more roomy and comfortable tent, which, of course, would weigh more. In this case I should suggest a wall-model tent about 6 x 8 ft. with a separate canvas floor.

CHOOSING A SLEEPING BAG

Question: I want a good sleeping bag for cold weather. Should it be filled with down or feathers?—G. P., N. C.
Answer: There is not much difference between the insulating power of a down-filled bag and one stuffed with the regular commercial grade of ground-up feathers. The down bags, however, are warmer, pound for pound, if you expect to sleep outdoors in temperatures of 20 degrees or more below zero.

HOW TO CHOOSE AND CARE FOR YOUR CAMP CLOTHES

CURE FOR STICKY OILSKIN COATS

Question: I have an oilskin raincoat which is very sticky and will not dry. Is there any method of drying it out so that it will be usable?—R. A., N. J.

Answer: Sometimes a sticky raincoat can be improved by dusting the surface with talc powder, then hanging the garment in the sun. Also, soaking the coat in weak limewater for an hour or two may convert the sticky layer into a powdery deposit which can be easily brushed off. A third stunt which has often proved effective is to paint over the surface with a mixture of equal parts of spar varnish and turpentine, then hang the coat in a cool place until completely dry.

In very bad cases it may even be necessary to remove all the softened coating to effect a cure. This coating can be dissolved with alcohol or acetone. A new application of linseed oil is then sprayed over the fabric. This treatment is rather costly.

DRESSING FOR LEATHER SHOES

Question: Will you please tell me the formula of beeswax and tallow or any good formula that is used as a dressing for leather hunting boots.—F. M. P., N. Y.

Answer: In my opinion a mixture of beeswax and tallow would be too thick and stiff to use as a satisfactory dressing for leather. Most of the popular formulas contain one of these materials, but not both.

There are two good combinations, equal parts of beeswax and neat's-foot oil; or equal parts of beef or mutton tallow and neat's-foot oil. If you particularly want to use both of the heavier substances, you could mix 1 oz. each of tallow and beeswax with 2 oz. of neat's-foot oil.

Personally, I do not care for the very thick dressings as they do not penetrate leather readily and thus have little action in softening the material and preventing cracks. A very heavy grease will merely glaze over the surface.

CLOTHING FOR COLD AND RAINY WEATHER

Question: Do you advise the use of horsehide clothes for hunting and camping purposes? What sort of clothing have you found best for hunting in wet weather and in cold weather?—C. E., Wis.

Answer: Waterproofed horsehide garments are splendid in cold, wet, and blustery weather, in temperatures ranging from zero to 40 degrees F. I've worn them quite a bit for fall shooting when winds were sharp and cold, and rain a frequent occurrence. The material is very soft and comfortable. One point to remember is that horsehide is slightly heavier than wool, which may or may not influence your choice.

For hunting in rainy weather, you also have the choice of waterproofed canvas, or of wool clothing covered with a lightweight raincoat or cape. Featherweight oilskin garments are very popular with hunters. They can be taken off when the weather clears, and carried in the hunting-coat pocket. Some woodsmen wear long coats, others buy jacket and pants to slip over regular clothing. Any of these types will serve you well.

CLOTHING FOR CANADA FISHING TRIP

Question: Will you tell me the most suitable clothing for a fishing trip in Alberta, Canada, in summer? I expect to be there for a month.—W. G. D., Tex.

Answer: I suggest that you pack two shirts, one of lightweight wool and the other of the stout, hard-weave cotton known as khaki or drill. The cotton shirt will be very useful on hot days when you may be active. The woolen one can be saved for possible chilly weather or for wearing around camp in the cool of the evening. It will give better protection, too, if you have to go out in the rain.

Take, also, two pairs of trousers made of very stout cotton, like whipcord or gabardine, a material that will resist wear and not catch burs and brush. The surface should be smooth and hard. Your hat can be of felt or canvas; in either case it should be waterproofed and have a wide brim to protect your face and neck from sun and rain. Cotton underwear should do; it can have long or half-length arms and legs as you prefer. Take a jacket for cold days; also a light sweater.

For shoes, an all-leather moccasin-type boot with 8 or 10-in. top, depending on your height. Tall men prefer the 10-in. size. Have these boots roomy and keep them well-softened with oil or grease. Wear wool socks inside. You will also need wading boots or wading pants if you do any fly-fishing. These should be of the lightweight type to prevent fatigue when worn for hours at a stretch. Socks are long and pull up over the outside of trouser bottoms. Take some cotton ones to wear around camp. You'll also need a rain suit or rainproof slicker; also take some large handkerchiefs to wear about your neck when the mosquitoes get bad.

CUTTING LEATHER FOR BOOT LACES

Question: I have some rawhide that I want to cut into thin strips for boot laces. How can I do this without getting cross grains?—S. W. H., N. Y.

Answer: So far as I know, leather has no cross grain that would make it necessary for you to cut thongs in one direction to retain maximum strength. The usual method of making thongs is to cut around the chunk from the outside, cut-

ting continuously so that you take off the thong in a single piece. Of course you must try to keep the width uniform.

CARE OF RUBBER BOOTS

Question: I have a new pair of rubber boots, and since I can't afford to get them often I'd like your advice on how to store them, say for six months at a time. Is there any preparation that will lengthen their life? Should they be hung up or left in the box?—H. W. S., Calif.

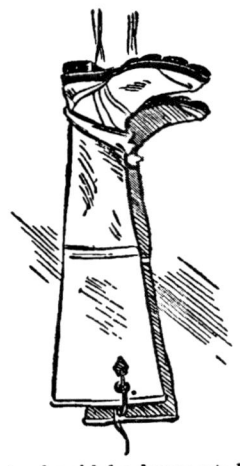

Stored boots should be hung up by the feet; preferably with stout cloth as wire would cut into the rubber.

Answer: You can do a great deal toward prolonging the life of your rubber boots by storing them properly and giving them an occasional application of the following mixture: Take 3 parts glycerine and 1 part grain alcohol and shake until well mixed. Apply all over the outside of boots with a small sponge. After five minutes wipe off excess mixture with a dry cloth. This will help to keep the boot material soft and pliable and postpone indefinitely the time they'll begin to crack and leak.

The best way to store rubber boots is to put shoe trees in them to keep the toes stretched out and free of wrinkles. Or you can stuff the feet full of dry, shredded newspaper. Then hang them by the feet in a cool, dark place; light and heat attack rubber. Never put the boots away folded, tops must be smoothed out and hang free. There are many ways to hang a boot by the foot—some sportsmen make hangers out of wire clothes hangers, or you can use a stout cloth about an inch wide; this won't cut into the rubber.

KEEPING FEET WARM

Question: I am troubled with poor circulation and weak arches, and want to know whether it is possible to wear arched bedroom slippers inside hip boots. I feel this would combine more warmth with better support for my arches. If this can be done, what size boot should I get to take an 8½ slipper?—R. B., N. J.

Answer: You should be able to do this without much trouble. I'd suggest a 10½ boot. If you buy by mail, sketch the outline of your slipper with your foot in it and send the drawing with your order to assure a satisfactory fit.

Two or three pairs of soft woolen socks usually provide ample insulation inside boots—but won't give you any arch support. Write for catalogues to firms making wool-covered insoles with spring-steel arches which are worn inside boots.

Massage your feet two or three times a week with rubbing alcohol to improve their circulation. If they're tender, soak them briefly in a salt-water solution on alternate nights to toughen the skin.

WATERPROOFING LEATHER BOOTS

Question: I have a pair of leather boots that I've used for hunting for three seasons and now find that the water seeps through the leather. Will a mixture of rubber cement and gasoline make a good waterproofing material?—C. H., Ga.

Answer: Ordinary rubber-tire cement, thinned with about 50 percent gasoline,

is often used to waterproof leather shoes and boots. The gasoline has no special virtue, merely being added as a thinner to make the cement easier to handle. The usual method is to brush on the mixture with a small paint brush. The rubber coats over the surface of the leather and seals its pores, thus excluding water.

However, this is the extent of its value —it does not soften leather or make it wear longer, as will a good animal fat or oil. For this reason I recommend that you give your boots liberal applications of neat's-foot oil or any commercial dressing made especially for shoes.

Sportsmen generally find it advisable to oil or grease their boots at least once a week during constant use. This keeps the footwear soft, prevents the leather from cracking and breaking, and in addition seals it against water. If your boots have not been greased for three seasons, a good dressing is evidently required. Apply plenty of oil and give it several days to sink into the leather. If you find then that the leather still allows seepage, you might try the rubber-gasoline treatment.

REPAIRING RUBBER BOOTS

Question: A pair of rubber boots about a year old have cracked a little in the up-

Pinhole leaks in boots can often be repaired with rubber cement thinned with gasoline.

pers and leak above the knees. What can I do to remedy this?—A. H. W., Calif.

Answer: Pinhole leaks can often be sealed by painting that part of the boot with pure rubber cement thinned with enough gasoline to make it brush easily.

Give bad areas several coats. Larger holes and punctures can be closed with automobile inner-tube cold-patch material. They detract from the appearance of the boot but will stick permanently and do the work. Of course, your local tire-repair man can vulcanize the bad parts, but the expense is hardly warranted.

SHOES FOR HIKING

Question: A friend and I plan a prospecting trip into the California mountains. What footwear would you advise us to get for such a trip?—D. P., Ohio.

Answer: You have a choice of two types of shoes. The first is a regular leather one of medium height with a stout leather sole. This sole can be fitted with hobnails. If you adopt this type, carry along an extra set of nails to replace those that are worn off or lost.

The second type of footwear is a stout leather shoe with a heavy crêpe-rubber sole. A great many prospectors and sportsmen are adopting this shoe because it is comfortable, lighter than the hobnailed shoe, and just as sure in slippery going. If your feet are not adversely affected by the rubber soles (you'll have to try them out to determine this), I'd recommend this type to you.

Shoes with leather leggings, worn with breeches, are often more comfortable than the more popular high-top leather boot, which I shouldn't advise. If you plan to wear regular trousers, get a shoe with a top not more than 8 in. high, and pull your wool socks up over the trouser legs. Whipcord trousers will probably give better service than wool.

SEWING MOCCASINS

Question: Can you give me some information about making Indian moccasins? My main difficulty is in the sewing of the upper to the sole.—F. F. G., Tex.

Answer: Your trouble in sewing uppers and soles together may lie in the use of a regular needle instead of the three-sided kind leatherworkers use. When the sole is fairly thick, it is necessary first to pierce each hole with an awl. Waxed shoemaker's "ends" or bristles can be used in place of thread in which case a needle is not needed, as this material is stiff enough to enter the holes without one.

Some moccasins call for lacing with leather thongs. Punch holes for these with a nail, draw the thong up very tight, hammer the seam flat, and the holes will close enough to keep water out.

CARE OF NEW BOOTS

Question: I am going to buy a new pair of boots, and I am wondering what type sole would be best for our country, where we have plenty of gumbo mud whenever it rains, and deep snow in the winter.

Also, how should I break in a new pair of boots?—D. R. R., Manitoba.

Answer: Usually a good leather sole is best for boots. One good way to keep the soles well greased, to prevent them from absorbing water, is to heat neat's-foot oil in a shallow pan and set the boots in it, letting them soak for half an hour. Also rub the warm oil into the uppers with a cloth swab. It will work best if the boots too are slightly warmed.

You can break in boots by oiling them heavily until they are soft, and then walk in them, wearing thick woolen socks. Another method is to soak the upper—all but sole and heel—with hot water. When the leather is saturated, put on over wool socks and walk. As the boots dry they shape themselves to your feet.

VARNISH FOR SNOWSHOE WEBBING

Question: The varnish is peeling and cracking on the webbing of my snowshoes. What is the best way to refinish these rawhide strips?—L. E. H., Pa.

Answer: Use a fine-wire brush, and it won't injure the rawhide when you scratch off the old varnish. *Don't* use varnish remover. When the webbing is clean, apply a high grade of exterior or spar varnish, and then set the snowshoes to dry in a warm room.

FOOTWEAR FOR MONTANA

Question: What type boot do you recommend for big-game hunting in the rough country of Montana? I'm considering 12-in. shoepacs. Should they be worn just with socks?—W. L. B., Mont.

Answer: For hunting in mountainous country I prefer a stout leather shoe with 7-in. or lower tops, constructed along the lines of the U. S. Army "Munson" last, and well hobnailed to cut down on slipping and sole wear. However, such a boot is not nearly so waterproof as the shoepac, even though you grease or oil the former.

But for the smoother going in the woods the rubber-bottom pac is excellent. I like this style with 10-in. tops. The shoepac is usually worn with wool socks —as many as three pairs sometimes. And in very cold climates a felt or sheepskin inner shoe is often worn inside the pac for maximum warmth.

WATERPROOFING COMBAT BOOTS

Question: How can I waterproof a pair of infantry combat boots which have the rough side of the leather out?—P. S., Pa.

Answer: Write any manufacturer of camping or hunting boots and get some fairly heavy-bodied shoe or boot-waterproofing compound.

RAWHIDE LACING

Question: Can you tell me how to make rawhide lacing suitable for use in snowshoes?—A. N., Minn.

Answer: First dehair the hide with a solution of hardwood ashes and water. After scrapping off all hair, deflesh the skin well, removing all cartilage, flesh, etc.

Then, while the skin is still wet, lace it into a stout wooden frame; take up on it as tightly as you can. As it dries it shrinks and gets still tighter. After the skin is thoroughly dry remove it from the frame, dampen it, and soften it by working it over the edge of a smooth board. Keep

Rawhide lacing for snowshoes can be cut out of the skin after it has been thoroughly processed and softened.

the hide damp and continue to work it, breaking down all fibers, until it dries soft and with no trace of stiffness. Next cut the hide into thongs of the proper width. Wet these thongs and pull and stretch them. The important thing is to get every bit of stretch out of them. Finally, lace the thongs wet in the shoes, let them dry there, and give them a coat of varnish.

CLEANING ELKSKIN JACKET

Question: My elkskin jacket, made by Indians in Manitoba, was soiled by soot and smoke on a recent train trip. How can I clean the garment without damaging its soft leather?—D. W. L., Toronto.

Answer: Unless you can find a dry-cleaning establishment which will guarantee satisfaction it will be difficult to restore the jacket to its original unsoiled condition. Nearly any home-cleaning method presents difficulties—fluids such as naphtha may stiffen the leather; saddle soap or similar material will keep it soft but will not remove bad stains.

If you must do the work at home, remove the worst grime with a cleaning fluid and then go over the whole jacket with saddle soap. However, don't expect too much success from this method.

SNOWSHOE FRAMES AND FILLING

Question: Trapping last winter I wore out two pairs of snowshoes, and now I want to make some myself. What can you tell me about the best time to cut ash, how to shape it, how to select a suitable tree, and what kind of hide to use for thongs?—J. R., N. Y.

Answer: I don't think it makes much difference when you cut ash for your purpose, but it is important that the wood be well seasoned before using. Woodsmen who make their snowshoes in camp usually cut 6-in. saplings, selecting straight-grained quarters that are free of knots and twisted fibers. While still green these are then whittled to size and bent to shape, sometimes with the help of steam, or after soaking in water for several days. Frames are usually made in the summer and set aside to dry until fall.

Cowhide makes the best filling. Woodsmen stretch a green hide very tight, let it dry, then shave off the hair with a sharp knife. A better method is to soak the hide in a solution of wood ashes and water, or lime and water, until the hair loosens. Then the hair is scraped off and the wet hide stretched tight. As it dries, the flesh side is rubbed vigorously with the dulled edge of a hand ax.

WATERPROOFING PARKA

Question: I have some blanket material which I'd like to make into a parka. Can I successfully waterproof and dye it at home?—M. Z., Mich.

Answer: Before you waterproof the parka you can dye it by first using Turkey red and then scarlet wool dyes. Naturally, it will be impossible to dye the parka after it's been waterproofed. For waterproofing use water-free lanolin, obtainable at your drug store. Mix it in the proportion of 2 oz. to a gallon of benzine or naphtha. Soak the parka in this mixture for 5 minutes; squeeze out gently and hang up to dry, shifting the parka several times so that the mixture doesn't accumulate in any one spot on it.

SELECTING HUNTING BOOTS

Question: I'd like to get a pair of hunting boots, both comfortable and waterproof. What do you suggest?—L. F., La.

Answer: If you expect to do your hunting in Southern states I believe an all-leather hunting boot of 14-in. height would be best for your purpose. The best all-round boot for Northern hunting, in my opinion, is the combination leather-top and rubber-bottom boot 10 or 12 in. high. But it would be rather warm for Louisiana and surrounding states.

The 14-in. top is popular with a great many Southern sportsmen because it offers protection against poisonous snakes. Leather boots can never be made absolutely waterproof like rubber, but if properly tanned and then greased or oiled regularly they become almost impervious to moisture, and for all practical purposes as good as rubber.

REPAIRING CUT IN BOOTS

Question: I had just had my hiking boots rebuilt, and they were like new, when I had an accident in camp. While I was splitting wood the ax slipped and cut through the edge of the rubber sole and also through part of the leather upper. (My foot wasn't touched!) I hope you can tell me some way that these boots can be repaired.—S. R., Pa.

Answer: The only way I know of to patch a cut or gash in the leather upper is to cover the place with a patch. That will be noticeable, of course, and will spoil the appearance of the boots to an extent. Formerly, shoe repairmen sewed all such patches in place, but they are now using some sort of vulcanizing process to attach half soles, and it may be that a shop could attach a patch on upper leather in the same way. If this could be done, and the edges of the patch carefully skived or feathered down, it would not be nearly so noticeable. The sole may have to be renewed, depending, of course, on the extent of the damage. You'll have to consult a repair shop about that.

DEER-HUNTING CLOTHES

Question: What in your opinion is the ideal outfit of clothing for deer hunting in the Northern states?—J. D. G., N. Y. **Answer:** My preference would be something like this: First, an all-wool hunting suit such as is furnished by many firms, which consists of rather a close-fitting coat and a pair of breeches which fold about the leg and are placed inside long wool hunting socks. The coat, really a jacket, can be belted or not to suit your own taste. The cloth should be resistant to rain, and I like a checked pattern using white, red, and black, or a similar combination which will identify you in the woods as a hunter and not a deer. In addition, you should wear a deer hunter's cap covered with red flannel, and it is a good idea to pin a large square of bright red cloth to the back of your jacket.

A lightweight flannel shirt, knee-length woolen socks, a light raincoat of thin material to be carried on wet days, and a pair of rubber-bottomed, leather-top hunting shoes about 8 in. high will complete the outfit. Buy a light boot or shoe, not the kind made for loggers, but the type designed for sportsmen.

All of these items will give you a comfortable and lasting hunting outfit.

WATERPROOFING CAMP CLOTHES

Question: How can I waterproof cotton and wool clothing?—W. B., Calif. **Answer:** Here is the best home process I know for waterproofing canvas clothes or any garment made entirely of cotton: Dissolve ¼ lb. paraffin in 1 qt. gasoline. The wax is first shaved and melted, then added to the gasoline, which has been warmed by setting its container in a pail of boiling water (outdoors and at a safe distance from flames). Mixture is painted on with an old brush. The main fault of this method is that it leaves the cloth slightly stiff in cold weather.

Linseed oil will waterproof closely woven canvas or cotton garments. You thin the oil with a little paint dryer, then paint it on the cloth. The garment must be hung up to dry about 3 weeks before it can be worn.

Don't use these processes for wool. Dipping the garment in a lanolin solution is the best way to waterproof wool at home. Some manufacturers of wool hunting clothes will re-treat their products to restore their water-repellent qualities.

PATTERNS FOR HOBNAILS

Question: What is the best pattern to use for hobnails on boots?—R. M., Calif. **Answer:** There is no specific pattern to use when driving hobnails into boots. They are usually staggered over the sole and heel, using perhaps nine for the sole and three for the heel. For safe walking, they should be set no closer than ¾ in. to the edges of sole and heel.

TO DRY RUBBER BOOTS

Question: How can I dry my rubber boots overnight?—E. H. R., Pa. **Answer:** Heat some oats in an oven and pour them into the feet. If this material is changed and reheated two or three times during the evening the boots should be well dried out by morning.

HOW TO CARE FOR YOUR CAMPING EQUIPMENT

STORING CAMP EQUIPMENT

Question: I'd like to know how to store my camping equipment properly. The chief articles that I want to keep in good shape are rubber air mattress, various canvas articles, leather and rubber boots, other leather articles, axes, knives, cooking equipment, and rifles. Please give me some advice.—A. T. S., Md.

Answer: Canvas articles like sacks, packs, and tents need only to be dry and free from dirt, mud, or grease. Brushing ordinarily will do this job. Tents should not be folded in hard creases. Roll loosely or fold a couple of times, hang over two wood crossbars or a couple of ropes, and store in a cool, dry place. Metal articles should be greased to prevent rusting.

Give all leather goods applications of neat's-foot oil or similar shoe dressing to keep them soft and free from mildew, and store in a dry place.

Rubber boots, air mattresses, and other rubber equipment should be cleaned with warm water. Then give generous application of 3 parts grain alcohol and 1 part glycerin, and after 10 minutes wipe off any surplus. Don't fold rubber articles. Hang up rubber boots and waders with tops fully extended. Treat rubber coats similarly. Partly inflate air mattress so the sides won't stick together.

MENDING HOLES IN TENTS

Question: Is there any method, other than sewing, to repair holes in canvas tents and covers?—R. W., Wis.

Answer: The only practical way to repair holes, tears, and rips in a tent is to sew the split together, if possible, and then sew a patch over it. The edges of the patch should be turned under neatly. Put the patch on the outside, then apply a waterproofing solution. Very small pinholes can be sealed with waterproofing dope which has a fairly heavy body; but it would obviously be impractical to patch a large number of such holes.

STOPPING TENT-SEAM LEAKS

Question: Last year I bought a tent, which leaks along the seams where it is stitched. How can I fix this?—D. N., Va.

Answer: Rub paraffin or beeswax along the leaking seams, and then melt the wax in with a moderately warm iron.

CLEANING SLEEPING BAG

Question: How can I clean a sleeping bag so badly soiled that it is past the sun-and-air cure?—G. W. F., Ind.

Answer: Write to the manufacturer. If he is unable to recommend a safe method for that particular bag, take it to a cleaning establishment specializing in such articles as feather-stuffed pillows.

KEEPING MICE OUT OF MATTRESSES

Question: The members of our camp have all had their mattresses damaged by mice. Do you know of any mouse-repellent available, or any treated mattress that we could buy?—F. E. M., Pa.

Answer: I have never heard of any material, or of any cloth or mattress, that would repel mice. Your letter leads me to believe that the damage to your mattresses occurs when the camp is closed. If so, why not store the bedding in mouse-proof containers? They could be large boxes in the form of a frame of 1 x 3 in. wood covered with wire screening. The screening would be impassable to mice yet allow sufficient ventilation to avert mold or dampness in the bedding. You could make up such a box for each mattress, or larger ones to hold several each. If the latter plan is followed, insert cross cleats to hold the mattresses apart and allow sufficient ventilation.

SLEEPING-BAG LINERS

Question: Do you recommend the use of a liner in a sleeping bag? Which type is best, cotton or wool?—J. E., Colo.

Answer: I like to use a bag liner, for it helps keep dirt and moisture from within the bag proper. In warm weather I use a cotton-fleece liner, in cold weather a rather thin all-wool or part-wool blanket. If these liners are regularly removed for washing and drying, the bag itself seldom requires cleaning.

WATERPROOFING TENT

Question: Kindly give me a formula for waterproofing an olive-drab tent. I recall one which I think specified 5 lb. of paraffin to 1 gal. of gasoline, but this would not give an olive color.—V. R., N. J.

Answer: The correct proportions for the waterproofing mixture are 1 lb. of paraffin, shaved fine, to 1½ gal. of gasoline. However, I prefer turpentine in place of gasoline, as it seems to leave the material less stiff in cool weather. This formula can be improved by the addition of a couple of tubes of rubber cement to the mixture. Warm your turpentine *outdoors* (its fumes are inflammable), stir in the paraffin until it is dissolved. Add rubber cement last. Apply the mixture to tent material with a brush and let the waterproofed cloth hang in the open air for a week or until the turpentine odor is gone.

I know of no home formula which combines waterproofing and dyeing in one operation, although some of the factory compounds can be purchased colored. I suggest that if you want to use the paraffin formula, you dye your tent first, using any commercial dye recommended for cotton.

TO PATCH AIR MATTRESS

Question: I have several air mattresses, canvas-backed, which have developed leaks, and I'm at a loss as to how to repair them. My garage man says applying heat would ruin them.—F. H. W., Sask.

Answer: Have had the same trouble myself. At first, when there were only a few pinhole leaks which let air out very slowly, I thinned pure rubber cement with gasoline and painted this over the leaking section. With larger leaks (you can locate them by holding the inflated mattress under water) I put on cold patches such as are used on inner tubes. I would not use any heat method. Try the cold patch, and if the spot is properly roughened with sandpaper and cleaned with gasoline I'm sure the patches will adhere.

BLOODPROOFING RUBBERIZED GAME POCKET

Question: The rubberized game pocket in my hunting vest is no longer bloodproof. Is there any way that I can remove the present rubber coating and apply a commercial waterproof and bloodproof material? I also have a new hunting coat with a bloodproof pocket which is not rubberized but appears to consist of a double layer of cloth. Can I apply bloodproofing material to it?—F. J. L., Ind.

Answer: If you can remove all traces of the old rubberized treatment from the pocket you probably can make it bloodproof by applying a coat or two of some good commercial preparation. However, it is difficult to take off the original coats and I don't think you'll have much success, especially since applying one type of waterproofing material over another is seldom satisfactory.

You can make a good bloodproofing coating by dissolving ¼ lb. of shaved paraffin in 1 qt. of uncolored gasoline. To do this, heat the gasoline by setting it inside a pail of hot water *outdoors*. Don't heat it inside a building or over a stove. Apply while warm to the pocket, if you succeed in removing the rubber.

If you think the pocket of your new coat isn't bloodproof apply a coat of this compound to the inside of it, then test the cloth.

STORING A TENT

Question: I have a large tent which I propose to store away in a bag. Are there any precautions I should take to protect the fabric?—L. D., Pa.

Answer: The first step in preparing a tent for storage is to clean it thoroughly, brushing off all mud and dirt and removing spots or grease with naphtha, clear white gasoline (don't use ethyl gas), or commercial cleaning fluid. Such spots might rot the fabric. Next, be sure the tent is absolutely dry; there must not be even a suggestion of dampness anywhere. If it leaks, this might be a good time to give it a coat of good factory-made waterproofing solution, but if not the treatment can be deferred.

Roll the tent rather loosely—never fold it in sharp creases that might cause the fabric to crack. Then when it is placed in its bag, store the shelter in a cool, dry place; not the attic if it is hot. Even extreme cold won't harm the tent as long as it is dry.

TO PROTECT TENT AGAINST SPARKS

Question: Will you please describe a treatment which will make a tent resistant to sparks.—C. J. F., Minn.

Answer: There is an alum-and-lead treatment which makes canvas resistant to sparks and also to water. It consists of two solutions.

First, mix 1 lb. alum in 1 gal. soft water that is nearly boiling hot. Then add 2 gal. cold water—rain water if possible.

In another container dissolve 1 lb. sugar of lead in 1 gal. boiling water, then when it cools add 3 gal. cold water.

Soak the tent in the alum solution first until completely saturated—about 5

hours should do it. Then wring out the surplus liquid and put the tent in the solution of sugar of lead, leaving it there for 5 hours. Wring it out lightly and hang it up to dry.

The quantities mentioned will do for a medium-size tent. In the case of a small one you might be able to get along with half the quantities. Both the alum and the sugar of lead may be obtained at drug stores almost anywhere.

PORCUPINE REPELLENT FOR TENTS

Question: How can tent walls be protected against hungry porcupines? I am planning to keep two pup tents set up for 6 weeks in a remote section of the Adirondacks, but they will be occupied only over week-ends.—C. R. S., N. Y.

Answer: I don't know any positive means of preventing porcupines from gnawing tents. One measure I have heard of is to dump a couple of pounds of salt over a low stump near the tent. The animals are supposed to lick the salt and not the tent.

Another system is to coat the tent, especially the lower edges, with some substance that porcupines don't like. The lower portions of wilderness cabins are often painted with a mixture of linseed oil and red pepper. This or a similar formula might work on tents. Linseed oil is a good waterproofing agent too. It takes a long time to dry but in drying would likely seal in the pepper so rain wouldn't wash it away, and a porky would taste it the instant he started to work on the cloth.

VARNISHING A PACK BASKET

Question: Recently, I bought a pack basket which is not varnished. If it should be, what kind of varnish should I use and how is it applied?—B. W., N. Y.

Answer: Varnish your basket: it certainly will do no harm and it probably will protect the material from moisture and wear.

Use the best grade of spar varnish, for this withstands weather better than other grades. Apply it with a small brush, brushing it well inside and out, and taking pains to cover all joints of the woven

Spar varnish applied to a pack basket will protect it from moisture and wear.

strips. Thin the first coat with a little turpentine to make it go on easier, then put two more coats on as the varnish comes from the can. I think a pint ought to provide three coats.

MILDEW ON CANVAS

Question: In pitching my wall tent a short time ago, I discovered several mildew spots. They form a regular ring around the canvas, varying in width from a foot to a few inches. I suspect that snow got at it while it was stored. Can the spots be removed?—R. J., Ill.

Answer: There is no sure way that I know of to remove mildew spots from canvas and most efforts to do so would probably affect the waterproofing treatment. Consequently, I would let them remain. They probably haven't seriously impaired either the strength of the fabric or its ability to resist rain, and they are not likely to get any worse. It might be a good plan to go over the mildew spots with a coat of some factory-made waterproofing preparation. This should block any possible deterioration of the cloth.

Be careful in the future to avoid laying the tent away when damp. Also be sure to store it in a dry place.

CLEANING GREASY TARP

Question: Do you know of any way to remove grease and dirt from tent material? I have a large tarp, but it is badly stained, mostly with grease, and I cannot seem to get these spots out. I also should like to know what size to cut the tarp to shelter two men and what style of tent you would recommend for packing on one's back for a 3-day trip.—G. H. B., Pa.

Answer: The best way is to give the tarp a thorough scrubbing with white gasoline which will soften and help remove the grease. A dry-cleaning plant might be willing to tackle the job if you explain what you want done.

To shelter two men, I'd cut the tarp about 9 x 14 ft. When you actually begin making the tent, you may find that you can cut that size down some without sacrificing roominess.

A good tent for short hiking trips is the hiker's model, similar to the explorer's but shorter and narrower.

LEAKPROOF WATER BAG

Question: Is it possible to waterproof a canvas water bag? Mine leaks so that it's worthless. I've been afraid to use ordinary compounds because they might be poisonous.—D. D. C., Calif.

Answer: The safest waterproofing material you can use on a water bag is paraffin. I believe commercial water buckets are sealed with it. Of course, you know that a water bag is made of canvas that will leak a little; that makes the bag self-cooling. If yours leaks too much you can remedy the situation by applying a mixture of $\frac{1}{4}$ lb. paraffin in 1 qt. white lead-free gasoline. Rinse bag out repeatedly, after applying the waterproofing, until all odor or taste of gasoline is eliminated. I'd put this compound on sparingly to avoid making the bag completely waterproof.

COOKING HINTS AND HELPS FOR CAMPERS

TO SMOKE GAME

Question: I would like a recipe for a satisfactory method of drying and jerking salmon and venison.—R. E. T., Ore.

Answer: Here is a very successful recipe to smoke fish. Clean them, leaving the skin on—also leaving heads on smaller fish. Split larger fish in half, fillet them if possible (which means carving a slab of meat from each side, cutting down close to the curved ribs so that few, if any, bones will be taken off with the fillet),

This smoke box and small stove make a satisfactory device for smoking or jerking fish and venison.

and soak overnight in brine strong enough to float an egg. Next, smoke eight hours over a very slow, smoky fire. Use damp sawdust to smother the flames and produce smoke. Birch and apple wood make good fuel, but use anything you have except strong-scented wood such as pine.

After eight hours of smoking, finish with 30 minutes of intense heat to cook the smoked fish. A good device for smoking is a box set up on legs so it is some 3 ft. above the ground. Fish can be laid on trays with wire-netting bottoms that slide into the box, or you can hang them from wires stretched from one side of the box to the other. Put a small stove under the box or to one side, and lead smoke pipe from stove into one side of the box. If fish are to be laid in trays rather than being hung from wires, turn them several times while they are being smoked.

Venison can be handled similarly only it is not soaked in brine nor is it finished off with intense heat for the 30 minutes mentioned. Dust thin strips of meat with salt and pepper, allow to stand overnight, then smoke until perfectly hard and brittle. Use less smoke, your object being to slowly dry all moisture out of the vension. When dry as a chip it's done.

BREAD OF THE TRAIL

Question: Please give me some recipes for bannock and camp biscuits.—J. S., Pa.

Answer: Here's a popular and successful recipe for bannock:

2¼ cups flour
4 tsp. baking powder
6 tbsp. shortening
¼ cup sugar
1 tsp. salt
1 egg or equivalent powdered eggs
⅔ cup liquid, half water, half canned milk.

Mix dry ingredients well, working in shortening with a fork. Add liquid, knead swiftly into a stiff dough, roll or press into a half-inch sheet. This may be baked as one sheet or cut into biscuits. Use more or less liquid to suit.

Camp biscuits (serving for one; multiply each item by number of campers):

1 cup flour
1 tsp. baking powder
¼ tsp. salt
1 tbsp. shortening
Water, or water and milk, to make a stiff dough.

Mix and bake as above.

The easiest way for inexperienced camp cooks to prepare good biscuits is to take along some of the prepared pancake or biscuit flour available at any grocery. All that's necessary then is the liquid to make a dough; all fuss of measuring and mixing is eliminated.

DUTCH OVEN COOKERY

Question: Can you give me an outline of the general method of cooking and baking in a Dutch oven?—F. L. C., Ont.
Answer: One general method can be followed for almost any meat. Put the oven on the fire to heat, putting a quantity of fat into it—bacon fat or salt-pork fat preferred. When the melted grease is hot you can brown an onion in it, or a couple of cloves of garlic, although this depends on your tastes alone and can be omitted. In the meantime, cut meat into serving pieces, season with salt and pepper, and roll in dry flour. When the oven and grease are piping hot put the meat in for a quick browning. Do not overbrown—this involves getting the oven too hot. Next put a little water in the bottom of the oven, set the lid on tight, and expose the oven to a mild heat. Cook the meat until it is tender—no matter how long that takes. From time to time, you should peek in to see if more water is required.

When heating an oven for baking get both body and lid very hot. Then grease the inside well and set bread or biscuits on bottom of oven. Place the covered oven over some glowing coals and heap more of them on top of it, doing that anew every 5 or 10 minutes. It takes some practice to get the oven to the right temperature for baking and to maintain that heat so that bread bakes evenly without scorching or burning.

KEEPING FOOD IN HOT WEATHER

Question: Can you tell me a method of keeping fish and other food from spoiling during a week's trip in warm weather to a region where it will be impossible to get ice?—A. A. T., Mo.
Answer: If your camp is near water, you might make a wooden rack and put your food, in cans or fruit jars, in it, and sink it under water. A flowing stream has a lot of cooling power. Some campers dig a little cellar in a cool spot, line it with leaves, and set their food inside, covering the hole with canvas and brush.

A water-evaporation cooler is a good stunt, too. It is merely a small set of shelves with the sides covered with strips of burlap. A pan of water is set on top and the upper ends of the burlap strips are placed in it. Water then seeps down the entire length of the burlap and cools the contents of the cupboard.

Fish offer a special problem, since both heat and moisture start spoilage. About the best you can do is dress the fish, wipe them dry, and hang them inside a coarse-mesh bag in a cool place.

Ice can be carried in if you have room for it. A 100-lb. cake will keep for some time if it is well wrapped in paper and then put in a fiberboard carton. The best plan is to dig a hole twice as large as the ice container, put the ice (carton and all) at one end of the hole, and place your food close to it. If you keep the pit well covered, the ice will function for 3 and sometimes 4 days.

TWO WAYS OF PREPARING BEAR MEAT

Question: What is the best method of preparing bear meat?—E. J. M., N. J.
Answer: There are two quite satisfactory ways of preparing bear meat. One is by braising the meat in a heavy utensil such as a Dutch oven, and the other is by frying. In braising, put the meat in the oven with about 2 in. of water, together with chopped onions or garlic, and salt and pepper. Cook slowly for several hours, with lid on the oven, until the meat is tender. This takes quite a while if the bear is old and tough.

Before bear meat is fried, it should be sliced and parboiled for about 20 minutes in water to which bicarbonate of soda has been added, one tablespoon to the quart. Next, pour off the soda water and simmer the meat in clear water until it is fairly tender. Then it can be fried in a little bacon grease.

Season the meat with the onions or garlic, and add a little Worcestershire before serving.

COOKING A CROW

Question: Please tell me the best way to cook crows.—W. E., Md.

Answer: Crows can be cooked in any way you'd prepare young chickens or pigeons. My favorite recipe is this: dress the birds; cut them in serving pieces; dredge with flour; salt; and brown both sides in a skillet with hot bacon fat. Put a little water in the skillet and cook very slowly until the meat is tender. Season with salt, pepper, Worcestershire sauce, and a little garlic if you like it. Try cooking a few crows at home to get the hang of it. A young bird is very tasty but some of the older ones are tough, even strong. If you get that kind, soak them 4 hours in cold water to which a little vinegar has been added, after they have been cut up. Wipe dry before browning.

COOKING COOTS

Question: A game warden told me last fall that coots were good eating.

What is the proper method of cooking them?—F. W. C., Nebr.

Answer: A coot can be cooked in any of the ways you would handle the smaller species of ducks. You should, however, remove some of the strong flavor that distinguishes these birds. One plan is to dust inside and out with black pepper, putting plenty on and setting the bird in an ice box for about five days. Then wash the pepper off and cook. Sometimes a coot is roasted with two apples and one onion inside it. Apples and onions absorb the strong flavor and are thrown away.

I prefer to use the pepper method and

to stuff the coots with a dressing containing much onion and sage. Strips of bacon spread over the birds before they are roasted make coots more appetizing.

SEASONING DUTCH OVEN

Question: My Dutch oven is about a year old. Every time something is cooked in it, rust forms—more so on the lid than on the oven—and drops into the food. When the oven is washed and put away it does not rust until used again. How can I prevent this?—J. W. H., Ariz.

Answer: New Dutch ovens, and other cast-iron cooking utensils, should have the following "seasoning" treatment to prevent rusting. Grease the inside of the the oven, and especially the underside of the lid, with a saltless grease or oil. Then put empty oven over a low flame and heat slowly for about ½ hour. This seems to drive the grease into the metal —at least I have had no rust form on mine after I used this method. If, later on, rust should begin again, you can renew the seasoning. After heating the oven, wash and dry it thoroughly.

HOW TO PICKLE FISH

Question: What is the best way that you know of to pickle fresh-water fish such as pike and bass?—D. S., N. Y.

Answer: Boil 2 cups vinegar, 2 cups water, 2 tsp. salt, 20 whole peppercorns, 18 whole allspices, 5 bay leaves and 3 slices onion for 30 minutes. Add 4 slices lemon and boil 5 minutes more.

Remove the lemon slices. Leaving fins and tails on the cleaned fish, simmer them in the mixture a few at a time until tender enough to pull a fin free. Pack the fish, with a few slices of lemon and onion, in sterilized jars. Fill jars with the boiling liquid. Cover with loose lids, but do not seal. The fish should keep 2 weeks if left in a cool place.

To preserve them for longer periods, get a canning guide and follow it.

POWDERED PARCHED CORN

Question: How do you prepare pinole, the old Indian condensed food? What is Indian Corn?—J. M. S., N. Y.

Answer: To parch corn and make what the pioneers called pinole, the corn must mature in the husk. Then it is dried by hanging the ears up by their husks. Shell the corn and put kernels in hot skillet. Toast until they're brown and you can crunch them easily with your teeth. The parched corn can be used in the whole grain or can be ground up into meal. Pioneers used the small hand coffee mill, then found in every kitchen, for this purpose. When I was a little boy we used to grind the corn, then cook in milk.

Indian corn was the ancestor of our developed strains of field corn. It had small ears, with many red kernels.

RECIPE FOR SOURDOUGH

Question: How do you make sourdough? —J. M. E., N. J.

Answer: Mix 2 cups flour, 2 tablespoons sugar, 1 teaspoon salt with enough water to form thin batter, then set in warm place to sour. Souring takes at least 48 hours, so anticipate needs for bread well in advance. Don't let the odor of the dough discourage you. Baking and the soda take the odor out of the finished product.

When mixture is well soured, stir in 1 teaspoon of soda, and enough flour to make stiff dough. Knead this into loaves or biscuits, and set in warm place until they have risen to twice their original size. Then bake in oven or cook in your frying pan with a little grease.

If you want to keep a sourdough mixture going for use on succeeding days, don't mix soda with all of it. Take out about ¾ of the soured batter, and mix that with soda and flour. Then stir more flour and water in what remains, and let it sour for the morrow.

CANNING RABBIT MEAT

Question: If possible, please give me a dependable method of cold packing rabbit meat?—E. P. C., Va.

Answer: Cut your rabbits in serving pieces and brown in hot fat, either in skillet on top of stove or in roasting pan in oven. No attempt is made to cook the meat, but browning it imparts a nice flavor. Next pack meat in clean, sterilized glass jars, adding a level teaspoon of salt to each quart jar. You can add a little water; sometimes I add a little water to the fat the meat was browned in and put this thin gravy in each jar. But you can omit the liquid entirely if you wish.

Now process the jars in a steam cooker at 15-lb. pressure for 1 hour, or in the hot-water-bath type of canner for three hours. Always use new rubber rings.

PRESERVING FISH

Question: Can you tell me how to preserve or keep fish for home use, other than by canning?—K. W. S., Mich.

Answer: Fish are sometimes put down in a salt brine, which is made strong enough to float an egg. Split your fish down one side, and place—split side down—in the brine to soak. Keep them submerged with a weighted board.

Another way to keep them is by smoking over a wood fire, burning wood sawdust to give off a good volume of smoke. The fish should be cleaned and scaled first, and the fins and tails cut off. Most sportsmen leave the heads on, and string or hang the fish through the gills. When preparing fish this way, continue to cure them in the smoke, with very little heat, until they are quite brittle.

RECIPE FOR PEMMICAN

Question: Please give me a good recipe for pemmican.— R. C. R., Ohio.

Answer: Dry strips of beef over a low fire or in an oven until all the moisture has been removed. Grind or pound the meat until it resembles meal, add 25 per-cent melted suet, and sugar—if desired—to taste. Pack in jars or wrap well in parchment paper. A mixture of these proportions should keep up to 15 days in warm weather.

TO KEEP FOOD FROM FREEZING

Question: My Nova Scotia fishing and hunting camp has no cellar. How can I prevent canned goods, left there all win-ter, from freezing?—J. P. C., N. H.

Answer: Install a trapdoor in the floor of the cabin and dig a pit below. If this isn't practical, dig the pit somewhere near by. Make it large enough to hold all your canned food, and deep enough so that the contents are below frost line.

Guard against moisture by covering the bottom of the pit with 2 ft. of dry straw, hay, or dead grass, or by installing a 1-ft.-high wooden platform on which to store the cans. Leave them in the cartons in which they come, and cover with a layer of hay.

If, next season, you plan to open the pit just once, emptying it completely, merely shovel dirt in on top of the hay. However, if you will remove the cans at intervals throughout the season, make a cover of boards. Place this atop the hay, then shovel on the dirt as before.

When the pit is filled, heap up the ground over it so surface moisture will drain away rapidly; also dig a few small ditches several yards long to lead the water off.

KEEPING BACON FRESH

Question: I am planning a long canoe trip. Can you tell me the best way to keep bacon from spoiling.—J. E. B., Ohio.

Answer: When bacon is taken on any camping trip that lasts two weeks or longer, it should be purchased in a chunk or side, and not sliced, because the solid bacon resists mold much better. If a little mold does appear it can easily be scraped or cut away. When sliced bacon begins to mold you have a tough time cleaning both sides of all the slices.

One precaution is to wrap the chunk of bacon in a cloth moistened with vinegar, then wrap in parchment paper and pack in a water-tight sack or in a metal can with a friction cover. If the inside of the sack or can becomes damp, dry it out well.

It is also a good plan to quickly dry off the bacon piece in the smoke of your camp fire every three or four days.

PROTECTING FOOD

Question: Can you tell me a method of keeping squirrels, skunks, and other small animals away from food in camp?

Food supplies can be kept safe from vermin by hanging it from a tightly stretched bare wire.

I don't mean one of those cumbersome platforms but something that is easily erected.—J. S., N. Y.

Answer: An easy way to keep food sup-plies safe from vermin is to stretch a tight bare wire between two trees. It should be about 10 ft. off the ground. Then tie bags or boxes of food to the wire, hanging them near its middle and away from any tree branch. Mice and squirrels won't be able to walk the wire and climb down to the food.

If, however, you intend to leave caches of food and supplies for long periods of time a well built platform is the best bet.

SPECIAL CAMPING PROBLEMS

MAKING KNIVES AND AXES

Question: What type of steel, available to the average person, would be best to use in making a hunting knife? I'd like to make one myself. Would a hack-saw blade be good material, or would a large butcher's knife of reliable make, ground down to size, be better?

Also, is there any difference in quality between blue and white steel? I bought a small ax recently, and was later told that it is not of good quality because the blade is of white steel.—A. B., La.

Answer: Handmade knives, as done by amateurs, are fashioned from hack-saw blades—the large power-saw type—and also from old files. Saw blades, even the common, carpenter's handsaw, will do. Or, as you suggest, it is quite practical to buy a butcher knife of good quality, and then work it down to the desired shape and size.

In grinding down a large knife, saw blade, or file, be extremely careful not to overheat the steel. If you do, the temper and cutting edge will be spoiled. Grind only a little at a time, then let the steel cool. If the metal turns blue or dark, then it's spoiled for knife purposes.

Of the several possibilities open to you, I'd prefer to grind down a large butcher knife.

As to the ax, don't pay any attention to that statement that blue steel is preferable to white. The one way to test an ax —if you have bought it of a good maker —is to see how long it holds its edge when cutting hardwood. A good ax will need whetting up every 20 to 30 minutes if used in chopping hard timber.

CARRYING WATER ON CANOE TRIPS

Question: On canoe trips I usually carry a 1-gal. vacuum jug of drinking water, but since this isn't enough I am thinking of getting a canvas water bag. Is the loss by evaporation very great and would the drip from such a bag be a problem in a canoe? Would it be better to carry another vacuum jug?—W. E. A., D. C.

Answer: I have always found canvas water bags very satisfactory. They keep the liquid moderately cool and there is no excessive loss by evaporation. There would be no drip problem in a canoe. Of course, the bags function best when hung up in the shade, exposed to a breeze. I'm not sure that their cooling properties would be sufficient if they were laid in a canoe or tied to a thwart. If you are not particular about the water's being cool, you could get a regular canvas canoe water bottle with a closed top. These too are very serviceable.

I'd suggest that you fill your present vacuum jug with ice cubes or ice chunks and carry along one of those canoe bottles. You could then mix ice from the jug with water from the bottle. This would give you plenty of drinking water and save much weight as compared with packing two jugs.

MAKING STRETCHER FOR BEAVER HIDES

Question: Please tell me the best way to go about making a simple but satisfactory stretcher for beaver hides.—J. P. L., Neb.

Answer: Most trappers stretch beaver skins on a round hoop made from a flexible limb. (The hides are supposed to be pulled as nearly round as possible.) The exact size of the hoop depends on the size of the pelt. Most trappers, however, make large hoops, then, when they catch a small beaver, use longer lacing cords to tie the hide inside the frame. Another stunt is to unlash the ends of the limb and shove them farther past each other to reduce the hoop's size.

TREATING DUCK FEATHERS FOR SLEEPING BAG

Question: I have some wild-duck feathers that I would like to use in a sleeping bag. How can I process them so that they can be used?—M. E. S., Colo.

Answer: The only treatment necessary is to dry the feathers thoroughly. You may have already done this; but if you haven't, it would be best to pack the feather loosely in open-mesh bags and to hang them in a dry, airy place. Feathers in commercial sleeping bags are often treated to make them mothproof but this is not a process generally available.

Your main trouble may come when you start to pack the feathers into your bag. An easy method is to quilt them in, the same way that cotton and wool quilts are made. Commercial bags have the feathers blown into series of long, narrow pockets or tubes. Some people have sewn tubes in their homemade bags and then blown the feathers in with a vacuum-sweeper attachment.

CHOOSING A SLEEPING BAG

Question: We are planning a hunting trip in the Montana Rockies. I want to get a good sleeping bag, one which will be warm even during zero weather. Since I have no previous experience with these articles, will you tell me what type would be best?—E. F. L., Mont.

Answer: I should advise you to get one of the better grades, preferably insulated with waterfowl down, weighing 13 or 14 lb. in a medium size. If you get one insulated with wool or kapok, you will need more filler to obtain the same warmth and your bag will weigh more.

COMPARING SLEEPING BAGS

Question: I want to buy a sleeping bag, which will seldom have to be packed from place to place, for deer hunting trips. We camp at 10,000-ft. elevations where the temperature drops to 5 degrees F. I do not want to invest too much money in a bag and would appreciate it if you would outline the advantages of the various types so that I might make an intelligent selection.—O. H. R., Colo.

Answer: Materials most often used to insulate sleeping bags are feathers or down; wool; and kapok. The main difference between them is their ratio of weight to efficiency. Feathers and down give the most protection for the least weight and are usually chosen for difficult packing conditions and extremely low temperatures.

Since packing is no great problem in your case, you can pick a wool or kapok bag and thus invest less money than if you bought one lined with feathers. A wool or kapok bag should weigh about 12 lb. for your use.

BLAZING TREES

Question: Please explain the system of marking trees with an ax to indicate the direction of camp.—M. M., Mo.

Answer: The custom among woodsmen in blazing trees is to make one blaze on

One blaze is away from camp, two blazes are toward camp.

the side of the tree that is away from camp, and two blazes on the side toward camp. This is easy to remember if you think of it this away: "a-way" (a blaze) and "to-ward" (two blazes). Make absolutely sure that any blazes you may make are pointing in the right direction.

LEATHER OR CANVAS PACK SACK?

Question: Have you any preference between leather and canvas as material for a pack sack? Do you think the frame sack has any advantage?—E. R. M., Calif.

Answer: The choice between leather and canvas depends very much on your own inclinations, and the amount of money you want to invest. So far as utility goes I'd just as 'soon have the canvas pack, since I doubt that there is much actual difference in strength and wearing qualities in relation to cost. My favorite pack has always been the waterproofed-canvas plain pack. Other campers like the pack frame and the pack harness. These two devices carry large-size canvas bags filled with the various articles you need to camp. A pack frame and harness combination is used on canoe portages where immense loads are carried for fairly short distances. For hiking, I would prefer the regular canvas pack which needs no frame or harness to be carried. However, if leather appeals to you, it's O.K. to use.

TENT PLATFORMS

Question: What size platform should be built for a 9 x 12 ft. tent? Also, how is the tent set up on the floor for best results?—W. C. C., N. Y.

Answer: If your tent is waterproofed and well pre-shrunk, then you can build a floor platform of practically the same size. I would recommend that you measure your tent carefully, then build a platform 1 in. smaller each way.

Usually a frame of 2 x 4-in. lumber is used to support the tent, placing the uprights in the same position as regular poles. Have the upper edges which bear against the canvas smoothly rounded. Then build sides about the platform, say 1 ft. high, draw tent sides down and outside this board siding, and secure bottom edge of tent to it with strips of lath nailed over the canvas.

BEST TENT MATERIAL

Question: I am going to buy a fairly large tent and am undecided as to material. Would you prefer 9.93-oz. duck over 12.41? And should I get treated or untreated material?—E. P. S., Va.

Answer: By all means specify treated duck for your tent. Plain duck will not shed water perfectly, at least not enough for camping. Order a tent that has been sealed with some good waterproofing compound.

As to your choice between the 9.93-oz. and 12.41-oz. material, that should be determined by the use to which you're going to put the tent. If you go canoeing, and run into lots of portages, the lighter cloth is preferable, but if carrying is not a problem the heavier duck is more durable and will last longer, especially if the tent gets rough usage.

CLEANING SMALL GAME

Question: What is the correct way to clean and skin small game?—A. H., Md.

Answer: I clean small game as soon as I pick it up. With rabbits I make a 5-in. slit down the belly with my knife, grasp

Small game is easily skinned by cutting the skin around the middle and then pulling the hide off in opposite directions.

head in one hand, heels in the other, and with a quick downward swing send entrails rolling out on the ground.

To complete the cleaning at home, chop off the head, legs at knees, and tail with a hatchet. After dipping the rabbit in cold water to keep hairs from flying, cut skin crosswise around middle of body, separate edges of it from flesh at the cut, then grasp skin and pull it off. Half comes over rabbit's neck, half over tail. Cut the carcass in two along spine, then cut off front and hind quarters to make six serving pieces.

To dress a squirrel, chop off feet, head, and tail. Cut skin in two across middle of back, insert fingers of both hands in this crosswise cut, and rip the skin off in two pieces. Split carcass down the spine and separate each half into quarters, leaving two ribs on the hind quarters.

KEEPING EQUIPMENT IN BAGGAGE TRAILER

Question: I have purchased a metal, trunk-type baggage trailer, in which I plan to store some of my guns, rod, and tackle, so that I can couple the trailer to my car and leave for a field trip on short notice. Have you any suggestions as to what would be the best method of securing my gear to prevent damage by jouncing and scratching?—E. C. S., Kan.

Answer: The idea of keeping your trailer packed and ready to go is good, but I wonder if you plan to leave your guns in it for any length of time. Guns are best kept in the house, and you might find room for them in your car, devoting the trailer's space to the regular camp outfit.

However, if you must keep your guns in the trailer, I'd suggest you pack them in cases that are well padded with cloth, and strap them to the floor, over to one side for additional protection against shifting. A partition might even be installed to separate guns from the other duffel, if you think this advisable.

The fishing rods should be inclosed in stiff cases, which can be strapped up against the underside of the trailer lid, where they would be well shielded. It might also be a good idea to fit a number of straps to the floor of the trailer, so other items of equipment could be tied down. Otherwise, they may be damaged.

A GOOD FIRST-AID KIT

Question: What do you consider the essentials for a first-aid kit on a camping trip which might take me some distance from medical aid?—B. N., N. Y.

Answer: Unless you visit sections where poisonous snakes are a risk you'll need only a simple kit. Take an antiseptic to cleanse slight wounds; ready-made and gauze bandages; adhesive tape; aromatic spirits of ammonia (a stimulant); laxative; toothache drops or gum; an ointment for burns or sunburn; aspirin.

In regions where poisonous snakes present a real menace you should undoubtedly have a snake-bite kit, consisting of tourniquet, suction cups, antivenin, etc. Lastly, if your water supply is of doubtful purity, take along commercial purifying tablets.

REMOVING STUMPS

Question: There are some ugly stumps about my camp that I'd like to remove. Do you know of any simple method that will help me get rid of them?—J. D. B., N. Y.

Answer: One old method is slow but sure; if you have time and patience it will do the job for you. Bore a number of holes down through the top of the stumps and fill them with kerosene. After the coal oil has soaked in, add more, and keep this up until the stumps are pretty well saturated. Then set fire to them.

This method won't work on green stumps, cuts made less than a year before. On dry wood, when you add kerosene place a piece of tar paper over the stump to prevent water from entering and slowing the penetration of the oil during the soaking-in period. If the stumps really bother you, it might pay to have a professional come in and remove them with dynamite. Another alternate is to cut the roots and have the stumps pulled out by horses or a tractor.

THWARTING BEAVERS

Question: How can we keep the beavers now working along a near-by stream from attacking the quaking aspen near our cabin? We don't want to have them trapped out.—M. E. S., Colo.

Answer: Inclose each aspen with wire netting just as orchard trees are protected against rabbits in the winter. Fashion a 3½-ft.-high cylinder out of ½-in. hardware cloth. Sink the bottom a few inches below ground and hold it there by driving stakes through the mesh and into the earth at an angle. Set the screen out a couple of inches from the tree.

PROTECTION AGAINST SNAKES

Question: I am planning a camping trip into country where I am likely to encounter rattlesnakes. People have told me that snakes will often crawl into your blankets while you're sleeping, but that they won't cross a rope looped around the camp. Is there any truth in either of these statements?—P. P., Wash.

Answer: There is no truth in the fairly common belief that a snake will not cross a rope, particularly a hair rope. This fallacy has been exploded many times by actual experience. On the other hand, it is true that snakes will occasionally crawl into a sleeper's blankets.

The best protection a camper can provide against snakes is a tightly made tent with a sewed-in floor. The door should be covered with strong net material to admit air and there should be a low canvas doorsill on the bottom to which the net curtain can be securely fastened so that no snakes can push through.

SINGLE VS. DOUBLE BLADE AX

Question: What is your opinion of the double-blade ax, compared with the single, for a belt ax?—B. C., Calif.

Answer: The single-blade ax is positively my choice for a belt model. Double-bitted axes are fine for heavy and frequent chopping, especially when one needs both a chopping edge and a splitting edge. But for camp use, and especially when a short-handle ax is selected, I prefer the single type. Frequent sharpening is required, of course, particularly for rough work, and it's wise to have a file and a two-faced carborundum stone along; a little attention will then keep your ax in fairly good condition. If you watch a professional lumberman you'll note that he touches up the edges of his tools at frequent intervals.

WATERPROOFING ROPE

Question: If you have a formula for waterproofing rope, I should very much appreciate having it.—E. S., Ill.

Answer: For many years ropes and lines on sailing ships have been waterproofed by treating them with tar. If you add 20 percent tallow to the tar, melting both materials so they combine evenly and spread over the rope easily, the rope will be more pliable.

I have waterproofed tent ropes with the same preparation used on the tent itself. Any tent manufacturer or dealer can furnish good tent waterproofing.

PLANNING A CANOE-CAMPING TRIP

Question: A friend and I are going to make a 14-day, 400-mi. canoe-camping trip. Do you think the distance is too great for the time? How can we prevent our hands from becoming sore from paddling? Do you suggest single or double paddles? Is it sufficient to hang our food supply out of reach of animals or must we hang up all our stuff? What size pack board do you suggest?—R. L., Manitoba.

Answer: A 400-mi. canoe trip in 14 days sounds all right, unless you are going to run into some long, frequent, and hard portages. Some days you may be able to travel 40 mi. on smooth water; others you may not cover 5 or 10. The canoeist usually figures on an average of 25 mi. a day under ordinary circumstances.

Start to toughen the skin on your hands a couple of months before the trip. Bathe the hands in cold salt water every night, and avoid wearing gloves as much as you can. If possible, do some kind of work that will give the skin more resistance to blisters—working around your garden or yard will help. On the trip you might try wearing leather gloves that fit snugly. A great many canoeists dislike gloves; this is only a suggestion for you to consider.

I suggest that you use single paddles in a regular canoe. The double blades are awkward in rough water. In camp it is not necessary to hang any of your food if you have room for it in the tent and don't leave the latter open for long periods of time. If there is any danger of visits from porcupines, mice, or other animals, then suspend the food bags on a wire stretched between two trees.

Pack boards run about 13 to 14 in. wide.

WAX GOOD FOR TRAILER TOPS

Question: Please suggest a treatment for the leather top of my trailer.—C. M., Ga.
Answer: Wax is good to restore life and color to leather or imitation-leather trailer tops. However, some of the trailer factories offer their own preparations.

TREATING UNPEELED LOGS

Question: I am building a cabin of unpeeled white-cedar logs. What can I use to preserve these logs and repel worms? Do you think linseed oil would be suitable?—J. D. S., N. J.
Answer: Linseed oil is excellent to preserve wood, but it will be difficult to get enough of it to soak through the bark to be of much value in your case. Creosote stain also is fine for preserving wood as

well as discouraging borers, although its objectionable odor hangs on for several weeks after each application. You might try spraying the logs with a half-and-half solution of this stain and linseed oil.

There are two things to remember in building with unpeeled logs. First, the bark encourages worms and borers, and looks messy after a time because some sections of it will loosen and drop off. Secondly, as it peels, it exposes untreated surfaces of bare wood which are at the mercy of insects and weather.

BEST LOG-CABIN TIMBER

Question: What is the best wood to use in building a log cabin?—A. W. L., Wis.
Answer: Most cabin builders consider Norway pine the best. The reason—it grows very straight and tall, so that long, shapely sticks can be cut from such trees. There is probably less taper in a Norway-pine log than in most of the others. Evergreen timber is always preferred because it grows straight, and also because the logs are lighter to lift up on walls, and easier to cut and fit. Spruce and balsam are good; so is Western cedar. Tamarack is nice but harder to work.

Hardwood trees are usually too branchy and crooked for cabins. Slight curves can, of course, be hewed out, but most of the hardwood trees are beyond even this treatment.

BUILDING A WOODS CABIN

Question: I am planning to build a cabin in the Pennsylvania mountains. It will be about 16 x 20 ft. and have a living room, kitchen, and bedroom. If natural logs are available should I use them, or should I use the Adirondack type of imitation-log siding? Which would be easiest and cheapest? Could one man build a cabin of this size alone?

I plan to insulate the cabin with rock wool and line it with imitation knotty-pine paneling. How much of the latter would I need?—L. J. H., Nebr.

Answer: The imitation-log siding would be easier to handle than regular logs and would, in addition, make a tighter job with less future upkeep expense. As far as comparative cost goes, it depends on the availability of suitable natural logs and the charges for delivery of the siding to your cabin site. Not many locations have enough suitable logs for building a cabin, and if you have to buy them and pay for hauling them in, the siding might be cheaper. If suitable logs are close by, however, they make for the cheapest kind of construction.

It really takes two men to handle logs of cabin size—12 ft. or longer. No one should attempt such a job alone, since an accident might leave him in a very dangerous position. One man can, however, handle frame-and-siding construction. With material on the ground, he should be able to erect the cabin in about 10 days. If he is a skilled carpenter, of course, he can do it more quickly.

Since you are planning to use insulation and knotty-pine paneling, it would seem to me that the siding would be the best for you. The uneven surface of logs always gives trouble when a cabin is lined. Roughly, you will need about 1,200 sq. ft. of paneling for the cabin walls and ceiling, 550 for both sub and finish flooring, and approximately 1,100 board feet of siding.

DRINKING-WATER PRECAUTIONS

Question: The rain water that falls on the roof of my summer lodge drains and flows through the gutters and leaders into a 1,000-gal. tank. The leaders are screened to prevent leaves from entering.

I have been placing several bags of charcoal in the bottom of the tank each year, and I boil the water and add a few drops of iodine to every gallon. Are these

sound purifying methods?—J. J. K., N. Y.

Answer: I'm not sure about the value of iodine. Any druggist can supply you with chloride of lime, which some cities use to purify water drawn from lakes. Also at hardware stores you can buy charcoal filters to use at the bottom of roof-drainage pipes. The charcoal you're using at the bottom of your tank might keep the water free from odors, but that's about all.

BEST PAINT FOR DECOYS

Question: My black-duck decoys need repainting. They are made of wood. What's the best type of paint to use?—N. T., N. Y.

Answer: I try to get a semigloss enamel for painting decoys, but failing that, I get full gloss in the shade I want. After it is dry I rub it dull with pumice and water. The surface must be sufficiently dull so light does not reflect from it. The black duck will have a gray-black body with a lighter-gray head, and neck with dark stripes from top of head and alongside each eye.

DECOY GROUPING

Question: How should two boats be grouped in relation to decoys? What is the safe distance for shooting between boats? What is the best method of concealing the boats?—R. W. W., N. Y.

Answer: A popular way of arranging duck decoys and boats is to place the three factors in the shape of a triangle; have the boats about 40 yd. from each other and 30 to 35 from the decoys. The exact range will have to be determined by a little experimenting. I like to face the boats in the direction from which the ducks will come, and if hunters will shoot forward only, the 40-yd. distance above can apply. But if there is any danger of a shooter swinging his gun toward the other boat they should be placed at least 100 yd. apart, or even more.

It is better to have not more than two shooters to a boat, no matter how big it is. There is liable to be confusion in handling guns, especially in moments of excitement. A boat may safely hold three or four men as far as stability is concerned but it's chancy with regard to gunning.

I suggest you disguise the boats by placing branches or brush upright around them, using plenty of foliage. Lacking such brush you can use cat-tails or dead marsh grass.

PAINTING DECOYS BLACK

Question: How can I paint my decoys black, so that they won't glisten on the water?—B. W., N. Y.

Answer: I have used two methods with success. The first way is to paint the decoys with ordinary black house paint or a semigloss mixture. Then after the paint has thoroughly dried I rub the surface with powdered pumice mixed with water. That cuts away all the shine.

I have also mixed my own black decoy paint, using a tube of lampblack ground in oil (obtainable at any paint store), to which I add a very small quantity of linseed oil and about twice as much turpentine. However, even this mixture will shine a bit sometimes, so I go over it lightly with pumice.

TANNING SMALL HIDES

Question: How can I tan small skins, such as those of squirrel and rabbit, so that the fur will remain firmly in place, with the pelt soft and flexible?—A. F., N. Y.

Answer: To tan such small hides, use the following formula: Mix 1 gal. soft water, 1 oz. commercial-strength sulphuric acid, and 1 qt. salt. Soak hide in this solution for about three days. Then remove, wring dry, soak overnight in a pail of water to which ½ cup sal soda has been added. This will neutralize any

acid remaining in the skin. Then rub and pull and stretch the hide until dry. If it dries hard, moisten it and rub and work again. Repeat this—it is a very important operation—until the skin stays soft and pliable when dry.

SILENT TREAD

Question: Indians and pioneers are reputed to have been able to walk through the woods without making the slightest noise, even though leaves, twigs, stones, etc., were scattered in their path. What do you think their secret was? Could it be done today?—R. M., N. Y.

Answer: A silent tread can be acquired only by much painstaking effort and practice. Although the ground over which Indians and pioneer woodsmen walked was strewn with twigs and leaves, these men carefully selected a clear spot for each step they took. It was as much a matter of selection as of walking, although slow lowering of the foot always aids in achieving quiet. However, I think it is safe to say that the silent walkers progressed as much by eye as by step.

SLEEPING BAG INSULATION

Question: My recently purchased sleeping bag has about 4½ lb. of insulation, 55 percent being down and the remainder reprocessed goose feathers. I am unable to get 100 percent down. Can you tell me the minimum temperature for which my sleeping bag is suitable.—B. B., Pa.

Answer: I'd estimate it would be efficient down to 40 degrees F. This is only approximate, because there are many factors involved. For instance, I assume you will use your sleeping bag inside a tent—outdoors it would not serve so well. You can add to the bag's efficiency by making an insert of wool-blanket material—loosely woven type—with one layer under you and one over. This adds considerably to the efficiency of any sleeping bag. You'll also be more comfortable in colder weather if you sleep in a heavy shirt or sweater and wear woolen socks.

WATERPROOF HUNTING PARKA

Question: I want to make a waterproof parka to wear when hunting ducks. Any advice you can give me will be appreciated. Are duck and canvas the same thing?—W. R., N. J.

Answer: I suggest you use 8-oz. canvas, as heavier material would be hard to sew. It could even be lighter since the primary purpose of a parka is only to turn rain and wind. If you buy waterproof canvas you will only need to treat the seams to make the garment moisture tight. A parka made of plain cloth would need to be treated all over. For this purpose any tent waterproofing such as is sold by dealers in camping equipment would be preferable to a home-mixed formula.

I have never seen a good pattern for a parka. I have often thought that if I were to make a parka I'd use an ordinary shirt pattern. It would have to be large enough to slip on over your other clothing and long enough to come midway between hips and knees.

Duck and canvas are practically the same material, duck being commonly used to designate heavy cotton fabrics used on seagoing equipment.

WOOL FOR SLEEPING BAG

Question: How many 2-lb wool bats will I need to make a sleeping bag which will withstand freezing temperatures? I plan to use it in a tent.—M. K., Mo.

Answer: Three. Be sure to quilt the wool at regular intervals so it won't bunch when in use. It also will help if you use a wool-cloth lining for the bed.

VARNISHING SNOWSHOES

Question: The rawhide stringing in my snowshoes is turning white. I know that snowshoes should be varnished, but wouldn't it be a good idea for me to treat the webbing with neat's-foot oil or a good leather dressing?—C. F. B., Minn.

Answer: Any application of oil or a dressing containing oil probably will stretch the webbing of the snowshoes and let the mesh sag. It is for this reason that varnish is recommended—it waterproofs without stretching the webbing. Use the best grade of spar varnish, once a season if the shoes are used a great deal, to prevent the thongs turning white or becoming water hardened.

B'AR GREASE

Question: A friend of mine, who collected a large black bear on a hunting trip, has given me a jar of bear oil. Is this good for greasing hunting boots, etc. Should any other ingredient be added? —C. H. T., Mich.

Answer: My advice is to forget the bear's grease and buy some standard brand of shoe and boot dressing. I like neat's-foot oil or castor oil or the commercial products sold by many shoe stores. I prefer a rather thin oil to the heavy, greasy salves, because the oil thoroughly penetrates the leather, makes it soft and supple, and prevents it from cracking and splitting.

The bear grease would be better than nothing in an emergency, but not a bit superior to lard or suet. Woodsmen used it when they were unable to obtain anything else.

ALL ABOUT BOATS

by J. A .Emmett

HOW TO CHOOSE YOUR BOAT

RIVER CAMPING TRIP

Question: We're considering a trip down the Susquehanna River from Sayre, Pa., to the Conowingo Dam by rowboat and outboard, camping on shore at night. The party will consist of my wife and me and our 9-year-old son, with perhaps another adult. Would a rowboat of 14 to 16 feet with a moderately rounded bottom and a one-lung kicker of about the $35 class do the job?—G. B. deM., Pa.

Answer: The boat you have in mind is most suitable for such a trip, but for such a load I'd advise a 2½-horsepower motor. Although you'll be going downstream you may want to buck the current at times, and very small motors are apt to be disappointing with heavily loaded boats. In any case, I'd confine the party to the family; four people and duffel will not leave much room in this size craft. Besides regular camping equipment, carry a supply of mixed fuel, shear pins, and ordinary tools, plus drinking water and food in cans or other compact form, since supplies may be hard to get.

NEW JERSEY OFFSHORE BOAT

Question: I want an inexpensive boat for fishing along the New Jersey shore—say, up to about 10 miles out. I've seen plans for a 17½-ft. motor dory, and wonder if this would be suitable. If so, how much would a builder be likely to charge me for it? Would a 5-horsepower motor be large enough to drive it 9 to 10 miles an hour? As an alternative, how about a 20-ft. sea skiff?—M. S., N. J.

Answer: Conditions vary so greatly at the different inlets along the New Jersey coast that the one you use will partly determine the type of boat. If conditions aren't too severe, the motor dory will do nicely; if they are, the 20-ft. sea skiff with good inboard power should be considered. Materials for the dory would probably cost you about $50, and the builder would charge you another $50 or so to build it—perhaps more.

As for an engine for it a 5-horsepower inboard will cost about $175 with fittings, plus about $70 more for a reverse gear if wanted. The 5 will give you the speed mentioned under favorable conditions, but for bucking head seas a 10-horsepower two-cylinder model would be better, costing you something more than $300 complete. As for the sea skiff, it would cost about twice as much as the dory, and should have about 25 horsepower. If you couldn't swing the cost of this engine, you might use a car conversion or a used boat engine to start with.

I suggest that you visit builders around the inlet you plan to use, getting their advice and prices on the best boat for your purpose.

BOAT FOR ONE-MAN CRUISING

Question: I would like to build a boat and use it to travel along the East Coast from Maine to Florida, with side trips to the West Indies. It would have to be small enough so that I could handle it alone.—E. W., Pa.

Answer: I would advise a small chunky cruiser about 32 ft. long, with a dependable marine-type engine, or, better still —especially if economy of operation is required—a chunky, rather shoal-draft auxiliary sailboat about the same size. The latter type invariably has a small marine engine aboard to give a speed of about 6 miles an hour. The engine comes in handy in canals and narrow waters or when there is no wind, while the sails are available for open-water work. This is a good craft to choose for getting used to handling sails, too, as the knowledge can be acquired gradually, with the engine to fall back on in a pinch.

BOAT FOR WEST COAST CRUISE

Question: What type of boat is best for a West Coast cruise?—E. C. O., Wis.

Answer: The most interesting part of the coast is from Seattle north. For that region you need a husky boat between 35 and 40 ft. in length, powered by a small diesel or twin gasoline motors.

NAVIGATING THE INLAND WATERWAY

Question: Three of us want to make a leisurely sailing cruise from Forked River, N. J., to Florida. What type sailing vessel would you recommend? Should it have an auxiliary engine? What charts

will we need? Roughly, what will we have to pay for a suitable used boat and how can we check on its worth? We would appreciate your opinion of the whole idea?—T. M., N. J.

Answer: Your trip through the Inland Waterway is practical, but you will do little sailing and dependable auxiliary power is a must. You could use sails, except possibly through the Chesapeake and Delaware Canal, to Norfolk, but from there on you'd use your engine 75 percent of the time, so I'd recommend that you buy a powerboat. Prices of such a vessel should be cheaper too; you'd probably have to spend $4,500 for a used sailboat with auxiliary power and living accommodations for three, whereas a power cruiser in the same condition and with similar accommodations would cost about $2,500. Running costs would be roughly equal for either, and although a person without sailing experience might run into trouble on the trip in a sailing craft, anyone with water sense or a love of boats probably will make out O.K. with power.

Unless you are familiar with boats you may take an awful beating in buying a used one. The best thing to do is place yourself in the hands of a reputable yacht broker. Lay your cards on the table and let him take care of you.

You can buy all the charts you need by ordering through the catalogue of the U. S. Coast and Geodetic Survey at Washington, D. C. The journey is about 1,000 miles and an average of 30 miles a day is good.

I'm sure this trip will give you something to remember always—and, I hope, pleasantly.

FISHING-CRUISING CRAFT

Question: What size seagoing craft would you recommend for fishing and cruising both coasts as far as Alaska and Argentina? I want it to be fast and maneuverable for fishing, sturdy and compact for cruising. I'd prefer a two-man, cabin affair, about 38 ft., for low upkeep.

Do you think batteries could power such a ship?—E. R., N. Y.

Answer: A sailboat with a small auxiliary engine, for use in calms and in negotiating narrow passages, should fill the bill. A 30-footer, with a cabin, ought to be even better than the 38-ft. model you mentioned. My next choice would be a power cruiser of the same size.

Electric propulsion would not work well in so small a boat. The weight of the batteries and the space required for their charging plant would be too great.

CANVAS OR WOOD BOAT?

Question: I plan to buy a lightweight 12-ft. rowboat for duck hunting and fishing on small lakes, but am undecided between a $\frac{7}{16}$-in.-planked smooth-built boat and one with canvas covering over $\frac{3}{16}$-in. planking. There's only 15 or 20 lb. difference in the weights of these craft. Which would you advise?—P. B., Iowa.

Answer: The important point here is the use to which you will put your boat. If it's to be out of the water a great deal of the time, or carried from one place to another by trailer, the canvas-covered craft will be better. A wood boat won't stay tight under such conditions.

On the other hand, if you're going to keep the boat in the water constantly throughout the season, the wooden one will do just as well as the canvas type and you won't run the risk of having the paint crack after a few years or snagging the covering.

PRAM FOR ONE MAN

Question: I do much of my fishing and duck hunting on a small river near my home, and in adjacent ponds and lakes. The river banks are thickly overgrown

with brush, the other waters are off the beaten track and in most cases not supplied with boats. To complicate matters, my car is a coupé and I can't carry large craft on its top.

I want to get a small, easily carried boat, preferably about 3 ft. wide and 6 ft. long. Would this be practical; would it carry one man safely? If so, where can I obtain plans?—W. C. S., N. Y.

A square nosed pram at least 7½ ft. long is ideal for one-man fishing and hunting on small rivers and creeks.

Answer: You'll need a square-nosed or pram-type hull, but it should be at least 7½ ft. long. If you were willing to make one 9 ft. long it would accommodate two persons and could still be carried atop your coupé for short distances if you used a reliable carrier. Several are now, or soon will be, on the market.

You might also consider a sectional rowboat. These craft, which are made in three sections, can be stowed readily in the back of a car and assembled when you reach your destination.

FOR CANOEING ON THE SUSQUEHANNA

Question: I want to get a canoe for use on a stretch of the Susquehanna where there are no rapids and only a few sections of rough water. Four of us will take week-end camping trips in it and occasionally two of us will go on longer jaunts up to 100 miles. What do you think of an 18-ft. guide model for this use? Do you think it should have a keel or sponsons?—R. G., N. Y.

Answer: A guide canoe should be fine for the use you have in mind, but get it in the 18-ft. length, not in the customary 20-ft. size, in view of the fact that only two people will go on some of your trips. Have a keel installed and, if possible, have half ribs built in; they avoid the necessity of using floor boards so long as you keep the spray sponged out, and they add considerable strength.

Don't buy a sponson model, however. Sponsons take much of the life out of a canoe and tend to make paddling work instead of pleasure. The added safety factor isn't of tremendous importance, since any overturned canoe will afford at least a handhold for its occupants. And with the type you have in mind there shouldn't be much danger of capsizing.

STAR-BOAT RACING

Question: Although I've had no experience, I'd like to get into the Star-boat racing class this summer, racing and cruising on Lake Michigan. Should I buy a used boat, and how can I gauge its condition?—T. L. K., Tex.

Answer: Stars are good boats to buy if you want keen racing competition—and it will be keen—but their deep keels make cruising difficult since you can't get in close to shore. Therefore you'll have to plan on landing at docks unless you tow along a small tender.

If you buy a used boat, investigate its past racing record. That has a lot to do with its value. Have the boat pulled from the water and examine vital points below the waterline.

The price will also depend in large part upon the condition and style of the rig and sails, and the reputation of the latter's manufacturer. An indication of the boat's worth may be gained from an inspection of rigging and sails. A com-

paratively new or a reconditioned boat may have stainless-steel rigging wire, linen running rigging, and sails by a well-known manufacturer.

BOAT FOR IN-AND-OUT USE

Question: I want to buy a boat to be used for fishing the streams, rivers, and lakes

A canvas covered canoe will stand much hard wear and can be easily carried atop a car.

(up to 5,000 acres) of the Midwest. It should hold three people, be powered by a 4-horsepower outboard motor, transported by trailer, and kept out of the water except when in actual use. Weight and price are relatively unimportant; the biggest consideration is safety. What type craft is best?—J. N. B., Ohio.

Answer: A 16-ft. canvas-covered boat is best, for it won't leak when continually alternated between service in the water and storage on land. The canvas type in this size is well suited to the power unit you have in mind and should drive at from 8 to 10 miles an hour—plenty of speed for sensible use. Given good care, such a boat will provide years of service.

MISSISSIPPI RIVER

Question: Four of us—my friend and his wife, and my wife and I—want to make a fall boat trip down the Mississippi from St. Louis, Mo., to the Gulf of Mexico, with fishing and hunting thrown in. I can spend about $400 for the boat and want to get one with a small cabin and a V-8 motor. Is such a trip practical, and what hints can you give me in planning it?—K. C. O'D., Ark.

Answer: This is a very popular trip which has been made by many boating enthusiasts in the past. Towns are fairly close together, so fuel is no great problem. However, I'd keep several 5-gal. cans filled as a reserve.

Buy your food at chain stores in the larger places so that you won't be dependent upon small shops. Also be sure to familiarize yourself with fishing and hunting regulations along the way, for they vary from state to state. Carry suitable gear so that if no camp sites are available you'll be able to sleep in the boat, as well as cook in it when under way.

You can obtain charts of the Mississippi by writing to the Mississippi River Commission offices at St. Louis, Mo., and at Vicksburg, Miss. These offices cover different sections of the river. You will also find pertinent books on this subject in any large-city libraries near the river.

The conventional canoe is by far the best to use if portages are to be made.

BEST CANOE FOR PORTAGE

Question: I am planning a 10-day canoe trip and want to know whether a sponson-type craft would be best. I will have to make several carries but, despite its extra weight, I like the sponson because I think its stability should prevent any loss of equipment through tipping. What do you think?—J. R., N. Y.

Answer: If you already have the sponson, by all means use it on your trip. However, if you have not made your purchase I should advise a conventional model—particularly if you plan future trips which also may involve portages.

Canoes without the sponson air chambers are used constantly. So long as they are loaded and handled properly they do not tip; therefore I do not think you need worry about losing your equipment. I am sure you will find the lighter weight and bulk of the regular model—both when paddling and carrying—will more than make up for its slightly less stability.

BOAT FOR TRIP TO ALASKA

Question: A friend and I are planning a trip to Alaska via the Inland Passage. Would it be very difficult for two inexperienced men to make such a trip in a small open boat? I understand it has been accomplished in boats of 18 ft. or less, with outboard motors. Of course we would travel only by day, pulling into shore each night.

What size and type of boat and motor would you suggest and what would the cost be? Also, will we require any special permit or license?—E. K., Wash.

Answer: Such a trip should be entirely practical if a motor of good size is used—you will need plenty of power to buck the currents in many places. Daily runs must be planned according to the tide, since many of the passages can be made only in the comparatively short slack periods between tides. That is something you will have to study out, of course, as you go along.

Gasoline may be a problem, as sources of supply in some sections are few and far between. Hence your boat should be large enough to carry spare cans of fuel, your camping gear, and still have a good measure of buoyancy for safety. I would suggest an 18 or 20-ft. boat with an outboard of about 15 horsepower. Perhaps $500 would cover the cost in normal times.

You also should have a good spray hood or similar cover—one that could be fastened down outside the rail over the forward half of the boat as a shelter for duffel? A boat with a short forward deck and narrow side decks would be all to the good.

As to a permit, I think you would only require clearance at a customs office at the border. And there might be some examination to determine whether your boat and outfit are suitable for the trip. All in all your journey should prove most interesting.

TRY A LAPSTREAK SKIFF

Question: With two adults and two children in my family, I am faced with the problem of selecting the right boat to go with my 5-horsepower outboard motor. We want to use the boat for pleasure riding and a little fishing on both fresh and salt water. Do you think a car-top model would be the answer?—J. V., N. J.

Answer: A car-top boat, at least in the conventional size and model, will not be best for the load you have in mind, especially if the salt water you speak of gets rough. You have a practical motor, neither too large nor too small, and you should be able to find a good boat to go with it.

Why not try a craft that can be carried on a light, underslung, self-loading trailer? A 16-ft. lapstreak skiff would have the necessary capacity and plenty of safety, although possibly a little less speed than you've figured on.

DUCK BOAT FOR ROUGH USE

Question: I want a duck boat suitable for hunting on Minnesota marshes and small streams. Would plywood or canvas over wood frames be the more durable? Can I handle a two-man model alone?— R. S. M., Minn.

Answer: A duck boat of plywood will stand up under bottom rubbing better than a framework and canvas boat, although the latter will be satisfactory if you order a double or heavy-service bottom. The two-man size in either type would work out better for hunting, even if you are using the boat alone a good deal of the time. Another good proposition for such waters would be a short trapper's type canoe, about 12 ft. long, rather full-bodied, and low-ended. This is easy to handle alone, yet will take two men plus light gear. It's a slightly more expensive type than the duck boat, but is growing more popular every year.

FLATBOTTOM VS. V-BOTTOM

Question: I have a flat-bottom plywood boat that is well-braced and of rather heavy construction. It is 12 ft. long, has a 47 in. beam, and 17 in. sides.

Is this boat seaworthy; is the V-bottom better than the flat?—G. R. M., Ind.

Answer: The dimensions given indicate a skiff-type boat of good model, although much depends on the rake or run-up of the bottom aft, the flare of the sides, and the way the latter are carried in at the stern, etc.

In general flat-bottom boats of this type have good initial stability and are good sea boats up to a certain point. Usually, however, the V or semi-V-bottom models row easier than the flat and certainly behave better under power, especially in rough water. The flat-bottom boat rows well except when bucking waves, in which case the bottom offers more resistance to the water than does one of V design. The speed limit of the usual skiff is about eight miles an hour, whereas a V-bottom boat can be driven as fast as 40 miles an hour with sufficient power.

FACTS ABOUT POWER UNITS AND ACCESSORIES

MOTOR FOR SECTIONAL BOAT

Question: Having built a sectional boat I'd like to know what size outboard motor the boat could take, which would be heavy enough to give fair speed and service.—J. H. G., Ky.

Answer: A 3-horsepower outboard should be very satisfactory as power for the boat you mention. It should give you speeds of up to 7½ miles an hour, depending on the number of persons in the boat. A 5-horsepower size, while usable, would give only an extra half-mile or mile of speed, which hardly would be worth the difference in price, running expense, weight, and size.

CLEANING GAS TANK

Question: How can I remove rust from inside the gasoline tank of my outboard motor?—C. M., Wis.

A small chain lowered into the gas tank of an outboard motor will loosen rust after the links have been swirled around vigorously inside the tank.

Answer: Tie a small chain or steel dog leash to one end of a short stick. Holding stick by the other end, drop chain in tank until it forms a loose pile. Insert end of stick to which chain is attached and use it to swirl the links around vigorously. Remove chain from tank. Rinse out tank with clear gasoline or kerosene. Repeat until rinsing liquid runs off clean.

There are commercial preparations for removing sludge left by some gasolines and these may also take off rust. In addition, the usual mixing of oil with the gasoline discourages rust from forming.

OUTBOARD MOUNT FOR DUCK BOAT

Question: I have built a double-ended 13½-ft. duck boat and would like to use an outboard on it. Would a 10-lb. motor be all right if mounted about 3 ft. forward of the stern?—H. D., Ill.

Answer: I see no reason why a 10-lb. outboard can't be mounted on your duck boat, using a bracket of the type sold for canoes. Having the motor 3 ft. forward of the stern should be an advantage, since it will keep the boat from squatting too much under power—one trouble of sharp-sterned boats—and will make the craft balance better in any case. On some kayaks a small motor is even mounted on the side, right alongside the cockpit, and its light weight does not tilt the boat appreciably.

ENGINE FOR TWENTY-FOOTER

Question: What should the horsepower of an engine be to drive a 20 to 22-ft. boat, about 5 ft. wide, from 8 to 17 miles an hour?—J. E. A., Calif.

Answer: So much depends on the lines of the boat that it's difficult to figure speeds from length and beam dimensions alone. I would say that 5 horsepower would give you 6 miles an hour; 10 horsepower, 8; 25 horsepower, 14. It would probably take 35 horsepower to drive your boat 17 miles an hour. The majority of hulls not intended for high speeds drive easily up to perhaps 8 miles an hour, harder from there on.

OUTBOARD FOR RENTED BOATS

Question: I am buying an outboard motor to be carried in my car and used on boats which I will rent on the spot at fishing resorts, for trolling. There will generally be two or three people in the boat. What horsepower would be best, and is a twin or single-cylinder model preferable?—R. F. P., Ill.

Answer: As the boats for hire at the usual resort are generally on the heavy side and hard to drive, I would advise your buying a 3 to 5 horsepower motor—preferably the latter. Weight will run between 30 and 50 lb., well within your ability to handle. I would prefer a twin for its smoother running and probable easier starting, twins being the usual type in this size motor anyway. As for trolling, although the new motors perform well at low speeds, you can always get an inexpensive little trolling attachment for yours if you want to go still slower.

CHANGING PROPELLER BLADE

Question: Some outboard owners replace the conventional two-blade propeller with a three-blade one of somewhat different pitch. What are the conditions under which one might change the propeller of his motor?—G. H. W., Mich.

Three-bladed propellers are often substituted for the two-blade type when a boat has to be driven against high seas.

Answer: Larger wheels and even reduction-gear drives sometimes are used on heavier boats or on craft which buck waves or a head sea. While the motor naturally turns such a propeller more slowly, it makes for more power than a smaller wheel revolving faster. The three-blade propeller offers a better hold

on the water and gives smoother running at low speeds. Normally you can obtain such propellers for several of the standard motors.

An especially easy-to-drive boat may well use a slightly smaller propeller or one of different blade pitch to increase speed by a knot or so. Racing motors are fitted with such props.

If you use your motor under average conditions the original propeller is probably the most efficient for it. If you do change, first write the service department of the manufacturer of your motor to get advice. Generally, though, the cost of the change is out of all proportion to its value—an extra-long shaft and heavy-duty propeller cost from $7.50 to $20 and a reduction gear about $30.

AUXILIARY FOR SMALL SAILBOAT

Question: I have a sailboat that's 13½ ft. long, 54 in. wide, and 14 in. deep. I live most of the year in Barnegat City, N. J., and use the boat in the bay. Would you be kind enough to advise me what size motor would be suitable for my boat and if the proper-size one would be light enough to carry?—J. H. H., N. J.

Answer: A motor of about 3½ horsepower would be ideal for the auxiliary use you have in mind. It shouldn't weigh much more than 35 lb., and certainly is as powerful as your needs require. If, however, you plan to run in and out of the inlets a good deal, a little more power might be advisable in order to make fair time against adverse tides. Unless this is the case, 3½ horsepower should prove adequate for your purpose. It doesn't seem to me that the extra weight would prove worth the slight advantage.

MIXING OIL WITH GAS

Question: The directions that came with my 6-horsepower outboard motor call for 1 pt. of oil to 1 gal. of gasoline. I think this sounds like too much oil. Shouldn't I cut down on the oil during cold weather to promote starting? I also wonder if an outboard can freeze during the winter when it is attached to the boat but not running?

One more thing: Will regular gasoline hurt my motor?—P. H., Ill.

Answer: A mixture with less oil than the maker specifies might give faster starting in cold weather, but it might be dangerous to run on. For cutting down on the oil may cause wear that you won't even notice till too late. It would be well, however, to shake the motor a bit before starting up, to remix the fuel in the tank. Also, you can squirt a primer of clear gas in the spark-plug holes to help the starting; but doing this repeatedly will wash oil off parts and make the motor hard to turn.

Some motors, supposedly, will drain all water out so you can leave them attached in freezing weather, but I would hesitate to chance it.

Regular gas will not actually harm a motor, but it makes operation more difficult as the residue it leaves gradually gums up the parts.

TROUBLE WITH PROPELLER

Question: Please tell me where I can have my outboard motor fixed. The groove in the propeller where the shear pin fits has enlarged.—P. F. C., Ga.

Answer: I believe you'll have to take the propeller to a machine shop to have it built up by brazing and a new hole the size of the original one bored to take the shear pin. Any good machine shop should be able to do this.

WHAT SIZE OUTBOARD?

Question: Would a 2½-horsepower twin-cylinder outboard motor stand up well if used on a 14-ft. boat? Could it power a 16 or 18-ft. craft.—D. A., S. D.

Answer: The 2½-horsepower motor should give a speed of about 7 miles an hour on a 14-ft. skiff, which is about all that type hull can accommodate. However, it would not be large enough to handle a 16 or 18-footer with any degree of satisfaction.

In any event, you'd do better to get a 3½-horsepower motor. Then you could develop 2½ horsepower with the engine running at three-quarter throttle. This would help the motor last much longer than if run at top capacity and would require less gasoline. The larger model also would have the reserve power needed to handle heavy loads or buck strong currents.

OUTBOARD FOR A 12-FT. ROWBOAT

Question: What horsepower outboard should I get for my 12-ft. flat-bottom rowboat?—H. B., N. Y.

Answer: An outboard of from 2 to 3½ horsepower should drive your rowboat satisfactorily, though you can't expect to get much more than 6 miles an hour with that type of hull. If the stern is very narrow, choose the lower horsepower, to avoid excessive "squatting."

OUTBOARD FOR HOUSEBOAT?

Question: Can an outboard motor satisfactorily propel a houseboat without damaging itself?—J. M. J., Okla.

Answer: In calm water an outboard of 5 or more horsepower, depending on the size of the vessel, should move a houseboat from one anchorage to another or over any other short distance. Against a wind or fairly strong current such an engine probably will be of little use even for this limited work.

You may attach the motor to a skiff and tow the houseboat; you can lash the skiff to the side of the boat and propel it from that position; or you can fasten the motor directly to the stern.

OUTBOARD FOR CANOE

Question: We have recently acquired an 18-ft. sponson-type canoe with square stern. We renewed the finish on it, and plan to use an outboard. But we have no opportunity to try out various sizes of motors, and do not know what horsepower would be most desirable. What would you suggest—and what is the maximum speed which may be expected? We use the canoe on the Mississippi River.

Mention has been made about using oars on a large canoe. How are oarlocks on this type of craft?—N. L. R., Mo.

Answer: I assume your 18-footer is a paddling-type craft, with a narrow, tucked-in stern which looks as though a couple of feet had been cut off a longer canoe. This type is supposed to take anything from a 1 to 5 horsepower motor with speed of 5 to 10 miles an hour. An easy driving speed is about 7 knots—obtainable with a 3½ horsepower motor.

There are also square-stern sponson-type boats of canoelike construction. These have an underbody better suited for driving under power. They will take a motor up to 9 horsepower with a speed of about 17 miles an hour.

As to rowlocks, these depend on the construction of the gunwale. Usually the plan is to fasten a hardwood block about 2½ x 6 in. atop the flat section of the gunwale, with its center well out from the inner gunwale strip or trim. Then a swivel-type rowlock is attached instead of the through pin found on the ordinary type, this has a base plate which is secured to the block. The rowing seat should be located about amidships, with the rowlocks about 1 ft. from its after edge.

A 12-FT. INBOARD OUTFIT

Question: I have a 12-ft. boat with a 50-in. beam, and I should like to install an air-cooled inboard engine of 1½ to 4 horsepower in it, instead of using a 5-horsepower outboard. With a 10-in. No. 6 propeller on a shaft, would that give me an approximate average of 10 to 12 miles an hour?—C. A. P., Calif.

Answer: I think you will be well satisfied if you use a small air-cooled engine in your hull, but the speed may not be so high as you expect. About 7 to 9 miles an hour would be about average.

Ordinarily, it would require a 5-horsepower engine to turn a 10-inch propeller, unless you used a reduction gear, in which case the wheel speed would be cut down in proportion. In any event, take that up with the maker of the engine.

Don't get too large an inboard. About 3 horsepower would seem about right. This would drive an 8-in. wheel with a 6-in. pitch. You will find this type very reliable, economical, and long-lived.

CONCERNING ELECTRIC OUTBOARDS

Question: Is it practical to use an electric outboard motor to replace a ½-horsepower gasoline outboard on a light fishing boat? I understand that electric outboards are not powerful enough to use for any purpose other than trolling. Is this true?—J. R. L., Jr., Ala.

Answer: I see no reason why you couldn't use an electric outboard motor to replace a ½-horsepower gasoline engine on a light fishing boat. Of course the power it will develop depends to a great extent on the condition of the batteries. Your mention of trolling suggests a speed of about 4 miles an hour; you should be able to get this and perhaps up to 6 miles an hour. The ½-horsepower motor wouldn't do much better.

In general, it has been my experience that the electric outboard serves well on a pond or lake where the use of gasoline engines is prohibited. Except for this, and for operation by children, I believe the regular gasoline type is the best.

BOAT CARE, REPAIR AND CONVERSION

RE-COVERING KAYAK

Question: My kayak is badly in need of re-covering. Can you give me any suggestions as to the material needed, and how to apply it?—R. E. W., Ohio.

Answer: If your kayak is a manfactured model I'd try to buy a new covering from the maker. These come all ready to be put on, requiring only final treating and finishing.

Otherwise, if your kayak is the usual framework type (not a planked model), get a piece of No. 10 (not 10 oz.) canvas, wide enough to come up as far as the gunwales all around.

If a kayak is a manufactured model, a new covering may be bought from the maker; otherwise it can be covered with No. 10 canvas.

As you remove the old covering, note how it was attached, so you can put the new one on the same way. If the cover is not fastened to the framework or keel in any way, you will have to stretch your canvas from gunwale to gunwale and toward the bow, with V-shape sections cut out so one edge can be lapped over and secured tightly with liquid marine glue. Then repeat the process with the other end.

If the original covering is secured by a keel strip down the bottom of the kayak, you will have to remove that strip, along with the gunwale strips; then replace them when the new covering is on. When the canvas is all attached, wet it in order to shrink the material and stretch out

any small puckers. Lastly, treat the covering with some coating which will remain soft (not with ordinary paint, which hardens and checks).

ALTERING A SLOOP

Question: I have a Cape Cod sloop, 15 ft. 9 in. long, with a 4-ft. 8-in. beam. She's a square-stern dory type, with practically a round bottom; a good sea boat. I want to change her over for offshore striper trolling, and plan to install about a 6-horsepower, air-cooled motor and remove the centerboard. How does this sound to you?—W. V. C., R. I.

Answer: I think your sloop could be converted to take inboard power satisfactorily, but I wonder if it would be wise. You should be able to save time and money by selling your sailboat in the present high market and purchasing a utility-type boat, which would have the advantage of being brand-new.

If you make the change, however, the only hard parts will be to lead the propeller shaft through the bottom at an efficient angle, and to fit the strut bearing outside and the adjustable stuffing box inside. It is seldom possible to lead the shaft through the center of the keel and skeg in an old boat, as fastenings interfere. It should be simple to remove the centerboard case, close the opening, and build simple beds for the engine.

I would prefer installing a motor of about 2½ horsepower, which should be powerful enough for bucking waves or head seas.

TO REPAIR GOUGE IN BOTTOM

Question: I have a planked boat and I want to fill in a spot below the water line where the wood rubbed against a rock. The white-lead putty with which it had been patched is beginning to wash out.

Any instructions you can give me will be appreciated.—R. B. D., N. Y.

Answer: Trowel cement would be handier to use than putty because the former sets more rapidly. First of all, be sure to clean the spot thoroughly and prime it with thin paint. Then whatever you use, do not crowd it all in at once. Apply a layer at a time and allow time enough for each layer to set.

When the gouge is a deep one and the thickness of the planking will permit, it is a good idea to drive in a number of small tacks just far enough so that their heads will remain exposed but will still be below the outer surface of the hull. The tack heads will help to hold the filling in place.

RENOVATING SAILBOAT HULL

Question: Do you think I should use tar below the water line on the outside of an old 42-ft. sailboat I recently purchased? This is often done on European fishing boats, both as a preservative and as an aid in sealing the seams. Can I use coal tar in place of pine-pitch, or would it be injurious to the wood?—R. C., N. Y.

Answer: Don't use any tar on the bottom of your boat! Its use in Europe is confined to fishing boats that are hauled out of the water between trips, for lack of sheltered anchorage. This makes it possible to keep the bottoms clean. Tar is good for wood but it is no protection against worms. Even in fresh water, growths will build up on it.

Some old sailboats are remarkably well built. If yours is a good model, I think you should do a complete job on her hull, either hiring someone or doing it yourself with help. Have her hauled out at a shipyard so you can examine the hull to decide what treatment is best.

I'd first burn the old paint completely off with a blowtorch, then search for rotten planking on both topsides and bottom. Dig out any serious rot and replank faulty areas; otherwise calking won't keep the hull tight for long. And I'd suggest having the boat completely recalked. Fill the underwater seams with red-lead putty after painting them with red-lead paint. Use some good marine seam composition in the topside seams.

Finally, sand well, then paint the topsides with a good grade of marine hull paint and the bottom with good copper bottom paint. Don't neglect painting the bottom, regardless of whether you plan to use the boat in salt or fresh water. It will help discourage growths attaching themselves to the hull in fresh water, and will be an asset if you ever desire to sell the boat for salt-water use.

I'll venture to say that this job will give you at least one or two knots' more speed than a tarred bottom would, especially after the boat has been in the water a couple of months.

TO MAKE PIPE FIT WATER-TIGHT

Question: Here are two questions concerning a metal inboard boat I have just purchased: 1. How best can I make the stern water-tight at the spot where the exhaust pipe fits through? 2. Is it all right to use graphited metal-covered packing (the type used in water pumps) for the stuffing box?—R. C., Ind.

Answer: To have a water-tight fit for the exhaust pipe, thread the pipe back far enough to permit the use of lock nuts inside and out, and also use disks of sheet packing on both sides. If the nuts should fit loosely, the thread can be burred with a cold-chisel to prevent the nuts from working loose.

If the hole is a very loose fit for the pipe, you can use two exhaust flanges—bronze disks 4 to 5 in. diameter which come in inside diameters to fit tight around the pipe. These flanges have screw holes for use in wood transoms, but they can be drilled out to take stove bolts entering from the outside and going through holes drilled in the steel stern, then through the inside flange. Use washers and nuts inside. The sheet packing should be used also, both inside and out.

Answering your second question, graphited metal-covered packing may be used in the stuffing box but will not stand up as well as the more expensive flax packing which comes square, rather than round. Whichever you select, be sure to get the right size. Both types come in diameters of from ⅛ in. up.

SPLINTERED PLANKING

Question: My 14-ft. lapstreak boat is bruised in two places—the result of a bang against rocks. The plank is not split clean through. How shall I treat the bruises and the slightly splintered bottom (caused by dragging) so I can paint the boat?—W. C. P., Me.

Planks which are bruised and splintered should be especially treated before the boat is repainted.

Answer: Sand off the protruding slivers with coarse sandpaper, but don't attempt to level the surface. If the worn spots are below the water line, prime them with thin red-lead paint, then level the places off using red-lead putty. When the putty is really hard, sand it smooth, then paint it along with the rest of the boat.

If the spots are above the water line, prime with thinned ordinary paint, level off with a mixture of common putty and

white-lead paste, sand when dry, then paint.

If you wish, you can screw ¾-in. oak half-round strips to the ridges of the lap-streak planking at the turn of the bilge and wherever serious chafing occurs.

Use marine hull and deck paint, rather than regular house paint or even outside enamel, for finishing the boat. Sand the boat before painting, but don't use an aluminum priming coat as it may seal moisture into the wood and cause rot. Apply the paint recommended in several thin coats rather than fewer thick ones.

REPAIRING PIROGUE BOTTOM

Question: My 11½-ft. pirogue has a new bottom of ½-in. cypress that leaks like a sieve. I've tried calking, marine glue, and even filling the boat with water to swell the wood at the seams, but nothing helps. What can I do?—E. J. D., La.

Answer: That thin bottom planking probably is to blame. Ordinarily planking of less than ⅝-in. will not hold calking. Planking as thin as yours should require battens or lapped seams such as are used in lapstreak construction, unless your boat has some patented form of seam joining. No filler or compound will keep the boat tight for any length of time.

Why not install a new bottom of ⅝ or ¾-in. cypress? Use planks not wider than 8 in. and they'll swell tight. If you prefer, use a panel of ⅜-in. waterproof plywood. Whichever you use, lay it on top of strips of paint-soaked flannelette which have been placed over the edge of the chines.

You also could cover the present bottom with canvas laid in heavy paint or marine canvas cement. Extend the fabric 1 in. up the sides to cover the seam there. Tack it, trim off, and conceal raw edge by applying hard canoe glue and ironing it out well with a hot iron.

Still another way: fasten over the present bottom a layer of paint-soaked muslin. Over this install a new bottom of ⅜-in. cypress, fastened with screws as in double-plank construction. The cypress can be laid either crosswise or fore and aft; the muslin will provide necessary tightness.

PAINTING OUTBOARD BOAT

Question: Will you please send me information on painting and conditioning an outboard boat. What kind of paint will hold up well and what would you advise for the inside of the boat? I should like the inside to have the appearance of natural wood. I have been told that after sanding I should apply aluminum paint as a first coat. Do you think this a good practice?—G. F. H., Pa.

Answer: To answer your last question first: I do not believe I would use aluminum paint but would employ instead any good grade of hull and deck paint. Apply this in two or three rather thin coats after thoroughly washing and sanding the hull. Allow ample time for drying between coats, even though this type of paint sets up fairly quickly. Also it is best to sand lightly between coats if a really good job is wanted.

Only the very best grade of hull and deck paint should be used in refinishing a boat.

In order to obtain inside work with a bright finish you will have to consider the condition of the old varnish. If this is in bad shape, remove completely with paint and varnish remover, used according to instructions on the can, then sand and finish with several coats of marine spar varnish. It would be best to get a marine varnish with a bakelite base if you can find a dealer who has such varnish on hand. If the old varnish happens to be in fair shape, merely sand and re-varnish with a couple of coats.

STRIPPING LEAKING GARBOARD SEAMS

Question: My 22-year-old 30-ft. cabin cruiser is in good condition, except where the garboards meet the keel and the planks next to them. There it leaks and caulking does not hold, for the vibration of the 36-horsepower engine always loosens the seams. Can you suggest a remedy?

New lumber can be had, of course, but it's 60 miles away, and it would take all my vacation to fit new planks, anyway. There are no boat yards within hundreds of miles of my Lake Superior camp where the boat is kept.—C.F.K., Wis.

Answer: Garboards, the planks next to the keel, are usually oak, and whenever the boat is taken from the water this wood shrinks more than the rest of the planking. The real remedy, of course, is to have new garboards fitted, but this is a hard job, and unless it is done properly you would be worse off than before.

The accepted remedy for this trouble, especially with a boat as old as yours, is to strip each seam with lead. Get sheet lead ¹⁄₁₆ or ¹⁄₃₂ in. thick and cut in strips 1 in. wide. Calk or fill the seam first, then cover it with white-lead paste or special seam composition, and tack the lead strip over it. Use ½-in. tacks, spaced about ¾ in. apart.

Then tap the lead strips in to follow the shape of the hull and to hug the wood tightly, giving a tighter job than would copper or galvanized-iron strips. Where one strip follows another, lap them about ½ in., bed in plenty of lead paste, paint, or seam composition, and tap down well. These strips not only give tightness, but prevent the calking from falling out. They should carry you along until you can have new garboards installed.

MAKING PUTTY STAY PUT

Question: The putty over the screw heads of my factory-made motorboat keeps falling out. Can you recommend something that will stay in place?—E. E. W., Okla.

Screw holes should be primed with paint before they are filled with a good grade of marine putty.

Answer: Common putty is seldom satisfactory for use in boats. Marine putty is better, and you can make this by carefully blending common putty and white-lead paste with a putty knife. However, the method of application has much to do with results. The wood should be perfectly dry and each hole primed with paint which is allowed to half-dry before the putty is set in. For best results fill holes more than flush, and sand down when hard. If this fails, I recommend using one of the marine seam compositions which can be obtained from marine supply houses. However, these compositions are messy to use and dry slowly.

OPEN SEAMS PROBLEM

Question: I have an almost new 14-ft. tongue-and-groove cedar boat, with 4-in. bottom planks running crosswise, which I keep on a trailer in the garage when not in use. Recently the bottom seams have opened up, and leak badly when put in the water.—L. E. B., Okla.

Answer: No doubt the heat in your section is too much for the boat. Since keeping it under cover doesn't work, another idea is to cut a piece of heavy burlap, or even felt, the exact shape of the inside bottom planking. When the boat is to be left out of water for some time, this cloth is put in and thoroughly wet down with water. Although it is a nuisance, this keeps the planking damp enough to counteract shrinking.

Or you might try painting the boat with a good grade of marine deck paint, when the wood is well dried out, the seams are slightly open, and all dirt is cleaned out of them. Put this paint on fairly thick both inside and out, brushing across the seams so they will take in as much as possible. Again, if the boat is varnished, try painting it, or if it is painted a dark shade switch to light gray or even white, and you'll find the wood will not swell and shrink so much. If it were an old boat I'd suggest covering the bottom with canvas neatly bonded in marine glue, but one of the other methods should be all that is necessary.

CRACKED LAPSTREAK

Question: How can I repair a cracked and badly leaking board in the side of my lapstreak boat?—W. C. M., Vt.

Answer: The best way is to take out a long section of the lapstreak and replace it with a new length—a job for a professional.

An alternative is to back the damaged spot with a piece of cedar the same thickness as, or slightly thicker than, the planking. Bed it in with thick white-lead paint or paste and fasten with small flathead brass screws, countersunk. Bore small holes for them, first.

Drive the screws both above and below the crack. Also drill a ¼-in. hole through the planking, right at the point of the V, and fit cedar plugs tightly in paint.

Use a marine-grade paint in a semigloss hull and deck type for repainting. Wash the boat, sand well, and apply the first coat thinned with turpentine. After it dries, apply the second, thicker coat.

REMEDY FOR LEAKING ROWBOAT

Question: A short time ago a friend of mine attempted to stop some leaks in my rowboat, but it still leaks. How can I make it tight without having it out of commission too long?—C. T., N. Y.

Answer: If your boat has been in the water for more than 2 weeks and still leaks after swelling, I doubt if a filler will end the trouble. The best thing to do is to have the seams calked. If you wish to try it yourself you will have to let the seams become fairly dry. Then procure several balls of candlewick and marine glue. Run a thin stream of the glue into the seam, and then force one or more strands (as necessary) of the candlewick into place with a screw driver or fine calking iron. Do not use too much force. Keep a little oil handy to dip the tool into, to prevent glue and candlewick from sticking to it. Finally, fill the seam with marine seam composition or red-lead putty. To shorten your work you can, of course, sponge out the boat, mark the leaks, and calk at those points.

CURE FOR LOOSE CANVAS

Question: The canvas has become loose here and there on my canoe. After I remove the paint from it, how can I tighten the canvas, or refasten it to the hull so it will stay?—E. J. M., N. Y.

Answer: When the entire canvas covering is bared, douse it with plenty of warm water to make it shrink. The success of this will depend upon how much "filler"

is in the canvas, for this determines whether or not the covering will absorb the warm water. This method works with new canvas, and the old may draw tight and not loosen again after painting.

Loose canvas can sometimes be tightened by removing the paint and then soaking the canvas with warm water.

REPAIRING RIPS IN CANVAS

Question: My brother has a canvas boat which we'd like to use—only it has a lot of small holes and rips in the covering. How can we repair them?—R. H., Neb.

Answer: Heat hard marine or canoe glue and daub it over the damaged spots, where it will harden at once. Lay a small piece of heavy unbleached muslin or twill over the glue. (Never use canvas; it's too heavy.) Now heat an iron and press against the patch, forcing it into the glue. Smooth the patch down and paint over it. These patches, properly applied, are barely noticeable.

STORING BOAT IN BASEMENT

Question: In storing a boat in a dry basement, out of the weather, is it best to keep the bottom of the boat covered with water or leave it dry?—A. B. R., Pa.

Answer: If the basement is unheated, the boat should come out in the spring in perfect shape. The air in the usual unheated basement is just right for proper storage—neither too dry nor too damp. But I would not leave any water in the boat. The paint on the inside may not be such as to satisfactorily withstand continous soaking in water, and may peel off or loosen its hold before spring. The only time I'd want to put water in the boat would be in spring, for a few days before launching, if necessary, to swell the seams tight.

Should the basement you have in mind be heated, I would not keep the boat in it in any case. Even with water inside, the boat would dry out. Instead, I'd pick any cool place, inside or out, where the boat is sheltered from rain or snow; in fact of the two extremes I'd rather leave a boat out in the open, entirely exposed, than in an overheated basement.

BULGE IN KAYAK

Question: I stored my kayak quite a while with the topside resting on a box. The other day I noticed that the pressure has warped the canvas and made the deck bulge out. What can I do?—J. P., Ohio.
Answer: First soak burlap bags in ordinary water, wring them out, and pack them in the kayak between the bulge and the floor. Then pour boiling hot water over the bulge to shrink it. Push the bulge in so it will retain the water, or else make a circular dam of putty around the spot. Persevere, renewing the hot water as it cools, and I feel you will get results despite the filling or waterproofing used in the fabric.

If this method shouldn't happen to work, make three razor-blade cuts radiating from the center of the bulge. Pare a tiny strip of canvas off each cut, just enough so when the three flaps are brought together the bulge is gone and the cuts closed. Use a small needle and fine thread to secure them, but no more stitches than necessary. Cut off each stitch and tie it separately; don't sew in a long line. Then fasten a patch beneath the repaired area with marine canvas cement. Keep it propped up from beneath till it sets. Let the cement ooze through

the seams, and sand it smooth when it hardens.

TO REMOVE OLD PAINT

Question: The paint has never been entirely scraped from a used rowboat I bought recently. It has had three or four coats and is now so badly blistered that I can't apply a new coat. How can I get all that old paint off?—B. G., N. Y.

A blow torch using uncolored gasoline is the most efficient and rapid device for removing many layers of old paint.

Answer: I think a blowtorch will do the job better than a paint remover in your case. If possible, use uncolored gasoline in the torch to insure better operation at the rather low flame which will be necessary in order to avoid charring the wood.

With one hand, hold the torch over an area of paint until it rises into blisters and begins to blacken, then run a putty knife under the paint and peel it off. A little practice will indicate just how long the torch must be held over each spot.

After removing the paint, go over the hull with a sharp hoe-type scraper to remove the last vestige of paint. Fill all dents in the wood and all places where fastenings have been countersunk. For this use a mixture of white-lead paste and putty. Follow this with coarse, then with medium sandpaper. Apply your first or priming coat of paint rather thin. Use a flat or semigloss marine paint, not a gloss paint or enamel. Sand after the first coat, then apply two additional coats.

BOAT BUILDING PROBLEMS

YELLOW PINE FOR HULL?

Question: Would yellow pine without knots be suitable for the hull of a 12-ft. lapstreak dinghy?—J. K., Ohio.

Answer: There are several grades of yellow pine, all of which are good boat-building woods except for their weight. If the wood you use has a heavy gum content (the grain will tell you this), you will find it on the brittle side and very heavy. I'd much prefer cedar, or even your local poplar, which stands up well on inland waters.

WOOD FOR ROWBOAT

Question: Disregarding cost, which do you consider the better wood for building a flat-bottomed rowboat: cypress or white pine?—A. L. F., N. Y.

Answer: I think you'll find cypress a better wood for boat building than most white pine, but much depends on the wood itself. Some cypress is inferior stuff, and kiln-dried wood of any kind must be avoided, as it swells so much the planking warps out of shape. In general, the grain of cypress has a tendency to rise, in spite of careful sanding and finishing, while white pine has the reputation of holding paint rather poorly on submerged parts of the boat. Better than either is white cedar, which has the extra advantage of being lighter in weight.

BUILDING CAR-TOP BOAT

Question: I am thinking of building a 12-ft. boat of marine plywood, to be powered by a small outboard or possibly later by a light inboard motor. Can such a boat be made light enough for car-top carrying?—R. L. B., Tenn.

Answer: While you can build a plywood boat for outboard use, light enough to be carried on a car, you'll find it difficult to keep the weight down on one designed

for inboard use. For the lighter boat, I'd advise a carrier fitted with rubber suction cups, but a trailer will probably be necessary with an inboard installation. The average weight limit for loading on a car top is 100 lb. The stronger construction required to put an inboard in the boat, together with the weight and bulkiness of shaft, strut, and propeller, makes a trailer advisable.

PLACING OF ROWBOAT SEATS

Question: I am building a 12-ft. rowboat in which I plan to install four seats. One seat will be in the bow, one in the stern. What are the best locations for the other two, and for the oarlocks?—H. B., Wis.

Answer: Two seats besides those in bow and stern may crowd your 12-ft. boat, but if you want them, locate one with its center 4 ft. from the bow, the other with its center 4 ft. from the stern. In other words, divide the space equally. The oarlocks should be fitted 12 in. astern of the seat from which they will be used for maximum rowing efficiency.

SASSAFRAS FOR PLANKING

Question: Would you prefer sassafras or cypress as planking for a cruiser to be used on the Mississippi?—W. S., Ky.

Answer: If the sassafras can be obtained in long enough and wide enough boards it should make perfect material for the job so far as its lasting qualities are concerned. How well it would finish I don't know, since the only sassafras I've worked with was small and was used only in small-size construction members, but you can test this for yourself by seeing if it will plane smoothly and take paint nicely. I do know that sassafras was widely used when larger trees were obtainable, and ranked with locust and mulberry as far as immunity to rot was concerned. As for cypress, I find it's apt to be pretty poor boat-building material unless one can get heartwood out of large trees. I certainly would try the sassafras.

REMODELING WITH MAPLE

Question: I am remodeling the top of my 15½-ft. inboard with raw maple and should like to know whether boiled or raw linseed oil is best for a base and if this would take a coat of varnish when dry. Also, I'd like to know whether water stain allowed to dry and coated with varnish would do the job.—W. K., Ill.

Answer: Maple is not often used for boat building because it is heavy and hard to work. I should not advise putting it under the water, and even for such use as you plan to make of it the wood must be kept well painted or varnished, or it will warp. Boiled linseed oil rather than raw would be preferable, as the former dries more quickly, especially if applied warm. Whatever staining is to be done should be attended to before using the oil, though it must be remembered that the oil itself will darken the wood. If you want as light a shade as possible, allow the oil to dry thoroughly and then apply several coats of marine varnish, preferably one with a bakelite base. I believe that varnish could be used directly on maple as the wood is so close-grained that oil will penetrate only slightly in any event. Some varnishes will adhere well over oiled wood; others will not. And one takes a chance on this. If you use stain, almost any type will do as maple hardly requires a filler.

PLYWOOD FOR PLANKING

Question: I'm going to build a 12-ft. boat, with a flat bottom and plenty of beam for stability, for use with an outboard motor or oars. Can I use ordinary plywood for planking, or will the layers of wood come apart when soaked?—E. F. S., Calif.

Answer: Since ordinary plywood is not made with waterproof glue, it isn't suitable for your boatbuilding, even if you paint it well or cover it with canvas. Get marine plywood, and use a plywood primer or aluminum paint for a priming coat; then your paint or varnish job won't develop hairline checks later.

BENDING CANOE RIBS

Question: I am building a 16-ft. canoe, the plans of which call for common straight-grained elm barrel hoops to be used as ribs; but I have been unable to locate any such hoops. What other wood would be suitable?—H. K., Pa.

Answer: You'll find straight-grained white oak, on the green side, good bending wood, but you'll have to steam or boil it to bend it, whereas the barrel hoops would be the approximate shape. Good spruce, free of knots, could also be used, to keep weight down, but is generally harder to get than the oak.

To steam the wood for bending, find a pipe as long as the ribs and as large in diameter as possible. Cap the lower end, fill the pipe ⅔ full of water, and incline it across a fire with its upper end in an iron crotch or some other support. When the water boils, put in as many ribs as you can at one time, allowing a little leeway for swelling of the wood, and stuff a cloth around the opening to keep the heat in. Let the wood boil for ½ to 1 hour, pulling it out from time to time for testing. When ready for use, it should be as limber as a switch and bend in any direction. Work quickly after taking it out of the water, as it stiffens again as soon as it gets cold.

PUNTS OR POINTED BOATS

Question: I plan to build a rowboat about 11 or 12 ft. long for use on a nearby river. Which is better material for the bottom, narrow boards 4 or 6 in. wide, or boards of 10 or 12 in.? Also, are tongue-and-groove boards recommended?

I have enough 12 x ½ in. clear white pine to build a boat. Would you suggest my using this—and would a punt-style boat with a narrow bottom row as easily as a pointed boat?—H. E. U., Mo.

Answer: The best width for bottom planking is about 6 in. Lumber that is too wide has a tendency to warp and open up. I would advise against using your tongue-and-groove material for the hull of a boat as the seams would never swell tight and there is no way that they could be properly calked. The clear white pine you have on hand can be easily ripped into narrower strakes for bottom planking and will make good building material. However, the ½ in. thickness seems a little light for the average flatbottom unless the plans call for closely framed or ribbed construction.

Speaking of plans, it seems to me that the only way to build a boat such as the one you have in mind is to choose a plan and to stick to it! Plans give full specifications regarding lumber and fastenings.

I think a narrow punt type will row quite as easily in smooth water as the usual pointed-bow boat. However, you cannot compare the punt-type boat to a semi-V-bottom or to a round-bottom one.

PREVENTION OF BUCKLING

Question: I am making a boat of ½-in. white pine. Since I will be unable to leave it in the water, please tell me how to treat the boards to keep them from buckling. I don't want the wood to soak up too much water.—P. L. H., Mo.

Answer: Whether or not the white pine buckles depends a lot on the construction of the boat and on the grade of wood. Some of the white pines used for houses (sugar pine, for example) will not hold paint well; blisters form when the boat is laid up. You should build only to a re-

liable design and not trust your own judgment or that of friends unless they are experts.

Building even the smallest of boats is an exact science. Always build from the plans of a tried and true design.

Generally speaking, wide boards are more likely to buckle than narrower ones. It is unsafe to lay bottom planking in widths wider than 6 in., because most woods—pine especially—swell a lot when wet and the excess wood must go somewhere. Narrower boards naturally have more seams to take the come and go of the wood. Fastening and inside supporting of the side and bottom planking help too. When framing members are close together and planking is well fastened to them there is less likelihood of buckling. Construction should be laid out so that fastenings go through the soft pine into some harder wood, such as oak, to give them a better hold.

A coat of linseed oil, heated well and applied before painting, may prevent the wood from soaking up excess water.

BUILDING BOATS FOR RENT

Question: What type rowboats would you advise me to build for rent on a small lake where they'll be used by families for fishing?—C. L. C., Mich.

Answer: Sharp-nosed, flat-bottom, 14-ft. skiffs. Later you can add better models to your line, should the customers prove willing to pay the higher rental you'd have to ask in order to make a profit.

WHITE PINE OR REDWOOD PLANKING?

Question: How does California redwood compare with white pine for boat planking?—C. W., Ohio.

Answer: Use redwood only if you can't get a good grade of white pine, cypress, or white cedar. Redwood will last longer than white pine and stand well alongside the other two. However, it splits easily and requires careful handling when being bent into place if it must be cut in narrow strips for certain planking.

In using redwood, bore for all fastenings as you would with any wood but be especially careful near the ends of the planks. Countersink screw heads in holes bored by a rose bit. Dampen the wood if it is too brittle.

Be sure to make all seams as tight as possible and paint all touching surfaces with white-lead paste or liquid marine glue because redwood does not shrink or swell to any extent—and it is the natural swelling of most woods when placed in water that tends to close poorly fitted seams.

RE-LAYING DOUBLE BOTTOM

Question: I'd appreciate some advice regarding a new bottom for my 16½-ft. inboard-powered boat. This boat makes about 40 miles an hour. Would a single bottom of ⅝-in. cedar with twice the amount of ribs be as strong as the original double bottom of ¼-in. cedar? I don't like the double bottom because it makes it difficult to locate a leak.

With single planking, would there be danger that continuous pounding would cause leaks?—B. MacA., N. Y.

Answer: I'd try to duplicate the original double bottom. If you try to lay out another type you're liable to get a weak bottom as a result of cutting into ribs or frames for the battens necessary to back

⅝-in. single planking. Or else, in trying to avoid that trouble, you may plan construction which will cut down speed.

After all, it's hard to beat double-bottom construction for craft of this class. If properly laid out, with two layers of white cedar (or cedar inside, mahogany outside, and canvas glued between) I believe you will have less trouble building this type bottom to remain tight despite pounding at high speeds.

The trouble with battened-seam construction is that with such thin planking you cannot depend on outside calking at all, but must rely on the planks being backed by the battens. These, of course, act as longitudinal stringers; but the inner of the two layers of planking fulfill that function even better.

I know leaks are hard to locate in a double bottom, but they shouldn't start until the boat is well on in years and the canvas rots. When that happens, you might be able to remove the outer layer of wood, replace the canvas, then lay a new bottom—using liquid marine glue or one of the special compositions for double-bottom construction.

BEST GLUE FOR BOAT

Question: I would like to know whether marine is better than casein glue for use on the transom frame, chines, and keel of a small rowboat.—C. D. W., N. J.

Answer: Casein glue adheres well, but will not stand up for long in underwater locations. If available, you might use powdered resin glue or adhesive, as it is handled in the same manner as casein, but really withstands immersion. However, it is difficult for the amateur to do a sound job, for even pressure is necessary to insure proper bonding, and clamps aren't always enough. Also, the glue should not be used when the temperature is less than 70 degrees F.

SPECIAL BOATING PROBLEMS

KAYAK STEERS BADLY

Question: I have built a 16-ft. kayak, and although I use a double-bladed paddle, find it very hard to keep on a straight course. Would a keel help?—A. A. P., Ill.
Answer: If the construction of your boat will permit, a light keel amidships—say ⅝″ wide and ¾″ deep—should help. You should also experiment with various paddling positions to get the best weight distribution. It is the cutaway ends which cause such a boat to go from side to side, and it must be properly handled.

OARS FOR DUCK BOAT

Question: I am building a 13½-ft. canvas duck boat, which is 36 in. wide from oarlock to oarlock. What length oars should I buy?—M. C., Mich.
Answer: Five-foot oars are considered correct for a boat of the beam you mention and are generally used on duck boats.

CHOOSING OARS

Question: What length oars should I buy for a 9 ft., 8 in. rowboat I recently built? It is 45 in. wide.—E. W. S., Ohio.
Answer: Six-ft. oars will be found about right. Several pointers occur to me which may be helpful to you: You'll find spruce oars much easier to handle than others, and it's a good idea to fit them with leathers. Wrap an 8-in. strip of leather around each oar at the point where it passes through the lock, then wind a ½-in. strip several times around the inboard end of the leather, and tack it securely. Protect tips of the blades by tacking on copper sheeting, and if you paint the oars, leave the handles bare—to afford a better grip. New oars should be put away carefully after using, at least until they've had time to season. If not stored flat,

properly supported their entire length, they are likely to warp.

SKIFF SHIPS WATER

Question: I have a 14-ft. flat-bottom rowboat, 14 in. deep at the stem and 15 in. amidship and at the stern, which I use with a 5-horsepower motor on Luke Huron. It does pretty well except that when the lake is rough a not-too-big wave, on hitting the bow, will splash up the side and into the boat. This will also happen on smooth water if I come about too quickly and get in my own wake. Would spray rails help?—E. M. M., Mich.

A canvas cover over the front part of a flat-bottomed skiff will prevent water from being shipped into the boat.

Answer: Shipping waves over the bow is a common fault of a flat-bottom skiff, but I am quite sure fitting spray rails will not prevent it. These rails help a boat to get up out of the water under power and so keep the bow higher and perhaps prevent its throwing spray, but they are seldom efficient on anything but a light boat, round or V-bottom and driven fairly fast. In your boat it is the lack of buoyancy forward and the absence of outward flare in the sides that cause the trouble, although any small boat will have the same trouble to some extent if the water is rough enough.

If you are in the habit of going out on rough water, I'd suggest making a spray hood of waterproof canvas to cover the forward third of the boat, having it arranged so it can be put on and taken off quickly. To hold this you would need a crosspiece in the form of an arch, its feet fitting into sockets inside each gunwale and its central part curving fairly high. A notch in the top of this would take the ridge pole, which would slant down forward to fit in a socket at the stem. This will raise the cover enough to throw off water. Edges of the cover can fasten down beneath the rub rail all around the outside of the boat, probably with snap fasteners which will be out of the way there. The whole thing can be rolled up in a small bundle to stow out of the way.

GRADING CANVAS

Question: The designations used by manufacturers to describe canvas—No. 6, No. 8, 24-oz., and all the rest—have me in a complete fog. Please tell me what these terms mean?—J. W. R., N. Y.

Answer: The ounce designation tells the weight of 1 sq. yd. of canvas. The number series also describes the canvas's weight, but not so directly. Here is a simple table to help you compare the systems—either one of which, but not both, should be used as a standard by manufacturers:

Weight in ounces of 1 sq. yd. of canvas—

No. 4   No. 6   No. 8   No. 10   No. 12
24½ oz. 21¼ oz. 18 oz. 14¾ oz. 11½ oz.

Numbers not shown can be computed by continuing out this table, deducting 3¼ oz. for each increase in grade number; for example, No. 14 canvas weighs 8¼ oz. a square yard.

TO ESTABLISH A BOAT LANDING

Question: I would appreciate some information on starting a commercial boat landing on a lake?—I. E. S., Ariz.

Answer: If there are no zoning laws to prevent a landing from being operated, determine who controls the water—a power company, some other corporation, or the state. Arrange with the owner to buy or lease the land. In the case of a lease, be sure to have it understood that you can build all necessary docks and floats.

If possible, the land should be served with electricity, water, and telephone; and have room for parking, with a good road entrance.

Start with a few boats and gradually expand as demand warrants, turning the bulk of the profits back into the business. The boat livery and service end of the business seems like a good line now if you have a little capital to live on, and if you know your stuff.

BEACH CRAFT ON INCLINED TRACKS

Question: My 14-ft. runabout and outboard motor weigh about 300 lb., and I have been hauling this load into my boathouse on rollers, by main strength. The boathouse is about 1 ft. above the high-water line; sometimes 18 in. above it.

Can you suggest some way of making this task easier, such as running the boat up on a rack attached to a truck on rails?—N. E. T., Iowa.

Answer: Arrangements for handling small boats such as yours are generally homemade. Make an inclined ramp of planks, and run the ends well down into the water. Support these ends with pilings.

Attach tracks to the ramp, and build a carriage with four flanged wheels to fit onto the rails. There should be two cradles on the carriage to conform to the contours of the boat. Haul the boat in with block and tackle, or by motor power.

MAKING SMALL-BOAT ANCHOR

Question: I should like to make an anchor for my 12-ft. boat. I plan to use this anchor in water of approximately 35-ft.

depth. Any instructions you can give me will be appreciated.—J. H. C., Colo.

A homemade boat anchor can be made from a metal disk and a solid piece of rod.

Answer: To make a good-holding anchor obtain an old disk from a farm disk drill or cultivator and fit it with an 18-in. piece of old shafting, drilling the center hole to take the piece of shaft so that it sets at right angles. The other end of the shaft should be drilled to take a ring for the rope. This anchor, of course, will bring up mud when pulled up, and the manufactured types are cleaner in this respect. Use shafting instead of pipe as a piece of shafting has more weight.

REGISTERING MOTORBOAT

Question: A friend and I are building an open motorboat, which will be about 18 ft. long. How should we go about registering her, and how much does it cost? Do you think we can have the boat registered in both names?—J. K., N. Y.

Answer: To register your boat, write the nearest Coast Guard office, asking for forms which you will have to fill out and return to them. It might be a good idea, at the same time, to request a copy of the latest regulations as to equipment you will be required to carry. There is no charge for these services, but I do not know whether you will be able to register the boat under two names.

If you don't know where the nearest office is, write the U. S. Coast Guard, Washington, D. C., for its location. The forms used to be issued by collectors of customs, but the Coast Guard has taken over the work.

WAKE OVERTURNS ROWBOAT

Question: I use a rowboat on the Allegheny River, and have often had it turned over by the wake of large boats passing. I've asked several boatmen how to take the waves with the most safety, but their opinions vary.—W. J. C., Pa.

Answer: You must study your own boat's behavior to know how best to meet waves from larger boats, since every craft has peculiarities of its own according to the shape of its bow sections and its freeboard, buoyancy, and balance. I see no reason why any small boat of decent design should be overturned by such a wave if met at the right angle and if the weight of those aboard is properly distributed. Study the way the boat goes over; if the bow comes up and completely back and over there is probably too much weight concentrated in the stern and too much buoyancy in the bow and the best way to take waves may be to run before them. However, you will probably find that the boat rolls over sideways, and that the best way to prevent this will be to head directly or almost directly into the waves. The way the boat is loaded will make a lot of difference; weight should be concentrated neither in bow or in stern but in the middle, and kept as low as possible. You may be able to help things by lowering the boat's seats.

If I were using oars at the time, I would carry on with them. If using an outboard, it might be best to throttle it down, but not enough so that it would stall.

MOLDED-PLYWOOD HULLS

Question: Before buying a molded-plywood hull, I'd appreciate some information. Would a round-bottom hull tend to capsize easily in rough water? And would a molded hull develop more speed, because of lessened friction against the water, than a conventional outboard-motor boat or sailboat?—M. W. B., Mass.

Answer: In the first place, round-bottom hulls are more seaworthy than either the flat or V types. They have less initial stability, and when you step in them they tend to roll, but they soon steady themselves and then are superior to the others in seaworthiness.

Secondly, speed is a matter of design. You wouldn't need a round-bottom hull in a speedboat, where the big consideration is planing ability which can be obtained even from a flat bottom. However, a round-bottom hull is better for a sailboat; the other types of sailboat hulls were developed originally to lower production costs.

INSTALLING SAIL ON CANOE

Question: Is there any easily stowed sailing rig on the market which I can install on my 16-ft. canoe, and would it be effective for a trip up the Ohio River this summer?—M. H. S., Ind.

Answer: A number of leading canoe and boat manufacturers can supply sailing rigs for the average canoe. You will need the mast step and mast seat to replace the bow seat, rudder, leeboards, and fastenings, and a lateen rig the spars of which will stow in the canoe with the sail wrapped around them. Sail areas vary from 40 sq. ft. to 75, and 55 sq. ft. should be about right for your trip.

You will certainly find it possible to sail up the Ohio River. I tried it, going downstream, a few years ago, figuring there would be a good deal of current to help the boat along, but found the current very slight while the wind was strong upriver three days out of four. I wished I was going the other way. The big trouble with sailing and camping on the Ohio, and the Mississippi too, is that the mud left from the annual high water makes the shore a mess and campsites difficult to find.

NEW YORK STATE CRUISE

Question: Another fellow and I are planning a canoe trip up the Hudson River from Yonkers, camping on Lake George or Lake Champlain for a week, but going on north to the Canadian border. Can we do this in a month? Are there any maps we can get, or previous arrangements we should make?—R. K., N. J.

Answer: With only a month to spend and a week of that passed in camp, I doubt that you could reach Canada and back even with an outboard on your canoe. The round trip from Yonkers to the international border is about 700 miles, and there are canal locks to contend with and tide to fight part of the time. I suggest that you find out about taking a steamer from Yonkers to Albany, taking your canoe or duffel on board, and thus giving yourselves far more time for the interesting country north of Albany. The steamer fare is moderate, especially when you consider the saving of gasoline for your outboard. Again, you might take a train to Lake Champlain or Lake George, carrying your duffel but hiring a canoe from one of the many outfitters at the other end.

However, if you want to stick to canoeing, charts for the Hudson River (Numbers 281, 282, 283, and 284) can be obtained from the U. S. Coast and Geodetic Survey, Dept. of Commerce, Washington, D. C., for a total cost of $2.25. These cover the route as far as Troy, and while not necessary would be useful and instructive. For a permit to go through the canal into Lake Champlain, and for charts of this section, write the Dept. of Canals and Waterways, Albany, N. Y. For the northern part of the cruise, or in fact anywhere along the way, you can get valuable data from the marine gasoline stations you will pass.

PERMANENT KEEL BEST

Question: I have a short, wide, flat-bottom boat, 11 ft. long, 58 in. beam, 16 in. high, and built of ½-in. spruce.

I am planning to use this boat on the lower Sacramento River. It's a mile wide at points and waves roll high. Except that the bow is rather sharp, I think the design is quite O.K. for my requirements. A front deck could be installed with a combing to exclude water from the hull.

Would you recommend a removable keel, attached by clamps, to be detached when in transit overland, or would you recommend a set of leeboards for each end of the boat?

My desire for a keel or leeboards is to avoid excessive side drift. I do not want to install a permanent keel. What do you advise?—A. J. S., Calif.

Fastening a shallow keel strip to the bottom of a boat makes it easier to handle both in and out of the water.

Answer: I am sure if you will add a shallow keel strip of oak ⅞ x ⅞ in., fastened aft atop a skeg and running the length of the bottom, your boat will behave satisfactorily. Fasten the skeg and keel with screws from *inside* the boat, and run a supporting strip up the transom. This will make a stronger job than attaching through the outside members.

The attachments holding leeboards or any sort of detachable keel are a nui-sance, making rowing harder and slowing down a power craft.

As a matter of fact, having a keel to skid on, will make your boat easier to handle out of the water. Also, the keel and skeg will strengthen the bottom considerably for use on a stream with shallows, gravel bars, and a rocky bottom.

STABILITY OF BOTTOM TYPES

Question: Other characteristics aside, which tips more easily, a round-bottom or a flat-bottom boat?—H. J. S., Minn.

Answer: The flat-bottom boat may be a little stiffer when you step into it or move from side to side, but when it comes to serious tipping—enough to take water over the gunwale—I think the round-bottom is the safer. That is, it may have less initial stability, but more final stability, and that's what counts. Of course, a round bottom with very little dead rise (upward curvature) will be stiffer, but that would defeat its easy rowing and handling qualities. Every boat is a compromise between handling ease and stiffness.

LOCATING WATERLINE

Question: How can I locate the waterline of my new boat?—J. H. W., Tex.

Answer: There is no simple way of doing this, although an experienced builder familiar with some simple type such as a skiff can tell pretty well by eye just where the waterline will come. Otherwise you'd really have to be a naval architect and calculate weights, bearing surfaces, and other factors.

The easiest thing is to launch the boat, load it with the weight it will carry, and mark the planking with tacks at the waterline. Then remove the boat from the water and paint on the waterline, working up for 1 in. more from the tacks, depending upon the size of the craft. For looks, the line often is slanted upward slightly toward the bow.

INDEX

CPSIA information can be obtained at www.ICGtesting.com
Printed in the USA
LVOW09s1533291215

468271LV00007B/345/P